Falling Monuments, Reluctant Ruins

Falling Monuments, Reluctant Ruins
The Persistence of the Past in the Architecture of Apartheid

Edited by Hilton Judin

Published in South Africa by:
Wits University Press
1 Jan Smuts Avenue
Johannesburg 2001

www.witspress.co.za

Compilation © Hilton Judin 2021
Chapters © Individual contributors 2021
Published edition © Wits University Press 2021
Images and figures © Copyright holders
Cover image: Back entrance to Pass Office hall from waiting yard, 80 Albert Street, Johannesburg, 2012. Photograph by Jo Ractliffe

First published 2021

http://dx.doi.org.10.18772/22021066673

978-1-77614-667-3 (Paperback)
978-1-77614-668-0 (Hardback)
978-1-77614-669-7 (Web PDF)
978-1-77614-670-3 (EPUB)

All rights reserved. No part of this publication may be reproduced stored in a retrieval system or transmitted in any form or by any means electronic mechanical photocopying recording or otherwise without the written permission of the publisher except in accordance with the provisions of the Copyright Act Act 98 of 1978.

All images remain the property of the copyright holders. The publishers gratefully acknowledge the publishers institutions and individuals referenced in captions for the use of images. Every effort has been made to locate the original copyright holders of the images reproduced here; please contact Wits University Press in case of any omissions or errors.

Project manager: Catherine Damerell
Copy editor: Lynda Gilfillan
Proofreader: Tessa Botha
Indexer: Sanet le Roux
Cover design: Hybrid Creative
Typeset in 10 point Garamond Pro

CONTENTS

LIST OF FIGURES
ix

FOREWORD
Muchaparara Musemwa
xv

ACKNOWLEDGEMENTS
xxiii

INTRODUCTION
Hilton Judin
1

PART ONE: LANDS
11

1 **LAND DISPOSSESSION AND THE GHOSTS OF THE MEDUPI POWER STATION**
Faeeza Ballim
13

2 **A COMMUNITY JOURNEY: RETURN TO JULIWE CEMETERY IN ROODEPOORT, JOHANNESBURG**
Eric Itzkin
29

3 **PUBLIC MEMORY AND TRANSFORMATION AT CONSTITUTION HILL AND GANDHI SQUARE IN JOHANNESBURG**
Temba John Dawson Middelmann
40

4 **EJARADINI: NOTES TOWARDS MODELLING BLACK GARDENS AS A RESPONSE TO THE COLONIALITY OF MUSEUMS**
MADEYOULOOK
62

PART TWO: BUILDINGS
81

5 JOHANNESBURG CENTRAL POLICE STATION AND THE PHOTOGRAPH AS EVIDENCE
Sally Gaule
83

6 THE PERSISTENCE OF ROBBEN ISLAND: ABOLITION AND THE PRISON MUSEUM
Kelly Gillespie
106

7 THE APARTHEID PASS OFFICE IN JOHANNESBURG AND A HERITAGE OF DESTRUCTION
Hilton Judin
124

8 INDIAN TRADING, ART DECO AND URBAN MODERNITY IN A SEGREGATED TOWN: JUBILEE HOUSE IN KRUGERSDORP
Arianna Lissoni and Roshan Dadoo
150

9 AN UNCERTAIN HERITAGE AND RESISTANCE: TRANSFORMING THE DRILL HALL IN JOHANNESBURG
Barbara Morovich and Pauline Guinard
173

PART THREE: STATUES, AS MONUMENTS
191

10 **CREATING SPACES OF MEMORIALISATION: NEW DELVILLE WOOD (FRANCE) AND SS *MENDI* (SOUTH AFRICA)**
Yasmin Mayat and Brendan Hart
193

11 **RE-HISTORICISING CREDO MUTWA'S KWA KHAYA LENDABA CULTURAL VILLAGE IN SOWETO**
Ali Khangela Hlongwane and Tara Weber
212

12 **FACING (DOWN) THE COLONISER? THE MANDELA STATUE AT CAPE TOWN'S CITY HALL**
Cynthia Kros
234

13 **'WHERE'S OUR MONUMENT?' COMMEMORATING INDIAN INDENTURED LABOUR IN SOUTH AFRICA**
Goolam Vahed
256

14 **DECOLONISATION, MONUMENTS, AND A NEW ARCHITECTURAL LANGUAGE**
Nnamdi Elleh
278

CONTRIBUTORS
299

INDEX
305

LIST OF FIGURES

Frontispiece
Passage from waiting yard to back entrance of Pass Office hall, 80 Albert Street, Johannesburg, 2012. Photograph by Jo Ractliffe   ii
Back page
Medical examination rooms and counter, 80 Albert Street, Johannesburg, 2012. Photograph by Jo Ractliffe   319

CHAPTER 2

Figure 2.1
A view of the Dobsonville History Exhibition at the Roodepoort Museum. Photograph by Carolina Geldenhuys (Roodepoort Museum)   31
Figure 2.2
The empty site where Juliwe township once stood, with the former cemetery in the south-east corner. Photograph courtesy Roodepoort Museum   33
Figure 2.3
A blue heritage plaque awarded by the City of Johannesburg stands alongside a community memorial. Photograph by Eric Itzkin   37

CHAPTER 3

Figure 3.1
The public square at Constitution Hill, with a few tourists and uniformed guards. Photograph by Temba Middelmann   46
Figure 3.2
Gandhi Square on a typical weekday morning, with the Gandhi statue opposite the Mall. Photograph by Temba Middelmann   52

CHAPTER 4

Figure 4.1
Archival photograph from the Ronald and Torrance Ngilima collection, exhibited as part of Ejaradini. Photographed in Benoni Old Location or Wattville Township, c. 1950. RN1302C, Ngilima Photo Archives   63

Figure 4.2
Archival photograph from the Ronald and Torrance Ngilima collection, exhibited as part of Ejaradini. Photographed in Benoni Old Location or Wattville Township, 1940–60. RN4058S, Ngilima Photo Archives   76

CHAPTER 5

Figure 5.1
View along Commissioner Street with Johannesburg Central Police Station, 2009. Photograph by Sally Gaule   84

Figure 5.2
John Vorster Square, 1972. © *Sunday Times*   85

Figure 5.3
Page from the police 'terrorist album'. Ronnie Kasrils has kindly permitted his image to be shown here. National Archives, Pretoria. Digital copy from Historical Papers Research Archive, University of the Witwatersrand   87

Figure 5.4
Former 'non-white' entrance of Johannesburg Central Police Station, 2019. Photograph by Sally Gaule   92

Figure 5.5
Johannesburg Central Police Station from M1 highway, 2017. Photograph by Sally Gaule   93

Figure 5.6
Corridor of Johannesburg Central Police Station, 2018. Photograph by Sally Gaule   96

Figure 5.7
Removal of the bust of B. J. Vorster, September 1997. Trevor Samson, © *Business Day*   98

Figure 5.8
Surveyor's chair, roof of Johannesburg Central Police Station, 2008. Photograph by Guy Trangoš   99

CHAPTER 6

Figure 6.1
Voorberg Correctional Centre Medium A section, with Mr Flynn
in the foreground. Photograph by Mikhael Subotsky   116
Figure 6.2
Voorberg Correctional Centre Medium B section, cell. Photograph
by Mikhael Subotsky   119

CHAPTER 7

Figure 7.1
Back entrance to Pass Office hall from waiting yard, 80 Albert Street,
Johannesburg, 2012. Photograph by Jo Ractliffe   125
Figure 7.2
'The queues at Albert Street are long and tedious, but for the man
in a hurry 50c slipped to the right cop can get him to the top of the
line…'. May 1968. Photograph by *Drum* photographer. APN252546.
DM2008103103: SAED. Baileys African History Archive   128
Figure 7.3 A–C
Top to bottom: DSCN1731 destroyed clinic, Diepkloof; DSCN1711
Orlando East beer hall; DSCN1726 WRAB building with collapsed
roof, Orlando East, Soweto June 1976   130
Figure 7.3 D–F
Top to bottom: DSCN2085 WRAB office, Dobsonville; DSCN1946
community hall inside after fire, Thokoza; DSCN1730 destroyed
WRAB building, Dube, Soweto June 1976   131
Figure 7.3 G–I
Top to bottom: DSCN1733 WRAB building fire damage, Diepkloof;
DSCN1737 fire-damaged building; DSCN1917 aerial view of building,
Soweto June 1976   132
Figure 7.3 J–L
Top to bottom: DSCN2151 WRAB building with graffiti; DSCN2167
WRAB office, Meadowlands; DSCN2522 WRAB office building, Soweto
June 1976. *Archives of the Commission of Inquiry into the Riots in Soweto and
Elsewhere, 1976–1978*. National Archives, Pretoria: K345 [missing file].

Digital Copies from Historical Papers Research Archive, University of the Witwatersrand   133

Figure 7.4
Main administrative hall, Pass Office, 80 Albert Street, Johannesburg, 2012. Photograph by Jo Ractliffe   140

CHAPTER 8

Figure 8.1
Solly's (formerly Jubilee House), corner of Market and Commissioner Streets, Krugersdorp, 2015. Photograph by Arianna Lissoni   151

Figure 8.2
Jubilee House, c. 1925. To this day, a copy of the photograph hangs in the 'office of the manager' in Solly's shop, the only trace of its former owners   160

Figure 8.3
Jubilee House, 1993. Photograph by Roshan Dadoo   161

Figure 8.4
'Magnificent New Department Store for Krugersdorp – M. M. Dadoo & Sons, Ltd.', *The Star*, 28 June 1940. Courtesy Roshan Dadoo   164

CHAPTER 9

Figure 9.1
Sketch of proposed renovation of Drill Hall by the architect Michael Hart   176

Figure 9.2
Map of the Drill Hall and its immediate surroundings, by Pauline Guinard   178

Figure 9.3
Skateboarding at the Drill Hall. Photograph by Pauline Guinard   184

CHAPTER 10

Figure 10.1
The new memorial looking towards the original memorial arch. Photograph by Anix Consulting   197

Figure 10.2
Thin members of the concrete pergola create a sense of enclosure when viewing the integrated display panels; they also repeat patterns and shadows that move through the day. Photograph by Papercut Photography   201

CHAPTER 11

Figure 11.1
Entrance of the Kwa Khaya Lendaba cultural village, c. 1974. Photograph by Gilbert Briscoe. Courtesy of the Johannesburg Art Gallery   213

Figure 11.2
Credo Mutwa and *amathwasa*, with tourist onlookers, c. 1974. Photograph by Gilbert Briscoe. Courtesy of the Johannesburg Art Gallery   223

Figure 11.3
A grass hut, with the Oppenheimer Tower in the background, c. 1974. Photograph by Gilbert Briscoe. Courtesy of the Johannesburg Art Gallery   227

CHAPTER 12

Figure 12.1
Taking 'selfies' in front of the statue of Edward VII on the Parade. Photograph by Cynthia Kros   237

Figure 12.2
Mandela statue on the balcony of the Cape Town City Hall. Photograph by Cynthia Kros   247

CHAPTER 13

Figure 13.1
Sketch by Nanda Soobben for the 1860 Monuments Committee for the statue of an Indian sugar cane plantation worker, 2013. Provided to author by Sinothe Thabethe, KwaMuhle Museum   267

Figure 13.2
1860 project sod-turning ceremony at the beachfront, Durban.
From the left are Vic Pillay, Mayor Zandile Gumede (partially obscured),
KZN Premier Willies Mchunu, A. V. Mahomed and Seelan Archary, 15
November 2016. Photograph by Gcina Ndwalane   268

CHAPTER 14

Figures 14.1A and B
Tiglachin (our struggle) monument was built in the Ethiopia–Cuba
Friendship Park, Addis Ababa, in 1984 to celebrate the 10th anniversary
of the socialist revolution of Ethiopia. Photographs by Nnamdi Elleh   286

Figures 14.2A and B
The 51-metre column of the Memorial for Martyred Freedom
Fighters and Patriots, Mek'ele, built by the Tigray People's Liberation
Front (TPLF) at the end of the Cold War (after the socialist government
had fallen in May 1991). Photographs by Nnamdi Elleh   288

Figures 14.3A and B
The medallion of Tiglachin and the coat of arms (insignia) of the
Memorial for Martyred Freedom Fighters and Patriots, Tigray People's
Liberation Front (TPLF), Mek'ele. Photographs by Nnamdi Elleh   289

FOREWORD

The themes explored in this book have evoked memories of growing up in post-liberation Zimbabwe, where the postcolonial state led by the late President Robert Mugabe engineered what the anthropologist Richard Werbner describes as a 'whole complex of *elite* memorialism'.[1] We witnessed in the early 1980s the construction of what turned out to be the majestic National Heroes Acre, built diagonally opposite the equally majestic National Sports Stadium in Harare, the capital of Zimbabwe. The National Heroes Acre monument was, of course, built to immortalise the ideals of the anti-colonial struggle and to commemorate the bravery of those who had sacrificed their lives for the liberation of Zimbabwe. But at this national monument only the elite lie buried, to be joined by those remaining in the Zimbabwe African National Union–Patriotic Front (ZANU–PF). This postcolonial monument to commemorate Zimbabwe's heroic elite has been described by Werbner as bringing together 'pre-colonial symbolism, colonial stereotyping, both cultural and racial, social realism imported from North Korea (whose government co-financed the monument), and national imagery which is at once divisive and unifying'.[2]

Yet in August 2019, former President Mugabe, Zimbabwe's longest-serving president until his overthrow in November 2017, surprised many Zimbabweans when he informed his family that he did not want to be buried at the National Heroes Acre monument. This, despite the fact that it was a structure which was to all intents and purposes his brainchild. The reason given was that he did not want Emmerson Mnangagwa, the president who displaced him, to officiate because of the way he had removed him from power and failed to apologise for what Mugabe deemed an assault on the Zimbabwean constitution, that is, overthrowing an elected president and his government. This refusal triggered a national debate, with social media comments ranging from the relevance of the monument and who is a hero to how Mugabe had ensured that a number of his contemporaries labelled as 'sell-outs' – such as Ndabaningi Sithole and James Chikerema – would not be declared worthy of burial at the National Heroes Acre.

But if some thought that Mugabe had minced his words because he was ill and bedridden in a hospital in Singapore, the unfolding conflict following his death on 6 September 2019 between the Mnangagwa government and his immediate family over his burial place showed that he was as obdurate in death as he had been in life.[3] A day after his death, the Zimbabwean president moved swiftly to declare Robert Mugabe a national hero – the country's highest posthumous honour. With only a few recent exceptions, declaration of national hero status automatically meant burial at the National Heroes Acre.[4] The official state funeral for the former president proceeded as planned, but did not take place at the national monument as with previous heroes. Instead, it took place at the National Sports Stadium, less than a kilometre away from the national shrine. From there, his body was taken to his house – the Blue Roof – and not to a military morgue. The government announced that the burial awaited the construction of a mausoleum befitting his status as the founding father of the nation. However, his family protested and reiterated that he would be buried in his rural birthplace, Kutama, in the Zvimba district of Mashonaland West Province.[5] After much shuffling between the government and the Mugabe family and traditional leaders from his clan, Mugabe was buried in a private funeral at his rural mansion on 28 September, 22 days after his death.[6]

The question that arises is whether Mugabe's snubbing of the National Heroes Acre in preference to being buried at his rural home diminishes the significance of the national monument? Does it now fall away completely or remain as a 'reluctant ruin' that testifies to this unforeseen episode featuring Mnangagwa and his government, on one hand, and the late president's family and his dead body, on the other? In his op-ed published in *Newsday*, Cyprian Muketiwa Ndawana responded: 'It is a lame conclusion that without Mugabe, Heroes Acre fizzles out to mere commonplace.'[7]

But one thing is clear: without Mugabe, the way the national shrine is viewed, its meaning and symbolism both within the ruling party and among the public, will change. Not least among the questions likely to be revisited are who exactly is a hero in Zimbabwe's political landscape, and which 'heroes' are deserving of laying to rest at the national, provincial and district-level commemorative shrines? Will a statue to commemorate Mugabe as the founding father of the nation be erected on a prominent street in Harare, as with the controversial erection in Bulawayo of the statue of his erstwhile political enemy, Joshua Mqabuko Nkomo, turned compatriot after the 1987 Unity Accord?

Such commemorative projects, as some of the chapters in this book highlight in South African history, are highly contested and have led to raging debates about their symbolism, and who benefits from their construction and display. As such, regardless of the august symbolism of the National Heroes Acre monument, commemoration was marked by painful polemics when it came to substituting colonial shrines with those of the liberation struggle. For all its sharp anti-colonial discourse, the ZANU–PF government was, as Werbner writes, 'reluctant to obliterate the Rhodesian memorials of the Second World War even for the sake of anti-colonial re-inscription. Zimbabwean nationalism was represented as being within internationalism, and the Second World War memorials were kept as anti-fascist and thus within the anti-colonial struggle.'[8]

Those who have visited the National Archives of Zimbabwe in Harare will have seen in its grounds the statue of Cecil John Rhodes, which used to stand tall on what is now Samora Machel Avenue in Harare. It stood between the Harare High Court and Munhumutapa Building, where the offices of the president are situated in the central business district of the capital. In the same grounds of the National Archives sits the statue of the gold and diamond magnate, Alfred Beit. Reflecting on 'the fate of Zimbabwe's colonial monuments', the Zimbabwean writer Farai Mudzingwa recently bemoaned the fact that, despite the initial swift changes of colonial names of streets, hospitals, schools and rivers by the black government of Zimbabwe, 'what once again raises eyebrows is the marble statue of David Livingstone, which stands in the courtyard of Munhumutapa Building, a short distance from where Rhodes' statue once stood'.[9] This prompts Mudzingwa to ask a pointed question that is at the core of this volume, whether the vestiges of colonialism are to be erased, preserved or celebrated? Mudzingwa concludes: 'What is clear is that Zimbabwe has a conflicted relationship with its colonial past and relics.'[10]

Clearly, this is not true only of Zimbabwe. Several other countries on the African continent and beyond have a contradictory relationship with their colonial past and its inherited monuments and architecture, which are a hauntingly enduring presence. Certain themes explored elsewhere in this book confirm these dilemmas in the postcolony in Africa; there are traces and vestiges of the past that are difficult to erase and, in fact, can barely be expunged. From the ashes and ruins of colonial memory arise the memorials of Zimbabwe, Mozambique, Namibia and South Africa – as does the violence of Zimbabwe, Zaire and many other independent African countries.

Zimbabwe, which attained its independence from British rule in 1980, some 14 years before apartheid ended in South Africa, has grappled with the same set of issues that this book seeks to confront. On 18 April 1980, when Prince Charles, representing the British government, lowered the Union Jack in Harare to make way for the new Zimbabwe flag, he also bequeathed to the new nation a colonial heritage of several buildings, reminders of a painful past that a fiery nationalist such as Robert Mugabe might have been expected to waste no time in erasing. But his reconciliation speech would see his government unable to exact vengeance against his erstwhile enemies by destroying colonial symbols and architecture across the country.

The Zimbabwe government could only concentrate on a symbolic and cosmetic erasure, such as the names of roads and buildings, most of which now bear the names of leaders of the liberation struggle, many of whose remains were entombed at the National Heroes Acre. Instead of destroying and replacing buildings, many were partially redesigned and renovated to reflect the new political order. Others have remained intact and regularly receive a fresh coat of paint.

While in South Africa the #RhodesMustFall campaign enlivened debates about what to do with colonial symbols, in Zimbabwe it has been a vexed question of what to do with Rhodes's grave in Matobo National Park in Matabeleland province, from time to time re-igniting public discourse. Calls for its removal preceded independence. The grave was petrol-bombed during the liberation struggle, and guerrillas swore that it would be among the first colonial symbols to be removed once independence was attained. As early as June 1961, Robert Mugabe threatened to disinter Rhodes's body and repatriate it to England.[11] He was to repeat this threat countless times when he became president of Zimbabwe, especially when angered by the British.

Yet he seemed acutely aware of the detrimental effects disentombing Rhodes's remains might have on tourism – a high foreign currency earner for the country – and how this might dent the image of a country he had built on the bedrock of reconciliation. There are several instances of Mugabe toning down his rhetoric against Rhodes, to the extent of censuring even his own war veterans in the late 1990s and 2000s when they had threatened to excavate Rhodes's remains.[12]

On one occasion in 1998, Mugabe had told Zambia's President Frederick Chiluba: '[Some people] want his bones removed. But I am saying the bones do not do us any harm ... I have said in the past that Rhodes should pay his taxes [but] our people don't want to promote tourism towards that grave. They are still a bit uneasy.'[13] This ambivalence about what to do with colonial as well as apartheid symbols and artefacts is a central concern of this volume. The empirical case studies are bold assertions of how controversial they continue to be. In Zimbabwe, one strategy was to turn a blind eye for a while and construct its own postcolonial symbols and monuments, such as the National Heroes Acre, to immortalise the ideals of the revolutionary struggle against colonialism. But as with all monuments, symbols and shrines, whether pre-colonial, colonial or postcolonial, they are often imbued with polemics, however much their sponsors may have rationalised them as necessary at the time. As historian Paul Maylam observes, 'African views about Rhodes's grave are ambivalent and changing, marked by contestation and paradox.'[14] So, too, did Mugabe's views about the National Heroes Acre he had established change once he had been ousted in a military coup.

Colonial ruins and derelict spaces in Zimbabwe are undergoing bitter contestation and continual negotiation as locations of remembrance, as are similar sites in South Africa. It would seem that the policy of reconciliation adopted by the founding fathers of Zimbabwe and post-apartheid South Africa, Robert Gabriel Mugabe and Nelson Rolihlahla Mandela respectively, continues to loom large in heated debates about whether to destroy, remove or integrate colonial symbols. Far from providing final answers to the questions raised in this book, the arguments are meant to arouse debate about the meaning and significance of structures that continue to overshadow the terrain, in particular, of South Africa's past.

Muchaparara Musemwa
September 2020

NOTES

1. Richard Werbner, 'Introduction: Beyond Oblivion: Confronting Memory Crisis', in *Memory and the Postcolony: African Anthropology and the Critique of Power*, ed. Richard Werbner (London: Zed Books, 1998), 8.
2. Werbner, 'Introduction: Beyond Oblivion', 8.
3. Cyprian Muketiwa Ndawana, 'Mugabe Obstinate in Death as in Life', *Newsday*, 17 October 2019, accessed 18 October 2019, https://www.newsday.co.zw/2019/10/mugabe-obstinate-in-death-as-in-life/.
4. The few exceptions include the musician Oliver Mtukudzi and the former military commander of the Zimbabwe People's Revolutionary Army, Dumiso Dabengwa; while grateful for the lavish state burial assistance accorded such heroes, their families opposed the burial of their loved ones at the National Heroes Acre as they would not be able to freely visit the grave due to intense security controls. Others declared before their death that they did not wish to be buried at Heroes Acre owing to political differences that had emerged between them and the ZANU–PF elite.
5. Macdonald Dzirutwe, 'Robert Mugabe's Family Pushes Back Against Zim Government's Burial Plan', *IOL*, 8 September 2019, accessed 18 October 2019, https://www.iol.co.za/news/africa/robert-mugabes-family-pushes-back-against-zim-governments-burial-plan.
6. Blessed Mhlanga and Everson Mushava, 'ED Loses Mugabe Burial Site Tussle', *Newsday*, 17 September 2019, accessed 18 October 2019, https://www.newsday.co.zw/2019/09/ed-loses-mugabe-burial-site-tussle/.
7. Ndawana, 'Mugabe Obstinate in Death as in Life'.
8. Werbner, 'Introduction: Beyond Oblivion', 8.
9. Farai Mudzingwa, 'The Fate of Zimbabwe's Colonial Monuments', *This is Africa*, 7 July 2016, accessed 30 May 2020, https://thisisafrica.me/lifestyle/fate-zimbabwes-colonial-monuments/.
10. Mudzingwa, 'The Fate of Zimbabwe's Colonial Monuments'.
11. Paul Maylam, *The Cult of Rhodes: Remembering an Imperialist in Africa* (Cape Town: David Philip, 2005), 38.
12. 'Robert Mugabe Blocks Cecil John Rhodes Exhumation', *The Telegraph*, 22 February 2012, accessed 31 May 2020, https://www.telegraph.co.uk/news/worldnews/africaandindianocean/zimbabwe/9098490/Robert-Mugabe-blocks-Cecil-John-Rhodes-exhumation.html; 'Mugabe Supporters Demand Exhumation of Rhodes Grave', *Bulawayo News 24*, 18 February 2012, accessed 31 May 2020, https://bulawayo24.com/index-id-news-sc-regional-byo-12287-article-mugabe+party+supporters+demand+exhumation+of+rhodes+grave.html.

13 As quoted in Maylam, *The Cult of Rhodes*, 40.
14 Maylam, *The Cult of Rhodes*, 40.

REFERENCES

Dzirutwe, Macdonald. 'Robert Mugabe's Family Pushes Back Against Zim Government's Burial Plan'. *IOL*, 8 September 2019. Accessed 18 October 2019, https://www.iol.co.za/news/africa/robert-mugabes-family-pushes-back-against-zim-governments-burial-plan.

Maylam, Paul. *The Cult of Rhodes: Remembering an Imperialist in Africa*. Cape Town: David Philip, 2005.

Mhlanga, Blessed, and Everson Mushava. 'ED Loses Mugabe Burial Site Tussle'. *Newsday*, 17 September 2019. Accessed 18 October 2019, https://www.newsday.co.zw/2019/09/ed-loses-mugabe-burial-site-tussle/.

Mudzingwa, Farai. 'The Fate of Zimbabwe's Colonial Monuments'. *This is Africa*, 7 July 2016. Accessed 30 May 2020, https://thisisafrica.me/lifestyle/fate-zimbabwes-colonial-monuments/.

'Mugabe Supporters Demand Exhumation of Rhodes Grave'. *Bulawayo News 24*, 18 February 2012. Accessed 31 May 2020, https://bulawayo24.com/index-id-news-sc-regional-byo-12287-article-mugabe+party+supporters+demand+exhumation+of+rhodes+grave.html.

Ndawana, Cyprian Muketiwa. 'Mugabe Obstinate in Death as in Life'. *Newsday*, 17 October 2019. Accessed 18 October 2019, https://www.newsday.co.zw/2019/10/mugabe-obstinate-in-death-as-in-life/.

'Robert Mugabe Blocks Cecil John Rhodes Exhumation'. *The Telegraph*, 22 February 2012. Accessed 31 May 2020, https://www.telegraph.co.uk/news/worldnews/africaandindianocean/zimbabwe/9098490/Robert-Mugabe-blocks-Cecil-John-Rhodes-exhumation.html.

Werbner, Richard. 'Introduction: Beyond Oblivion: Confronting Memory Crisis'. In *Memory and the Postcolony: African Anthropology and the Critique of Power*, edited by Richard Werbner, 1–17. London: Zed Books, 1998.

ACKNOWLEDGEMENTS

This book had its origins in a 2018 colloquium that included the work and efforts of many individuals, as well as some important collaborations. I wish to thank Noor Nieftagodien, Lukas Spiropolous and Antonette Gouws of the History Workshop; also, at the School of Architecture and Planning, the former head of the School, Paul Jenkins, and the current head, Nnamdi Elleh. For the colloquium, I thank our part-funders, IFAS (French Institute of South Africa) and the Goethe Institute, as well as the University of the Witwatersrand, and Roshan Cader and Kirsten Perkins at Wits University Press. Above all my thanks are due to Arianna Lissoni who was instrumental in developing and organising not only the colloquium but this book which she encouraged and supported.

INTRODUCTION

HILTON JUDIN

In traversing the stubborn landscape of South Africa's oppressive past, we are confronted with the ambivalent ruins and seemingly innocuous buildings of the forgotten architecture of colonialism and apartheid. What we observe in this neglected infrastructure is the lingering presence of architecture's largely hidden yet pervasive everyday structures. The buildings and spaces are a powerful reminder of the everyday bureaucracy of colonialism and apartheid – and how this history of subjugation and planning continues to shape life in post-apartheid South Africa.

Such conflicting spatial claims raise a number of haunting questions: What are we to do with these buildings, remnants and abandoned sites? How are we to remember what happened in these places? Which, if any, of these edifices should remain and which be dismantled? Could these buildings and vacant sites serve as inspiration, or offer solace, of battles won and adversity overcome? Should they be made conciliatory, exemplary or explanatory as a space for restitution and justice sought? These spaces are fraught with incomplete resolution as much as ambivalent reverence, for restoration is often conflated with reconciliation since the threat they once implied is mute.

In the first decade of the post-apartheid period a relatively small number of books examined memory, museums and monuments as part of a national reckoning and reconciliation that was also applied to heritage.[1] In the following decade, this grew to address built environment tasks in the increasing debates and conflicts around the politics of the public, community and commemoration.[2] Challenges to the presence of colonial and apartheid symbols in democratic South Africa were further highlighted by the #RhodesMustFall campaign and the charged public anger and discourse that followed. There have subsequently been many animated debates about the place of historical names, statues and art in public spaces, with calls for their removal as an integral part of decolonisation. These debates have taken on global salience just as this volume is being prepared for publication. Statues in countries across the world have been attacked in a spate of protests inspired by the Black Lives Matter movement against the persistent structures of racism and oppression, rooted in painful histories of colonial violence. It is in this context that questions raised by this book acquire particular urgency.

Through these chapters, we are seeking to understand in what ways history and architecture might ameliorate, contest or subvert these protracted conditions in terms of social justice, land reclamation, heritage, and urban rehabilitation. In examining the oppressive built environment of South Africa, from the burial grounds of Lephalale in Limpopo to the Albert Street Pass Office in Johannesburg, we are asking what is the influence of memory and activism on such anguished places and sites of resistance and defiance? The decades following the dismantling of apartheid are examined in the light of contemporary heritage projects, in which building ruins and abandoned spaces are being contested and renegotiated as sites of remembrance, and historical practices re-examined for the lessons and inspiration they hold.

All of the writers in this volume have made distinctive contributions, based on the colloquium 'Falling Monuments, Reluctant Ruins' held by the History Workshop and the School of Architecture and Planning at the University of the Witwatersrand, Johannesburg, in November 2018. Collectively they tell the story of a country still deeply engaged in the task of commemoration a generation after the demise of apartheid, with all its contradictions and conflicts. They individually show how the intricate, intractable and haunting historical legacy of colonialism and apartheid continues to play out in our collective cultural politics and everyday life. In this, our buildings and institutions are implicated, as much instigators as reflections of both our fraught relationships and shared heritage. This volume and the colloquium from which it draws reflect in some ways back to the conference 'Myths, Monuments, Museums: New Premises?' held by History Workshop in 1992; at this time, during the transition to democracy, cultural optimism balanced the political reality of negotiation and pending reconciliation. That early focus on the Voortrekker Monument has given way here to the cemeteries, abandoned buildings and peripheral spaces that are vital to questions of social identity, heritage and belonging.

For the editor, it is also notable that it was with the History Workshop in 1994 that the archive and video testimony project 'setting apart' was jointly developed (with Deborah Posel and Sue Parnell) to examine and expose the intricate aspects of apartheid spatial planning by placing in the public realm confidential official documents, maps and plans so as to expose the detailed and intimidating bureaucracy of racist state planning at all levels of the state. As with other histories of the present, it is periodically necessary to revisit and revise early debates and assumptions, in these particular cases around communities of remembrance. Disputes in the cultural realm continue to resonate alongside moments of resolution and catharsis. Decades of visions and projects now dot the country – museums, monuments, statues and parks – often surprising and optimistic, and in sharp contrast to the bleak structures and damaged environment from which they arose.

In examining buildings and sites within segregationist and apartheid infrastructures, the contributors to this volume show ways in which formerly oppressive structures still retain some of the physical elements – and social stigma – through which they had symbolically and functionally operated. In South Africa, these racist regimes of operation and representation have not fully retreated: they continue to operate, though in subdued but exhausting and debilitating ways. The focus on state administration buildings, public spaces, memorials and monuments allows for an interrogation of this uncomfortable architecture, in its broadest sense, and the ways in which it is currently being negotiated and treated. An infrastructure of everyday oppression is addressed through the three spatial structures that are the organising themes of this book: Lands, Buildings, and Statues, as Monuments. Even as the functions of many of these edifices has changed – prisoners freed, offices closed and buildings abandoned – their history, which is still unfolding, needs to be continuously gathered and told.

Moving from the absence and erasure of some of the painful everyday urban histories to the architectural confrontations recorded in this book is a necessary shift in moving past an early era of reconciliation and indifference. The chapters in the book employ case studies, community histories and visual analysis to describe the ongoing processes of cultural confrontation. Photographs, oral testimonies, plans, documents, interviews, as well as letters from archives, homes and offices have all been used in different ways by the historians, architects, anthropologists, heritage specialists, curators and artists engaged in this practice. The book seeks to build on confrontations over a conflicting colonial and apartheid history, which includes segregation and forced removals, acts of defiance, the memories of those caught up in it all (even as they moved on with their lives), and a past still seeping into our public life and conscience.

In Part One, which focuses on Lands, the historian Faeeza Ballim examines claims to land in the town of Lephalale in Limpopo province, which are centred around the violation of burial grounds on the construction site of the massive Medupi power station and coal mine. Conflicts over land and belonging are also central concerns in heritage practitioner and writer Eric Itzkin's exploration of efforts by ex-residents of Juliwe for the recognition and restitution of their cemetery. The chapter is a case study of a little-known and neglected local community standing their ground to preserve their cemetery in the face of bureaucratic indignities. Such sites of remembrance and contestation are also apparent in the transformation of public space after apartheid, such as in Constitution Hill and Gandhi Square in Johannesburg as described by the historian and planner Temba John Dawson Middelmann, with the demands of memory and reconciliation rubbing up against those of regeneration and privatisation. The problem of accessibility over managed heritage sites is also raised. The artists Molemo Moiloa and Nare Mokotho challenge such notions of heritage through their collaborative artist practice MADEYOULOOK in the project Ejaradini, which researches black urban gardening and reclaims models of belonging and place-making in the city, while also imagining the Johannesburg Art Gallery beyond mere preservation.

Part Two looks at Buildings, and here the photographer Sally Gaule focuses on photographic representations of the notorious John Vorster Square police station in Johannesburg's central business district to ask about the meaning of the building and the shadow it still seems to cast today. The continued existence, and in many cases rehabilitation, through restoration and repair, of buildings leaves much of the historical legacy of colonialism and apartheid intact and dormant. Rather than a distancing from the past, political and legal anthropologist Kelly Gillespie suggests that the transformation of Robben Island into a museum offers the possibility of reflecting on the violent history of colonialism and apartheid; the prison museum itself poses a problem for history given the escalation in incarceration and ongoing criminalisation in the country. The former Johannesburg Pass Office at Albert Street bears witness, for the architect Hilton Judin, to a terrible past, and continues to silently serve as a space of provocation rather than conciliation and forgetting. Remembrance is all that is left in the wake of the burning of hundreds of West Rand Bantu Administration Board buildings in Soweto during the 1976 uprising. In the West Rand town of Krugersdorp, a building such as Jubilee House could serve heritage as a site of resistance, according to Arianna Lissoni, a historian, and Roshan Dadoo, whose family owned the building: it is emblematic of the history of an Indian trading family and the segregation it was forced to confront. At a building on the other side of the city, engagement with the social and cultural associations of Johannesburg's Drill Hall, as described by urban anthropologist Barbara Morovich and geographer Pauline Guinard, continues to invigorate a long-contested site, keeping practices of memory production alive in the city.

In Part Three – Statues, as Monuments – remembrance, as discussed by architects Yasmin Mayat and Brendan Hart, emerges from community engagement and interaction rather than the consolidation of objecthood in traditional memorial architectural development. The historian Ali Khangela Hlongwane and curator Tara Weber, on the other hand, offer the lesson of the cultural village of Credo Mutwa in Soweto, where the invisibility of the site comes to us today as a living reference and home of indigenous knowledge, a tourist attraction as much as a landscape of bloody repression. In the following chapter, the statue of Mandela, by its placement on the balcony of the Cape Town City Hall, is destined, according to heritage specialist and historian Cynthia Kros, to orientate visitors more towards the colonisers than those who were repressed. Commemoration of the dispossessed, which would be at the heart of the postcolonial memorial project, is examined by social historian Goolam Vahed with regard to the descendants of Indian indentured migrants to Natal, in this case in relation to the building of a statue and the factors driving such a project. Lastly, architectural historian Nnamdi Elleh unpacks the powerful and fraught relationship between memorials, memorial practice and the political battles that surround their erection and removal across Africa, most recently in the wake of global anti-racist movements.

In this book, contributors ask what form rehabilitation takes in mediating between antithetical poles: containment and restoration of distressing sites as opposed to disbursement and dissemination of new narratives. In what sense do these historical forms engage with the political, addressing the demands of polarising conditions of repression and remembrance, pitting official public remembrances against private individual experiences? They investigate historical architectural preservation, community engagement, visual practice, and performance models employed as engagements with spaces still convulsive with meaning. Instead of researching buildings alone in considering heritage history and memory, they further consider the events, songs, practices, actions and aspects of forgotten communities that do not always experience historical recognition. Ultimately, this re-engagement of heritage opens up a space to rethink and reassert the role and place of ideas, imaginaries and communities long marginalised.

We no longer have to cast histories in bronze, carve images out of stone, or place memories on record in concrete. Instead, we can turn to patterns of behaviour and social practices as much as historical figures, we can observe nature and listen to each other, and we can watch plants grow and buildings decay. We can turn the soil and reflect on a shared landscape rather than dig trenches in commemoration of battles and war, remembering as well, marches, dances and acts of defiance. For remembering itself is active, and it is to these living processes to which we need to return again and again. So, alongside historical commemorations and official ceremonies, we might find everyday activities and resistances recalled, and people and practices embraced. Clearly, we are not only talking about buildings and memorials but also about what was not built or erected, designs and communities not considered worthy of attention, and memories not coming to rest on anything like a singular national narrative or history.

What these contributors are doing is contesting our very notion of heritage: Whose it is, how it came about, where we find it, and how we are going to distinguish and weigh it; how we are going to retain it, in some cases, and lose it in others, put it aside or make it central. Who of us will record it and who preserve it? In each of the areas addressed, from burial sites and abandoned buildings to public places, from forgotten sculptures and sites of defiance to reconstituted statues and plaques, who gets to decide, and by what means is our heritage to be interrogated and constituted? If heritage is not merely to be a record of history and a collection of old edifices and objects, its value will depend on the ways it reflects a community's daily practices, recollections and cultural activities. And this in ways that communities have responded collectively and are considered, understood and regularly engaged. There is no easy way to move past conflicts over commemoration or the communities embodied therein. In the end, it is debates and sagas, historical embroilments and conflicting and conciliatory views which constitute a deeper sense of heritage as a shared cultural practice passed on to a nation not haunted but strengthened by its past.

The chapters that follow point to changes undergone in politics and society in South Africa over the last decade that have brought new groups into solidarity to confront conflicting interests and memories. Recognition given to past generations, events and individuals is being challenged just as stories once buried and censured are becoming more central to an evolving public space. As many of the contributors have found, the past has remained a haunting presence even as the absence of an intimate unconventional heritage has become increasingly apparent. The present, in turn, is hardly able to address all the horrors of the past. Increasingly, however, there is clarity that there is no place where racist historical statues, monuments and memorials can remain standing. Statues are falling in protests around the world against racism, colonialism and slavery. From the toppling of the statue of Edward Colston in Bristol, to attacks on confederate statues across the southern states of the USA, from the burning of a statue of Leopold II in Antwerp to another toppling of Cecil John Rhodes this time at Oxford University, outrage and revulsion are everywhere evident. The very act of pulling down statues has brought about and confirmed for many that things are indeed changing. These granite and bronze structures no longer speak, and nor do they serve any meaningful purpose. There is no more time for further discussion or debate, as those finding a voice must instead be heard. Suddenly all talk has given way to action and communal affirmation, a burning activism that cannot be dampened.

Buildings have in reality never been able to bear witness to the past, speak poignantly, or offer testimony to a public or a historical period. There seem few ways they can be rearticulated, reassigned meaning, or thoroughly recontextualised. Monuments are not history. Statues, while mute, are not completely silent, and can either rebuke or sneer. Moreover, while they do not fully transcribe the historical figure they mimic, instead resonating with meanings they evoke or commemorate, statues are fixed in time; as such they no longer retain the right to a public place. As long as they stand, they remain reflective of the politics, power and period of their erection. Increasingly, and instead of these, participation and inclusion of a new public have proceeded as violent confrontation which is not simply recorded in stone, brick and mortar. Histories are never neatly expunged, as repressive and violent pasts continue to echo in public spaces and buildings. From such a traumatic past, it is hard to imagine anyone desiring to preserve associated places and buildings, reminders of the horrors and urban structures that continue to stifle social life. Given this, perhaps all statues and commemorative projects need a periodic reckoning?

The complexities of public space and representation, as examined in this book, have not been mitigated by the distance and neglect that many of these lost spaces of apartheid – the cemeteries, renovated government edifices, districts and historical statues – continue to reflect. Instead, we are witnessing battles over urban space and monuments preceding newly emerging memories. Many of the places discussed in this volume are embroiled in ongoing conflict, not only over their historic meaning or the commemoration that gave rise to them, but also over communities and the changing uses of these spaces. Contributors have highlighted the extraordinary and rapidly changing practices that have evolved to meet these challenges, reaching beyond architecture and history to take on shared social tasks such as gardening, burial, advocacy and healing. We have in these chapters a growing sense that it is the activities, acts of defiance and stories people tell themselves that need to be preserved. This search for new narratives and strategies to challenge the legacy of apartheid demands the diverse practices exemplified in the contributor's research of landscapes and buildings caught up in the contemporary cultural and social challenges of South Africa.

NOTES

1   See Sarah Nuttall and Carli Coetzee, eds, *Negotiating the Past: The Making of Memory* (Cape Town: Oxford University Press, 1998); David Goldblatt, *South*

Africa: The Structure of Things Then (Cape Town: Oxford University Press, 1998); Annie E. Coombes, *History after Apartheid: Visual Culture and Public Memory in a Democratic South Africa* (Durham: Duke University Press, 2003); Noeleen Murray, Nick Shepherd and Martin Hall, eds, *Desire Lines: Space, Memory and Identity in the Post-Apartheid City* (London: Routledge, 2007); Sabine Marschall, *Landscapes of Memory. Commemorative Monuments, Memorials, and Public Statuary on Post-Apartheid South Africa* (Leiden and Boston: Brill, 2010); and Jonathan Noble, *African Identity in Post-Apartheid Public Architecture: White Skin, Black Mask* (London: Ashgate, 2011).

2 See Martin J. Murray, *Commemorating and Forgetting: Challenges for the New South Africa* (Minneapolis: University of Minnesota Press, 2013); Derek R. Peterson, Kodzo Gavua and Ciraj Rassool, *The Politics of Heritage in Africa: Economies, Histories, and Infrastructures* (Cambridge: Cambridge University Press, 2015); Kim Miller and Brenda Schmahmann, eds, *Public Art in South Africa: Bronze Warriors and Plastic Presidents* (Bloomington: Indiana University Press, 2017); Lesley Witz, Gary Minkley and Ciraj Rassool, *Unsettled History: Making South African Public Pasts* (Ann Arbor: University of Michigan Press, 2017); and Ali Khangela Hlongwane and Sifiso Mxolisi Ndlovu, *Public History and Culture in South Africa: Memorialisation and Liberation Heritage Sites in Johannesburg and the Township Space* (London: Palgrave Macmillan, 2019).

PART ONE
LANDS

1 LAND DISPOSSESSION AND THE GHOSTS OF THE MEDUPI POWER STATION

FAEEZA BALLIM

In 2007, South Africa faced the reality of the country's electricity shortage with the introduction of 'load-shedding', a term used to describe scheduled blackouts that affect both households and businesses. In response, Eskom embarked on the construction of two new power stations, Medupi in Limpopo province and Kusile in Mpumalanga, although more than ten years later, these have yet to be completed. The Medupi Power Station is the subject of this chapter. Once complete, it is expected to be the largest power station of its kind in the world. It was built at a time when the growing consensus around climate change had made clear the unsustainability of fossil fuel-based energy. The power station is situated in an arid, bushveld region, near to the South African border with Botswana, on the outskirts of the small town of Lephalale. Medupi is situated about twenty kilometres away from another power station called Matimba, which the electricity public utility Eskom built in the 1980s. To the north of these power stations lies the Grootgeluk coal mine, built by South Africa's former state-run steel corporation Iscor in the late 1970s. The mine produced coking coal, commonly used to manufacture steel, as well as the bituminous coal that Eskom burnt in its power stations. The Lephalale region has thus for decades been the site of state-driven, sophisticated engineering projects, rooted in the tail end of the apartheid government's period of high modernism[1] and brutal social engineering.

The construction of the Medupi Power Station began in 2008, and its completion date has been regularly postponed. In 2015, community members resident in the township of Marapong, adjacent to Lephalale, complained that the Medupi construction site contained graves that had not been exhumed and were likely destroyed during the construction period. They claimed that the angry spirits were responsible for disruptions at Medupi. The chairperson of one of the organisations representing community members, the Commission for the Promotion and Protection of the Rights of Cultural, Religious and Linguistic Communities (CRL Rights Commission), Thoko Mkhwanazi, said: 'It's the bones underneath and in the vicinity. Some of the graves were destroyed there. The belief systems of some people will tell you that this Medupi dream of yours will never happen. It will be another 10 years.'[2] The allegations were met with scepticism and disdain from some quarters, with one online news report stating that the CRL commission 'firmly believes that strikes, political infighting, unionist sabotage and general mismanagement has no role to play in the delays at Medupi. Rather, they spent tax money – the CRL commission is a chapter 9 institution [state institution supporting constitutional democracy] – to compile a report claiming that the ancestors are unhappy as their graves have been disturbed by Medupi's construction.'[3]

Eskom had conducted a heritage assessment in 2006 before it began construction and this assessment had not taken account of the graves at the Medupi site. Heritage consultants, Mbofho Consulting and Project Managers, who investigated Eskom's handling of the community claims in 2018, concluded that there was no ill-will or evidence of a cover-up on the part of Eskom. The graves were for the most part unmarked, with just one bearing a concrete head and slab that melded into the surrounding bushveld seemingly without a trace. While noting the absence of malicious intent, the heritage consultants chastised Eskom for failing to engage community members sooner or paying appropriate attention to local sensitivities.[4]

'PLACE OF BONES'

This tale of the restless spirits is shot through with a history of profound and lasting dispossession. This legacy is a part of the founding mythology of the African township, whose name Marapong translates to 'place of bones'.

It is also linked to a historical process of racially delimited technological modernisation, driven by state corporations. In the aftermath of the Sharpeville Massacre of 1960, the apartheid government became increasingly concerned to ensure the country's economic self-sufficiency in the face of its deepening international isolation. State corporations produced the base inputs, in this case electricity and steel, that could support industrialisation and the mining sector.[5] While tied to the national developmental project, these corporations also enjoyed an organisational autonomy from the state bureaucracy, and at times defied the precepts of spatial segregation practised by the apartheid government in the interests of financial efficiency. In this way, while circumscribed by the dictates of racial segregation, technological modernisation in the region could not be strictly identified with the brutality of forced removals that occurred under the Group Areas Act.

Heritage studies in South Africa is intimately linked to the conception of the new nation that emerged after the democratic elections of 1994. In what Leslie Witz, Gary Minkley and Ciraj Rassool term the 'heritage complex', it has tied particular pasts to 'governmentality and the nation-state'.[6] These pasts have assumed a regional dimension, with each province being renowned for a particular heritage symbol. As a peripheral, border region, Lephalale has not featured in the national heritage conversation, and the contestation over the graves at Medupi marked the first major engagement between the legitimating authority of heritage consultants and local community histories. The search for missing human remains is also closely bound up with South African nationhood after 1994. Ciraj Rassool has documented the role of material remains in the Truth and Reconciliation Commission, a body set up to usher in the new nation that would emerge in the era of democracy. Rassool writes that 'again and again, witnesses made claims in respect of body parts and human remains, making their visibility, recovery and repossession a metaphor for the settlement of the pasts of apartheid'.[7] But more than a need to settle the past injustice, the restless spirits aroused by the disturbance of graves at the Medupi construction site are seen to actively curtail the economic prosperity of community members. After a century of capital and land dispossession of Africans in the region, those who seek redress for the dead couch their claims for inclusivity in the continued deleterious effects of the restless spirits in their lives, as well as in the construction of Medupi itself.

On the one hand, these complaints are not reducible to claims of land ownership, yet they also indicate a hidden history of autochthony and belonging.[8] In their report entitled 'Medupi Power Station Graves – Towards Healing and Closure' of October 2018, the heritage consultants Mbofho state: 'It has not been possible to get an accurate measurement of the social impact of the crisis among the affected people as individuals, as families and as a community.'[9] The immeasurable nature of the inflicted hurt creates the impression of an incalculable malaise. In her edited collection entitled *Imperial Debris: Reflections on Ruins and Ruination*, anthropologist Ann Laura Stoler urges the adoption of a more historical approach to studies of the remnants of colonial rule and consequently to the 'connective tissue that continues to bind human potentials to degraded environments, and degraded personhoods to the material refuse of imperial projects'.[10] Stoler's focus is avowedly on the ruins of empire, and while Medupi is a contemporary construction project, the principle of dispossession through a history of large technical projects and of social engineering in the region remains.

In an interview with the South African news station eNCA, a traditional healer, Lazarus Seodisa, who has been one of the main drivers of the reburial process, stated the importance of the completion of Medupi's construction: 'The company needs to be successful so our children will have jobs.' While Seodisa expressed no antipathy towards the construction of Medupi, he lamented the lack of educational opportunities for the young people of the community. He stressed that Eskom should have consulted with community leaders before commencing with construction in order to ensure that the remains of the dead were properly laid to rest. Another community member interviewed by eNCA, Johannes Tibanyane, said that his three-day-old infant had been buried at the Medupi site. He was, however, unsure of the fate of the remains once construction began in 2007, and noted: 'My wife has many problems, she is always complaining about pains on her wrist.'[11]

Eskom's defiling of the graves at Medupi constricted the lives and livelihoods of the residents of Marapong, both spiritually and materially. People believed the restless spirits caused mysterious ailments among living family members and contributed to the continual delay of the completion of Medupi, so harming the prospects for employment and economic prosperity among community members. In July 2016, Eskom unveiled a memorial site to commemorate the dead, a site chosen in consultation with community members and traditional leaders.¹² But since many of the graves were destroyed during the construction, rendering them unrecoverable, it remains unclear whether this was enough to appease the affected family members.

ISCOR'S ARRIVAL

Iscor began to show an interest in the coal reserves of the Waterberg in the 1970s, bringing its full financial and technical expertise to bear on a region that had escaped state regulation and significant capital investment for much of the twentieth century. While organisationally distinct from the state, the population growth it brought in its wake meant that the Group Areas Board had to ensure an 'orderly' urban development, which manifested in racial segregation and the forced removals of Africans living in nominally white areas. In so doing, it cemented decades of the capital dispossession of Africans. In the early 1970s, Iscor began prospecting work at various sites in the vicinity of the town of Ellisras. Lazarus Seodisa had been a part of these prospecting teams. He argued that angry spirits had sabotaged the establishment of coal mines at sites that Iscor deemed unfeasible for the development of a coal mine. At a prospecting site close to the Seleka village, and another close to the dumping grounds in what is now Onverwacht, water flooded out of the first holes that workers dug. Seodisa interpreted this as a sign of the displeasure of the spirits at being disturbed.

At the site of the Grootgeluk coal mine, excavated during the early 1970s, workers insisted that the bones of the deceased known to lie beneath the soil were first exhumed and relocated to nearby gravesites. A former manager of the coal mine and Iscor employee, Joe Meyer, recalled in an interview that Iscor's managers watched as traditional healers performed cleansing ceremonies during the exhumation and burial. Seodisa argued that the spirits had to be approached with caution and reverence if the mine was to successfully sink a shaft. The restlessness of the spirits has become an important interpretive theme for Seodisa in his narrative of events. As part of his work as a traditional healer in the community, he has lobbied the Department of Traditional Affairs to consider the relocation of graves at the site of the Medupi Power Station. When I interviewed Seodisa in March 2015, he maintained that the spirits of bodies were not laid to rest at Medupi; they have been the cause, he claims, of supernatural incidents and freak accidents at the power station, and he was especially fearful for workers on the night shift.

When Iscor's workers excavated the site for the establishment of the Grootgeluk coal mine, they uncovered the bones of people who had not received proper burials and were likely to have perished alone. Lazarus Seodisa was one of those workers, and he went on to describe how, while digging up the soil at the site of one of the mine shafts, they uncovered numerous sets of human bones. Community members were able to identify one of these, by the cloth found in its immediate surrounds, as a woman named Sara Moloantoa. She hailed from the nearby village of Seleka and had gone missing after she left her family on 24 December 1953 to visit her brother, who lived on a nearby farm, over Christmas. When she failed to return, her family assumed that she had lost her way and perished. This was a likely occurrence because travellers on foot would have faced a vast expanse of dry bushveld and intense darkness after sunset. Furthermore, workers uncovered other bones at the site which they believed to be the remains of travellers from the neighbouring countries of Botswana and Zimbabwe who crossed the border into South Africa in the hope of finding employment either at the iron ore mine in Thabazimbi or further south on the gold mines around Johannesburg. Seodisa contended, moreover, that fighters from the ANC's armed wing Umkhonto we Sizwe (MK) who had passed away in the Ellisras district were buried at the current site of the Medupi Power Station: 'Remember they were using their fighter names ... Now the veterans they start to say, we know this number with this name, they are the ones who we buried – we buried them there.'

When Iscor's engineers arrived in Ellisras in the early 1970s they encountered a vast expanse of bushveld. The land they sought to mine formed part of some smallholdings owned by white farmers, which Iscor acquired after some legal wrangling. For most of the twentieth century, the region that was to become known as Ellisras was untouched by state regulation, mainly due to the small number of white settlers. Arid environmental conditions made successful agriculture difficult and prevented dense residential settlement. It was only with Iscor's arrival and the imminent prospect of large-scale industrial development that state officials grew attentive to the direction of the town's development. Officials who visited the district during the 1960s found that its material conditions offended against the principles of apartheid. The scarcity of basic services meant that whites could not attain the standards of living necessary to set them apart from the surrounding African communities. Government officials insisted that for Ellisras to be formally declared a town, residents had to ensure that service provision was in place. But this required significant investment in urban infrastructure. Early private initiatives were shoddy and inadequate. It was only with Iscor's financial muscle that the residents of Ellisras could fulfil the infrastructural requirements for the government to grant the town municipal recognition.

WHITE SETTLERS

According to the official history of the town, Ellisras was named after two white settlers who established the farm of Waterkloof during the 1930s. These early settlers, Patric Ellis and Piet Erasmus, merged their last names to form the name Ellisras. The Waterkloof farm also included a railway stop for a line that passed from Vaalwater in the south to Stockpoort in the north. In line with the historian Bill Freund's description of African cities historically forming around the nodes of transport networks, the embryonic town developed around the railway stop.[13] Patric Ellis hailed from the Marico district, roughly 300 kilometres south-west of Ellisras. He was a member of the underclass of Afrikaner settlers who did not own land, and worked as a tenant farmer, or bywoner, and had fought in the South African War.[14] Ponk Ellis informed me in August 2013 that his grandfather, Patric Ellis, had migrated to the inhospitable territory of the Waterberg in search of a new beginning. Ellisras itself consisted of a rudimentary commercial centre, and barter was a common form of exchange. Ellis described the system that operated when his grandfather settled in the district: white settlers hunted the bushveld game for their survival, and exchanged biltong (dried meat) for agricultural crops such as grain and peanuts with nearby African chiefdoms. For the townsfolk, the only source of cash was the town's sole storekeeper. Ellis went on to describe farmers exchanging chicken, bones and 'anything you could give him' for money or household supplies. It is not clear how the nature of commercial exchange changed over the decades, but by the time a resident named Michael Deats arrived in Ellisras in the early 1970s, he found an unremarkable scattering of buildings. In an interview in September 2013, Deats gave me the following description: 'There was a bottle store. And there was a little kind of hotel and when I say little, I mean little. And a few houses. And I think there was a magistrate …'

The Waterkloof farm was a natural magnet for residential settlement because of its proximity to the Mogol River, a tributary of the Limpopo to the north of Ellisras. Before Iscor built the Hans Strijdom Dam to supply water to its Grootgeluk coal mine in the 1970s, the Mogol River served as a crucial water supply for farm dwellers. But the river was not an entirely reliable irrigation source because of its limited and temperamental flow. Until the arrival of Iscor, there was little sustainable crop farming in the region. The Mogol Dam, which Iscor built in the 1970s, was the first reliable and consistent irrigation source for farmers in the region. While under government ownership, Iscor maintained the dam and controlled the flow of water to the Grootgeluk coal mine, the town of Ellisras and to farmers, on a quota basis. Dam building had at the time proceeded across the country to encourage crop farming. The historian William Beinart estimates that by 1970 the proportion of South Africa's 'channelled water' that was used for irrigation was among the highest in the world.[15]

Because commercial agriculture was not wholly viable, the region did not attract large numbers of white settlers. Low white settler density is one of the reasons that the settlers failed to form a formidable front against the African communities residing in the district during the early part of the twentieth century. For Africans in the district, the story of the twentieth century is one of the gradual erosion of their economic autonomy. Sam Sekati, whose parents were born in the Ellisras district, told me that the 1940s saw a discernible shift in the balance of power towards white settlers. This coincided with the National Party's assumption of power in 1948 and its efforts to improve the lot of Afrikaners in rural areas, a constituency that had proven decisive in its electoral victory. The struggling white farmers of Ellisras received material and legislative support from the state to promote their economic prosperity. Ponk Ellis had informed me that, after 1948, the government assisted farmers by drilling boreholes on their land and parcelling out additional plots of land to white settlers. Sekati, on the other hand, described the abrupt manner in which rights to land utilisation were wrested from the resident African communities:

> You must remember the government was for the whites. So they came here, they're staying with you, you borrow [lend] them your cows to plough a portion and later on one morning when you wake up they will call all of them and tell them as from today I'm the owner of the farm … it's up to you to stay with me or go and look for another place. And white people were scattered all over now. Wherever you go you see the white owner is the owner of that place.

White settlers eventually won the land by dispossession through bureaucratisation. They demarcated property boundaries by pegging corners and then drawing up title deeds to serve as proof of land ownership. Title deeds were backed by the legislative power of the state. This allowed white settlers to acquire economic power by gradually acquiring cattle from the African communities. African farmers had historically used the entire region to roam and graze their cattle, unconstrained by the demarcated property boundaries. Sekati described the dispossession as a gradual process, where white farmers settled on the land in apparent parity with their African neighbours for a time before claiming ownership of the land and presenting a title deed as proof. Once in positions of authority, they ordered individual Africans to reduce their cattle stock:

> And then he will buy your cattle for far less, he will keep on reducing your cattle until you are left with nothing … until they kicked you out. But they don't just kick you out – they make sure the conditions are so difficult for you to live there then at the end you say, no I better go and not live here with all these conditions. And then you will go to another place. You have one hundred, two hundred cattle and then you are left with only four or five. And their tactic was that if you refuse to buy [sell] your cattle and then you decide to move to another place, another farm, the farmers will communicate, they will say: if a black person is coming to your farm, don't allow him to bring so many cattle. So that was the strategy, that there is nowhere to run.

This process of the gradual dispossession of cattle is a familiar tale in the district, with one interviewee, Johannes Mfisa, lamenting the fact that while his father owned a large herd of cattle, he was left without even a chicken to his name.

Nonetheless, despite some initial victories, white farmers failed to form an entirely triumphant front. African settlement on white farmlands in Ellisras, along with various marginal and under-capitalised farmlands in the former Transvaal province, stretched into the 1970s. Elsewhere in the Transvaal and in the Orange Free State province, black tenancy had been largely eradicated by 1969.[16] In an interview at Lephalale, Willie Loots, a long-time resident of the town, recalled the presence of African informal settlements on the farmlands surrounding Ellisras alongside the road to the village of Shongoane before forced removals occurred, encompassing a distance of roughly 25 kilometres.

FORCED REMOVALS

Once Iscor arrived, the black families living in informal settlements on white-owned farmlands surrounding Ellisras were banished to the Lebowa homeland. On the outskirts of the town, an informal black settlement known as the Pahama location had formed. Government officials also targeted Pahama for forced removals. There are two possible reasons for this. The first is Iscor's need for mining labour. Soon after Africans were forcibly removed from the white-owned farms, Iscor constructed its hostel for single males. Thus, the migrant labour system in existence almost everywhere else in the country was finally extended to its north-western border. The second is the threat of an insurgency from the neighbouring African countries. Certain municipal and government officials thought that an African settlement within the town could easily be infiltrated by terrorists, posing a security risk to the white town.

The forced removal of African families from white-owned farms was traumatic. In 1979, the *Sunday Express* detailed the mass removals of an estimated 20 000 Africans from small towns in the Northern Transvaal, including those residing in black townships and locations.[17] Apart from Ellisras, the Northern Transvaal towns of Naboomspruit, Nylstroom, Vaalwater and Louis Trichardt were also affected. The removals were therefore part of the broader segregationist plans which involved relocating Africans from white urban areas to the homelands. Relocation was also necessary to bolster the viability of formally established black local authorities. However, correspondence over 'black spot' removals in Ellisras reveals the frustration of the Commissioner for Bantu Affairs at the fact that he held no authority over Africans who resided on white-owned farms. When these reporters visited Ellisras to report on the forced removals, they struggled to locate the site of Pahama location: 'We had difficulty in finding the site of the former Ellisras location, two kilometres outside the town. At last we realised we had driven past it – it had been bulldozed flat, the ground surrounded by a two-metre game fence. A few ostriches were stalking among the ruins.'

The newly erected hostel – painted a 'vivid pink' – reportedly lay 20 kilometres out of town, close to the Grootgeluk coal mine, and was described as already populated with black single men. Their wives and children lived in Stelloop, which was in the Lebowa homeland and provided few employment opportunities. The government subsidised the cost of four-bedroomed houses but, Sekati informed me, living conditions remained unbearable. As a result, those who were financially able departed as soon as the dissolution of the apartheid regime rendered residential restrictions obsolete.

Ellisras officially fell under the ambit of the Group Areas Board in 1966 and the unregulated presence of informal settlements on white-owned land then swam into the government's focus. An inspector from the Group Areas Board who visited the town in 1966 found to his dismay that African families were spread all over the general district of the town. Many of the 'squatters' occupied farmlands with the consent of the owners in tenancy arrangements. The inspector insisted that a black township be established and began discussions with the Ellisras Area Committee to demarcate land.[18] While local officials dragged their feet, by the early 1970s the arrival of Iscor was no longer in doubt, and the need for ordered urban development in response to the coming industrial activity became more urgent. Government officials cast renewed attention on the black families scattered in the general vicinity of the town.

There is a clear link between the industrialisation thought to follow from Iscor's activities and the intense concern over health and hygiene in the town. On 8 March 1976, the Health Inspector reported that unhygienic conditions generally prevailed in the African 'squatter camp', daily generating complaints from the Ellisras white 'public'. The squatter camp in question was the informal settlement known as the Pahama location. In addition, he wrote, the arrival of Iscor heralded a more chaotic residential situation that would create perfect conditions for the spread of infectious diseases such as polio, chicken pox, tuberculosis and diphtheria. The health inspector also visited two farms on which Africans lived – one owned by a Mr van Rensburg and the other by a Mr Horn – and reported that, while the immediate surroundings of the 'Bantu' huts were clean, their occupants on Horn's farm were dumping their rubbish over the border fence. In addition, African residents drew their drinking water from the Mogol River, and suffered from a general lack of sanitary services. The Chief Medical Health Officer duly wrote to the Commissioner of Bantu Affairs, hoping for co-operation in providing latrines and proper water supply. But more importantly, to put an end to the sanitary problems associated with informal dwellings, the health officer sought assurance that plans for the township had been finalised.[19]

While health officials continued to expressed their concerns, the Commissioner of Bantu Affairs for the Northern Transvaal succeeded in expediting the forced removals. This was in line with a broader national move to eradicate 'black spots'. His chief concern was that the office of the Commissioner for Bantu Affairs could not control the Africans living on white-owned land and had no authority to dictate to the white farmers how these Africans should be treated. The Bantu Trust was about to purchase land in the vicinity of the town of Marken, roughly 70 kilometres from Ellisras, for the construction of a black township. This proposed site would eventually become Stelloop. Since it was situated inside the Lebowa homeland, government officials intended it to house the families of single males otherwise resident in the town's hostel.[20] In 1976, Iscor promised to build accommodation on the Grootestryd farm; of this, three per cent would be family housing for African employees, with a hostel for single males. In the meantime, the matter was finalised: Pahama was declared a temporary location and its residents earmarked for later relocation to the homeland.[21] The Northern Transvaal Bantu Affairs Administration Board applied to purchase a tiny section of the Grootestryd farm from Iscor to be used for a hostel that would house 600 single men who were ordinarily employed in the town.[22] Iscor retained 502 hectares of the property where the hostel providing temporary housing for workers employed by its sub-contractors would be situated.[23] The Administration Board intended to move families out of the Pahama camp as it had not provided them with suitable housing facilities or bus services. The necessity for a township remained, only to be finally resolved in the 1980s with the arrival of Eskom.

FAILURES AND FUTURE FEARS

This chapter has reconstructed a history of dispossession in the Lephalale region, which has been the site of large technical projects since the 1970s. Driven by South Africa's state corporations, these projects have entailed a large amount of capital expenditure with limited downstream material advantages to the people living in their vicinity. The power stations made their appearance at the tail end of a period of dispossession of Africans over the course of the twentieth century. In the absence of ownership of land or cattle, despite a history of residence in the region, graves and burial sites have become the only claim of belonging in the region for certain community members.

As a dry and derelict border region, the Waterberg stayed off the official map for much of the twentieth century, so much so that it escaped the iron fist of the Group Areas Board for some time. It was only with the economic and population growth heralded by the arrival of the state corporations in the 1970s that local officials paid concerted attention to racial segregation in the small town of Ellisras. While cementing land dispossession of Africans in the region, the state corporations also promised economic development, and the claims for grave restoration in the post-apartheid period contain within them a fear of spiritual sabotage of this prosperity. The graves at the burial site of the people of Marapong were largely unmarked, with the result that Eskom failed to perform the appropriate rites on the human remains before it began construction on the Medupi Power Station. To a large extent, heritage studies in the post-apartheid period, focused on casting certain local histories into the mould of the story of the new democratic nation, has neglected the role that the restoration of historic symbols and human remains plays in informing the way that people make sense of their material conditions, both in the present and in the future.

NOTES

1. James C. Scott, *Seeing Like a State: How Certain Schemes to Improve the Human Condition Have Failed* (New Haven: Yale University Press, 1998).
2. 'Medupi Delays: "It's the Bones Underneath"', *Capricorn Voice*, 28 May 2015, accessed 1 June 2019, https://capricornreview.co.za/48966/medupi-delays-its-the-bones-underneath/.
3. 'Medupi Will Never be Completed, because "the Ancestors are Unhappy" … Official Report', *The South African*, 27 May 2015, accessed 1 June 2019, https://www.thesouthafrican.com/news/medupi-will-never-be-completed-because-the-ancestors-are-unhappy-official-report/.
4. 'Medupi Power Station Graves – Towards Healing and Closure: An Integrated Management Plan (IMP)', Report prepared by Mbofho Consulting and Project Managers, 1 October 2018, accessed 17 June 2020, http://www.eskom.co.za/OurCompany/SustainableDevelopment/EnvironmentalImpactAssessments/MedupiGraves/Documents/MEDUPI%20POWER%20STATION%20GRAVES%20IMP%20FINAL%2001102018.pdf.

5   For further discussion, see Nancy L. Clark, *Manufacturing Apartheid: State Corporations in South Africa* (New Haven: Yale University Press, 1994); and Ben Fine and Zavareh Rustomjee, *The Political Economy of South Africa: From Minerals-Energy Complex to Industrialisation* (London: Hurst & Company, 1996).

6   Leslie Witz, Gary Minkley and Ciraj Rassool, *Unsettled History: Making South African Public Pasts* (Ann Arbor: University of Michigan Press, 2017), 221.

7   Ciraj Rassool, 'Human Remains, the Disciplines of the Dead, and the South African Memorial Complex', in *The Politics of Heritage in Africa: Economies, Histories, and Infrastructures*, eds Ciraj Rassool, Derek Peterson and Kodzo Gavua (Cambridge: Cambridge University Press, 2015), 139.

8   This tenuous relationship has been noted, inter alia, by Joost Fontein, 'Graves, Ruins, and Belonging: Towards an Anthropology of Proximity', *Journal of the Royal Anthropological Institute* 17.4 (2011): 706–27; Michelle Hay, '"The Last Thing that Tells Our Story": The Roodepoort West Cemetery, 1958–2008', *Journal of Southern African Studies* 37.2 (2011): 297–311; and Deborah James, 'Burial Sites, Informal Rights and Lost Kingdoms: Contesting Land Claims in Mpumalanga, South Africa', *Africa* 79.2 (2009): 228–51.

9   'Medupi Power Station Graves', 14.

10 Ann Laura Stoler, ed., *Imperial Debris: On Ruins and Ruination* (Durham: Duke University Press, 2013), 10.

11 'Medupi Built on Several Burial Sites', *eNCA*, 3 September 2015, accessed 1 June 2020, https://www.enca.com/south-africa/burial-sites-medupi-was-built.

12 'South African Families Gather to Commemorate Deceased with Memorial Near Medupi Power Plant', The World Bank, 8 July 2016, accessed 17 June 2020, https://www.worldbank.org/en/news/feature/2016/07/08/south-african-families-gather-to-commemorate-deceased-with-memorial-at-medupi-power-plant.

13 Bill Freund, *The African City: A History* (Cambridge: Cambridge University Press, 2007), 6.

14 Hannes Engelbrecht, *Ellisras: My Dorp* (Ellisras: Ellisras Nuus Uitgewers, n.d.). This publication is held by the Lephalale Public Library.

15 William Beinart, *Twentieth-Century South Africa* (Oxford: Oxford University Press, 2001), 207.

16 Beinart, *Twentieth-Century South Africa*, 210.

17 '20 000 Are Banished to Dumping Grounds', *Sunday Express*, 29 July 1979.

18 'Ellisras: Instelling van Groepsgebiede', 14 October 1966, National Archives of South Africa, GMO 1/177 4.

19 Letter: Hoofmediese Gesondheidsbeampte aan Hoofbantoesakekommissarie, 20 March 1976, National Archives of South Africa, TRB 2/4/57 G31/13/0.
20 Head Bantu Commissioner for Native Affairs to the Chief Medical Health Officer of the Transvaal Peri-Urban Areas Board, 22 September 1976, National Archives of South Africa, TRB 2/4/57 G31/13/0.
21 Memorandum: Aan Onafgehandelde Sake, 4 May 1976, National Archives of South Africa, TRB 2/4/57 G31/13/0.
22 Letter from N. A. Lombard, Streekverteenwoordiger, to [recipient unclear in document], 8 May 1977, National Archives of South Africa, GMO 1/177 5.
23 Memo: To the Hoofdirekteur Bantoesake Administrasie, 9 February 1977, NASA, BAO 3/4074 A12/2/6/E10/15.

REFERENCES

Beinart, William. *Twentieth-Century South Africa*. Oxford: Oxford University Press, 2001.

Clark, Nancy L. *Manufacturing Apartheid: State Corporations in South Africa*. New Haven: Yale University Press, 1994.

'Ellisras: Instelling van Groepsgebiede'. 14 October 1966, National Archives of South Africa, GMO 1/177 4.

Fine, Ben, and Zavareh Rustomjee. *The Political Economy of South Africa: From Minerals-Energy Complex to Industrialisation*. London: Hurst & Company, 1996.

Fontein, Joost. 'Graves, Ruins, and Belonging: Towards an Anthropology of Proximity'. *Journal of the Royal Anthropological Institute* 17.4 (2011): 706–27.

Freund, Bill. *The African City: A History*. Cambridge: Cambridge University Press, 2007.

Hay, Michelle. '"The Last Thing That Tells Our Story": The Roodepoort West Cemetery, 1958–2008'. *Journal of Southern African Studies* 37.2 (2011): 297–311.

James, Deborah. 'Burial Sites, Informal Rights and Lost Kingdoms: Contesting Land Claims in Mpumalanga, South Africa'. *Africa* 79.2 (2009): 228–51.

'Medupi Built on Several Burial Sites'. *eNCA*, 3 September 2015. Accessed 1 June 2020, https://www.enca.com/south-africa/burial-sites-medupi-was-built.

'Medupi Delays: "It's the Bones Underneath"'. *Capricorn Voice*, 28 May 2015. Accessed 1 June 2019, https://capricornreview.co.za/48966/medupi-delays-its-the-bones-underneath/.

'Medupi Will Never be Completed, because "the Ancestors are Unhappy" … Official Report'. *The South African*, 27 May 2015. Accessed 1 June 2019, https://www.thesouthafrican.com/news/medupi-will-never-be-completed-because-the-ancestors-are-unhappy-official-report/.

'Medupi Power Station Graves – Towards Healing and Closure: An Integrated Management Plan (IMP)'. Report prepared by Mbofho Consulting and Project Managers, 1 October 2018. Accessed 17 June 2020, http://www.eskom.co.za/OurCompany/SustainableDevelopment/EnvironmentalImpactAssessments/MedupiGraves/Documents/MEDUPI%20POWER%20STATION%20GRAVES%20IMP%20FINAL%2001102018.pdf.

Rassool, Ciraj. 'Human Remains, the Disciplines of the Dead, and the South African Memorial Complex'. In *The Politics of Heritage in Africa: Economies, Histories, and Infrastructures*, edited by Ciraj Rassool, Derek R. Peterson and Kodzo Gavua, 133–56. Cambridge: Cambridge University Press, 2015.

Scott, James C. *Seeing Like a State: How Certain Schemes to Improve the Human Condition Have Failed*. New Haven: Yale University Press, 1998.

'South African Families Gather to Commemorate Deceased with Memorial Near Medupi Power Plant'. The World Bank, 8 July 2016. Accessed 17 June 2020, https://www.worldbank.org/en/news/feature/2016/07/08/south-african-families-gather-to-commemorate-deceased-with-memorial-at-medupi-power-plant.

Stoler, Ann Laura, ed. *Imperial Debris: On Ruins and Ruination*. Durham: Duke University Press, 2013.

Witz, Leslie, Gary Minkley, and Ciraj Rassool. *Unsettled History: Making South African Public Pasts*. Ann Arbor: University of Michigan Press, 2017.

'20 000 are Banished to Dumping Grounds'. *Sunday Express*, 29 July 1979.

INTERVIEWS

Deats, Michael. Personal interview with author. Johannesburg, 2 September 2013.

Ellis, Ponk. Personal interview with author. Lephalale, August 2013.

Loots, Willie. Personal interview with author. Lephalale, 6 August 2014.

Meyer, Joe. Personal interview with author. Onverwacht, 17 March 2015.

Mfisa, Johannes, with Hellen Kekae, Hendrik Ndebele, April Selema, and Kgantshi Makubela (translator). Group interview with author. Marapong, 25 August 2015.

Sekati, Sam. Personal interview with author. Lephalale, August 2014.

Seodisa, Lazarus. Personal interview with author. Merapong, 18 March 2015.

2 A COMMUNITY JOURNEY: RETURN TO JULIWE CEMETERY IN ROODEPOORT, JOHANNESBURG

ERIC ITZKIN

As the only part of the old Roodepoort West location to be spared demolition, Juliwe Cemetery became the centrepiece of a story of forced removals under apartheid which, for over 50 years, remained unknown to the wider public. This chapter explores the layered meanings attached to the cemetery as well as efforts to recognise the significance of the site, which has only recently begun to be acknowledged in the public sphere.

According to the historian Michelle Hay, 'The cemetery is the ghost of Roodepoort West. It is the last vision of the vibrant African location that once stood where the suburban houses now stand. Like a ghost, the cemetery continues to haunt the people, now living miles away in Dobsonville, who remember its past'.[1] When the rest of the old African location of Roodepoort West was destroyed in the eleven-year period from 1956 to 1967, the cemetery alone remained after threats of protest concerning the proposed destruction of the graves persuaded the authorities to leave it alone. After the rest of the location was erased and covered over by a whites-only township, the cemetery stood as evidence of an entire community forced to move to Dobsonville, which was merged into the vast, sprawling segregated African township of Soweto in 1994.

Roodepoort, located to the west of Johannesburg, began as a gold-mining village, and the Roodepoort–Maraisburg urban district became a municipality in 1904. By the 1950s and 1960s, during the heyday of apartheid, forced relocation of African communities was driven by the municipality under the banner of economic progress and development. These goals of economic growth and prosperity for the burgeoning white population – together with the expunging of African settlements – came to the fore in a long quest for official city status, which was eventually conferred on Roodepoort in 1977. Roodepoort was incorporated into the Greater Johannesburg Metropolitan Council in the late 1990s, together with Randburg, Sandton and Soweto.

At a Heritage Month event hosted by the City of Johannesburg in 2017, ex-residents returned to the cemetery in the Roodepoort suburb of Horizon View. This old location cemetery is all that remains of the Roodepoort West township, which was called Juliwe by its residents. In an emotional ceremony, a memorial was inaugurated to acknowledge and interpret this black cemetery, now surrounded on all sides by residential development. Near the edge of the cemetery, a blue heritage plaque was unveiled by the City's mayoral committee member for community development, Councillor Nonhlanhla Sifumba, giving a mark of recognition from the City to a community whose dead had most often been treated with official disregard and neglect. The City of Johannesburg heritage plaque carries the inscription below:

> In this cemetery lie the remains of residents of Juliwe Location, established in the early 1900s. By 1959, the cemetery contained the graves of some 3 000 adults and 2 635 infants. African residents of Roodepoort West were removed to Dobsonville, and their location destroyed from 1956–1967, but they resisted the removal of the cemetery, which they insisted should remain as a sacred memorial.

Buses were laid on to bring senior citizens from Dobsonville to the unveiling at Juliwe Cemetery that was held in the early morning. After the official ceremony at the gravesite, hundreds of community members gathered at the Kopanong Community Hall in Dobsonville for a day-long session of community dialogues, with reminiscences of past lives in Juliwe, and the early days of displaced residents starting over in Dobsonville. The gathering at Juliwe Cemetery and at the hall in Dobsonville marked a first step of according

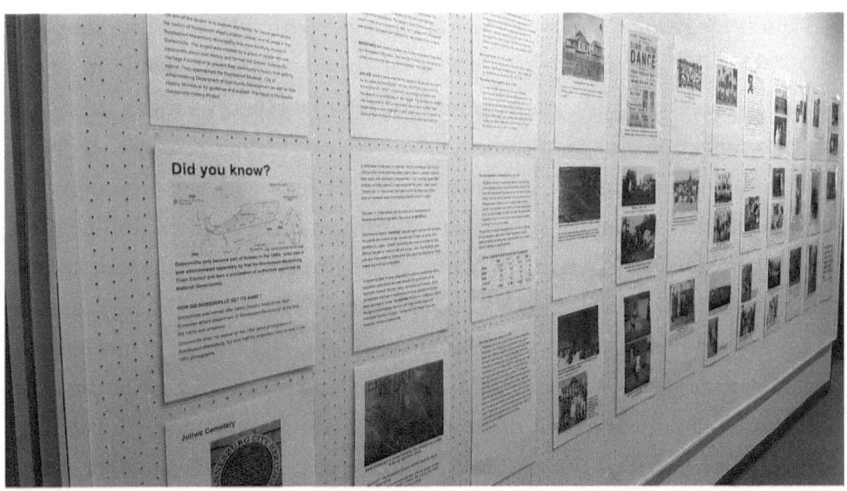

Figure 2.1. A view of the Dobsonville History Exhibition at the Roodepoort Museum. Photograph by Carolina Geldenhuys (Roodepoort Museum)

public recognition to a long-neglected story of displacement and loss in the annals of apartheid-era forced removals. It came about through a City initiative, responding to a long quest by a group of Dobsonville residents, organised under the auspices of the Greater Dobsonville Heritage Foundation (GDHF), to make their history known. At the heart of these efforts was a desire to raise a memorial at the site of the old location cemetery.

The story of Juliwe was again brought into the public space a year later, with an exhibition launched at the Roodepoort Museum on Heritage Day, 24 September 2018.[2] Displays featured personal photographs and documents from Dobsonville residents, reflecting disrupted lives. Images show people first going about their activities in Juliwe, and later re-establishing themselves in Dobsonville. The museum exhibition and cemetery memorial form part of the Greater Dobsonville History Project (GDHP), which began as a community initiative, led by the GDHF, to recover and make known the history of Roodepoort West location. The public history elements have drawn on an oral history project, based at the Wits History Workshop, as well as a more recent focus on the development of a community archive. With its various strands, the project has involved the Roodepoort Museum, the City's Heritage Unit, and the Wits History Workshop, while also engaging with community groups from Dobsonville.

A quest for recognition by ex-residents began with a land restitution claim in 1998–2000. The potent symbolism of the old cemetery made it a focal point for the land claim. The Greater Dobsonville History Project developed out of applications for land claims, as a group of former residents of Juliwe tried to help claimants find information. This began with the formation of a committee in Dobsonville by a group of former stand-holders, and children of stand-holders, of Roodepoort West. The claimants achieved some success, and each claimant received R60 000 in compensation. Such compensation was, however, restricted to stand-holders, or the children of stand-holders, while former lodgers were excluded from the land claims process at the time.

The land claims came at a time when little was known about Roodepoort West or Dobsonville. There were no studies done, and the story of Juliwe hardly came up at all in the literature. The claimants looked for points of support for recording the linked history of Roodepoort West and Dobsonville. To this end, they sought help from the City of Johannesburg's Arts, Culture and Heritage Directorate, which also linked them to the History Workshop. In the course of this project, efforts by community members to recapture lost lives led to locally produced histories, community dialogues, museum displays and the development of memorials. All of these activities and expressions – from producing local histories, to exhibitions and memorials – are ways of recapturing, sharing and sustaining memory. By 2007, a groundbreaking study had been produced by the History Workshop, with oral histories revealing many aspects of township life.[3] A prominent issue which came to the fore, in both community narratives and official documents, was about the fate of the Roodepoort West cemetery.

The roots of the Roodepoort West location go back to the early 1900s, when an informal settlement of African mine labourers was taken over by the town council, and soon became known as Juliwe. Like many old African townships, Juliwe was predominantly poor, with many living in slum-like conditions, with no electricity, overflowing latrines and dirt roads. By the 1940s, parts of the location had increasingly become overcrowded. Despite the hardships, Juliwe is remembered as a vibrant place, with a strong sense of community. The desire of ex-residents to record their history by re-igniting fading memories bears testimony to the attachment people feel for their historic home, and the sadness with which they look back at the loss of it.

Figure 2.2. The empty site where Juliwe township once stood, with the former cemetery in the south-east corner. Photograph courtesy Roodepoort Museum

Early on in the life of Juliwe, the cemetery was located on a spot surrounded by gum trees, with a communal cattle kraal nearby. As early as 1929, the council's advisory board expressed anxiety about the shortage of burial space in the cemetery, with the reminder that council had previously consented to the use of this space as a public burial ground.[4]

In the decade from 1936 to 1946 the African population of Roodepoort was increasing fast, at a time when the white population was growing at an even faster rate. The massive economic and demographic upsurge in Roodepoort, marked by a doubling of the white population between 1937 and 1947, brought increasing pressure to dislodge African communities so as to make way for the growth in white settlement.[5] The financial opportunities presented by white expansion were not lost on the registered owner of the land on which the African location was established in 1907, the Horizon Development Company. Consequently, the company proposed that a white township (later named Horizon View) be established on the site. With the backing of the local authority, this solidified into a scheme to remove African residents to the distant township of Dobsonville.

When Roodepoort West was declared a 'black spot' and ordered to make way for the fast-expanding white suburbs of Roodepoort, the reaction of African residents was somewhat ambivalent. As Hay explains, many residents looked forward to better housing in more spacious surroundings: 'The general mood was sadness tempered with expectation. Dobsonville offered something that many residents, particularly lodgers, of Roodepoort West could only dream of: running water, one tap per house, one latrine per house, brick walls, four rooms, a little garden.'[6] The first phase of the removals began in 1956, and by 1967 the whole of Juliwe township had been destroyed, with the sole exception of the cemetery. While removals from Roodepoort West took place without organised or widespread resistance, there was one issue that had the potential for conflict: the intended removal of the cemetery. In negotiations over the removals, the future of the cemetery became the most contested issue, with African residents determined to resist the removal of the cemetery.

The party which was most adamant that the cemetery had to go was the Horizon Development Company. The company planned to lay out a white township, Horizon View, on the land where the old location stood, and insisted that the location cemetery was a 'discouraging factor' which should be removed.[7] In 1956, the town council began negotiations with the Horizon Development Company over the removal of the old location, and the future of the old location cemetery. These negotiations dragged on for several years, and from 1958 onwards there was a clash of interests between the town council, Horizon, and African residents whose dead were treated by the authorities with painful disregard.

In 1958, the town council moved to close the cemetery, and rumours reached Juliwe residents about the proposed destruction of their burial site and the planned exhumation of the human remains which were to be re-interred in a mass grave.[8] The impassioned response of African residents was conveyed in a memorandum from the Roodepoort Advisory Board, towards the end of 1958. Writing to the town clerk, Mr Mashao, the chairman of the advisory board, warned:

> The residents feel very strongly about the removal of the cemetery. The cemetery has been in existence for a considerable time. Generations, forebears of the residents, rest in that cemetery, and the cemetery has come to be regarded as a most sacred institution among residents. The veneration with which the

residents regard their 'DEAD' is common knowledge. The residents, therefore, feel that a great wrong and injustice would be committed if this sacred institution would be desecrated …⁹

How do we account for this sense of horror being aroused in particular by the threatened bulldozing and desecration of graves? At a time when the impending destruction of peoples' living spaces – including homes, schools and churches – was in a sense more easily accepted, why is it that the cemetery, more than anywhere else, came to be held up by the embattled community as 'a most sacred institution'? The matter of death, in most societies, is revelatory of deeply held community values. The case of Juliwe was no exception, and strong emotions were stirred, influenced by an interplay of Christian faith and African ancestral beliefs. The cemetery played a great role in cultural, community and religious life, and was the focus of much ritual activity – a place where both Christian and African ancestral rites were carried out. Funerals were occasions for social solidarity, attended by churchgoers as well as traditionally minded people. Ministers from different churches would attend and all church denominations would unite.¹⁰

As pointed out by Hay, the heated response in relation to the cemetery has in some measure to do with the continuing role of ancestral beliefs, and the importance of the cemetery as a place of communication with the ancestors.¹¹ Nonetheless, ancestor beliefs are varied and complex, often defying easy generalisations. The majority of community members coming from Roodepoort West were members of various Christian churches, with some rejecting the belief in ancestors as contrary to Christianity. As a place of final rest, as well as an abode of the ancestors, the cemetery was viewed as almost sacred ground. So, when rumours began to spread among the community that their cemetery had been sold off and people could no longer visit, there was much anxiety and indignation.

In its memorandum to the town council, the advisory board requested assurances to allay the fears of residents.¹² It asked for the following: that the cemetery be properly enclosed, and left intact as a sacred memorial institution; that, in the event of the removal of the residents from the location, the residents would always be accorded the right to enter the cemetery, and pay homage to their dead; and that the ground of the cemetery would not at any time in the future be converted to other use. The final paragraph of the memorandum sounded a warning which would have been noted by the town clerk, who was the official responsible for the orderly removal of the old location: 'We would respectfully urge that unless such assurance is given by the Council, a grave and permanent sense of injustice and wrong would be bred, that would pass from generation to generation and would never be forgotten.'

The Roodepoort Council took the memorandum seriously, and sent it to the Horizon Development Company in March 1959 for their consideration. Still, the company remained unmoved by the concerns of the residents, insisting that the cemetery be removed. The council was concerned to maintain the 'goodwill' of African residents, and ensure the smooth and unhindered removal of the location. Furthermore, after considering the high cost involved in doing away with the cemetery, the council decided that there would be no such removal.[13] This shift shows the flexibility exercised by the town council of Roodepoort in defusing what could have become a serious threat.[14]

By 1961, after further argument over costs and details, the developer finally relented, agreeing with the council that the cemetery would not be removed. As an alternative to the removal, the graves would be levelled, and numbered markers would be provided at each grave. The cemetery would be grassed, a wall would be built around it, and the area would be maintained by the council. Objections by residents had succeeded in preventing the removal of the cemetery, although the outcome also carried loss and bitterness. While the graves of the old cemetery were not bulldozed, former residents relocated to far-flung Dobsonville would struggle to visit the graves of their ancestors. Together with the actual distance between the old cemetery and the new location, the provisions of the 1950 Group Areas Act presented a barrier to visiting the cemetery.

After Juliwe location was removed, actions taken by the town council in relation to the cemetery were profoundly disrespectful to ex-residents and their dead. Graves were flattened, and numbered pegs used to identify individual graves were removed. The effect was to desecrate graves and depersonalise the cemetery, making it increasingly difficult to locate where individuals were buried.[15] Further indignities came from vandals knocking over tombstones, disturbing the grounds and leaving behind piles of refuse.

By the late 1990s, the group advancing land claims pushed for a memorial to mark the cemetery as a site deserving of respect. By 2000, a simple stone memorial was erected by the group. It was surrounded on three sides by granite plaques, each with the following inscription (one in English, one in Setswana and the third in isiXhosa): 'In loving memory of the fathers, mothers, brothers and sisters / of the old Juliwe location. / God bless all dear people for things they have done with / love and real kindness, each day, the year through. / For a thousand years in thy sight is but a yesterday and as a watch in the night. / RIP / Psalm Ch 9 vs 4.' This modest memorial, the product of the community initiative, was later considered inadequate by ex-residents, who called for a more substantial intervention from the City of Johannesburg. The subsequent introduction of a blue heritage plaque in 2017 brought greater presence and recognition to the memorialisation of the cemetery. The community memorial was re-mounted alongside the City heritage plaque which was raised on a brick column.

Figure 2.3. A blue heritage plaque awarded by the City of Johannesburg stands alongside a community memorial. Photograph by Eric Itzkin

For ex-residents of Juliwe, the maintenance and dignity of the cemetery remained an ongoing concern during the apartheid period, and continued long after 1994. Still in 2019, community members complain of poor maintenance, with tall grass being cut only infrequently during the rainy season. The wall which enclosed the cemetery has long since come down, and many local people habitually walk along a well-worn path to cut across the cemetery, trampling over graves as they go about their daily lives. Yet in a quiet corner of the cemetery, some sense of dignity has been restored with a memorial giving recognition to the defiance that rescued the cemetery, and remembering past injustices which the community refused to be buried and forgotten.

NOTES

1   Michelle Hay, '"The Last Thing that Tells Our Story": The Roodepoort West Cemetery, 1958-2008' *Journal of Southern African Studies* 37.2 (2011): 297.
2   The author thanks Carolina Geldenhuys, senior curator at the Roodepoort Museum, for her insights into the history of Roodepoort, and for making images from the museum available.
3   Phil Bonner, Michelle Hay and Sello Mathabatha, 'Roodepoort-Maraisburg Location: A History', unpublished paper presented at the Wits History Workshop, University of the Witwatersrand, Johannesburg, 2007.
4   Bonner et al., 'Roodepoort-Maraisburg', 16.
5   Bonner et al., 'Roodepoort-Maraisburg', 26, 30.
6   Hay, '"The Last Thing that Tells Our Story"', 300.
7   Roodepoort Council Minutes. 'Memorandum from Horizon Development Company Limited to Roodepoort-Maraisburg Municipality', September to December 1956, 2.
8   Roodepoort Council Minutes. 'Report on Negotiations Between Council and Messrs. Horizon Development Co. Ltd. Re Contribution towards Cost of Removal of Old Location, Roodepoort', September to December 1958.
9   Roodepoort Council Minutes. 'Memorandum of the Roodepoort Location Residents Re: Cemetery', September to December 1958.
10 Bonner et al., 'Roodepoort-Maraisburg', 17.
11 Hay, '"The Last Thing that Tells Our Story"', 306-07.
12 Roodepoort Council Minutes. 'Memorandum of the Roodepoort Location Residents Re: Cemetery.'
13 Exhuming and re-interring the graves was estimated to cost £20 000. Roodepoort Council Minutes, Non-European Affairs Committee Meeting 08/06/1959.

14 Michelle Hay, 'A Social History of Roodepoort West and Dobsonville' (Honours diss., University of the Witwatersrand, Johannesburg, 2008).

15 Hay, 'A Social History of Roodepoort West and Dobsonville', 307.

REFERENCES

Bonner, Phil, Michelle Hay, and Sello Mathabatha. 'Roodepoort-Maraisburg Location: A History'. Unpublished paper presented at Wits History Workshop, University of the Witwatersrand, Johannesburg, 2007.

Hay, Michelle. 'A Social History of Roodepoort West and Dobsonville'. Honours diss., University of the Witwatersrand, Johannesburg, 2008.

Hay, Michelle. '"The Last Thing that Tells Our Story": The Roodepoort West Cemetery, 1958-2008'. *Journal of Southern African Studies* 37. 2 (2011): 297-311.

Roodepoort Council Minutes, 1955 to 1975 (90 volumes).

3 PUBLIC MEMORY AND TRANSFORMATION AT CONSTITUTION HILL AND GANDHI SQUARE IN JOHANNESBURG

TEMBA JOHN DAWSON MIDDELMANN

Memorialisation practices involving public memory and history are usually located in public space. Such practices and their impact are therefore tied up with key public space dynamics and tend, as a result, to respond to a wider variety of imperatives than simply heritage preservation and representation. A crucial part of this is how memorialisation practices presume things about the nature and trajectory of the public or publics being planned for. Relatedly, the way public space shapes who counts as part of the public acquires further salience in heritage discourses.[1] Those who are or feel excluded from intendedly publicly accessible heritage sites are thus excluded from spaces and discourses of public memory, culture and identity, which is 'an explicit form of denial and assertion of power'.[2] This itself is linked to how memorialisation practices are tied to political processes or motivations.

The histories of contestation over how to remember heritage sites display both arbitrariness and contingency in how we remember. These histories also remind us of the political importance of how memorialisation practices are carried out. These practices may thus obscure as much as they reveal. They can be devices of forgetting and obliteration as much as remembering and conservation, often intentional as part of nation-building projects, 'an ongoing tension between collective memory and selective amnesia' in the words of Martin J. Murray.³ While memory is certainly built into architecture, it also exists in many other places, practices and cultures. As such, this chapter seeks to explore current and historical contestation over two spaces in central Johannesburg, in the context of how the spaces are used in South Africa's largest city, itself located in Gauteng (place of gold), a province that was renamed in the democratic era. The two spaces are Constitution Hill, a former colonial and apartheid prison-complex since transformed into a museum and human-rights precinct, and Gandhi Square, the main central bus terminus in Johannesburg's Central Business District (CBD).

Constitution Hill and Gandhi Square represent two early transformations of public places in the post-apartheid era – important sites in the narratives of the downtown 'regeneration' of Johannesburg and the elaboration of a new national identity in South Africa. Thus, they are also bound up in discourses and representations of public memory and identity. Constitution Hill aims at confronting and situating colonial and apartheid history by juxtaposing it with a vision for the future. It has its own long history of contestation over how to use and remember the space, an ebb and flow of conservation and neglect.⁴ It acts as a powerful site of remembrance and memorialisation as well as of imagining the future, and also as a human-rights precinct housing several institutions engaged in important public work. However, as a public space it is ambiguous, and has remained something of an enclave in the city, an ironic continuation of its closed-off origins as a prison.

Despite the importance of the Constitutional Court's jurisprudence in advancing transformative rights,⁵ these rights are not necessarily felt to exist by users of the Constitution Hill precinct or local residents in the immediate vicinity. In seeking to respond to various questions of memory, transformation, history and reconciliation, the precinct's vision has been drawn in many directions, resulting in an ambiguous public space, thereby highlighting rather than integrating fractured publics. That the space feels private to many – despite its public ownership and mandate – is a significant paradox. This contrasts with Gandhi Square, which is generally experienced as more public, despite being privately leased, managed and controlled as part of an insidious global trend towards privatisation of public space.

Gandhi Square has engaged its history and public memory in a different way to Constitution Hill, with several name changes that have shed layers of its history. Having started briefly as Church Square, it was renamed Government Square, then Van der Bijl Square, and since 1999 it has been known as Gandhi Square, reflecting changing functions and the tendencies of remembrance and memorialisation tied to political legitimisation practices.[6] While the most recent change might have been seen as replacing a colonial segregation-era figure with one profoundly involved in struggles against oppression, the conversation has again shifted. With the emergence of racist remarks from his early years, Gandhi is no longer simply a figure of veneration, resulting in debates about his memorialisation at Gandhi Square. However, the links between these debates and how the space is used are unclear. In both cases, symbolic engagements with history have a limited, though not necessarily insignificant, impact on the patterns of daily, public use, which are still haunted by the lingering presence of coloniality extant in the built environment and spatial practices of the city, as well as the domination of neoliberal capitalism. Both are examples of how public space is shaped by broader spatial, socio-economic and symbolic realities, but are key sites in terms of how the management, use and perception of public places play an important role in shaping and contesting the nature and composition of the public itself.

Exploring histories of memorialisation practices and their consequences evokes the passion and energy that drives these processes, the anxiety and tension that undergirds them, and thus their inherent subjectivity.[7] Key to this is how the nature of memories, and the way public places and monuments are used and felt, continue to change over time. The tension and hope of the early years of democracy gave rise to heritage practices which aimed at making a break with the colonial and apartheid past and its figures, while simultaneously aiming at celebrating and imagining a newfound freedom. Early post-apartheid memorials and monuments were thus linked to the political and emotional moment of transition in which the spirit of reconciliation was strong. However, how much did the designs of new public places in the context of heritage practices reckon with the nature of the publics they were planning for? How much did they anticipate – and allow for – these publics and their sentiments to change? As the dream or myth of the rainbow nation has lost some public currency,[8] how has the relevance of monuments in the context of that ideal changed?

BACKGROUND ON BOTH SITES

Constitution Hill is a mixed-use heritage precinct located on the highest ridge in Johannesburg, a continental watershed, at the northern edge of the inner city. Conflict between Afrikaners and the British shaped much of early Johannesburg and its heritage landscape throughout the twentieth century. The South African Republic (ZAR) built a fort and a prison in the 1890s, largely to control foreigners. It was used as a prison complex until the prison was closed in 1983. A period of relative abandonment and sporadic occupation followed, and from 1983 to the mid-1990s the precinct was occupied, inter alia, by the Rand Light Infantry, the notorious Civil Co-operation Bureau (CCB), and the traffic department, which impacted debates concerning how to use and remember the site. In the mid-1990s, the Department of Justice decided to erect the new Constitutional Court on the site. These plans merged with those that were gradually developing for the rest of the site, and in the early 2000s the new court building was developed in tandem with the restoration of several of the key prison buildings which were turned into museums. The concept involved remembering the painful history of the country through interpreting the prisons, as well as envisioning a future based on constitutional democracy and freedom, represented by the Court itself.

Gandhi Square is a major bus terminus in the southern part of Johannesburg's CBD. It is one of relatively few large open spaces in the inner city, and is bordered by a variety of shops and fast-food outlets. Initially named Church Square in terms of an agreement between the government and the Dutch Reformed Church, soon afterwards, in 1893, it was renamed Government Square as it housed several government offices and the Dutch Reformed Church had secured alternative premises.[9] After 1948, the new apartheid government redeveloped the space as the main bus terminus and called it Van der Bijl Square. The terminus suffered neglect and deterioration in the wake of business disinvestment in the inner city in the 1980s and early 1990s, though in the late 1990s the terminus was renovated by a property consortium led by Olitzki Property Holdings (OPH). Renamed Gandhi Square in 1999, it was the 'first major public space to be re-named in Johannesburg' in the democratic era.[10]

Constitution Hill and Gandhi Square represent early and significant instances of Johannesburg inner-city renewal and heritage representation.

While both are examples of public space transformations of South Africa's democratic era, Constitution Hill was steered by a dense mix of state bodies and individuals. Private involvement and development, despite its alleged importance for the funding model of the precinct, has been denied throughout its recent history. At Gandhi Square, regeneration and heritage representation were conducted as a public–private partnership. And yet the space, which is technically private, having been leased from the City by OPH, is experienced by many contemporary users as more public and open than Constitution Hill. To what extent is Gandhi Square, then, beholden to public interest? What does this mean for its supposed status as a heritage site, or a public space, given that a key element of genuinely public space is held to be freedom from small-group control?[11] Its importance as a transport node, commercial centre and open space is more pronounced than its significance as a heritage site.

CONSTITUTION HILL'S CHANGING MONUMENT STATUS

Constitution Hill – formerly the Johannesburg Prison, generally referred to as the Old Fort – has a long history of debates over how to use and remember the site.[12] In the 1960s the city council advocated for its demolition, which sparked a debate with the National Monuments Council (NMC), which argued for its importance, given its history as a military fort constructed by the old Afrikaner republic. It is now one of two buildings left in Johannesburg from the ZAR period. While this particular debate ended in 1964, concern over the heritage value has ebbed and flowed throughout its history. This began as early as 1904, when a commission of enquiry found it to be unfit for use as a prison, as Flo Bird, chairperson of the Johannesburg Heritage Foundation, who was at the time working for the NMC, revealed in an interview with Cheryl Stevens. Nevertheless, it was used as such for close on 80 years, until the new Johannesburg Jail was opened in Soweto in 1983. When the prison was abandoned that year, concerns over how to use the site again emerged, with calls for the preservation and unearthing of its heritage value.

It was only in the late 1980s and early 1990s, however, that concerns over the site's national heritage status began to grow. Bird describes how her growing realisation of the importance of the rest of the site beyond the Fort was at odds with the NMC leadership, many of whom were Afrikaner nationalists: 'We had to disguise our feelings about it politically.' This dynamic made it difficult to push for the whole site to be declared, which resulted in parts of it further deteriorating. The situation was indicative of the lines around which South Africa's publics were fractured in the period before the fall of apartheid. Realising the heritage importance of the political prisoners of Constitution Hill, Bird found it difficult, arguing on these lines: 'It was not the kind of significance we were going to be able to sell, not even to our own regional committee, let alone to a wider public.'

In the mid-1990s, the new Constitutional Court decided to erect their building on the site. In the context of the newly democratic state, as Graeme Reid, then working for the Johannesburg Development Agency (JDA), revealed in an interview with Karen Martin, those involved in redevelopment plans generally agreed that declaring the rest of the prison complex a national monument was important, given its social and historical significance in terms of the struggle against apartheid. The complex institutional arrangements in the build-up to, and construction of, the new precinct began to have an impact on the process. It was decided that no construction tenders would be awarded until the whole site was declared. However, soon afterwards, after several stumbling blocks in the planning and construction process, plans to declare the whole site seemed to fall away. In part, this was to do with the urgency of starting construction, and perhaps also for easing demolition permission for certain buildings that were in the way of new construction. Negotiations between the JDA and the Department of Public Works over who would run the project saw a donation reversed, and it is possible that in this tension and confusion the proviso to declare the monument either got lost or was discarded.

The site was finally declared a national monument in 2017, 13 years after the precinct was opened. Debates over the heritage value have thus expanded from an emphasis on the site's military history and its history of housing ordinary criminals, to include the social history value in the context of oppositional politics, both before and during the apartheid era. However, while it has been used as an important site of oppositional politics in the post-apartheid era, this is not signified on the site. Also, the precolonial history of the space does not seem to have entered the discourse. Its first developers after Johannesburg was established were themselves apparently unconcerned with conservation on the site, as shown during feasibility studies and archaeological surveys prior to Constitution Hill's construction.[13] Accordingly, while precolonial use of the ridges was common for 'settlement or resource acquisition', owing to 'the intensity of landscape modification and construction since the late nineteenth century, it is doubtful that any precolonial sites or remains from within the precinct are preserved in any coherent form'.[14]

This discussion is intended to show the shifting and contingent nature of heritage importance, as well as the way it changes in accordance with the political context and development concerns. Layers of history are continuously revealed and obscured, remembered and forgotten, always contingent on a range of factors and impulses. Part of this is to do with how buildings on the site are constructed, preserved or demolished. The environment and public space of the precinct are, indeed, imbued with the contestation and debate about Constitution Hill's past as well as its future. While the experience of the heritage aspects of the site is incredibly powerful for many, people's feelings towards the public space are often less positive. Many users find it unsettling, in part due to the strong presence of uniformed security. This relates to the uncomfortable relationship of many local residents to the justice system and the Court building, a feeling that the built environment is inherently oppressive to black people.[15] Despite Constitution Hill's careful planning and sensitive thinking, it succumbed to common tensions around balancing security and accessibility, as I have discussed elsewhere.[16]

Figure 3.1. The public square at Constitution Hill, with a few tourists and uniformed guards. Photograph by Temba Middelmann

If it is agreed that heritage – and, thus, collective memory – is something to be preserved and shared among all citizens, accessibility is crucial at heritage sites. Because such sites are generally also intended as public spaces, this ties into broader debates around accessibility. This, in turn, is complicated by how heritage sites are funded and managed. In the case of Constitution Hill, government funding comes largely through the Gauteng Growth and Development Agency, but since its inception it has battled with balancing needs for commercial viability and preservation of the symbolic integrity of the space, as I have previously indicated.[17] The main museum sections of the site are only open to paying customers, and so, as several locals have told me, experiencing this important heritage is beyond their means.

A conversation I had with a young man at Constitution Hill in 2018 reveals the extreme effects of the situation. During a 2017 visit to the precinct with his uncle, who had been a prison inmate some 50 years before, his uncle was refused entry to the museums unless he paid – this despite the fact that the memories of former prisoners form the basis of the museum experience.[18] This is a powerful indicator of a particular public remembrance – in part intended to legitimise the new state – given precedence over an individual whose experience it is meant to commemorate. Perhaps this is an instance, in the words of the historian Annie E. Coombes, of 'the fissures that develop as soon as there are attempts to integrate personal with national history, private with public memory, and the small stories of everyday refusal to comply with the apartheid state with the grand narratives of heroic resistance'.[19]

RUINATION AND DEVELOPMENT AT CONSTITUTION HILL

Parts of the prison complex were abandoned following its closure in 1983. In the period between then and the mid- to late 1990s, when the Constitution Hill project gained real momentum, layers of a sinister and obscure history were added to the site at the same time as parts of it deteriorated. However, especially in the case of the Fort, there were also efforts towards conservation and renovation. These processes are revealing of heritage debates around the impact and value of preservation, conservation or ruination. The manifestations of these questions in the history of Constitution Hill are revealing of the importance attached to different parts of the site, and therefore different aspects of its history, by various interested parties over time. Memorialisation practices are to some extent inherently arbitrary, with decisions made about the site clearly contingent on various other processes.

The deeply contingent nature of the entire process is evident from decisions around which buildings to keep or demolish, and whether to move a certain tree.[20] While decisions tended to focus on what the most important buildings were, in terms of their own particular histories, interviews with people formerly imprisoned there also show that, to them, the heritage value of the site was not necessarily captured in any particular structure, but rather in a part of a wall, perhaps, or an experience, sound or memory. As artist Clive van den Berg, who was involved in interpreting the site for the museums, revealed in an interview with Lauren Segal: 'One of the most constant laments is from prisoners who come back to the site and literally want to locate a memory – try and literally find the space – the piece of dirt or concrete where they slept or ate.'

In the case of the Women's Jail, Van den Berg stated that the 'destruction of cells in the northern courtyard was an event which caused enormous trauma for people coming back'. Furthermore, historians involved in researching the site to ascertain the relative importance of different buildings argue that there was insufficient time to fully understand the wide-ranging importance of the site's history.[21] Early construction and landscaping obliterated material traces of precolonial use, while renovation of the Fort in the 1990s saw important graffiti painted over, with some buildings – apparently without the correct permissions – being demolished.[22] Bird observed that the funding delay to the Constitution Hill project effectively permitted more careful conservation thinking between the late 1990s and early 2000s. However, the construction of the Court saw not only the Awaiting Trial Block demolished but also other smaller buildings such as the black wardens' quarters, each with their own traces of the nation's past, notwithstanding contestation over all buildings on the site.[23] And yet, as revealed in the debates over the mortuary building, exploring the social history of these buildings – which, as structures, are relatively unremarkable – does not necessarily rely on their continued presence. As implied by the spatial practices of users, history can be more powerfully expressed in terms of consciousness, relationships and interactions. The past can figure especially powerfully, for instance, in a symbolic relationship with city space; it also figures on broader levels than with a specific building. The subjectivity of both public memorialisation and private remembrance complicates these processes.

By the time the Constitution Hill development was genuinely underway at the start of the 2000s, issues around how to balance interpretation, development and ruination resurfaced. This intended balance was expressed by the Historical Task Team of the project as follows: 'Do as much as is necessary and as little as possible.'[24] Despite this intention, different perspectives emerged throughout the process. One suggestion was to leave the buildings to decay for future generations to watch;[25] Architect Nabeel Essa, who was involved in the Heritage and Education Team, stated in an interview with Cheryl Stevens that the deterioration of the site had been 'reflective of our society' and thus shows how the 'decay was very powerful'. Though appreciative of this position, Albie Sachs, a former Constitutional Court justice who was closely involved in the process of development, supported intervention:

> It had a totally ruined, derelict character, which was overgrown. In fact it was the worst of all worlds, because it wasn't ancient enough to be a real ruin which has its own mystery and magic and not pristine enough to look like a useable contemporary area ... it was the knowledge of what the hill represented and the recall through imagination of those who had been there, with its potential as a site for renovation and resurrection – renaissance – that was so captivating.[26]

According to Essa, it was a struggle by those involved in interpreting the site 'not to sanitise' the place. While the museum interventions were careful, sensitive and powerfully evocative of the intensity and brutality of prison life under colonial and apartheid rule, the securitised feel of the public access areas of the site sully the aim of avoiding a sanitised atmosphere. This relates to a key tension in public memorialisation, and paradoxes within public space:[27] attempts to create a publicly accessible and open space can sit uneasily with attempts at memorialisation. As noted by a heritage official in debates over how to construct the new precinct, 'The architects are trying to make it a friendly place which goes against its historical record. The site was always kept invisible for several reasons and the drive to make it pedestrian friendly goes against its history.'[28] Clearly, contestation related to multiple imperatives in the planning for Constitution Hill resulted in ambiguities of use, as well as meaning.

GANDHI: A CONTESTED ICON

Although the initial preference of the consortium that renovated the old Van der Bijl Square was to rename it Renaissance Square, the proposal by Museum Africa to name it Gandhi Square was accepted by the City.[29] Nonetheless, in 2019 a senior employee of OPH told me of the company's desire to name it Nelson Mandela Square, lamenting the fact that Sandton City had beaten OPH, thereby gaining the competitive edge that came with the Mandela name. It is interesting to note that the name was not changed because of a public outcry against Hendrik van der Bijl, who was an electrical engineer during apartheid, and that the town of Vanderbijlpark in Gauteng province still bears his name. This demonstrates some of the arbitrariness in the way names and iconography are used, discarded, changed, remembered or forgotten. Important support for the name Gandhi Square came from a member of the Johannesburg City Council who was also a member of the Gandhi Centenary Council, which aimed to 'promote [Gandhi's] legacy'.[30]

Part of the political background to this process was the Indian Consulate's commissioning of Museum Africa to research Gandhi's time in South Africa, a task undertaken by heritage specialist Eric Itzkin. Correspondingly, a statue of Mahatma Gandhi in legal attire, reflecting his occupation in Johannesburg in the early twentieth century, was unveiled in 2003, though to mixed reaction. Itzkin, who was then working for the City of Johannesburg's heritage department, drove this process as a forerunner to the city's 2006 Public Art Policy. While Gandhi's statue and other artworks linked to this programme have aimed at 'speak[ing] to the public', the reception of such artworks has often been ambivalent.[31] Individual championing, political motivation and marketability in memorialisation and public art practices are, thus, important aspects of the process.

Debates around problematic iconography have been expressed at Gandhi Square through contestation of the statue of Gandhi itself. Public debate has, however, been sporadic since it first erupted in 2003.[32] In 2015, a man was arrested after defacing parts of the statue with white paint and placing placards alongside it that read 'Gandhi statue must go.'[33] While Itzkin admits to the validity of such critiques, he argues that proper contextualisation of Gandhi's racial comments is crucial, and that a wider view of Gandhi's life mitigates negative views of his character.[34] However, the plaques around the statue mention neither Gandhi's racist remarks nor his changing attitude during his time in South Africa. Indeed, it is worth bearing in mind historian Patrick French's observation: 'The point is not that someone born in the 19th century should be expected to have 21st-century racial attitudes: it is that, even by the reformist standards of his own time, he was regressive. Gandhi's blanking of Africans is the black hole at the heart of his saintly mythology.'[35] The issue here is not to enter into a debate around whether or not Gandhi was racist, but to show that his legacy remains contested, indicative of the persistence of fractures among publics. While practices that glorify *any* figure may provoke similar contestation, such contestations are always contingent on a range of processes. Nevertheless, we are left with pertinent questions about how we remember, and why we monumentalise.

The changing relationship of Gandhi to South Africa and its indigenous inhabitants is expressed in the following passage related by Albie Sachs, describing Gandhi's period of incarceration at the Johannesburg Prison: 'They were ordered to wear caps, like the black prisoners, and [Indes Naidoo's] grandfather objected and Gandhi said "No, we must experience life as the most humble amongst us do and we will wear that cap as a badge of honour", and when he went back to India afterwards, he took the cap with him and the Gandhi cap became the symbol of the Indian independence struggle.' Sachs thus suggests that this 'prison played a big role in [Gandhi's] transformation'.[36] However, [Gandhi] is also quoted as saying of his time in prison: 'Many of the native prisoners are only one degree removed from the animal and often created rows and fought among themselves.'[37]

These debates are not unique to South Africa. This statue and others have prompted an international debate around how Gandhi is remembered and honoured. A statue of Gandhi was removed from a university campus in Ghana in 2016 following a petition citing his racism and the importance of honouring African leaders.[38] Similarly, in Malawi in 2018, a court stopped construction of a Gandhi statue as part of a development of a convention centre to be named after the figure.[39] That the statue was a condition of the development agreement again shows the blurring of heritage practices with both public and private interests, and displays the increasing heterogeneity in the concept of publicness. Such debates also link to ongoing discussions around iconography more broadly, which in South Africa were prompted by activism under the banner #RhodesMustFall, which started in 2015 at the University of Cape Town.[40]

The sporadic nature of challenges to such iconography begs the question, why only these statues? Gandhi statues stand all around the world, and despite recent events that have challenged colonial statues and iconography, statues of Cecil John Rhodes and Jan van Riebeeck remain standing in South Africa and elsewhere. Part of the answer may be in the fractured nature of South Africa's publics and society. In line with this, more statues of Nelson Mandela are built around South Africa and elsewhere at the very moment his legacy is contested in increasingly complex ways, especially by younger people in this country.[41] Thus, perhaps the question has shifted: why are we continuing to put up statues at all, when, as argued by Sabine Marschall, a professor in cultural and heritage tourism, these reflect Euro-American commemoration practices more than African traditions?[42] Often, this is due more to political and economic considerations than careful deliberation of how such a heritage site or monument might be used or felt.

While some protest and anger has been directed to the monumentalisation of Gandhi, most people who use the square react ambivalently or not at all to the presence of the statue. Many pass by without looking up, either oblivious, uncaring or simply busy; some sit on benches around the statue with their backs to it; occasionally, tourists come to see it; others, still, campaign for further change. Clearly, the idea of collective memory takes on a fractured

Figure 3.2. Gandhi Square on a typical weekday morning, with the Gandhi statue opposite the Mall. Photograph by Temba Middelmann

nature in a country with many publics. Choosing to privilege a memory of Gandhi signals the obscuring of other aspects of the site's history, for example the symbolic handing over of power from the Afrikaner state to the British when the South African War ended in 1902.

Furthermore, this choice speaks neither to historic nor current realities of black experience in the city. As David Bunn argues, '[T]he absence of any engagement [in the South African architectural tradition] with questions of black citizenship means that no monument can claim to represent "nationhood" fully.'[43] Thus, the statue of Gandhi is likely to remain contested, or at least contestable in light of the ambivalence demonstrated towards many statues and place names around the country. For as Itzkin himself suggests, 'Gandhi Square offers a malleable terrain where multiple narratives contend for recognition and influence.'[44] In this way, statues can become valuable sites of public discourse and political mobilisation, though they run the risk of further polarising the debate in a global moment where people who disagree seem to move further from each other's viewpoints while clinging ever more rigidly to their own.

This discussion of Gandhi Square brings up the contingent nature of history and of remembering. It also highlights, though not necessarily in straightforward ways, debates around symbolic reparation as opposed to redistributive justice.[45] Older users – irrespective of race – remember the bus service being better 'in the old days' while others recognise the improvements to the ailing infrastructure resulting from the redevelopment of Gandhi Square. Currently it is a hub through which thousands of South Africans pass daily. The relative unreliability of the bus service unintendedly promotes the sort of integration so strongly desired by South African planners and politicians. Commuters range widely in terms of race, class, gender and age, and I have frequently overheard conversations shift from a mutual complaint about a late bus to a discussion covering a range of topics.

For many, however, the passage through Gandhi Square on the way to work and home again to the peri-urban fringe is reminiscent of Johannesburg in the days of apartheid, when the city was either a thoroughfare or a place of work where full rights to the space were denied. Sharlene Davis is fairly typical in that she commutes daily from Protea Glen, over 30 kilometres south-west of Gandhi Square, and from there on to the city's new 'CBD', Sandton, some 20 kilometres to the north. This compels her to leave home before her children do, and by the time she returns they are already asleep. Gandhi Square is thus a space where proximity to others is real, but where distance and the spatial injustice of the city are also keenly felt. While Sharlene Davis appreciates the space in Gandhi Square, the enduring spatial reality of apartheid continues to shape her daily life.

ONGOING CONTINGENCIES OF COMMEMORATION

The memorialisation practices at Constitution Hill and Gandhi Square – along with their reception – demonstrate the conflict, contradiction and contingency embodied in the sites, which reflect and refract a society still very much in transition. And though many users may be unaware or uncaring of the history and heritage value of each site, this indicates that the social history of the city and its spatial legacies are remembered in private and unknown spaces as much as they are in particular *sites* of remembrance.

Comparing these two sites elucidates different approaches to representing the past and demonstrates how memorialisation practices are often more heavily influenced by the present political-economic moment than by careful consideration of the collective past and future, and their impact on contemporary publics. Gandhi Square is about monumentalising Gandhi and portraying a certain version of him in a gloried manner, partly to facilitate the marketing of the space. Constitution Hill, on the other hand, is about memorialising the past, using minimal intervention and trying to allow it to speak for itself. Furthermore, Constitution Hill is about monumentalising a vision of the post-apartheid future, using the Court and its representation of this noble future, to which South Africans are believed to aspire. This brings up further questions, which Marschall raises, about a potential disjuncture between what monuments mean, what they are intended to mean, and what they come to mean over time.[46] Part of this dynamic, in the words of the historian and cultural critic Michel de Certeau, is about how 'renovation does not, ultimately, know what it is "bringing back" – or what it is destroying – when it restores the references and fragments of elusive memories. For these ghosts that haunt urban works, renovation can only provide a laying out of already marked stones, like words for it.'[47] The way these dynamics relate to the recent history of Constitution Hill speaks to how the precinct unsettles the distinction between memory and history.[48] In doing so, it further highlights ambiguity in the space.

Constitution Hill had a multilayered vision for its future, which was tied to hoped-for trajectories for the city and nation, and thus their publics.[49] As such, with a more complex and wide-ranging vision, the ambiguities of the space are more pronounced. Gandhi Square was perhaps more modest in its assumptions about the public, as the space has been strongly shaped by its use as a bus terminus. Therefore, it may be unsurprising that different people interact in queues while waiting for the bus. Nevertheless, assumptions were made about the public in positioning the monument there, and the responses to Gandhi's statue are as wide-ranging as the public itself.

These conclusions may themselves prove to be transitory, given that perceptions of any memorial or monument will change over time, as individual and national sentiments change. Uses of the spaces will not stay the same, as people and the city they live in change. While there are no immediately apparent prospects for the heritage presentation at Gandhi Square to change, Constitution Hill continues to erect new monuments and exhibitions. Along with the events regularly hosted by Constitution Hill, the precinct aims to contribute to public history and memory in a more conscious manner than Gandhi Square appears to do. Gandhi stands as a monument on the square, albeit a quiet one, and the square itself has been distanced from a period of near failure. Constitution Hill, on the other hand, embodies some of the dynamics of monuments and ruination on the site, even as their significance and meaning continue to shift.

NOTES

1. Lynn Staeheli and Don Mitchell, 'Locating the Public in Research and Practice', *Progress in Human Geography* 31.6 (2007): 793.
2. Marc H. Ross, 'Cultural Contestation and the Symbolic Landscape: Politics by Other Means?' in *Culture and Belonging in Divided Societies: Contestation and Symbolic Landscapes*, ed. Marc H. Ross (Pennsylvania: University of Pennsylvania Press, 2011), 1–24.
3. Martin J. Murray, *Commemorating and Forgetting: Challenges for the New South Africa* (Minneapolis: University of Minnesota Press, 2013), viii–ix.
4. Temba John Dawson Middelmann, 'Imagining the Future Through the Past: A Political History of Constitution Hill Since 1983', *South African Historical Journal* 71.2 (2019): 150–69.
5. Eric Christiansen, 'Transformative Constitutionalism in South Africa: Creative Uses of Constitutional Court Authority to Advance Substantive Justice', *Journal of Gender, Race & Justice* 13.3 (2010): 575–614.

6   Eric Itzkin, 'The Transformation of Gandhi Square: The Search for Socially Inclusive Heritage and Public Space in the Johannesburg City Centre' (Master's thesis, University of the Witwatersrand, Johannesburg, 2008).
7   Annie E. Coombes, *History after Apartheid: Visual Culture and Public Memory in a Democratic South Africa* (Durham: Duke University Press, 2003); and Sabine Marschall, 'Memory and Identity in South Africa: Contradictions and Ambiguities in the Process of Post-apartheid Memorialization', *Visual Anthropology* 25.3 (2012): 189–204.
8   Fred Khumalo, 'Rainbow on a Paper Sky: Fault-lines on Post-Racial Rhetoric in South Africa', *African Journal of Rhetoric* 10 (2018); and Sisonke Msimang, 'The End of the Rainbow Nation Myth', *New York Times*, 12 April 2015, accessed 25 October 2019, https://www.nytimes.com/2015/04/13/opinion/the-end-of-the-rainbow-nation-myth.html.
9   Itzkin, 'The Transformation of Gandhi Square', 37.
10 Itzkin, 'The Transformation of Gandhi Square', 29.
11 Karina Landman, *Evolving Public Space in South Africa: Towards Regenerative Space in the Post-Apartheid City* (New York: Routledge, 2019).
12 Middelmann, 'Imagining the Future', 6–8.
13 Simon Hall, 'Proposal for an Archaeological Assessment of the Constitutional Court Precinct', 26 July 1999, SAHA, AL2395, D4, File 5, E1.4, n.p.
14 Hall, 'Proposal for an Archaeological Assessment', n.p.
15 Edward Kgosidintsi, 'Decolonising the African Landscape', *The Con Mag*, 16 September 2015, accessed 2 August 2019, http://www.theconmag.co.za/2015/09/16/decolonising-the-african-landscape/.
16 Middelmann, 'Imagining the Future', 16–18.
17 Middelmann, 'Imagining the Future', 14–17.
18 See Lauren Segal and Clive van den Berg, eds, *Mapping Memory: Former Prisoners Tell Their Stories* (Johannesburg: David Krut, 2007).
19 Coombes, *History after Apartheid*, 114–15.
20 RFB Architects, 'Letter to Fort Foundation', 21 July 1992, SAHA, AL2395, D4, File 5, E1.4: n.p.
21 Jennifer Kitto, 'Fax to Herbert Prins Re: Western Portion', 10 May 2002, SAHA, AL2395, D4, File 5, E1.4: 2.
22 David Emery, 'Letter to Hillary Bruce', 11 July 1991, SAHA, AL2395, D4, File 5, E1.4: n.p.; and Fort Steering Committee, 'Minutes of First Meeting', 16 August 1994, SAHA, AL2395, D4, File 5, E1.4: 2.
23 See South African Heritage Resource Agency, 'File note, ref: 9/2/228/35, Re: Constitution Hill ATB application for Demolition permit', 24 May 2001, SAHA, AL2395, D4, File 5, E1.4: n.p.; and P. Mills, 'Fax to SAHRA', 14 January 2002, SAHA, AL2395, D4, File 5, E1.4: n.p.

24 Historical Task Team of Constitution Hill Heritage Subcommittee, 'Minutes of Workshop', 20 June 2000, SAHA, AL2395, D4, File 5, E1.4: 2.
25 Segal, *Number Four*, 117.
26 Albie Sachs, 'Interview on the History of Constitution Hill', interview by Lauren Segal, 15 June 2005, SAHA, AL2395, D4, Interviews: 5–6.
27 Peter Marcuse, 'The Paradoxes of Public Space', *Journal of Architecture and Urbanism* 38.1 (2014): 102–06.
28 Jean Beater, 'Email to Jennifer Kitto', December 2001, SAHA, AL2395, D4, File 5, E1.4: n.p.
29 Itzkin, 'The Transformation of Gandhi Square', 51–2.
30 Itzkin, 'The Transformation of Gandhi Square', 53.
31 Kirsten Harrison and Potsiso Phasha, 'Public Art: Aesthetic, Evocative and Invisible?' Report produced by South African Research Chair in Development Planning and Modelling, University of the Witwatersrand, and the Johannesburg Development Agency (2014), 15, accessed 26 October 2020, http://wiredspace.wits.ac.za/bitstream/handle/10539/17150/Report7_Harrison_1006LR.pdf?sequence=1&isAllowed=y.
32 Itzkin, 'The Transformation of Gandhi Square', 54.
33 Jennifer Etheridge, 'Man Held After Damaging Gandhi Statue in JHB', *News24*, 12 April 2015, accessed 25 October 2019, https://www.news24.com/SouthAfrica/News/Man-held-after-damaging-Gandhi-statue-in-JHB-20150412.
34 Itzkin, 'The Transformation of Gandhi Square', 56–8.
35 Patrick French, 'Gandhi Before India by Ramachandra Guha – Review', *The Guardian*, 9 October 2013, accessed 25 October 2019, https://www.theguardian.com/books/2013/oct/09/gandhi-before-india-ramachandra-guha-review.
36 Here Sachs is referring to Indes Naidoo's grandfather. See Sachs, 'Interview on the History of Constitution Hill', 2.
37 Rory Carroll, 'Gandhi Branded Racist as Johannesburg Honours Freedom Fighter', *The Guardian*, 17 October 2003, accessed 25 October 2019, https://www.theguardian.com/world/2003/oct/17/southafrica.india.
38 Jason Burke, '"Racist" Gandhi Statue Banished from Ghana University Campus', *The Guardian*, 6 October 2016, accessed 25 October 2019, https://www.theguardian.com/world/2016/oct/06/ghana-academics-petition-removal-mahatma-gandhi-statue-african-heroes.
39 'Malawi Court Halts Work on Statue After Gandhi Branded Racist', *BBC News*, 31 October 2018, accessed 25 October 2019, https://www.bbc.com/news/world-africa-46051184.

40 Brenda Schmahmann, 'Monumental Mediations: Performative Interventions to Public Commemorative Art in South Africa', *de arte* 53.2-3 (2018): 142-59.
41 Sisonke Msimang, 'Rescuing Mandela from Sainthood', *Africa is a Country*, 27 April 2019, accessed 25 October 2019, https://africasacountry.com/2019/04/rescuing-nelson-mandela-from-sainthood.
42 Marschall, 'Memory and Identity', 191-2, 201.
43 David Bunn, 'Whited Sepulchres: On the Reluctance of Monuments', in *blank_____ Architecture, apartheid and after*, eds Hilton Judin and Ivan Vladislavić (Rotterdam: Nai Publishers, 1999), 100.
44 Itzkin, 'The Transformation of Gandhi Square', 77.
45 Marschall, 'Memory and Identity', 200.
46 Marschall, 'Memory and Identity', 191.
47 Michel de Certeau, Luce Giard and Pierre Mayol, *The Practice of Everyday Life, Volume 2: Living and Cooking* (Minnesota: University of Minnesota Press, 1998), 143.
48 Pierre Nora, 'Between Memory and History: Les Lieux de Mémoire', *Representations* 26 (1989): 7-24.
49 Middelmann, 'Caught Between', 37-9.

REFERENCES

Bunn, David. 'Whited Sepulchres: On the Reluctance of Monuments'. In *blank_____ Architecture, apartheid and after*, edited by Hilton Judin and Ivan Vladislavić, 93-115. Rotterdam: Nai Publishers, 1999.

Burke, Jason. '"Racist" Gandhi Statue Banished from Ghana University Campus'. *The Guardian,* 6 October 2016. Accessed 25 October 2019, https://www.theguardian.com/world/2016/oct/06/ghana-academics-petition-removal-mahatma-gandhi-statue-african-heroes.

Burton, Antoinette, ed. *Archive Stories: Facts, Fictions, and the Writing of History.* Durham: Duke University Press, 2006.

Christiansen, Eric. 'Transformative Constitutionalism in South Africa: Creative Uses of Constitutional Court Authority to Advance Substantive Justice'. *Journal of Gender, Race & Justice* 13.3 (2010): 575-614.

Coombes, Annie E. *History after Apartheid: Visual Culture and Public Memory in a Democratic South Africa.* Durham: Duke University Press, 2003.

De Certeau, Michel, Luce Giard, and Pierre Mayol. *The Practice of Everyday Life, Volume 2: Living and Cooking.* Minnesota: University of Minnesota Press, 1998.

Etheridge, Jennifer. 'Man Held After Damaging Gandhi Statue in JHB'. *News 24*, 12 April 2015. Accessed 25 October 2019, https://www.news24.com/SouthAfrica/News/Man-held-after-damaging-Gandhi-statue-in-JHB-20150412.

French, Patrick. 'Gandhi Before India by Ramachandra Guha – Review'. *The Guardian*, 9 October 2013. Accessed 25 October 2019, https://www.theguardian.com/books/2013/oct/09/gandhi-before-india-ramachandra-guha-review.

Harrison, Kirsten, and Potsiso Phasha. 'Public Art: Aesthetic, Evocative and Invisible?' Report produced by South African Research Chair in Development Planning and Modelling, University of the Witwatersrand, and Johannesburg Development Agency, 2014. Accessed 26 October 2020, http://wiredspace.wits.ac.za/bitstream/handle/10539/17150/Report7_Harrison_1006LR.pdf?sequence=1&isAllowed=y.

Itzkin, Eric. 'The Transformation of Gandhi Square: The Search for Socially Inclusive Heritage and Public Space in the Johannesburg City Centre'. Master's thesis, University of the Witwatersrand, Johannesburg, 2008.

Kgosidintsi, Edward. 'Decolonising the African Landscape'. *The Con Mag*, 16 September 2015. Accessed 2 August 2019, http://www.theconmag.co.za/2015/09/16/decolonising-the-african-landscape/.

Khumalo, Fred. 'Rainbow on a Paper Sky: Fault-lines on Post-Racial Rhetoric in South Africa'. *African Journal of Rhetoric* 10 (2018): 192–204.

King, Tony, and Mary K. Flynn. 'Heritage and the Post-Apartheid City: Constitution Hill, Johannesburg'. *International Journal of Heritage Studies* 18.1 (2011): 65–82.

Landman, Karina. *Evolving Public Space in South Africa: Towards Regenerative Space in the Post-Apartheid City.* New York: Routledge, 2019.

'Malawi Court Halts Work on Statue After Gandhi Branded Racist'. *BBC News*, 31 October 2018. Accessed 25 October 2019, https://www.bbc.com/news/world-africa-46051184.

Marcuse, Peter. 'The Paradoxes of Public Space'. *Journal of Architecture and Urbanism* 38.1 (2014): 102–06.

Marschall, Sabine. 'Memory and Identity in South Africa: Contradictions and Ambiguities in the Process of Post-Apartheid Memorialization'. *Visual Anthropology* 25.3 (2012): 189–204.

Middelmann, Temba John Dawson. 'Caught Between the Past and Future: Layers of Meaning at Constitution Hill'. Master's thesis, University of Oxford, 2016.

Middelmann, Temba John Dawson. 'Imagining the Future Through the Past: A Political History of Constitution Hill Since 1983'. *South African Historical Journal* 71.2 (2019): 150–69, https://doi.org/10.1080/02582473.2019.1610037.

Msimang, Sisonke. 'The End of the Rainbow Nation Myth'. *New York Times*, 12 April 2015. Accessed 25 October 2019, https://www.nytimes.com/2015/04/13/opinion/the-end-of-the-rainbow-nation-myth.html.

Msimang, Sisonke. 'Rescuing Mandela from Sainthood'. *Africa is a Country*, 27 April 2019. Accessed 25 October 2019, https://africasacountry.com/2019/04/rescuing-nelson-mandela-from-sainthood.

Murray, Martin J. *Commemorating and Forgetting: Challenges for the New South Africa*. Minneapolis: University of Minnesota Press, 2013.

Nora, Pierre. 'Between Memory and History: Les Lieux de Mémoire'. *Representations* 26 (1989): 7–24.

Patel, Zarina, and Clinton van der Merwe. 'Understandings of Urban Regeneration, Heritage and Environmental Justice at Constitution Hill, Johannesburg'. *Urban Forum* 16.2–3 (2005): 244–58.

Patel, Zarina, and Clinton van der Merwe. 'Constitution Hill: Just Space or Space of Justice'. In *Architecture and Justice: Judicial Meanings in the Public Realm*, edited by Jonathan Simon, Nicholas Temple and Renée Tobe, 115–30. London: Routledge, 2013.

Ross, Marc H. 'Cultural Contestation and the Symbolic Landscape: Politics by Other Means?' In *Culture and Belonging in Divided Societies: Contestation and Symbolic Landscapes*, edited by Marc H. Ross, 1–24. Pennsylvania: University of Pennsylvania Press, 2011.

Schmahmann, Brenda. 'Monumental Mediations: Performative Interventions to Public Commemorative Art in South Africa'. *de arte* 53.2–3 (2018): 142–59.

Segal, Lauren, ed. *Number Four: The Making of Constitution Hill*. Johannesburg: Penguin Putnam, 2006.

Segal, Lauren, and Clive van den Berg, eds. *Mapping Memory: Former Prisoners Tell Their Stories*. Johannesburg: David Krut, 2007.

Staeheli, Lynn, and Don Mitchell. 'Locating the Public in Research and Practice'. *Progress in Human Geography* 31.6 (2007): 792–811.

Weszkalnys, Gisa. *Berlin, Alexanderplatz: Transforming Place in a Unified Germany*. New York: Berghahn Books, 2010.

INTERVIEWS

Bird, Flo. 'Interview for Number Four'. Interview with Cheryl Stevens, 27 July 2005. South African History Archives (SAHA), Constitution Hill Collection AL3295, D4, Interviews: 2.

Essa, Nabeel. 'Interview for Number Four'. Interview with Cheryl Stevens, 2005. SAHA, AL3295, D4, Interviews: 3.

Reid, Graeme. 'Interview for Number Four'. Interview with Karen Martin, 16 August 2005. SAHA, Constitution Hill Collection AL3295, D4, Interviews: 13.

Van den Berg, Clive. 'Interview for Number Four'. Interview with Lauren Segal, 15 August 2005. SAHA, Constitution Hill Collection AL3295, D4, Interviews: 4.

4 EJARADINI: NOTES TOWARDS MODELLING BLACK GARDENS AS A RESPONSE TO THE COLONIALITY OF MUSEUMS

MADEYOULOOK[1]

Ejaradini is a multi-sited art project that builds and grows gardens in the courtyards of South African museums. The gardens serve as sites of exploration of the potential of black gardening and its histories, as a way to rethink museums. Black gardening, as an existing practice of refiguring a colonial inheritance, offers us ways to think through how we might reimagine our relationships to inherited colonial infrastructures more broadly.

The first iteration of Ejaradini was an 18-month project that sought to understand, practise and model the socialities of urban black gardening. In so doing, it took up residence at the Johannesburg Art Gallery (JAG) in 2018 and the Wits University Anthropology Museum in 2019, as both a garden installation and a series of social engagements, experiences and happenings. Ejaradini thus unearthed the political potential that emerges in the social experiences and connections offered by urban black gardening.

Select engagements and conversations with people we have met through the research and production process form our focus. In this way, the depth of social practice that emerges through the everyday practice of growing, as well as communal ties, becomes evident. The application of the socialities of urban black gardening practice connects to a wider spectrum of discourse, unlocking potential for institutions. These parallel lines of enquiry – the one conversational and descriptive, the other discursive – bring together a deeply affective experiential positionality, on the one hand, and a critique orientated towards modelling that selfsame affect and experience on the other. These two aspects are intended to be read simultaneously, and the reader will find references to various elements that cut across both.

Figure 4.1. Archival photograph from the Ronald and Torrance Ngilima collection, exhibited as part of Ejaradini. The photograph reflects the different forms of sociality forged within the urban, black garden between individuals, as well as between people and other-than-human life. Photographed in Benoni Old Location or Wattville Township, c. 1950. RN1302C, Ngilima Photo Archives

MAM' SUSAN

Mam' Susan grows chomolia, pumpkin, mielies, sweet potato and sugar cane, as well as lilies and marigolds. Her main garden, on the street outside her home, is approximately a metre wide and two metres across. It is enclosed with a high fence to protect it. She is forced to garden on the pavement largely because the plot that her house is on is tiny, and any spare space in the yard has been filled with back rooms. When we come to meet her, entering through the back door, she is sitting in her dark kitchen-cum-spaza shop, next to the old Welcome Dover stove. She is softly spoken, and funny. She speaks humbly about her giant pumpkins, and says that she hasn't cooked the rest of them because they don't taste that great.

She walks us over to her other garden, leading us across the street and on to the banks of one of the many small streams criss-crossing Soweto. This garden is larger, salvaged out of the dumpsite that the other side of the road has become. Surrounded by trash but fenced off, this little patch of reclaimed land is filled with sugar cane, potatoes, a grapevine and peach trees. The reeds that have completely claimed the shallow vleis of Soweto threaten the edges of her patch, encroaching ever further and making it more difficult to access the water she needs for the garden. The rats rummaging in the trash always get to her peaches before she does.

Throughout our conversation, Mam' Susan continues to tell us about the many difficulties and setbacks she faces in growing and caring for her gardens. She has little access to water in her gardens and has to rely on the rain. Her children aren't so keen on gardening either and don't really assist her even though she is growing old. The soil quality has deteriorated and has many layers of trash from long-term dumping. Being self-taught, Mam' Susan is largely experimenting, and her experiments don't always succeed. Unprompted, she answers the question that remains unuttered and hanging in the air: why would she continue to tend to her gardens when her labour yields so little fruit?

What becomes apparent is that cultivation has always been a central feature of Mam' Susan's life. It is attached to many personal memories of childhood and generations of gardeners in her family. For Mam' Susan, gardening as a vocation of care is a point of identification. Who is she if she does not garden? she asks. Gardening is therefore a way for Mam' Susan to connect the past, present and future. The act of growing, although not her primary motivation, is reason enough to garden even when there are few other gratifications for her labour. The challenges she faces in maintaining her gardens are a measure of the degree to which Mam' Susan values the processes of gardening and places value on the non-material fruits of her labour.

Mam' Susan's garden is, in fact, quite different to the many gardens of Soweto one sees on the roadside. The many manicured lawns, with beds of roses and pelargoniums, reflect European gardening practices – and the skills some have honed in the suburbs of Johannesburg. These gardens are obvious points of pride and neighbourly swagger. Mam' Susan's gardening is a labour of love, but also of sustenance. Many of the more manicured gardens of Soweto are ornamental and are therefore, too, a labour of pleasure and aesthetics, yet they are also potential reclamations of an alienated labour of the suburbs to an affective labour for the self.

ENTANGLED HISTORIES: THE BLACK GARDEN AND COLONIAL COERCION

The terms 'black garden' and 'black gardening' are used to refer to a variety of growing practices undertaken autonomously by gardeners of black African descent in rural as well as urban spaces such as townships, which were previously designated as black areas. We are specifically interested in South African practices, but have also touched on similar practices further afield. In addition, we very specifically focus on small-scale domestic gardens in urban settlements as opposed to, for example, rural subsistence farming. These gardens and practices display a set of shared features that loosely connect them. They are gardens with a multi-generational history, and have evolved over time to display their own aesthetic and conceptual paradigms. Although the term may suggest uniformity, black gardening encompasses a plurality of stylistic conventions often determined by their locale. Importantly, many black gardens do not recognise strict borders between plants used for nutritional, spiritual, medicinal and decorative purposes, choosing instead to cultivate a sociality among plants. Many black gardens exhibit an entanglement with inherited colonial gardening models rather than being oppositional to them. That said, these gardens are not simply imported wholesale from European perspectives.

There is an abundance of scholarship on the garden as colonial construct, and how plants have figured in processes of imperial expansion. Many of the principles inscribed in contemporary gardening trace back to the earliest stages of the European colonial project and voyages of discovery. The first of these was the collection and classification of living and preserved plant specimens from around the world, often motivated by the Christian desire to gather in one place all the creations which, they believed, had been scattered to the corners of the world at the fall of Eden.[2] This 'cabinet of curiosities' approach to collecting and ordering the natural world is imprinted and replicated in today's greenhouses, botanical gardens and, certainly, domestic gardens. Much like the 'cabinets of curiosities' of the sixteenth century, today's gardens attest to the careful ordering of multiple species and examples of the natural world into one confined space. It is commonplace to find an array of exotic plants – such as rose bushes, wisteria and bottlebrush collected from other colonies and introduced to South Africa – adorning suburban and township gardens.

In contrast to this desire for paradisiacal reproduction, gardening was also a means for recreating a sense of home in the colonies, made plain by the prevalence of ivy, daisies and English lawns in South African gardens. Manicuring, hedging, pruning, as well as mowing the lawn are all unassuming, everyday forms of control routinely exercised, and are couched within hierarchies of control. The differentiation of plants according to use and the demarcation of garden beds unfolds into the conception of the 'pleasure garden', a form of landscaping aimed specifically at pleasure for the land-owning gaze. Here the master, who has dominion over the land, surveys his work and is pleased by what he sees. We are less concerned, however, with an engagement on the specificities of colonial control and what Agnese Fidecaro describes as the 'embeddedness of gardening in a variety of discourses and practices of power'.[3] This is not to ignore the colonial legacies of gardening but rather to acknowledge its complicated and conflictual nature by looking to the urban black garden, not as a reproduction of colonial values of mastery over the natural world, but as a still-emergent model for the formation of new relations to colonial ruins and past oppressive spaces.

MAM' SIMANGELE SIKO

It is a Sunday morning and we are seated around Mam' Simangele's dining room table having a short chat about the Ejaradini project, and about the possibility of her working on it with us. Instead, the conversation drifts to Mam' Simangele's musings on the roles of gardens in her environment and, over time, the ways in which her own imagination was being broadened by surrounding herself with a community of local cultivators. Mam' Simangele lives in Dube, Soweto, in a house whose outside wall sports the blue circular heritage plaque more usually found in the leafy older suburbs of Johannesburg. The plaque commemorates her father, Theo Mthembu, who was a leader in the development of professional sports in Soweto and a stalwart of the non-racial sports movement in South Africa. The house is on an average sized Dube plot, with the expanded house taking up much of it, and very little garden to speak of. Mam' Simangele doesn't garden, though she hopes to start soon. She spends much of her time supporting growers and farmers in the broader Soweto area, and runs the local farmers' market.

Mam' Simangele often looks up, tilts her head a little to the right, as she remembers the gardens she grew up with. Gardens have disappeared in her neighbourhood, she says, and there used to be more of them. Neither she nor her sisters understood how important growing one's own food would become, and she laments that, as third generation inheritors of the house, they paved over the small matrilineal garden. She now, out of her regret, appeals to her neighbours and friends not to cut down their trees, and insists that they keep a little spot for growing when they pave. It's a way of summoning her lost garden and the labour of the women who raised her.

The generations of gardening that Mam' Simangele summons track the changes of Dube, of Soweto, and of black life more broadly. Her recollections trace the symbolic role gardens play in genealogies of black life, and especially its aspirations. She says, for example: 'For some reason roses are a favourite. If you've got a rose bush, you're made. It's like having – before I understood – paving.' She specifically references Dube Village, a very early Soweto development, which was established in the 1950s for black professionals and more affluent families. Over time, though, this has shifted somewhat. Newer, more affluent areas have since been developed, and a number of families have moved to neighbourhoods such as Diepkloof and, importantly, have taken their gardens with them. Mam' Simangele describes how the elaborate gardens of Dube gradually migrated to Diepkloof Extension in the 1980s and 1990s, and then on to neighbourhoods such as today's Dobsonville: 'So, you see the standing in the community from the garden, and lately from the paving. You know what area you're in simply by looking at the garden.'

REFIGURING GARDENING INHERITANCE

When it comes to black urban gardening, many of the tropes of the colonial garden are present. Yet their very manifestation brings to bear a complexity and life-giving vitality that is in direct contradiction to those very tropes. It is this space of contestation that provides some interesting tools. In some gardens, for example, we also see the inclusion of plants for spiritual and sacred use – many taken from indigenous wilderness areas – alongside plants used for medicinal purposes, sustenance and for aesthetic pleasure. These point to some of the myriad functions that the black garden performs.

In such gardens, with their various plant lives and roles, function and place flow from one into the other, unsettling boundaries. Spiritual and medicinal plants within some urban black gardens emphasise African traditions in cosmology and the natural ordering of the universe.[4] We see this in the seemingly chaotic gardens planted to the mutual benefit of all the vegetation. These gardens feature an assortment of plants, some in plastic tubs and bottles, worn tyres and tin pots, living and growing among neatly tended rows and beds of indigenous vegetables, herbs and decorative plants. There is, for example, a modest, albeit unsuccessful, attempt at the domestication of nature in Mam' Susan's struggling gardens. The ordered row system for vegetables comes into contact with untamed growth and uncoordinated planting practices. While gardeners like Mam' Susan may have particular desires and ideas of how they would like their gardens to manifest, they do not always have the capacity for control. Lack of resources and environmental factors are among many elements that undermine any grand ambitions for mastery over nature.

Additionally, there is the recurrent element of unsystematic cultivating on the part of many black gardeners, which further undermines the concept of conquest. For Fidecaro, the establishment of a home garden belonging to Jamaica Kincaid began with an unskilled experimentation with seeds, which itself follows a tradition of small-scale learning that keeps knowledge within the scope of the home.[5] For gardeners like Kincaid and Mam' Susan, this unsystematic approach is founded on a praxis of self-teaching located outside of Eurocentric knowledge systems and the unvaried voices of gardening catalogues, planting guides and classic literature on botany. By contrast, their approaches are sustained by interpersonal connections and the goodwill of fellow growers through gifted seeds, cuttings and practical information.

Even in the cases of the more manicured lawns of aspirant gardeners, with roses and paving, as described by Mam' Simangele, it becomes clear that, while operating in the modality of dominion over nature, these gardens exist in a very different space of symbolic potential. This symbolic potential is one within a genealogy of black aspiration, and is closely connected to the complexities of what it means to make a home within the histories of black urban settlement. Dube, after all, would have been settled by those forcibly removed from other areas. Furthermore, rather than an act of control and order of the obvious colonial type, these signifiers of perfectly trimmed hedges and European flowers are used for an altered form of respectability politics, one that is more inclined towards a humanising and dignifying practice of the self than a subjugation of the other. This is not to deny that the practices of class symbolism and conspicuous aspiration, not to mention a black respectability politics of the professional classes, are not problematic; rather, their problematics are noted as being one step removed from their initial colonial visualities.

MPHATHI MOTHA

With Mphathi, a comparatively much younger grower – our own age, in fact – many of the complexities of an older generation of growers are seen to collide with a newer, more globalised politics of growing. Mphathi and his business partner, Zakhe Dhlame, are small-scale food farmers who sell their herbs, fruit and vegetables at various markets and to various stores. As landless young men themselves, they cultivate on a number of sites in different parts of Soweto, making use of land through networks and familial relationships. They use a combination of familial inheritances of gardening practices together with more contemporary permaculture strategies for their farming. Mphathi states, for example, that he believes farming was 'originally' done the way he and Zakhe do it today, that they have taken it 'from our ancestors'. One of the sites on which he farms is where his grandmother used to grow food, he says, 'so I guess I took over from that legacy and I'm continuing with those methods, trying to bring in that force'.

Both Mphathi and Zakhe are forthright about the independence that growing gives them, not simply in relation to being able to grow their own food, but also in terms of a strategy of self-reliance and a connectedness to natural life which creates a different sense of selfhood. Mphathi explains:

> For me, since our garden is all natural, I look forward to waking up in the morning. I look forward to being in the garden and having interactions with birds, insects – because we always invite beneficial insects. We have different birds, we have reptiles roaming around, beautiful spiders that come visit us to do work. We've got bees. We've created our garden where we have a whole lot of flower power, because we want bees. Bees are doing wonders for us. Sometimes you find people with knowledge of growing tomatoes. You need a bee to have that fruit. Without a bee in your garden you'll just grow a tomato plant with no fruit because a bee is what pollinates that plant to give you that tomato. So that's what we realised. That's what we see on a daily basis. I see it as a hotspot to connect, just like you have your Wi-Fi hotspot, it's a hotspot to connect with nature ... It is that interaction with your spiritual world and understanding your wellbeing. That's where true connection starts.

Mphathi frames a sense of interconnectedness, of farming, to natural life broadly, and more specifically to a sense of selfhood driven by this connection and the sense of 'consciousness' it affords. Importantly, this is not simply a kind of self-centred escapism; it has a strongly political imperative. Both Zakhe and Mphathi speak emphatically of the problematics of current state support systems and their complicity with large-scale agribusiness and the undermining of small-scale farmers' independence. They are determined to use personally sourced seeds, and to get seeds from other permaculture farmers in particular, as well as from those involved in inherited African farming practices. Growing is a very self-articulated way of life, a kind of self-making, and also a political position.

REIMAGINING RUINATION

Operating within the tradition of artists such as Lonnie Graham and works such as his 'Enlightenment' and 'African-American Garden', Ejaradini hopes to engage the garden from the perspective of black people who grow their own gardens, and the possibilities they offer. In addition, Ejaradini considers how we might learn from the subversion of the colonial garden by black gardeners in ways that equip us to think through the afterlives of colonial ruins. The Ejaradini project brought together different forms of socialities through exhibitions and accompanying happenings and events. The exhibitions – made up of a living garden and archival photographs – transformed the usually austere courtyards of institutions into temporary garden installations open for use by staff, students and the public as spaces of encounter, reflection and repose. At the JAG, an open invitation was extended to inhabit and care for the garden during the hot summer months of the exhibition, forging an intimate sociality between people and plant life. The supporting social programme included plant-growing workshops for young people, while a series of public talks and lectures were held, both within the garden installations and in Soweto gardens, engaging with questions relating to plant socialities and growing in the wake of colonial collapse. DJ sets were specially created for the listening pleasure not only of visitors but also of plants, and a series of get-togethers completed the scheduled social engagements.

Responding to the JAG invitation to occupy the garden installation, the pan-African feminist publishing house and collective, Impepho Press, held a poetry reading in the garden. Apart from hosting a number of discussions on other exhibitions on view at the time, the JAG held their annual year-end staff party in the garden, in addition to a number of formal and informal events. All these social and interpersonal encounters reflect the project's orientation towards the myriad socialities that inform black gardening. These socialities are manifest at multiple registers. They range from indigenous naming conventions predicated upon black people's everyday relationships with plants,[6] to the historical significance of black gardens in making place for people historically displaced through dispossession.

The broad context of this project is the development of the JAG between 1910 and 1915 by Lady Phillips, the wife of a Johannesburg mining magnate.[7] The gallery's initial building and collection – including works by Rodin, Rembrandt and Pierneef – were entirely colonial, with the building itself being designed by Edwin Lutyens, an architect of the British Raj.[8] The JAG has sought to modernise over time, acquiring its first work by a black artist – Gerard Sekoto – in 1940, and developing a new wing in the 1980s. Today, the JAG stands in the busiest precinct of Johannesburg, nestled in its largest public transit node bustling with peoples and goods. While life throbs outside its walls, the gallery remains largely quiet, with very few visitors. Increasingly neglected by the City of Johannesburg authorities, it has suffered flooding, crumbling and overburdened staff.

The JAG appointed its first black chief curator, Khwezi Gule, in December 2017. His arrival serves as the first instance of viable and valuable reclamation being led by someone openly critical of the JAG's longstanding identity and its attendant collection and architecture. Rather than a continued support of these, Gule has sought to reimagine the gallery for a public previously kept at arm's length by its colonial origins. His arrival has enabled a reassessment of the gallery's traditional commitment to its material contents and refocused its efforts on the introduction of different socialities into its practices and culture. The question becomes therefore how life might emerge from the metaphorical ruins of the JAG under the new chief curator. Also, to what systems, models and precedents might its team look to develop a gallery that arises out of a colonial identity, becoming something valuable for a contemporary decolonised space.

For us, the socialities of black gardening serve as an important space to begin answering some of the questions currently at the forefront of the JAG's concerns. Black gardening offers possibilities for a new engagement with museums as places of growing and 'lifehood', given nature's ability to create life directly out of ruination and rot. Although museums around the world represent a vast accumulation of objects, there is generally limited public access to the artefacts they house. Large parts of collections are stored within museums and remain unseen by those who work within their walls, let alone by the wider public. It is no wonder then that the metaphor of the museum as mausoleum comes to mind, connoting a place of death, or a Derridean 'death drive';[9] within its walls, cultural objects are transformed into relics. However, in the case of the JAG, this notion of death is also present in the metaphorical ruination of the building itself. In an inversion of this metaphor, the collapse of the building comes to stand for the death of established values and attendant museological thought built on colonial notions of collection, categorisation and knowledge formation.

By using urban black gardening practices as a model, we can reflect on the idea of death as an integral part of growing and lifehood. We choose to deploy the garden as a model rather than emphasise the need for the restoration of the JAG's building, which is often spoken of in nostalgic terms, recalling the gallery's former glory, with the Edwardian architecture representative of a 'simpler past'.[10] Instead, we find the idea of the cycle of rot, germination and growth a far more generative possibility. By comparison, restoration and preservation as models merely recognise the physical integrity of the building and its collection, with a return to the status quo.

The current disintegration of the JAG can serve as fertile ground for different potentialities and new relations to form. As anthropologist Marc Augé contends, we must 'forget in order to remain present' and 'forget in order not to die'.[11] Augé's formulation suggests that material erasure and processes of change might help facilitate remembrance through transience, and so create a more dynamic relation to the present and future. More recently, more speculative approaches to heritage have adopted this perspective and have sought to call into question the contemporary preservation paradigm by recognising the generative potential of processes of decay and disintegration.[12] The deterioration of material sites, as some of these speculative approaches suggest, does not necessarily lead to the loss of memory but may in fact enable the creation of new models. The JAG finds itself at a crossroads: cling to prevailing conservation patterns that equate material stasis with memory, or embrace entropy and death as a blueprint for how things might otherwise be.[13]

BELONGING-MAKING

In a similar sense to the ways in which gardening can be reclaimed as a political space of self-making for many growers – articulated so clearly by Mam' Simangele and Mphathi – the JAG has the potential to become a space more closely engaged with its immediate environment and the people who live and work there. In so doing, it potentially becomes more relevant to the relations not only of people within the JAG, but also possible and actual 'audiences'. The black garden serves as a powerful modality for belonging-making under duress. The commitment, resources and labour of garden-making is a long-term investment in landedness, and a statement of belonging that is fixed and spatially based. This was a radical act in early black urban spaces in South Africa, where black subjects were strongly determined as migratory and not of a fixed belonging within the urban fabric. To plant a garden, then, was to physically stake a claim. Furthermore, it was to stake a claim of individualised and domestic place-making and home-making. This affective labour was one aimed at a determination of belonging, using the practices associated with those who chose to keep one out. Today, Mphathi and Zakhe point to ways in which historical forms of gardening that are inherited can be actively entangled with black historical practices and innovations of global forms. The JAG has the potential, too, to challenge the idea that an art gallery does not belong in Joubert Park, or that local residents do not belong in art galleries. There is the potential in the model of the urban black garden to use a foreign tool to claim home out of perceived or actual hostility, and to create selfhood through a claiming and reconstructing of one's practice. These socialities already float through the JAG as a number of young people in particular amble through its galleries and hallways after school. During the Ejaradini project these young people were invited to join a regular planting programme in the garden, and took to watering (and even over-watering) it for the duration. For most of them it was the first time they had been invited into programming at the JAG.

A SANCTUARY IN THE CITY

There is an undeniable correlation between the sanctuary offered by gardens and the 'wellbeing' articulated by Mphathi. This is another role of gardens that can be extended to the JAG. As with gardens, the JAG might become a space that people turn to in the midst of urban chaos for a different kind of affective experience and relation to the city. In fact, this is already happening, albeit to a limited degree. On several occasions, we have encountered groups of young people who come to the gallery not simply for the purpose of viewing art but to utilise the premises as a recreational space after school and over weekends.

The various ways in which they do so — some practising their dance choreographies for school, others using the building as a photographic backdrop, and still others revelling in the quiet of the exhibition halls — is an indication of the many ways in which the surrounding community find a moment for themselves, but also the ways in which they can help shape and define the role of the JAG. There is significant potential to harness this kind of experience, to identify where the public see value for it, and to heighten it. During the Ejaradini programmes, young people had many suggestions, and a number were extended by the JAG team beyond the framework of the project. The programmes also have the potential to change, reflecting the multiple ways we use and derive pleasure from gardens, which offer a space for play, solitude, reflection and reprieve from the temporalities and demands of city life.

AN AFFECTIVE LABOUR

The reaping of fruit and a conscious engagement with the future orientation of one's labour and its products further serve as a potential point of entry for the JAG. It has, until now, primarily served an audience associated with colonial interests, and an arts practice linked to that same legacy. There is potential for the workers at the JAG to move away from an alienated form of labour, disconnected from their immediate benefit, and to realise the potentialities of their labour for the broader benefit of their environment. An example of this emerged through the socialities of the Ejardini installation, in which JAG installation staff made suggestions for future iterations and programming, such as music sessions and public talks that attract jazz-loving audiences. These cultural events would not only attract more residents who were immediate neighbours to the JAG, but the new audiences would also enjoy such events. Making programming proposals is usually the domain of the 'intellectual' curatorial staff. Disrupting these inherited hierarchies could enable very different possibilities for the JAG. Thinking through Mphathi's radical claim of selfhood, we ask: What can black gardening teach us about a reclamation of labour from suburban alienated labour to a practice of pleasure and productivity for the self as well as the local environment? For the JAG, this becomes a labour less inclined to the proclivities of bureaucracy and hierarchy and the cycle of exhibition openings. Instead it is a labour driven by a sociality, a revision of the powers of knowledge production, and by the intrinsic value of its products.

A RADICAL POSSESSION OF TIME

Closely related to this reclamation of labour is the potential for the radical possession of time through gardening and growing. The act of gardening compels us to re-examine the impositions of capitalist time in relation to natural time scales, and potentially to yield to the slowed rhythms and temporalities of plant life. The temporalities of botanical life extend to seasonal change, growth, and to the cyclical nature of repetition and reproduction. These coalesce in the processes of gardening and encourage a critical examination of a linear, deadline-orientated clock time. Much like gardening, the

Figure 4.2. Archival photograph from the Ronald and Torrance Ngilima collection, exhibited as part of Ejaradini. The portrait reflects traditions extending from Victorian-era portrait photography, using subtle signifiers within the images such as clothing – and importantly, in this case, the garden – to convey indicators of the sitters' subjectivity and selfhood. Photographed in Benoni Old Location or Wattville Township, 1940–1960. RN4058S, Ngilima Photo Archives

reconfiguration of the JAG's colonial inheritance is likely to be a gruelling labour involving dedicated time and care. Formulating new models will seem, at times, a futile enterprise, while, at others, the meagre fruits of this labour will appear not to justify the disproportionate efforts and hours spent tilling the soil. Gule's appointment, and his shift towards practices engaged in different forms of sociality, signal a new season still in its infancy. Imagining the JAG beyond preservation will require the resolve of growers such as Mam' Susan and the patient assumption of the repetitious and cyclical temporalities of gardening.

GROWING NEW LIFE

What urban black gardening practices bring to the fore are the everyday entanglements with colonial legacies that black people continue to have in post-1994 South Africa. As a form of engagement with the ruinations of colonial architectures, black gardening serves as a means by which we might model this entanglement, offering us ways of claiming an unwanted inheritance and reimagining it, renegotiating it, and making it grow into something else. This entanglement is vital, for it enables the potential of lifehood to emerge from things that rot. It gives us an already existing vocabulary that functions outside of the Preservation vs #MustFall dichotomy. This vocabulary offers not a 'third way' per se, but rather a way of understanding the realities of ruination as they currently exist, and the agency that ruination enables for a reimagined time-space of black lifehood. It highlights sociality, and the people who live life, over and above the framing of physical infrastructures, their psycho-social origins, and whether they should stand or not. Too often this sociality, the humans who labour in these spaces and the ways in which they work, is overlooked, whether it might be in favour of, or in contention with, the structure of power itself.

Museums and art galleries and their collections are inherently infrastructures of time – of history and of perpetuity. However, in considering what might be done with the reluctant ruin of the Johannesburg Art Gallery we look neither to the building nor the collection, both of which usually serve as the main point of contention and mourning in contemporary art circles. We consider rather the in-between spaces, the lifehood within the JAG, its staff, its 'audiences', as well as its potentially relation-focused programming. We are interested less in architecture as buildings but rather as infrastructures of social relations, places of engagement. We are interested also in the interspaces as the often-overlooked sites of green life that are scattered among people going about their everyday. Even more so, we are interested in the activity of people who spend time in the in-between spaces and commit labour and love to their growth. In particular, we are interested in what we might learn from urban black gardening as practices of deep, affective spatial labour, often under challenging circumstances and within a fraught historical paradigm.

NOTES

1. MADEYOULOOK is a Johannesburg-based, interdisciplinary artist collaboration comprising Nare Mokgotho and Molemo Moiloa. The works often reference everyday innovations, aspects of inner-city life that find simple solutions to ordinary challenges. With its broad interest in the relation of art to audience and concepts of publics, a central concern is notions of knowledge production and access to ownership in the wider sense.
2. Jason T. W. Irving, 'Botanical Gardens, Colonial Histories and Bioprospecting: Naming and Classifying the Plants of the World', in *Theatrum Botanicum*, eds Shela Sheikh and Uriel Orlow (Berlin: Sternberg Press, 2018), 75.
3. Agnese Fidecaro, 'Jamaica Kincaid's Practical Politics of the Intimate in *My Garden (book)*', *Women's Studies Quarterly* 34.1/2 (Spring/Summer, 2006): 250–51.
4. A similar practice occurred in the United States, according Dianne D. Glave, 'A Garden so Brilliant with Colours, so Original in its Design: Rural African American Women, Gardening, Progressive Reform, and the Foundation of an African American Environmental Perspective', *Environmental History* 8.3 (July 2003): 401.
5. Agnese Fidecaro, 'Jamaica Kincaid's Practical Politics of the Intimate', 250–51.
6. Narendran Kumarakulasingam and Mvuselelo Ngcoya, 'Plant Provocations: Botanical Indigeneity and (De)colonial Imaginations', *Contexto Internacional* 38.3 (September 2016): 843.
7. Robert A. Beauregard et al., eds, *Emerging Johannesburg: Perspectives on the Postapartheid City* (New York: Routledge, 2003).
8. Jane Ridley, 'Edwin Lutyens, New Delhi, and the Architecture of Imperialism', *The Journal of Imperial and Commonwealth History* 26.2 (1998): 67–83.
9. Jacques Derrida, 'Archive Fever in South Africa', in *Refiguring the Archive*, eds Carolyn Hamilton et al. (Dordrecht: Springer, 2002), 38.
10. Recent media attention has bordered on alarmist, even suggesting that the collection be moved to affluent areas that would be more easily accessible to the white audiences who

care about it. See, for example, Lynsey Chutel, 'One of Africa's Largest Art Collections is Under Threat', accessed 1 July 2019, https://qz.com/africa/911421/the-johannesburg-art-gallery-suffers-from-neglect-despite-its-impressive-history-and-collection/.

11   Marc Augé, *Oblivion*, trans. Marjolijn de Jager (Minneapolis: University of Minnesota Press, 2004), 89.

12   Caitlin DeSilvey, *Curated Decay: Heritage Beyond Saving* (Minneapolis: University of Minnesota Press, 2017), 5.

13   Rike Sitas, 'Becoming Otherwise: Artful Urban Enquiry', *Urban Forum* 31 (2020): 157–75.

REFERENCES

Augé, Marc. *Oblivion*. Translated by Marjolijn de Jager. Minneapolis: University of Minnesota Press, 2004.

Beauregard, Robert A., Lindsay Bremner, Xolela Mangcu, and Richard Tomlinson, eds. *Emerging Johannesburg: Perspectives on the Postapartheid City.* New York: Routledge, 2003.

Braziel, Jana Evans. 'Daffodils, Rhizomes, Migrations: Narrative Coming of Age in the Diasporic Writings of Edwidge Danticat and Jamaica Kincaid'. *Meridians* 3.2 (2003): 110–13.

Chutel, Lynsey. 'One of Africa's Largest Art Collections is Under Threat'. Accessed 1 July 2019, https://qz.com/africa/911421/the-johannesburg-art-gallery-suffers-from-neglect-despite-its-impressive-history-and-collection/.

Clifford, James. *Returns: Becoming Indigenous in the Twenty-First Century*. Cambridge: Harvard University Press, 2013.

Cooper, David E. *A Philosophy of Gardens.* Oxford: Clarendon Press, 2006.

Craig, Lauren. 'Thinking Flowers? As Black Eco-Feminist Activism'. *Feminist Review* 108 (2014): 71–80.

Demos, T. J. *Decolonizing Nature: Contemporary Art and the Politics of Ecology.* Berlin: Sternberg Press, 2016.

Derrida, Jacques. 'Archive Fever'. In *Refiguring the Archive*, edited by Carolyn Hamilton, Verne Harris, Michèle Pickover, Graeme Reid, Raziah Saleh and Jane Taylor. Dordrecht: Springer, 2002.

DeSilvey, Caitlin. *Curated Decay: Heritage Beyond Saving*. Minneapolis: University of Minnesota Press, 2017.

Dungy, Camille T., ed. *Black Nature: Four Centuries of African American Nature Poetry.* Athens: University of Georgia Press, 2009.

Fidecaro, Agnese. 'Jamaica Kincaid's Practical Politics of the Intimate in *My Garden (book)*'. *Women's Studies Quarterly* 4.1/2 (2006): 250–70.

Glave, Dianne D. 'A Garden so Brilliant with Colours, so Original in its Design: Rural African American Women, Gardening, Progressive Reform, and the Foundation of an African American Environmental Perspective'. *Environmental History* 8.3 (2003): 395–411.

Haynes, Duncan, Michelle Cox, and Charlie Shackleton. 'Biocultural Features of Urban Gardens and Yards Enhance Place-Making and Belonging in South African Townships'. *Landscape Magazine* 7.1 (2018): 10–14.

Irving, Jason T. W. 'Botanical Gardens, Colonial Histories and Bioprospecting: Naming and Classifying the Plants of the World'. In *Theatrum Botanicum*, edited by Shela Sheikh and Uriel Orlow. Berlin: Sternberg Press, 2018.

Knepper, Wendy. 'How Does your Garden Grow?' or Jamaica Kincaid's Spatial Praxis in *My Garden (Book)*: and *Among Flowers: A Walk in the Himalaya*'. In *Post-Colonial Space: The Politics of Place in Contemporary Culture*, edited by Andrew Teverson and Sara Upstone. London: Palgrave Macmillan, 2011.

Kumarakulasingam, Narendran, and Mvuselelo Ngcoya. 'Plant Provocations: Botanical Indigeneity and (De)colonial Imaginations'. *Contexto International* 38.3 (2016): 843–64.

Marder, Michael. *Plant-Thinking: A Philosophy of Vegetal Life*. New York: Columbia University Press, 2013.

Mhlongo, Niq. *Soweto, Under the Apricot Tree*. Cape Town: Kwela Books, 2018.

Orlow, Uriel, and Shela Sheikh, eds. *Theatrum Botanicum*. Berlin: Sternberg Press, 2018.

Ridley, Jane. 'Edwin Lutyens, New Delhi, and the Architecture of Imperialism'. *The Journal of Imperial and Commonwealth History* 26.2 (1998): 67–83.

Simone, AbdouMaliq. 'People as Infrastructure: Intersecting Fragments in Johannesburg'. *Public Culture* 16.3 (2004): 407–29.

Sitas, Rike. 'Becoming Otherwise: Artful Urban Enquiry'. *Urban Forum* 31 (2020): 157–75.

Stouck, Jordan. 'Gardening in the Diaspora: Place and Identity in Olive Senior's Poetry'. *Mosaic* 38.4 (2005): 103–22.

Wendt, Dennis, and Joseph Gone. 'Decolonizing Psychological Inquiry in American Indian Communities: The Promise of Qualitative Methods'. In *Qualitative Strategies for Ethnocultural Research*, edited by D. K. Nagata, L. Kohn-Wood and L. A. Suzuki, 161–78. American Psychological Association, 2012.

INTERVIEWS

[surname unknown], Mam' Susan. Personal interview with authors. October 2018, Soweto.

Motha, Mphathi, with Zakhe Dhlame. Personal interview with authors. 1 December 2018, Soweto.

Siko, Mam' Simangele. Personal interview with authors. 25 November 2018, Soweto.

PART TWO
BUILDINGS

5 JOHANNESBURG CENTRAL POLICE STATION AND THE PHOTOGRAPH AS EVIDENCE

SALLY GAULE

A solitary figure pulling his cart in Johannesburg is reminiscent of a prospector with a small load of precious metals. In a curious way, this image reflects one attribute of photography – to stretch past and present. The arc of the gold-bearing reef below that gave rise to the city is echoed by another prospector, a century later, who will hawk his load by weight to scrap-metal dealers in the city. In this photograph, the building that terminates the street is Johannesburg Central Police Station, and from this vantage point, the building seemingly blocks the path of the road. This is unusual for Johannesburg, since its grid layout created views down its roads that extended as far as the eye could see. As a metaphor, the building terminates the road, giving the appearance of a dead-end that resonates with the building's history. Our view is blocked and our mobility is curtailed by the building which was itself the end point for many under apartheid.

The building faces Commissioner Street, a central artery that cuts through the old financial district and connects to Main Reef Road at each end. It is arguably the oldest road in Johannesburg. Immediately to the west of the building lies De Villiers Graaff motorway, constructed in 1972, which skirts the city, forming a boundary between city and veld, and city and mining land.

Figure 5.1. View along Commissioner Street with Johannesburg Central Police Station, 2009. Photograph by Sally Gaule

Commissioner Street marks the southernmost line of the *uitvalgrond* – a small triangle of surplus ground on which the city arose. On this line, two dominant landscape forces that shaped the city rub against each other: the grid of the cityscape, and the mine dumps deposited over a century ago. Commissioner Street marks the invisible line of the gold-bearing reef beneath and a boundary that cuts the city in half, separating Soweto in the south from the wealthier, historically white, land to the north. On this juncture still stands one of the most notorious buildings of apartheid, the Johannesburg Central Police Station, which was previously named John Vorster Square.[1]

One of the characteristic features of a metropolis, as the philosopher Achille Mbembe and literary and cultural theorist Sarah Nuttall note in 'Writing the World from an African Metropolis', is an *underneath*. They write that 'beneath the visible landscape and the surface of the metropolis, its objects and social relations are concealed or embedded in other orders of visibility'.[2] During apartheid, underground movements operated below the radar of visibility so that the underneath, the underground, and the Johannesburg Central Police Station remain intimately connected. A range of photographic depictions of Johannesburg Central Police Station are examined through the lens of forensics, detective work and the architecture of the panopticon, which bears stark comparison in terms of surveillance and the building's history, and, following the philosopher Michel Foucault, 'its very materiality as a vector of power'.[3]

Figure 5.2. John Vorster Square, 1972. © *Sunday Times*

John Vorster Square was designed by a commercial architectural firm, Harris, Fels, Jankes and Nussbaum, and completed in 1968, the era of high apartheid. Its construction comprised standardised modular windows. It is essentially a commercial office project, according to the architect Clive Chipkin, forming a strategic headquarters with a police barracks, prison cells, interrogation centre and offices.[4] Thus, the architects attempted to echo the modernity of the city, modern methods of construction, standardised units and elements that denote 'business as usual'. When the building was opened by John Vorster, then Minister of Justice in South Africa, he heralded it as a 'state of the art' modern police station, boasting that it was the largest in Africa.[5]

The *Sunday Times* photograph, from the archives of the Tiso Blackstar Group, is like a mugshot of the building, prosaic and unremarkable. Yet in the eyes and minds of citizens of Johannesburg, the building represents what Hannah Arendt famously termed 'the banality of evil'. It is where countless people were detained without trial, brutalised, intimidated, tortured and killed by the apartheid regime. It displays monotony and repetition as the organising feature of the building, evoking the template for prison life itself which makes one day elide into the next. Writer and photographer Teju Cole discusses the building in *Known and Strange Things*: '"Yes, they tortured people here," my friend says. She points out the building. In the old days people went into this building and came out lessened, if they came out at all. It was an evil place.'[6] Former detainee Barbara Hogan called John Vorster Square 'the iconic institution of the apartheid years, of the years of torture, of the reign of the security police, of the reign of the mad forces …'.[7]

THE MUG SHOT

The technology of photography and the science of criminology emerged virtually simultaneouly as parallel cultural phenomena, Sandra S. Phillips asserts in 'Identifying the Criminal'.[8] Moreover, as beliefs about physiognomy and the physical appearance of criminal types gained prominence as diagnostic tools for identifying criminals, these were applied to the new study of phrenology in the mid-1800s. The mug shot came into being in the 1860s, not long after the invention of photography. It still plays a role in police work, intended as an aid to identify suspects by their facial features. Police mug shot albums are considered an effective way to identify a suspect, and are the most commonly used method of identification.[9] As early as the 1850s, a 'Rogues' gallery' album compiled by the New York Police Department formed part of its practice in identifying lawbreakers.[10]

South Africa had its own version of the well-known Rogues' gallery. In 1985, in Pretoria, the security branch of the South African Police assembled a secret *Foto Album van RSA Terroriste* (photo album of South African terrorists, known as the 'terrorist album').[11] The album comprised as many as 7 000 photographs of individuals who had been branded as dangerous political extremists. Of the 500 copies that were circulated, only 3 survive. It consisted of a nondescript brown cardboard cover with nine mug shots per page identified by a number below each image. At the back, lists of names correlate with the number below each photograph. The mug shot appears as a neutral record, severed from the confused action, emotional stress, divided attention or poor lighting that may be a feature in the witnessing of a crime.[12] Yet many of the images in the 'terrorist album' are not conventional mug shots. Instead, some have been appropriated from other pictures, snapshots or ID photos, and some were taken secretly by the security police.¹³ The effect of this is to undermine the uniformity and seeming neutrality of the mug shot. Moreover, we know in retrospect that the only crime of those appearing in this album was to oppose apartheid.¹⁴

The photograph's ability to record surface rather than depth remains its major limitation. However, since its beginnings photographers have sought to show more than just appearances and surface detail. From the daguerreotype to contemporary portraits, viewers search for something more than the surface manifestation. Susan Sontag, in her seminal book, *On Photography*, writes about the essential aspects of the medium as 'a trace, something directly stencilled off the real, like a footprint or a death mask'.¹⁵ She likens it to an imprint that has made physical contact with its subject. It is this inscription and the fact that real people are depicted in it that forms part

Figure 5.3. Page from the police 'terrorist album'. Ronnie Kasrils has kindly permitted his image to be shown here. National Archives, Pretoria. Digital copy from Historical Papers Research Archive, University of the Witwatersrand

of the power of the photograph. It asks viewers to consider who the person photographed was, and the circumstances of their life. It is unlike a painting which is, in a sense, a fiction. Reinforcing the point, Walter Benjamin argues that photographs

> fill you with an unruly desire to know what her name was, the woman who was alive there, who even now is still real. No matter how artful the photographer, no matter how carefully posed his subject, the beholder feels such an irresistible urge to search the picture for a tiny spark of contingency, for the Here and Now, with which reality has so to speak, seared the subject, to find the inconspicuous spot where in the immediacy of that long-forgotten moment the future subsists so eloquently that we, looking back, may rediscover it. For it is another nature that speaks to the camera than to the eye: other in the sense that a space informed by human consciousness gives way to a space informed by the unconscious.[16]

Photographs are evidence of lived reality, depicting actual people. Yet their fragmentariness and the ways in which photographs are severed from the continuum of time makes them difficult to read and decipher. Moreover, there is no before or after represented in a photograph. The meanings of direct instantaneous views that are precisely recorded by the camera in perfect detail are neither obvious nor neutral. Their great detail is a paradox. Everything is there to see: every car on the street, every brick on the façade, every window and every passer-by, but regrettably not the interior lives of people and buildings. The vagaries of time and experience take their toll on us, and on buildings. The marks of age, weather, use and neglect inevitably mar façades as they do faces. Although an ID photograph is used as an accurate representation of a person, it remains an unreliable witness.

By slowly piecing the information in the photograph together, like a detective gathering evidence, meanings within an image gradually emerge. Like the detective, the photographer is trained to notice details within the whole picture. Since photographs are often cryptic and ambiguous, and require interpretation to be understood, their metaphorical meanings and traces need close examination. They demand a slow viewing for the spectator to uncover their secrets. They might be read for their broad detail, marks of wear and tear on the surfaces of things, stains, neglect, footprints, the transfer of substances and, on occasion, omissions. All may yield significances in our understanding of the scene. What the meticulous and all-embracing attention to detail reveals, however, is how little the minutiae show of reality. The photograph's evidential force may give way to metaphor. We might see the scars and wounds on the surface as analogies for other wounds, other experiences.

Like the mug shot, forensic photographs seem like straightforward documents, but their meaning is rarely self-evident, as Larry Sultan and Mike Mandel's *Evidence* demonstrates.[17] The images in this collection, sourced from the photographic archives of the Beverly Hills Police Department, government agencies, as well as educational, medical and technical institutions, are technically perfect and intriguing, but ultimately their evidentiary dimension is illusive and uncertain. In addition, no captions or text accompanies these images, reinforcing their mute conceptual form. Although we understand that the images were taken for a specific purpose, to convey evidence of some sort, it is unclear exactly where such evidence might lie. The images resist interpretation, and their ambiguous subject matter leaves the viewer unsure of what it is they are looking at. As South African forensic art practitioner Kathryn Smith points out, 'forensic photographs embody a beguiling paradox: they perform as evidence yet they are not self-evident. We demand that they act as arbiters of empirical data, while knowing that they require expert interlocution to reveal their truths.'[18]

PUNISHMENT

Prior to the eighteenth century, the penal system in Europe had been openly violent, cruel and punitive, using torture practices and exposing the body to public view. It was intended to inflict unbearable pain combined with ruthless public humiliation. But from the beginning of the nineteenth century, a number of changes in the treatment of criminals occurred, the most significant of which was the disappearance of torture as a public spectacle. Consequently, physical retribution became a less visible part of punishment. As Foucault maintains, punishment became 'the most hidden part of the penal process', the consequence of which was that 'its effectiveness was seen to be the result of its inevitability rather than its visible intensity'.[19] This also implied a move away from the body of the convict and the process of inflicting pain to an economy of 'suspended rights'.[20]

By the end of the nineteenth century, this shift from the excesses of vindictive and punitive treatment of criminals coincided with a more tempered approach to judging and punishing crimes. Motives and intentions for crimes were assessed and evaluated, which led the way to the appraisal of criminal acts by another group of individuals, namely warders, doctors, psychologists and educationalists, who attempted to ascertain the extent to which the offender's own will was involved. Circumstantial evidence was also introduced as part of the equation, serving to gauge the extent of the individual's culpability. This in turn introduced intangible and ambiguous components of crime that related to knowledge of the offender and came to fall beyond the scope of visibility, which focused on judging the 'soul' of the accused person.[21]

In South Africa from the 1950s, a regulated legal process was central to the rule of law, and was the primary apparatus through which apartheid laws were administered and maintained. Nevertheless, as the sociologist Deborah Posel puts it in *The Apartheid Project*, 'the simultaneity of law and violence is crucial to understanding how apartheid worked', and, while elaborate laws formed the basis of apartheid, it was the police who controlled the boundaries of racial segregation.[22] Thus, the police were authorised to exact the rule of law as part of the authority of government, which gave them unwarranted powers to impose punishment as they saw fit. Over time, this elided into unchecked gratuitous violence towards the populace which progressively increased in intensity, and was facilitated, especially, by the sustained secrecy of police practices.[23]

Indeed, we know in hindsight that many of the actual crimes in South Africa during the apartheid years occurred within the confines of John Vorster Square. The successful reopening of the inquests into the deaths of Ahmed Timol and Neil Aggett are mute testimony to the secrecy and callousness that lay behind the practices of the security police. Regarding this paradox in the power of the police, John Tagg writes: 'Here in the everyday scuffle, as criminality is brought to boot by the police, the separation of law-making and law-preserving violence is suspended and surpassed. The police force does not just administer the requirements of the law. The police force embodies the force of law, the violence whose legitimacy institutes the legitimising violence of law enforcement.'[24] What Tagg points to is the illegitimate exercise of power wielded by the police prevalent in totalitarian states.

FRAMES OF PERCEPTION AND DECEPTION

The rectangular viewfinder frames the scene, while the photographer selects the view according to the dictates of composition and the inclusion of that which forms their statement, be it a section of the building or the whole façade, or attempts to omit these. The scene might be framed perpendicular to the building or tilted to produce an unstable ground plane. All these decisions of framing have bearing on the image. What is outside the frame and what is excluded from view might also have been worthy of note. Moreover, omissions may be made subconsciously by the photographer, pointing to occlusions in their awareness or perception. But framing in photography refers to more than just compositional principles that define the physical limits of the image.

As photographer and writer Allan Sekula points out, photographic meaning itself is largely dependent on context.[25] Hence, the systematic organisation of photographs catalogued according to certain models such as family albums, police documents, or heritage and archives, form the basis for collections, tempering and shaping our reception of the photographs themselves. Related to this, Tagg links the frame to a form of power, 'a machinery of capture and expulsion', conjoining 'the image and the economy of power in which it comes to resonate and in which interpretation takes place'.[26] Moreover, laws themselves might be seen as frames that control or regulate behaviour – or even decree punishment, as suggested by the power assumed by the South African Police Force. In a strange twist to the frame metaphor, I was told in an email message by Marc Latilla on 13 May 2020 that, prior to the erection of John Vorster Square, a framing company had its premises on the site.

Relatedly, the philosopher Judith Butler asserts that '"to be framed" can also mean to be subject to a con, to be set up, or have evidence planted against one that would ultimately prove one's guilt'.[27] This 'framing' was one of the organising principles of apartheid itself. Writing during the 1950s, Lewis Nkosi notes that 'Africans have accepted the status of being outlaws from society and have evolved an elaborate system of escaping, hoodwinking and baffling the law'.[28] He thus highlights the impossibility of living as a law-abiding citizen under apartheid, suggesting that ways to subvert the rule of law or fall through the cracks was a strategic means of survival.

Figure 5.4. Former 'non-white' entrance of Johannesburg Central Police Station, 2019. Photograph by Sally Gaule

After 1948, the National Party government of South Africa enacted a raft of laws, which included the Reservation of Separate Amenities Act (1953). This law forced segregation in all public amenities with the aim of eliminating contact between designated races. It was part of the system of 'petty apartheid', concerned with the regulation of day-to-day life. Many liberation struggle photographers sought to document signs proclaiming the separation of races, whether on beaches or railway stations and bus stops, entrances to public buildings, and even park benches. In the photograph above (figure 5.4), the former non-European entrance to John Vorster Square was fenced off from public access, with the public prohibited from using it as an entrance after the end of apartheid.[29] Yet, this prevention of access – presumably a pragmatic rather than symbolic decision – remains a poignant reminder of the building's history.

The laws that governed separation pervaded all aspects of life. So ubiquitous were they, that the meanings of those signs passed as normative too. As artist Colin Richards points out, 'apartheid's supreme visibility worked to create its own normalisation. Part of the mystery of apartheid is the hold it had in normalising the starkest and most obstinate cruelties and contradictions.'[30] Perhaps it is only in revisiting the building, in recording prosaic features in a perfunctory manner, that we are able to fathom some of the effects of apartheid on everyday life. Indeed, many of the daily indignities, humiliations, invisibility and second-class citizenship experienced by black South Africans during apartheid simply went unnoticed and unacknowledged by whites. In photographs such as the ones in this chapter, no obvious spectacle is made manifest. Instead, by depicting palisades, balustrades and security bars – elements associated with physical restraint – the materiality of the architecture of prison life is evoked.

The building's proximity to the elevated M1 highway proved problematic to the authorities and in 1982 a louvred aluminium screen was attached to the open facades to facilitate secrecy. Over time, parts of these screened structures were damaged or cut away to reveal the windows they covered. On the north façade, the leaves of the blinds are still visible from the highway. Whether broken or bent, they give an impression of those inside looking out. But this is a paradox of the building: while it was

Figure 5.5. Johannesburg Central Police Station from M1 highway, 2017. Photograph by Sally Gaule

impossible to see what was going on behind these louvres, it also prevented those inside from seeing out, occluding their view and promoting an inward-looking gaze. The broken blinds convey a dimension of the violence to the building itself and stand as a synecdoche for all that the period continues to summon up.

PANOPTICISM

Jeremy Bentham's panopticon was designed as a structure for surveillance with the aim of controlling subjects who were the object of its containment. It was composed of a tower at the centre with cells radiating around, separated by walls that prevented any contact between inmates. Indeed, Bentham's intentions for the structure were far-reaching and were intended to include more than criminals. He believed that this structure of separation and control could be applied to hospitals, schools, sanatoriums, asylums and workplaces. As Foucault affirms in *Discipline and Punish*:

> If the inmates are convicts, there is no danger of a plot, an attempt at collective escape, the planning of new crimes for the future, bad reciprocal influences; if they are patients, there is no danger of contagion; if they are madmen, there is no risk of their committing violence upon one another; if they are school children, there is no copying, no noise, no chatter, no waste of time; if they are workers, there are no disorders, no theft, no coalitions, none of those distractions that slow down the rate of work, make it less perfect or cause accidents.[31]

Thus, one of the principle features of the panopticon was separation and exclusion – keeping people apart – which is in keeping with the racial mixing the apartheid government sought to prohibit and regulate. The thinking behind the panopticon itself arose out of measures taken to control the plague, to prevent contagion, and, like apartheid legislation, it sought to ensure physical separation and distance, penetrating the smallest details of everyday life. Following Foucault, Deborah Posel writes: '[T]his was apartheid's central and defining biopolitics: focusing the exercise of power on the regulation of large units of population, designating spaces for authorised residence, pathways of authorised migration, channels of authorised employment and the terms of political and communal organisation.'[32] In this way, the self-regulation and discipline fostered by the panopticon could be likened to the template of power and control that the apartheid state sought to impose.

One major effect of the panopticon was for the inmate to be consciously and permanently aware of being observed. That would in turn promote their own self-regulation. They would never know for sure whether they were being watched or not. Windows faced the inside of the tower for purposes of surveillance by the guard. Bentham envisaged Venetian blinds on the windows of the central observation hall and on the inside partitions to ensure that the presence of the guard would be undetectable by the inmate. The materiality of its construction and the organisation of its structure, with the guard at its centre, held absolute authority over those within: 'Visibility', Foucault asserts, 'is a trap.'[33]

It is well known that prisoners in John Vorster Square were brutally and viciously treated. Torture, solitary confinement, interrogations and 'accidental' deaths occurred within its walls. We are still learning about harrowing deaths in detention that were described as 'accidents' during apartheid.[34] The effect of being under constant surveillance is allied strongly with apartheid's omnipresent gaze. As the historian Philip Bonner put it, 'the sense of Apartheid's suffocating embrace, of its unceasing surveillance and pervasive control virtually paralysed urban blacks into submission and observance of every petty apartheid regulation.'[35] Within John Vorster Square, as former political prisoner and academic Raymond Suttner has written, 'all cells were openly monitored through video and audio systems … One could do nothing in private.'[36]

OPACITY AND TRANSPARENCY

From the east, Johannesburg Central Police Station appears as two buildings linked by a corridor. We can see figures passing along this corridor from the street below, with cars passing by on the M1 highway on the western side of the building.

Figure 5.6. Corridor of Johannesburg Central Police Station, 2018. Photograph by Sally Gaule

I am reminded of the anti-apartheid activist and writer Hugh Lewin's words in his memoir *Bandiet: Seven Years in a South African Prison*:

> Essentials only. You are stripped of everything inessential. You are stripped bare and given back only what they think is necessary. They strip you at the beginning and they go on stripping you, endlessly to ensure that you have only what is necessary. You are stripped bare of anything that you make your own; you are stripped bare in an endless process of peeling off your protective covering and leaving you naked. So they can watch you. So that you, like the corridor, are without decoration, without covering, with nothing behind which to hide, nothing they can't see into and watch.[37]

Here, paradoxically, is a building we can see through from one point of view, with, on the other side, a metal carapace of blinds covering its façades. Yet, the condition of the blinds on the west façade were never robust, ironically following Bentham's notion that the simple economic geometry of panoptic institutions could 'be so light'.[38] The very transparency of the building from one point of view, and the blinds required for secrecy, were flimsy.

EMPTINESS AND THE SCENE OF THE CRIME

Emptiness in early photographs of architecture arose from limitations of technique and the need for long exposures. But this aesthetic endured long after faster film and cameras permitted figures to be included without blurring. The reasons for this are twofold: firstly, architects preferred images uncluttered by people, and secondly, empty spaces and buildings convey a feeling of isolation and loneliness, reflecting a well-known psychological dimension emphasised by modernity in the early twentieth century. However, images of the empty city also have a dual purpose, as art historian Steven Jacobs points out:

> While some artists and photographers associated the motif of the empty city with a mysterious and threatening obscurity, others exploited this same motif for its qualities of clarity and transparency. For these artists the portrayal of the city as unpopulated and vacant was a way to suggest utopian urban spaces. The goal being to document the architecture as precisely and in as great detail as possible.[39]

In the city of Johannesburg, emptiness is a liability. Vacant buildings are mothballed to prevent invasion by the homeless. Empty streets are threatening as places where crimes are committed unwitnessed, and the presence of people might denote safety. Although early architectural photographers would strive for clarity and order, exploiting emptiness to highlight the form and structure of buildings and streets, the inevitable chaos and unpredictability inherent in the city was largely absent. For Jacobs, 'the emptiness of the city coincides with the harmonic fullness of the photographic composition'.[40] Here, the paradox of street photography is made manifest. Where there is pandemonium, the photographer strives for coherence. Where there is noise, the photograph offers silence.

Our view and experience of the city is thus a sanitised one, erased of all traces of human life: sounds and odours, violent confrontations, the roar of traffic, the capriciousness of the street. Yet, in the silence and emptiness of photographs of the city, signs of human presence are eerily felt and implied. Crime photographs are nearly always empty of people so as to preserve evidence, and such images are bound by silence and emptiness. The philosopher Walter Benjamin, observing that Parisian photographer Eugene Atget photographed the city like the scene of a crime, pertinently asked: 'But is not every square inch of our cities the scene of a crime? Every passer-by a culprit?'[41] This raises the question whether, at the intersection of building and highway, as in the photographs above, we come close to witnessing the crime of apartheid.

The bust of B. J. Vorster, former Minister of Justice and Prime Minister of South Africa, was removed in 1997 when the building was renamed. Vorster's set expression and heavy brow echo the physical heft of the bust, and the straps tethered to a small crane are like a noose from which he is suspended. Behind the bust, peeling paint and damaged plaster convey the state of disrepair of the building, betokening his unceremonious end. The practicalities of removing the bust appear perfunctory and efficient. The ostensible ease with which the bust was lifted off its plinth deceptively undercuts the decades of struggle that it took to dismantle apartheid.

Figure 5.7. Removal of the bust of B. J. Vorster, September 1997. Trevor Samson, © *Business Day*

OUTSIDE THE LIMITS OF SURVEILLANCE

During apartheid, it was forbidden to photograph restricted public buildings without permission, and today it is still illegal to photograph police stations, airports and bridges. Such images are regarded as stolen photographs, seized without permission. Surveillance has come to form much of the modern condition, which speaks in a way to the photograph of an empty chair on a rooftop with a view of the street below.

The top floor of John Vorster Square was where detainees were held.[42] Yet, in this photograph, the view of the chair on the rooftop might also be read in another way: instead of surveillance, a quiet place away from observing or being observed, a break from an oppressive daily grind, or a place to gaze at everyday life. It might offer a space outside the confines of the building and the apartheid / post-apartheid system. It has a parallel in Suttner's recollection of washing his clothes on the roof of the building when he was detained there: 'I could walk around the yard and look out onto the highway while my clothes were soaking. I tried to imagine it was not the road to Braamfontein but really a Seapoint beachfront.'[43]

Figure 5.8. Surveyor's chair, roof of Johannesburg Central Police Station, 2008. Photograph by Guy Trangoš

In the contemporary city, the presence of surveillance cameras is by now commonplace. Those behind the cameras observe the behaviour of citizens from an undisclosed control room. Cameras have become a form of security, assumed to curtail criminal activity because it is never certain if one is being observed or not; this is a grim parody of the panopticon, making us all 'criminals' in our own city. The architecture of Johannesburg Central Police Station has enabled the analysis of photographs for their metaphorical import. But what these photographs cannot depict is the prison of the mind: invisible mindsets, bigotry, racism, intolerance, xenophobia, the beliefs and prejudices that shape much of our behaviour and determine how we go forward. It is more than five decades since the Johannesburg Central Police Station was built, but it has not endured. While it has neither been abandoned nor burnt down, unlike many other government buildings that were targets during apartheid[44] – security police themselves bombed and destroyed buildings associated with resistance to apartheid, including Cosatu House in 1987 and Khotso House in 1988 – what it stood for has slowly been erased from public memory. Unlike the Constitutional Court,[45] which was imaginatively adapted and repurposed from a prison into a symbol of hope and justice, the Johannesburg Central Police Station building has remained unchanged, and in its fixed state the past continues to haunt us.

POSTSCRIPT

This chapter is dedicated to the memory of Philip Bonner (1945–2017), founding member and former head of the History Workshop, who spent a week in detention at John Vorster Square in 1986 during the second state of emergency. He rarely spoke to me about this experience, saying that it was not as extraordinary for him as it was for a lot of other people. The cells held people charged with a range of offences, and he was able to take on the task of helping them write statements for their defence.

NOTES

1   John Vorster Square was named after B. J. Vorster, Prime Minister of South Africa from 1966-1978.
2   Achille Mbembe and Sarah Nuttall, eds, 'Writing the World from an African Metropolis', *Public Culture* 16.3 (2004): 363-64.

3   Michel Foucault, *Discipline and Punish: The Birth of the Prison* (Harmondsworth: Penguin, 1977), 30.
4   Clive Chipkin, *Johannesburg Transition: Architecture & Society from 1950* (Johannesburg: STE Publishers, 2008), 180.
5   Barbara Hogan, 'Detention Without Trial in John Vorster Square', South African History Archive (SAHA), accessed 26 May 2020, https://artsandculture.google.com/exhibit/detention-without-trial-in-john-vorster-square-south-african-history-archive/gQ-1o9MM?hl=en.
6   Teju Cole, *Known and Strange Things* (New York: Random House, 2016), 334.
7   Hogan, 'Detention Without Trial'.
8   Sandra S. Phillips, 'Identifying the Criminal', in *Police Pictures, The Photograph as Evidence*, eds Sandra Phillips, Mark Haworth-Booth and Carol Squiers (San Francisco: San Francisco Museum of Modern Art, 1997), 11.
9   Eric Lee et al., 'Suspect Identification by Facial Features', *Ergonomics* 47.7 (2004): 720.
10 Allan Trachtenberg, *Reading American Photographs* (New York: Hill and Wang, 1989), 29.
11 I am grateful to Gabriele Mohale at Historical Papers, University of the Witwatersrand, for alerting me to the existence of this document; it forms the focus of Jacob Dlamini's book, *The Terrorist Album: Apartheid's Insurgents, Collaborators, and the Security Police* (Harvard: Harvard University Press, 2020).
12 Lee et al., 'Suspect Identification', 720.
13 Ronnie Kasrils, pictured on this album page, related in an email to me on 26 May 2020 that the photograph was taken by the Bureau of State Security (BOSS) agent Gordon Winter in London during a solidarity event of France's student uprising.
14 One such victim was trade unionist and medical doctor Neil Aggett, who rejected a lucrative career in private practice, choosing instead to work in public hospitals in Tembisa and Soweto, and to live in a worker's cottage that had neither electricity nor hot water. He died in detention in John Vorster Square in 1982 at the age of 28. See Steven Friedman, *Building Tomorrow Today. African Workers in Trade Unions 1970-1984* (Johannesburg: Ravan, 1987), 279.
15 Susan Sontag, *On Photography* (Harmondsworth: Penguin, 1977), 154.
16 Walter Benjamin, 'A Small History of Photography', in *One-Way Street and Other Writings*, trans. Edmund Jephcott and Kingsley Shorter (London: Harcourt Brace, 1970), 243.
17 Larry Sultan and Mike Mandel, *Evidence* (New York: Distributed Art Publishers, 2004).

18 Kathryn Smith, 'Under the Influence of Paul Stopforth's Biko Painting Called "Elegy"', accessed 30 September 2019, https://www.theconversation.com/under-the-influence-of-paul-stopforth's-biko-painting-called-elegy-64031.
19 Foucault, *Discipline and Punish*, 7.
20 Foucault, *Discipline and Punish*, 11.
21 Foucault, *Discipline and Punish*, 19.
22 Deborah Posel, 'The Apartheid Project, 1948–1970', in *The Cambridge History of South Africa, Vol II,* eds Ross Robert et al. (Cambridge: Cambridge University Press, 2011), 346.
23 Posel, 'The Apartheid Project', 347.
24 John Tagg, *The Disciplinary Frame: Photographic Truths and the Capture of Meaning* (Minneapolis: University of Minnesota Press, 2009), xxv–vi.
25 Allan Sekula, *Mining Photographs and Other Pictures* (Nova Scotia: The Press of the Nova Scotia College of Art and Design, 1983), 195.
26 Tagg, *The Disciplinary Frame,* 5.
27 Judith Butler, *Frames of War: When is Life Grievable?* (London: Verso, 2010), 8.
28 Lewis Nkosi, *Home and Exile* (London: Longmans, 1965), 40.
29 Guy Trangŏs, 'In the Shadow of Authority' (Master's thesis, University of the Witwatersrand, Johannesburg, 2008), 31.
30 Colin Richards, 'Retouching Apartheid, Intimacy, Interiority, and Photography', in *Rise and Fall of Apartheid: Photography and the Bureaucracy of Everyday Life*, eds Okwui Enwezor and Rory Bester (New York: International Centre of Photography, 2013), 234.
31 Foucault, *Discipline and Punish,* 201.
32 Posel, 'The Apartheid Project', 323.
33 Foucault, *Discipline and Punish,* 200.
34 Lauren Segal and Paul Holden, *Great Lives: Pivotal Moments* (Auckland Park: Jacana, 2008), 141–45. Among those who died in detention at John Vorster Square were Ahmed Timol (27 October 1971), Wellington Tshazibane (December 1976), Elmon Malele (20 January 1977), Mathews Mabelane (15 February 1977), Neil Aggett (5 February 1982), Ernest Dipale (8 July 1982), Stanza Bopape (5 June 1988) and Clayton Sithole (30 January 1990).
35 Philip Bonner, 'Race, Politics and the Quotidian in South African Photojournalism in the Era of High Apartheid', paper presented together with Sally Gaule and Katie Mooney at the Burden of Race Conference, Wits Institute of Social and Economic Research, and History Workshop, University of the Witwatersrand, Johannesburg, 8 July 2001.
36 Raymond Suttner, *Inside Apartheid's Prison* (Pietermaritzburg: University of Natal Press, 2001), 125.

37 Hugh Lewin, *Bandiet: Seven Years in a South African Prison* (Harmondsworth: Penguin, 1976), 29. In 1964, Hugh Lewin was sentenced, together with other members of the African Resistance Movement (ARM), to seven years imprisonment for sabotage activities in protest against apartheid.
38 Foucault, *Discipline and Punish*, 202.
39 Steven Jacobs, 'Amor Vacui: Photography and the Image of the Empty City', in *History of Photography* 30.2 (2006): 111–12.
40 Jacobs, 'Amor Vacui', 112.
41 Benjamin, 'A Small History of Photography', 256.
42 Chipkin, *Johannesburg Transition*, 180.
43 Suttner, *Inside Apartheid's Prison*, 127.
44 See Philip Bonner and Lauren Segal, *Soweto: A History* (Cape Town: Maskew Miller Longman, 1998), 86.
45 The Constitutional Court is located at the site of a former high security prison which was imaginatively transformed into a fragmented rather than monolithic manifestation of justice, already enshrined in the new constitution adopted in 1994. See Temba Middelmann's discussion in chapter 3.

REFERENCES

Barthes, Roland. *Camera Lucida: Reflections on Photography.* New York: Hill and Wang, 1981.

Benjamin, Walter. 'A Small History of Photography'. In *One-Way Street and Other Writings*, translated by Edmund Jephcott and Kingsley Shorter, 240–57. London: Harcourt Brace, 1970.

Bonner, Philip, and Lauren Segal. *Soweto: A History*. Cape Town: Maskew Miller Longman, 1998.

Bonner, Philip, Sally Gaule, and Katie Mooney. 'Race, Politics and the Quotidian in South African Photojournalism in the Era of High Apartheid'. Paper presented at the Burden of Race Conference, Wits Institute of Social and Economic Research and History Workshop, University of the Witwatersrand, Johannesburg, 8 July 2001.

Butler, Judith. *Frames of War: When is Life Grievable?* London: Verso, 2010.

Chipkin, Clive. *Johannesburg Transition, Architecture and Society from 1950.* Johannesburg: STE Publishers, 2008.

Cole, Teju. *Known and Strange Things.* New York: Random House, 2016.

Foucault, Michel. *Discipline and Punish: The Birth of the Prison.* Harmondsworth: Penguin Books, 1977.

Friedman, Steven. *Building Tomorrow Today: African Workers in Trade Unions, 1970–84*. Johannesburg: Ravan, 1987.

Hogan, Barbara. 'Detention Without Trial in John Vorster Square'. South African History Archive (SAHA). Accessed 26 May 2020, https://artsandculture.google.com/exhibit/detention-without-trial-in-john-vorster-square-south-african-history-archive/gQ-1o9MM?hl=en.

Jacobs, Steven. 'Amor Vacui: Photography and the Image of the Empty City'. *History of Photography* 30.2 (2006).

Lee, Eric, Thomas Whalen, John Sakalauskas, Glen Baigent, Chandra Bisesar, Andrew McCarthy, Glenda Reid, and Cynthia Wotton. 'Suspect Identification by Facial Features'. *Ergonomics* 47.7 (2004): 719–47.

Lewin, Hugh. *Bandiet: Seven Years in a South African Prison*. Harmondsworth: Penguin, 1976.

Mason, Judith, Anne Sassoon, Leora Maltz-Leca, and Kate McCrickard. *Paul Stopforth*. Parkwood: David Krut Publishers, 2010.

Mbembe, Achille, and Sarah Nuttall, eds. 'Writing the World from an African Metropolis'. *Public Culture* 16.3 (2004): 363–64.

Nkosi, Lewis. *Home and Exile*. London: Longman, 1965.

Phillips, Sandra S. 'Identifying the Criminal'. In *Police Pictures, The Photograph as Evidence*, edited by Sandra S. Phillips, Mark Haworth-Booth and Carol Squiers, 11–31. San Francisco: San Francisco Museum of Modern Art, 1997.

Posel, Deborah. 'The Apartheid Project, 1948–1970'. In *The Cambridge History of South Africa, Volume 2, 1885–1994*, edited by Robert Ross, Anne Kelk Mager and Bill Nasson, 319–69. Cambridge: Cambridge University Press, 2011.

Richards, Colin. 'Retouching Apartheid, Intimacy, Interiority, and Photography'. In *The Rise and Fall of Apartheid, Photography and the Bureaucracy of Everyday Life,* edited by Okwui Enwezor and Rory Bester, 234–47. New York: International Centre of Photography, 2013.

Segal, Lauren, and Paul Holden. *Great Lives: Pivotal Moments*. Auckland Park: Jacana, 2008.

Sekula, Allan. *Mining Photographs and Other Pictures*. Nova Scotia: Press of the Nova Scotia College of Art and Design, 1983.

Sontag, Susan. *On Photography*. Harmondsworth: Penguin, 1977.

Sultan, Larry, and Mike Mandel. *Evidence*. New York: Distributed Art Publishers, 2017.

Suttner, Raymond. *Inside Apartheid's Prison*. Pietermaritzburg: University of Natal Press, 2001.

Tagg, John. *The Disciplinary Frame, Photographic Truths and the Capture of Meaning.* Minneapolis: University of Minnesota Press, 2009.

Trachtenberg, Allan. *Reading American Photographs.* New York: Hill and Wang, 1989.

Trangoš, Guy. 'In the Shadow of Authority'. Master's thesis, University of the Witwatersrand, Johannesburg, 2008.

6 THE PERSISTENCE OF ROBBEN ISLAND: ABOLITION AND THE PRISON MUSEUM

KELLY GILLESPIE

On 27 March 2004, in commemoration of ten years of democracy in South Africa, Cape Town Opera, in conjunction with the Norwegian National Opera, staged a performance of Beethoven's *Fidelio* in the main courtyard of the Robben Island prison museum. This was the first time a large theatrical production had been mounted on Robben Island, the prison island where apartheid South Africa's high-ranking black political prisoners were incarcerated from the 1960s to the 1990s. The prison had been decommissioned after the last apartheid-era political prisoners were released, and in 1997, three years after the first democratic elections which officially ended formal apartheid, Robben Island prisons and other infrastructure from the island's long colonial history as a place of banishment were transformed into a museum.

I begin with the staging of Beethoven's 'liberation opera' as a means of addressing the prison museum as a problem both of and for history. At the heart of the problem is the use of the prison as a scene of liberation and as a monument to apartheid, when the end of formal apartheid presaged an escalation in incarceration and an ongoing operation of criminalisation and racialised violence. The conversion of the famous prison into a museum, simultaneous with the ongoing-ness, the prolonging, of the prison as a mechanism of continued apartheid relations into the post-apartheid period, converge as anachronism, a contradiction in time and in politics. Leaning into a global politics of prison abolition, I seek to treat the prison museum as an open question about the decommissioning not of one particular infamous prison, but of prisons in general as institutions of the extended and ongoing history of racial capitalism.

The production of *Fidelio* was staged on one night only. Audience members included high-ranking government officials, glitterati of the Cape Town social circuit and opera lovers from South Africa and elsewhere, who were taken across the water in boats departing from Cape Town's Victoria and Albert Waterfront. After disembarking, the guests were taken by bus to the prison, through which they were led to the auditorium set up in one of the large maximum-security courtyards. Adjacent to the prison, a massive marquee had been erected, in which a buffet dinner was served to guests before the show. High heels, elegant suits and wine were at odds with the histories of the island emerging in autobiographies and circulating in political discourse. These were stories of Nelson Mandela's eyesight ruined from futile labour in the island quarry, stories of prisoners on hunger strikes against chronic ill-treatment, of common-law prisoners being used by warders to humiliate political prisoners.[1] The juxtaposition of this vicious recent history of racial subjugation with the elegant night out at the opera was striking. A series of angled walkways comprising the stage were built around one of the high guard towers of the prison. In the distance, the other stone towers of the prison were lit up to enhance the spectacle of the prison as mise en scène.

Fidelio is known as Beethoven's 'freedom opera' and tells the story of a political prisoner, Florestan, the victim of a corrupt regime, imprisoned in a dungeon and presumed dead. The programme notes go on to describe his wife, Leonora, disguising herself as the prison worker Fidelio before she searches for her captive husband in the hope of freeing him. As the evil governor of the prison plans to bury his prisoner in a dungeon grave, Florestan, 'chained in his gloomy cell … turns to despair and he sinks exhausted to the floor'. Just as the governor begins making his murderous advances on the abject Florestan, Leonore casts off her disguise and leaps at the tyrant with a pistol, creating a spectacular ending where husband and wife escape the dungeon, the dark, the disguise, and emerge into freedom. Then, into the cold night air over Robben Island floats Florestan's aria (quoted in the programme notes):

> But do I not feel a balmy // softly stirring breeze? // And is not my tomb filled with light? // I see an angel, rosy-hued // standing by my side in comfort // An angel like Leonore // just like Leonore, my wife // who leads me to freedom // in the Heavenly Realm!

At that moment in the opera, a trumpet sounds, and a new minister of state arrives to free not only Florestan, but all the prisoners, from the dungeon. Angelo Gobbato, who was at the time Chief Executive Officer (CEO) of Cape Town Opera and artistic director of the *Fidelio* production, choreographed the chorus to emerge from the dungeon at the sound of the trumpet, singing jubilantly, toyi-toying, as each waved the newly designed South African national flag. Gobbato, an Italian immigrant to South Africa during the apartheid period, had been working for years towards producing *Fidelio* on Robben Island. For him, *Fidelio*'s reputation as an opera of liberation, thought to have been inspired by Beethoven's reading of the French Revolution, seemed a perfect way to commemorate the end of apartheid. As one critic of the opera explains: '[*Fidelio* reveals an] obsessive concern with before and after, the beginning and the end, the old order and the new. Indeed, more emphatically than any other opera I can think of, *Fidelio* conveys a sense of historical transformation, of movement from one realm of existance to another, from a defective to a pacified world.'[2]

Even by the standards of the camp and truncated world of opera narrative, Gobbato's flag-waving ending was absurd, drawing on the most banal images of freedom to represent the end of apartheid. And yet, something about the banality of the image worked to express, unwittingly to be sure, an increasingly withered politics of freedom that had taken shape in South African society, demobilised and fed into a liberal capitalist consensus. The final scene of canned happiness in fact worked perfectly to represent and consolidate the kitsch and unrealistic politics of rainbowism, reconciliation and patriotic history at play in the prison museum and in national politics at large.[3]

In *Fidelio*, it is the prison, as mise en scène as well as within the internal narrative of the opera, that is utilised as the prelude and precondition to freedom, as the space of past oppression. The performance of the opera in the prison, as indeed the very project of making museums out of prisons, positions the past as a space of incarceration, and the relations of warder to prisoner as the relations of a former era. The prison becomes a powerful metaphor in the establishment of historiography, a chronotopic scene in which the prison congeals as a time of past suffering and cruelty, a time from which we have been liberated: 'Time, as it were, thickens, takes on flesh, becomes artistically visible',[4] in the words of literary critic Mikhail Bakhtin, as the prison is made to play the part of history, marked as the past. Floating in Table Bay, Robben Island prison becomes a place to memorialise the atrocities of apartheid, requiring the maintenance of apartheid *as history* for purposes of post-apartheid national pedagogy. As Ahmed Kathrada, ex-prisoner on the island and former chairperson of the Robben Island Museum Council insists, the island should be 'a monument reflecting the triumph of the human spirit against the forces of evil, a triumph of freedom and human dignity over repression and humiliation'.[5] Circumscribed, touristed, opera'd, universalised, its political energies have been arranged into a diorama of nationalist liberation history.

DECOMMISSIONING AS RELOCATION

The release of political prisoners from Robben Island and other South African prisons after the unbanning of political parties in 1990 created the conditions for the Robben Island prison to be decommissioned as a functioning prison. The process of turning the prison into a museum involved working with ex-political prisoners to develop an archive of narratives on the history of that particular prison, exceptionalising it as a place of racial violence, broadly symbolic of apartheid. Robben Island becomes a singular infamy, the place that must, to use Nelson Mandela's phrase, 'never again' happen, a place of repugnant history. But the decommissioning of one infamous prison takes shape against the continuation of all the other prisons across the country, with all 240 being a product of colonial and apartheid histories in southern Africa. To singularise one prison while allowing the mass of others to go unremarked, unfamous, is an ideological event with serious materialist and historical implications. In particular, this use of the singular prison as a way to metaphorise the past brutality of the apartheid regime, while prisons in general continue to operate in real time with almost no interruption to their historical mandate, is a historic sleight of hand – an ideological trick that allows for the persistence of prisons into the democratic era even as they are recognised as institutions crucial to the creation and maintenance of colonial and capitalist hierarchies.

When Robben Island was decommissioned, most of the warders – all white and trained in the belly of the apartheid security state – were redeployed to a newly built medium-security prison some 150 kilometres away on the mainland. Voorberg Correctional Service Medium B, near the small farming town of Porterville in the Boland region north of Cape Town, was the last prison to have been planned by the apartheid administration. It was completed in 1996, a large single-story prison built to house 1 000 prisoners, with serialised cell wings containing some single occupancy but mostly large communal cells. It is a classic warehousing-style medium security prison built in the rural farmlands to service the towns established over the past 300 years by white settler communities, and to accommodate the overflow from older overcrowded rural prisons. Voorberg Medium B was built on an existing prison farm to augment the capacity of Voorberg Medium A prison, a corrugated-iron structure built in the 1970s that the state has planned to decommission for at least 20 years but which still stands, housing approximately 500 prisoners.

From when it was first established in 1976, Voorberg was, like all apartheid prisons, managed according to principles of racial difference and hierarchy. This ordering was of course not unique to the former Prison Service, but the product of an explicitly racialised ideological project that pervaded all aspects of South African life. Thus, the relations between white and black warders at Voorberg were typical of social relationships in the prison's nearest town, Porterville, some seven kilometres away. The town of Porterville was established as a meeting place for settler farmers, descendents of the vryburgers who had left the Dutch East India Company in the late seventeenth century to settle permanently in southern Africa, and it still accommodates one of the oldest white agricultural co-operatives in the country. Settler agricultural colonialism required the creation of cheap farm labour, which was originally provided by the incorporation of imported slaves and indigenous inhabitants (all to be later classified under the category 'Coloured') into the labour force.[6] This arrangement was enabled by means of a pacifying cocktail of alcohol and Christianity.

All around Porterville, missionaries developed small 'Coloured' towns called *sendingsgemeenskappe* (mission communities) in which residents were also congregants of the churches around which the towns were founded. The infamous '*dop* system', the remuneration for farm labour in alcohol, has an insidious history in this area and is still, despite its post-apartheid illegality, widely used. As Porterville grew, and labour was required, a township was established on its outskirts, forming a typically South African racial geography between white town and black township; the circulation of farming and business capital benefited the lifestyles and resources of the white town, and barely sustained the lives of township residents.

The farm labour system was a cornerstone of the development of racial capitalism in South Africa.[7] It functioned alongside migrant labour for the urban mines and industries to massively swell the profits of white landowners. Farm labour, an often-hidden history of super-exploitation in South Africa, is frequently overlooked in favour of urban labour relations, which have accrued higher levels of unionisation and historiography.[8] At the beginning of the apartheid period, the Afrikaner state wanted to ensure that white farmers – who, unlike the English-speaking urban industrialists, were predominantly Afrikaans-speaking – were given greater access to capital. Thus, the state began to augment the existing farm labour system with prison labour, achieving this through the building of rural prisons across the country.[9] While there were a few brave journalistic exposés on the prison labour used on farms – notably Ruth First and Henry Nxumalo's *Drum* magazine coverage in 1959 – rural prison labour remained almost entirely hidden from public view, despite being crucial to the development of apartheid's racial capitalist project.

Continuing to exist in the shadows of the church spire and grain silos, Porterville has not been much touched by post-apartheid social change. Although there are a few black children who now attend the 'white school' (the term is still used by township residents), and despite local government posts being subject to affirmative action policy, the relationship between town and township persists. Indeed, the history of impoverishment and *dop*-labour can be read in the alcohol-ravaged faces of black workers and the unemployed who spend their days waiting outside the entrances to the four liquor stores on Porterville's short main street. Even the town's historiography is unreconstructed. Along one of the central tree-lined streets of the white town is the Porterville museum. Its rooms and walls carry carefully designed displays of the history of white women's fashion and handiwork; medical instruments used by generations of Porterville's white doctors; and scores of old photographs of the white founding fathers of the agricultural board, church committees and sports leagues. Right in the centre of the museum, hidden at the end of a dim little passage, so that one might visit the museum without knowing of its existence, is a diorama of a 'bushman', spotlit in a small, heavily darkened room, appearing to hover like a shrine in space and time. A fitting disclosure: in the centre of an unreconstructed museum in the centre of an unreconstructed town, stands a sacred, secret admission to a history of racism and violence.

Voorberg prison was, from its early beginnings in the mid-1970s, sustained by a division of labour and life along racial lines: fifteen newly trained 'Coloured' warders transported and oversaw prisoners from the nearby Tulbagh prison in the laying of water and sewage lines and the building of Voorberg's first corrugated-iron cells. The warders themselves were supervised by white prison administrators, whose office jobs precluded them from working directly with black prisoners. The hierarchy between white and black prison staff was so clear that those first 15 warders recall having better relationships with the prisoners under their watch than with their white colleagues: '[The white management] treated us like prisoners at that time … We felt closer to the prisoners than to the white officials, the members of the management, because the prisoners realised that we are also prisoners, and they treated us better than the management did.'[10]

In fact, as a warder recalled in an interview with me, a sense of solidarity between black warders and prisoners at Voorberg during the 1980s sometimes produced unsettling alliances:

> In the afternoons the prisoners came together after work, and they would *sabela* [a prison-gang language[11]] or make new Numbers. We were also interested and we would watch how they did things. We were curious – 'Oh, you do this' … 'Now this one is also a 28.' Later the warders also began being drawn in. And that is how they got Europa [the name of one of the 15 warders]. One afternoon, after lunch they made him a 28, with a 28 tattoo on his leg …. I said to Europa, 'And now, what are you going to do now?' He said his task is to shoot dead Captain Kirsten [the white head of Voorberg] tomorrow morning at six o' clock … At that time it was very hot, and we were all wearing short sleeves to work. But that next morning Europa had to put on his full uniform, as the prisoners said he must. He also had a gun. I said to him, 'Hey, man, you are a dog handler. Where is your dog?' That man's eyes stood deadstill. When the Captain was seated the man made for his gun. He was really going to shoot the Captain … Then we all fell onto Europa and took him away. And afterwards we decided that we weren't going to play gangster games any more. We played cards and we bought a hi-fi to listen to music. And Europa left the service.

Isolated high up on the prison farm, with little access to transport, the young black warders at Voorberg began to plan forays into the township of Porterville to seek out entertainment, firstly in the form of access to the local 'Coloured' rugby league, where they filled all the positions in Porterville township's top rugby team, and secondly in the form of disco parties involving local women. Later, when the construction of a small hall for the black warders was completed, the warders invited the township's young women to come and dance, with the hi-fi turned up to full volume. The hall formed part of a compound for black warders at Voorberg, and was surrounded by tiny accommodation units, built far above the prison, on the periphery of the white-controlled farm.

The warders called the place *Mossienes*, or Mossie Nest – a mossie being a small brown bird. High up on the farm, it was situated among trees, where the 'brown' inhabitants of Voorberg were forced to live. White prison staff had their own separate accommodation, hall and recreation area, including a bar, to which black warders were denied access. Barred from moving freely around the white part of the farm after work, black warders were allowed onto the premises only to buy drinks through a small sliding window in a sidewall of the bar, and only once the barman had finished attending to the white managers inside. Contiguity between black and white staff was such a taboo at Voorberg that when a white staff member discovered that a black warder had used a glass meant only for whites who frequented the bar, he smashed it against a wall, along with other glassware and crockery he thought might possibly have been 'contaminated'.

FROM ROBBEN ISLAND TO VOORBERG

Boetie du Toit was one of the Robben Island warders who moved to Voorberg after the island prison was decommissioned. Born in 1963, he was raised in Pollsmoor prison in Cape Town because his stepfather worked in the Prison Service and had a house in the prison compound. He arrived as a toddler just after the first small prison was opened at Pollsmoor in 1964, and spent his childhood playing on building sites as Pollsmoor developed into the sprawling prison complex it remains today. When Boetie completed his schooling at the all-white government school in 1981 he wanted to join the army to fight black 'communists' on the border between Angola and the former South West Africa, but instead was recruited to the training college of the Prison

Service, where he was inducted into its military structures. He was sent to Robben Island with very little knowledge of the prison or who was held there. His accompanying cohort of young Afrikaans men also 'didn't even know there was such a thing as politics'. Many of the warders recruited at the time came from small-town white schools, and from white working-class families seeking secure employment for their sons. The apartheid state was a haven of sheltered employment for young men such as Boetie.

'They were a rough crowd', Boetie recalls of his cohort of warders. '*Braai en brandewyn* [barbecue and brandy], especially the young guys that lived in the single quarters.' Despite the heavily militarised culture of the Prison Service with its ranked hierarchies of command, parade marches and military-style drills, the petty charges against Robben Island warders were many and frequent, mostly 'staying away from duty, being drunk on duty, excessive drinking, assaults on prisoners and on each other'. And yet Boetie recalls his years on the island as the best years of his life. It is a refrain that many of the island's white warders repeat. Most describe the extraordinary natural beauty of the island as paradisiacal, with opportunities to dive for crayfish and perlemoen, to braai them fresh out of the water, and to spearfish without permit limits. 'The island is like a nature park, with eland, springbok, ostriches, penguins.' Boetie became a practised long-distance scuba diver, recalling six-hour underwater adventures across Table Bay. As with many of the warders facing relocation when the prison was decommissioned, Boetie was affronted at having to leave the island for mainland prisons, and especially under a change of government. Those warders who could afford it retired or left the service, though many stayed on to face the new policy and governance frameworks of the post-apartheid state.

When Winston M'bula first arrived at Voorberg in 1997 to take up a job in the new prison, he was horrified by the racism he found in the prison compound. Although new accommodation was in the process of being built to house Voorberg's growing number of warders working in the new Medium B prison – at that time black warders were still being housed at *Mossienes* – the children of white and black warders were being driven into Porterville in separate school buses. Little headway had been made in transforming the militarism of the prison. M'bula represented a new kind of warder. Having grown up in Ceres in a very poor household, with an isiXhosa-speaking father and an Afrikaans-speaking mother, he had become involved in struggle politics when he was a young schoolboy, developing a political consciousness through the teachings of his local pastor. Fiercely committed to the anti-apartheid movement, and the African National Congress (ANC) in particular, M'bula had been among the young comrades who boycotted school and took to the streets in protest, so that he himself was detained in prison for political activity on more than one occasion. He arrived at Voorberg in 1997, a newly minted member of the renamed Department of Correctional Services, and he drew on his own experience of being incarcerated to hone a commitment to changing the quality of prison life for inmates.

He was met by some of the most unreconstructed racists he had ever encountered, racists with whom he would have to live and work every day. Barry Kruger, for example, arrived at Voorberg with a long and proud history in the apartheid security forces. After serving his first few years of compulsory military service in the early 1970s as a member of the Parachute Batallion, he joined the Permanent Force of the South African Defence Force (SADF) and trained as a weapons instructor: 'There I was trained as a bomb expert – demolitions expert, terrorists weapons expert, normal specialised weapons in national defence force – all kinds of weapons. I also trained in rural warfare as well as guerrilla warfare.' Kruger served many years fighting 'terrorists' and 'communists' on the Angolan border, the battleground between the South African apartheid state and African liberation forces. On one mission, he was captured and held as a prisoner of war by South West Africa People's Organisation (SWAPO) forces, and upon release he was awarded the Pro Patria campaign medal for service in an operational area. This medal, among many others earned during his service to the apartheid government, hung in a frame on the wall of his house on the Voorberg compound.

When the new houses being built at Voorberg were finally completed, Barry Kruger and Winston M'bula were given houses next door to each other. Each was for the other an embodiment of the force he had spent his life combating. One of the first interactions between the two warders involved a contestation over Kruger's medals. Under military regulations, members of the apartheid Prison Service had to wear their rank and decoration on their uniforms. Rank was the fundamental organising principle of prison staff, and an important duty of every member was to learn the practice of that hierarchy: when to stand, how to salute, in what order members should enter and leave a room. Because military rank was mapped directly onto racial hierarchy in the apartheid Prison Service, at the end of apartheid it was scrapped through a process of demilitarisation and racial integration.

But Barry Kruger came to work at Voorberg every morning with his apartheid rank decorating the front of his uniform. It was an act of racist insubordination that infuriated his neighbour. While still at training college, M'bula had become a member of the Police and Prisons Civil Rights Union (Popcru), a new union for black police and prison warders that grew out of the anti-apartheid movement in the dying years of apartheid. He had already begun organising for Popcru at Voorberg. So he arranged a protest action about Kruger's decoration, drew up a memorandum, made placards, and led an angry group of toyi-toying black warders to Kruger's office, demanding that he remove the medals from his uniform. Kruger eventually relented, but above his breast pocket he continued to wear a green pin emblazoned with the image of a golden gun, a defiant reminder of his years in apartheid infantry. The rest of his medals continued to hang in his house, barely ten yards from Winston M'bula's front door.

UNMEMORIALISED VIOLENCE

Figure 6.1. Voorberg Correctional Centre Medium A section, with Mr Flynn in the foreground. Photograph by Mikhael Subotsky

While I was doing fieldwork in the old Voorberg Medium A prison in 2003, I needed a place to write up fieldnotes during the day. I asked Mr Flynn, an older white warder who had been in the prison service for 33 years, if he could help me find a quiet place to write. The old prison is constructed as a corrugated-iron square of squat communal cells and administrative offices around a grassed courtyard. It is neither large nor complex in its design, but Mr Flynn led me to a section that I had not seen before. It was a small corridor of single cells. The cells on the right-hand side of the corridor were long disused, declared a safety hazard many years before because of the broken and rusted walls. The foundations had sunk, causing the floor to crack. The cells on the left had, however, been in use up until a few years before, for inmates with chronic medical conditions. As with the rest of the prison, Boland temperatures meant that the uninsulated metal cells are extremely hot in summer and freezing cold in winter, making them unlikely places for recovery from chronic illness. Nowadays, all of the single cells are used for storage: old metal bed frames, a broken filing cabinet, a drum kit, hosepipes, dartboards, boxes of old material filled the rooms. One cell was half filled with old prison shoes. In each cell the toilet and sink serve as shelves for the discarded detritus of prison life.

At cell number 5, amidst a pile of old, boxy TV sets, Mr Flynn paused, as if signalling to me that it might be a good place for me to write. Instead, he told me a story from 1989. An inmate had been placed in the cell for aggressive behaviour, and left there for a very long time. When the cell door was finally opened to let him out, the inmate threw a bucket of his own excrement at the warders opening the door. Mr Flynn told me how a team of warders went into the cell and beat him with batons until he was bleeding and unconscious on the floor. Such incidental stories of violence meted out to prisoners by warders and by fellow prisoners, often unspeakably gruesome, were commonplace not only in the accounts of Voorberg that warders shared with me, but also in their conversations with one another in the prison compound. They point to a mostly unwritten history of brutality and torture that the prison system in South Africa has overseen since the beginning of colonial rule.

During British rule and later in the apartheid era, prisons were built at a rate of at least one each year for over 200 years, with exponential investment in upkeep, renovations and expansions. The network of prisons is a geography of racial capitalism, crucial to the production of a compliant and plentiful source of cheap black labour for the white colonial state and its white crony capitalist class. The mining economy as well as an expanding monocropping infrastructure required prisons as mechanisms for the production of cheap labour and capital accumulation. Prisons were built adjacent to mining compounds and agricultural areas, with prison labour used to drill and harvest, and to build road infrastructure for the colony.[12] The terror and constraint that prisons visited upon black urban life in the production of value for white capital was fundamental to the dynamics of the colonial and apartheid projects.

Post-apartheid prisons are no longer reservoirs of labour, given that restrictions on the use of prison labour were written into the new legislation; that the significant rise in the level of unemployment and underemployment in South Africa reconfigured the relationship of capital to the prison; and that prisons were identified early on as easy sites for privatisation and tender manipulation. Nevertheless, prisons remain warehouses for black working-class and poor lives. They remain venues for a systemic repetition of violence and disposability that entrenches the relationship between black township and prison, and sustains one of the most unrecognised continuities between apartheid and post-apartheid society.[13]

In the summer of 2003–2004, as part of an effort to improve its public relations, Voorberg management decided to host a large fair on the prison grounds, to which all surrounding communities were invited. It was to be a carnival event, with jumping castle, swing rides, Ferris wheel and many food and goods stalls crewed by warders and their families. Staff had even arranged to buy fireworks for a grand finale at midnight. The success of the event rested on how many people the fair could attract from the neighbouring rural villages and towns, so a marketing plan was drawn up by warders, including posters in local supermarkets and a word-of-mouth campaign.

A few days before the weekend event, a group of about 15 warders met in the parking area just inside the main prison gate to set out in a convoy advertising the fair throughout the nearby towns of Porterville, Piketberg and Saron. Seven cars left the prison compound together, each with a loudhailer and a throbbing sound system, and snaked towards town. '*Lekker! Lekker! Lekker! Carnival hierdie naweek by Voorberg! Die ding gaan ruk!*' (Fun! Fun! Fun! Carnival this weekend at Voorberg! It's gonna shake!). From a car window, Winston M'bula yelled into a loudhailer as the convoy drove along the main street of Piketberg, hooting and flashing car headlights. *'Lekker! Lekker! Lekker!'* he shouted down the broad streets of the white town. A few white people peered out from their spacious verandas to see what all the noise was about, but other than that, the unfamiliar entourage elicited little interest or concern.

'Carnival hierdie naweek by Voorberg!' The cars made their way out of the wide paved streets and into the black township on the edge of the white town. Onto the streets, from small patched-together houses, emerged dozens of people. What time would the fair start? How much it would cost to buy tickets? Will there be transport? But more importantly, as the cars weaved through the narrow streets of the township, men from the township began shouting greetings to the warders in their cars, greetings that were reciprocated by warders who recognised these men as ex-prisoners who had slept in the cells they oversee. Sitting on street corners, standing in the doorframes of their mothers' homes, sitting on crates outside their girlfriends' places, were men whose lives were intimately connected to the prison, an intimacy displayed by their prison tattoos as they eyed, waved or shouted at the passing warders.

Figure 6.2. Voorberg Correctional Centre Medium B section, cell. Photograph by Mikhael Subotsky

The unmemorialised violence that resides in the broken cells, the histories of torture, the apartheid residues, the continued brutalities of hundreds of prisons *still* operational, *still* warehousing black life, remains in every one of South Africa's 243 prisons. This ongoing violence, the systemic as well as the everyday kind, is nowhere recognised in the Robben Island prison museum, even though this national museum is dedicated to memorialising the very same violence. It neither reflects on the redeployment of racist warders to other prisons, and nor does it mention the post-apartheid increase in prison population, which remains disproportionately poor and black. The museum marks the prison as a metaphor for a political project that is past, overcome, historic. The type of museumification at work on Robben Island functions not so much as a refusal of colonial and apartheid violence, but as an ideological veil on the continuation of the long history of racial capitalism through the institution of the prison.

In *Fidelio*, as the trumpet sounds, it is not just Florestan who is released from the prison, but all of the prisoners, who then emerge from the dungeon into the light. The opera in the decommissioned prison museum makes the poignant suggestion that the release of the Robben Island prisoners was part of a historical process that liberated all South Africans into a new historical moment. But the unmemorialised working prisons that have inherited the daily, relentless violence of the racial project in South Africa, these places – hidden as much by old racisms as by new ideologies of liberation – stand in testimony against this historiography. Unless the decommissioning of one infamous prison leads to a fundamental reckoning with all of them, given South Africa's repetitive, punitive ways of routing and contending with the centuries-long histories of violence and harm, it should be sounding no trumpet.

NOTES

1   Govan Mbeki, *Learning from Robben Island: The Prison Writings of Govan Mbeki* (Suffolk: James Currey, 1991); Nelson Mandela, *Long Walk to Freedom* (Philadelphia: Little Brown & Co., 1994); Fran Lisa Buntman, *Robben Island and Prisoner Resistance to Apartheid* (Cambridge: Cambridge University Press, 2003); and Ahmed Kathrada, *Memoirs* (Cape Town: Struik, 2004).

2   Paul Robinson, '"Fidelio" and the French Revolution', *Cambridge Opera Journal* 3.1 (1991): 33.

3. Terence Ranger, 'Nationalist Historiography and Patriotic History', *Journal of Southern African Studies* 30.2 (2004): 215–34.
4. Mikhail Bakhtin, 'Forms of Time and of the Chronotope in the Novel', in *The Dialogic Imagination: Four Essays*, ed. Michael Holquist (Austin: University of Texas Press, 1981), 85.
5. Harriet Deacon, 'Remembering Tragedy, Constructing Modernity: Robben Island as National Monument', in *Negotiating the Past: The Making of Memory in South Africa*, eds Sarah Nuttall and Carli Coetzee (Cape Town: Oxford University Press, 1998), 164.
6. The term 'Coloured' is used here to mark the apartheid racial distinction between 'black / African' and a separate racial category that was invented to encompass people the racial state deemed to fall between black and white. I use the term 'Coloured' when explaining the specific logic of the apartheid project, but use the undifferentiated 'black' in general descriptions. See Hermann Giliomee, *The Afrikaners: Biography of a People* (Cape Town: Tafelberg, 2003).
7. Harold Wolpe, 'Capitalism and Cheap Labour Power in South Africa: From Segregation to Apartheid', *Economy and Society* 1.4 (1972): 425–56.
8. Andries du Toit, 'Farm Workers and the "Agrarian Question"', *Review of African Political Economy* 21.61 (1994): 375–88.
9. Dirk van Zyl Smit, *South African Prison Law and Practice* (Durban: Butterworths, 1992); and Kelly Gillespie, 'Containing the "Wandering Native": Racial Jurisdiction and the Liberal Politics of Prison Reform in 1940s South Africa', *Journal of Southern African Studies* 37.3 (2011): 499–515.
10. The interviews used to write this chapter were conducted during PhD dissertation fieldwork research at Voorberg Correctional Facility in 2003–2004. The author was hosted for part of that time by the Prisons Transformation Project of the Centre for Conflict Resolution, and would like to acknowledge the Social Sciences Research Council and the Wenner-Gren Foundation, which funded the research.
11. For further information on the practices of the Numbers gangs and their 140-year history across South African prisons, see Nicholas Haysom, *Towards an Understanding of Prison Gangs* (Cape Town: University of Cape Town, Institute of Criminology, 1981); Jonny Steinberg, *The Number: One Man's Search for Identity in the Cape Underworld and Prison Gangs* (Cape Town: Jonathan Ball, 2004); and Jonny Steinberg, *Nongoloza's Children: Western Cape Prison Gangs During and After Apartheid* (Cape Town: Centre for the Study of Violence and Reconciliation Monograph Series, July 2004). One of the practices of the Number gangs is that recruits must symbolically 'dress' themselves in full military uniform before performing an act of violence on behalf of the Number, as is indicated in the story about the warder 'Europa' described in this quotation.

12 Van Zyl Smit, *South African Prison Law and Practice*; and William Worger, 'Convict Labour, Industrialists and the State in the US South and South Africa, 1870–1930', *Journal of Southern African Studies* 30.1 (2004): 63–86.
13 Gabeba Baderoon, 'Surplus, Excess, Dirt: Slavery and the Production of Disposability in South Africa', *Social Dynamics* 44.2 (2018): 257–72.

REFERENCES

Baderoon, Gabeba. 'Surplus, Excess, Dirt: Slavery and the Production of Disposability in South Africa'. *Social Dynamics* 44.2 (2018): 257–72.

Bakhtin, Mikhail. 'Forms of Time and of the Chronotope in the Novel'. In *The Dialogic Imagination: Four Essays*, edited by Michael Holquist, 84–258. Austin: University of Texas Press, 1981.

Buntman, Fran Lisa. *Robben Island and Prisoner Resistance to Apartheid*. Cambridge: Cambridge University Press, 2003.

Deacon, Harriet. 'Remembering Tragedy, Constructing Modernity: Robben Island as National Monument'. In *Negotiating the Past: The Making of Memory in South Africa,* edited by Sarah Nuttall and Carli Coetzee, 161–79. Cape Town: Oxford University Press, 1998.

Du Toit, Andries. 'Farm Workers and the "Agrarian Question"'. *Review of African Political Economy* 21.61 (1994): 375–88.

Giliomee, Hermann. *The Afrikaners: Biography of a People*. Cape Town: Tafelberg, 2003.

Gillespie, Kelly. 'Containing the "Wandering Native": Racial Jurisdiction and the Liberal Politics of Prison Reform in 1940s South Africa'. *Journal of Southern African Studies* 37.3 (2011): 499–515.

Haysom, Nicholas. *Towards an Understanding of Prison Gangs*. Cape Town: University of Cape Town, 1981.

Kathrada, Ahmed. *Memoirs.* Cape Town: Struik, 2004.

Mandela, Nelson. *Long Walk to Freedom.* Philadelphia: Little Brown & Co., 1994.

Mbeki, Govan. *Learning from Robben Island: The Prison Writings of Govan Mbeki.* Suffolk: James Currey, 1991.

Ranger, Terence. 'Nationalist Historiography and Patriotic History'. *Journal of Southern African Studies* 30.2 (2004): 215–34.

Robinson, Paul. '"Fidelio" and the French Revolution'. *Cambridge Opera Journal* 3.1 (1991): 23–48.

Steinberg, Jonny. *Nongoloza's Children: Western Cape Prison Gangs During and After Apartheid*. Cape Town: Centre for the Study of Violence and Reconciliation Monograph Series, July 2004.

Steinberg, Jonny. *The Number: One Man's Search for Identity in the Cape Underworld and Prison Gangs*. Johannesburg: Jonathan Ball, 2004.

Van Zyl Smit, Dirk. *South African Prison Law and Practice*. Durban: Butterworths, 1992.

Wolpe, Harold. 'Capitalism and Cheap Labour Power in South Africa: From Segregation to Apartheid'. *Economy and Society* 1.4 (1972): 425–56.

Worger, William. 'Convict Labour, Industrialists and the State in the US South and South Africa, 1870–1930'. *Journal of Southern African Studies* 30.1 (2004): 63–86.

7 THE APARTHEID PASS OFFICE IN JOHANNESBURG AND A HERITAGE OF DESTRUCTION

HILTON JUDIN

The former Pass Office at 80 Albert Street in Johannesburg is sufficiently nondescript and untethered to any evolving national narrative to have remained abandoned decades after apartheid. Seen as neither redemptive nor exemplary, the building sits neglected and forgotten, a social and historical cipher yet to be unravelled. Such an incongruous apartheid facility was significant, reaching pervasively into the lives of every single black male living in Johannesburg but containing as it does a history few seek to remember or commemorate. Yet in its absence from our architectural heritage there is an incomplete record of the thoroughly damaging racist urban path once wrought within its corridors: the hated pass book that this office was responsible for issuing, controlling African migration to the city and making urban life temporary through influx control, maintaining segregation through the planning of all surrounding townships, administering at times all official aspects of black life.

There is little to distinguish this banal office block from other more notorious apartheid edifices, except for the seemingly innocuous set of entrance doors to the main administration hall: invisible to the white public beyond the building itself, the doors can only be accessed by the black public from

Figure 7.1. Back entrance to Pass Office hall from waiting yard, 80 Albert Street, Johannesburg, 2012. Photograph by Jo Ractliffe

the back courtyard of the building (figure 7.1). Has the abandonment of this building obfuscated the ominous work of segregation and deprivation of a generation ago? In striving against forgetting through architecture, should this building remain vacant rather than being preserved for posterity or reduced to a brick carcass with a sombre history? At times, it has served as a shelter for women, a creche and a city clinic. With no certainty and minimal preservation, tenants are vulnerable, the paint and panels peeling away, walls crumbling, and windows and railings coming loose. The question lingers as to what relevance the building might hold for a new generation of South Africans, faced as they are with a growing dissociation of historical events with sites such as this once embodied. Why is it ignored, absent from our collective memory, in its current condition remaining as neither ruin, rubble nor memorial? What does 80 Albert Street reveal to us today?

It was here that the remorseless system of apartheid was brought together for the city of Johannesburg, with operations relating to influx control, housing and employment of African men centralised in the building. Here, confrontations between the black public and the state were most tragic and urgent: in this place, it was required to seek permission to reside in the city, hold onto a job, or join one's family, as both husband and wife had to qualify for urban residence. Although legislation was in place from 1952, labour regulations were applied to African women from January 1959, initially at Albert Street, and later that year at a nearby facility in Polly Street. A complex web of laws, directives and regulations was developed as the migrant labour system of apartheid attempted to control everything from streets and houses to commerce and migration to the city. Officially opened for the City of Johannesburg by the chairman of the Non-European Affairs Committee, Councillor Leslie Hurd, in April 1954, the nondescript office building became the central site of the administration of the city's black population.

The building was the offices of the Non-European Affairs Department (NEAD) and, from 1973, the West Rand Administration Board (WRAB) with the shift to the planning and regulation of the urban development, housing, social welfare and recreation of all African residents in Johannesburg. Previously subsidised services and infrastructure had suddenly to be paid for by these residents. Officials collected rents for housing, as well as fines, fees, levies from employers, and revenue from beer halls, in part to finance influx control and supervise African urban accommodation, and in part to set off losses from these township housing schemes. These historical experiences can be understood as reflective and constitutive of current cultural debates around race and identity, commemoration, urban disparities, divisions and deprivations. In focusing on historical memory and building, it is important to continue to reflect on what should be remembered and retained, what put aside and re-examined, and what ultimately forgotten.

'PASS OFFICE'

The writer Mtutuzeli Matshoba speaks in his story from 1980, 'To Kill a Man's Pride …', of the pain and humiliation this building elicits: 'Registration for work is such an interesting example of a way of killing a man's pride that I cannot pass it by without mention. It was on Monday, after two weeks of unrewarded labour and perseverance, that Pieters gave me a letter which said I had been employed as a general labourer at his firm and which I had to take to the notorious 80 Albert Street.'[1] He wakes up that day and takes the train to Faraday Station. He then walks to his new employer's office to get the requisite signed employment forms and makes his way to the Pass Office. Matshoba continues: '"*Esibayeni*". Two storey red-brick building occupying a whole block. Address: 80 Albert street, or simply "Pass Office". Across the street, half the block ... taken up by another red-brick structure. Not offices this time, but "*Esibayeni*" (at the kraal) itself. No question why it has been called that. The entire black population of Johannesburg above pass-age knows that place.'[2]

Matshoba gathers with others sitting on both sides of Albert Street who are desperately waiting for a temporary piece-job from white employers driving by:

> The queue to '*Esibayeni*' was moving slowly. It snaked about thirty metres around the corner of Polly street. It had taken me more than an hour to reach the door. Inside the ten-feet high wall was an asphalt rectangle, longitudinal benches along the opposite wall in the shade of narrow tin ledges, filled with bored looking men, toilets on the lower side of the rectangle, facing wide bustling doors. It would take me another three hours to reach the clerks.[3]

After proceeding by bribing his way to the front of the queue, he is confronted by a young white clerk speaking in Afrikaans. Matshoba gives him his letter of employment and pass, and he gets his E and F cards stamped, giving him permission to work in Johannesburg. He then has to proceed to a room in the adjacent block, walking up a sloping cement pathway that rises to a green double-door: 'Here too it was full of the same miserable figures that were buzzing all over the place, but this time they stood in a series of queues at a long counter like the one across the street, only this one was L-shaped and the white clerks behind the brass grille wore ties.'[4]

A clerk takes his E and F cards, checks his pass against a photostat record, and then begins to interrogate him as to his whereabouts in the previous nine months. By not arguing or challenging the clerk, Matshoba is given a

Figure 7.2. 'The queues at Albert Street are long and tedious, but for the man in a hurry 50c slipped to the right cop can get him to the top of the line. The bribe virus has even affected ordinary municipal cops. Every municipal office has miles and miles of queues for one thing or another. If you can't afford wasting five hours standing in a queue doing nothing all you have to do is quietly to pass a 50c piece to a cop. That's the price for quick service.' May 1968. Photograph by *Drum* photographer. APN252546. DM2008103103: SAED. Baileys African History Archive

pass to move on to the next queue for the medical examination, vaccination and X-ray:

> The last part of the medical examination was the most disgraceful. I don't know whether it was designed to save expense or on some other ground of expediency, but on me it had the effect of dishonour. After being X-rayed we could put on our shirts and cross the corridor to the doctor's cubicle. Outside were people of both sexes waiting to settle their affairs. You passed them before entering the cubicle, inside which sat a fat white man in a white dust-coat with a face like an owl, behind a simple desk. The man who had gone in ahead of me was zipping up his fly. I unzipped mine and stood facing the owl behind his desk, holding my trousers with both hands. He tilted his fat face to the right and left twice or thrice. 'Ja. Your pass.'[5]

After dressing, Matshoba gets a maroon stamp on his pass, which means he is seen as fit for work: 'The medical examination was over and the women on the benches outside pretended they did not know. The young white ladies clicking their heels up and down the passages showed you they knew. You held yourself together as best you could until you vanished from their sight, and you never told anybody else about it.'[6]

What comes to us today in this singular searing indictment is a powerful testimony from which we cannot turn away or hide behind a façade of indifference or oblivion. The Pass Office was, as Matshoba told me in an interview on 20 September 2018, a 'station for deportation' under the migrant labour system of apartheid sustaining the impermanence of African urban life. What endures from his testimony are the public acts of daily humiliation and estrangement. And what remains today is less the ruin of perpetrators than a lingering apartheid structure.

After apartheid, 80 Albert Street was never able to fulfil any evidential role in truth-seeking or reconciliation during the early phases of democracy and nation-building. Here, we can distinguish this mundane administrative office from the prisons and sites of struggle of the past, and from more recent memorials and museums that have been consecrated in preserving and publicly constructing a national narrative. What we are considering is a site of trauma not readily reconciled to preservation nor easily accessible to any community. The building itself never had a constituency nor was it drawn into any collective historical narrative. Instead, it was made redundant by historical events and urban reconfigurations that followed the decommission of its offices.

BURNT TO THE GROUND, SOWETO, 1976

Looking back to June 1976, we might recall that nearly all of the West Rand Administration Board buildings across Soweto were destroyed. The Albert Street Pass Office, however, continued to operate unscathed, and in a central but distant position. In the official *Report of the Commission of Inquiry into the Riots at Soweto and Elsewhere* (Cillié Commission), this centrality was noted for the evening of Wednesday 16 June 1976: 'A control room was set up during the night at the WRAB head office in Albert Street, Johannesburg.'[7] The photographic evidence accompanying the Report was gathered by officials at

Figure 7.3 A-C. Top to bottom: DSCN1731 destroyed clinic, Diepkloof; DSCN1711 Orlando East beer hall; DSCN1726 WRAB building with collapsed roof, Orlando East, Soweto June 1976

Figure 7.3 D-F. Top to bottom: DSCN2085 WRAB office, Dobsonville; DSCN1946 community hall inside after fire, Thokoza; DSCN1730 destroyed WRAB building, Dube, Soweto June 1976

Figure 7.3 G–I. Top to bottom: DSCN1733 WRAB building fire damage, Diepkloof; DSCN1737 fire-damaged building; DSCN1917 aerial view of building, Soweto June 1976

Figure 7.3 J-L. Top to bottom: DSCN2151 WRAB building with graffiti; DSCN2167 WRAB office, Meadowlands; DSCN2522 WRAB office building, Soweto June 1976. *Archives of the Commission of Inquiry into the Riots in Soweto and Elsewhere, 1976-1978.* National Archives, Pretoria: K345 [missing file]. Digital Copies from Historical Papers Research Archive, University of the Witwatersrand

the time, and shows the enormous anger directed at the WRAB and surrogate buildings. The offices in the Central Business District (CBD) remained untouched, but in the townships WRAB buildings, recreation centres and beer halls were targeted and burnt to the ground.

The Inquiry followed the terrible events of 1976, which had begun with police shooting high-school students marching peacefully against the introduction of Afrikaans as the primary medium of instruction. During the following days, WRAB buildings in Soweto were razed in a series of incidents that followed the violent response of the teargas, dogs and bullets of the police (figure 7.3).[8] Early in the day, the station commander of Jabulani Police Station had ordered officials of the WRAB and other whites to leave the area. WRAB's new sheltered employment workshop was being officially opened that morning, attended by senior officials who were told to leave urgently. From then onwards, a number of WRAB offices were set alight: at 13:00 in Phefeni and Dube; at 14:30 a WRAB bottle store in Phefeni and WRAB offices and bottle stores in Orlando East; at 15:00 WRAB offices in Diepkloof and Meadowlands; from 15:00 to 17:00 bottle stores at Nhlanzane, Moroka, Mofolo, Chiawelo, Senaone and Zola; and at 16:30, the clinic and administrative offices in White City.[9]

Early next morning, at around 00:15 on Thursday 17 June, the WRAB's regional offices in Meadowlands were set on fire. At 07:00 WRAB offices for Areas 2 and 3 in Meadowlands were set alight; at 07:30 a WRAB sanitary depot in Area 2 was set on fire; and at 09:00 the WRAB offices in Klipspruit were burning; at 09:10 police shot dead two persons in a stone-throwing crowd at the WRAB offices in Diepkloof; and at 10:00 the WRAB library and offices in Area 1 Meadowlands were burnt down, the Diepkloof beer hall was set on fire, and the WRAB maintenance offices in Orlando East were burnt down.[10] While vehicles as well as other buildings were burnt, the sheer number of WRAB buildings targeted was powerful testimony of people's anger at the role of the WRAB in Soweto.

That anger had been directed by students at WRAB buildings. Most forcefully it was directed at WRAB beer halls as these were blatant sites of ongoing exploitation of the community. Profits from liquor sales – two-thirds of which was set aside for housing – went to the Department of Bantu Administration. The design and operation of the beer halls was in fact carried out by the WRAB from its Albert Street premises. Opposition had long been focused on these government businesses, as activist Randwedzi Nengwikhulu explained to historian Paul la Hausse: 'You have more bottle-stores than clinics. Every railway station ... has a bottle-store. When our parents leave work with their pay which is very meagre, they immediately buy liquor and then go home without money ... If you go to Soweto, you will find that every small location has a bottle-store and a big beerhall. But since 16th June bottle-stores no longer function because the first targets were bottle-stores.'[11]

At 09:00 on Friday 18 June 1976, as stated in the commission report, Mr J. C. de Villiers, Chief Director of the WRAB, 'travelled through the streets of Soweto in a motor vehicle under police escort. He made use of an interpreter and loudhailer and asked the public to keep their children at home, because, according to him, 'conditions had degenerated into wholesale thuggery.'[12] Later that day, at 14:00, De Villiers met with a group of Soweto leaders (including members of the Urban Bantu Council and churchmen) at the WRAB administrative offices in New Canada to 'discuss the rehabilitation and reconstruction of Soweto' in a meeting that was 'stormy at times' as 'the Blacks present asked to speak to the Minster of Bantu Education themselves'.[13] The photographic evidence of the commission bears testimony to the destruction of these hated symbols and offices of apartheid. With these buildings destroyed, there was never a need to resolve these conflicting urban heritage artefacts. Instead, 80 Albert Street, where plans of the township were drawn up, facilities designed, and legislation enforced, was never brought to reckoning.

REPARATION

Public historical recollections and personal experiences offer a means for collating and addressing other remnants of apartheid. This could function as a record of the passing of apartheid and its ongoing destructive effects, though without recuperating materials many see as better left discarded. Johannesburg makes little allowance for nostalgia, given the speed with which any historical urban fabric is discarded and the shame in which it is still steeped. Even so, addressing this past could serve memory across generations. For we commemorate the bravery and organisation that defied apartheid even as we look to ordinary everyday events and individuals involved in resistance, in all its complexity.

The significance of the question of historical preservation became apparent in the reconciliatory 1990s, as architects grappled with the practical concerns around addressing previously oppressive buildings and spaces. Social transformation and reconciliation were inherent in projects developed during that period. While not always served by focusing on these oppressive spaces, justice was more immediately done by government meeting society's demand for houses and urban reparation. Yet a historical reckoning was never absent from these urgent calls for building a more inclusive nation. Here, architects sought a form to buildings which neither negated nor diminished the terrifying past with its debilitating conditions – and though these have not disappeared, they are no longer in the forefront of public consciousness. Given the imperatives of a hopeful narrative in the built environment, bringing innocuous, yet pressing, urban conditions into question could never be a straightforward task.

Such preserved oppressive spaces are offered as stripped-down and stark objects. Scrubbed of historical traces, the rough-hewn red face-brick building in Albert Street would hardly demonstrate or recall the relentless daily bureaucratic humiliations recorded by Matshoba, for example. Architects might feel compelled to respond to traumatic events by overt symbolism, employing harsh elements or reducing any material embellishment. Curiously, it is never given to them to engage strategies powerfully employed in other cultural responses – the visual arts, music and literature. These have allowed the unspeakable to be pronounced, or offered nuanced examinations of a subject without resolution. Such cultural responses, however, call for individual expression more than the collective accommodation and practical resolution required of public space and building.

There is seldom a consensus about which events or what aspects of the past to remember and therefore commemorate in monuments and memorials. There is often public conflict over how these events ought to be represented, which elements to retain, and which to discard. How such pasts, memories and histories are to be negotiated often remains uncertain without the legitimacy of shared claims or some common sense of a particular building as having heritage value. It is clear that there is not always a common societal need to remember. What a certain element, building or object might mean, or what remembrance of such entities would entail, needs to be given time and space for different constituencies to proclaim.

Investigating the preservation and memorial models used to determine a contemporary confrontation with repressive architectures leaves us with objects torn by historical events from their original purpose. A building might degenerate and seem inconsequential, but it is still convulsive with a meaning many can never forget. As Can Themba recorded in an article 'Nude "Pass" Parade' in *Drum* magazine of 1957: 'Like so many others he [John Raditsebe] had to go fix his "passes." He too, had to walk the gauntlet of humiliation. "This pass, however," he says, "is so precious that one shuts one's eyes and goes through with the miserable experience."'[14] The building at 80 Albert Street could be imagined as still bearing witness and providing testimony. Conciliating or offering relief to communities might be seen as a step too far for architecture, overly objectifying the political and reinforcing the fetishisation inherent in the monumental.

Claims of white ignorance are difficult to reconcile with the centrality of such mechanisms as the WRAB to everyday life and labour during apartheid. The overwhelming silence of the white population in relation to this brings to every gesture or pronouncement an air of nostalgia as violence. Any attempt at preservation is a step too far. Although dependent on who is inaugurating the commemoration, buildings would require provocation taking the place of consolation. Evoking a destructive heritage would require care and consideration. Buildings have the scale and presence to be as consequential as judicial evidence, as powerful as the primary validated documents, photographs and testimonies of historical events.

Without explanatory inscriptions or the knowledge we bring to these structures, they remain meaningless, serving merely to corroborate in the last instance whatever was inscribed or attributed at the time. It does little, then, to fixate on how much of the original building or site the architect needs to retain or restore for it to convey its original purpose. This oppressive role is mirrored both in the nature of the actions carried out on its premises and the symbolism originally intended. As much as it is to the documents and plans that we turn for evidence of wrongdoing, the building itself is proof of the apartheid system at work, its power and beliefs made manifest in stone, brick and concrete. The actual building is the embodiment of the accumulated demands and intent recorded in the correspondence, charts and schedules for which 80 Albert Street serves as a repository of South Africa's apartheid heritage.

COUNTER-MEMORY

What, then, does our national heritage encompass? How we are to reconcile its conflicting expectations and expressions? Against forgetting, must 80 Albert Street remain as it always was: untouched, offering itself up as evidence? Can it be restored as a sombre space reflective of an obscene past, or uncovered to project its current seriousness? Is keeping as much of the original building – stripped down and painstakingly preserved – the best way to retain memories? Does restoring the building to its former notorious phase preserve its original ignominy? Just as official documents and testimonials are understood to embody a certain authenticity, starkly presented buildings seem to provide an authentic material presence, even under the deteriorating conditions of the building itself. Alternative strategies to built form might be considered, requiring deeper and at times painful engagement, in search of what is actually at stake in challenging interventions.

What possible relationship could a visitor today have to a once-infamous building and the events embedded therein, the objects and meanings having passed away, with only the faintest traces left behind? As the historian Sifiso Mxolisi Ndlovu asserts in *The Soweto Uprisings: Counter-Memories of June 1976* with regard to commemoration:

> Societies differ in the degree to which their citizens can contest the hegemonic practices of commemoration. In democratic societies we at least acknowledge in principle that previously established commemorative practice should be open to critique and contention. Thus democracy entails an ongoing tension between retaining affirmed shared memories and preserving the possibility that such memories can be opened to contestation. In other words, most democrats cherish, rather than dismiss, the practice of counter-memory. This calls into question both the social imagination previously secured by particular commemorations as well as the social interests and ethical visions supported by such imaginations.[15]

In calling for a process of seriously listening to and considering claims on our understanding of the present – of counter-memory and commemorations, according to Ndlovu – our social identities may be constructed and constantly renewed. We need as well to understand, given the enormity of past events, who encompasses this community and which generations are being called upon and addressed. What forms would participation entail as a project of radical consultation and involvement? For architects, it is a political framework within which any act of preservation might operate. The ignorance produced by 'forgetting' 80 Albert Street would leave us bereft in distinct ways. For within this building, white employers had to confront their complicity with the state, not as bystanders but as perpetrators. These are tasks that need to be taken on that were never previously considered for architecture. We know that it was not the building itself, but the vast machinery of apartheid legislation through which the country was forced into an oppressive and relentless confrontation. But it was in this building that we were forced to confront our complicity as perpetrators, our victimhood, or our seeming indifference.

'EMPATHETIC UNSETTLEMENT'

More than two decades after the end of apartheid there are few obvious concrete remnants of the racist urban order planned and maintained by the bureaucracy at 80 Albert Street. Few tangible traces of the territories and paths that were laid out are visible. In Johannesburg, in remembering and observing glaring disparities and ongoing segregation, we are faced with uncomfortable questions about our city. Unresolved aspects of our divisive urban spaces, fragmented and unjust, neither recede nor go unchallenged. Accordingly, ignoring previously oppressive spaces, leaving them as ruins, would diminish their capacity to recall past events, what the historian Dominick LaCapra refers to in *Writing History, Writing Trauma* as 'empathetic unsettlement':

> Empathy is important in attempting to understand traumatic events and victims, and it may (I think, should) have stylistic effects in the way one discusses or addresses certain problems. It places in jeopardy fetishized and totalizing narratives that deny the trauma that called them into existence by prematurely (re)turning to the pleasure principle, harmonizing events, and often recuperating the past in terms of uplifting messages or optimistic, self-serving scenarios.[16]

Although never hidden or demolished, 80 Albert Street receded from public view as it was subsumed into the urban fabric of the eastern section of the CBD. Just as a generation who could give first-hand testimony of the building passes on, so the most visible elements of the building – signs, furniture, documents and demarcations – have disappeared or been undone by time and change. In the main administration hall, only the beige floor tiles remain, exposed and blistered; silently, they reveal the outlines of the bureaucrats' counters and cabinets that had once stood facing the set of three double-doors, hinting at long-gone queues (figure 7.4). But in addressing another generation we again face the question of what to do about this building – confrontation or continued neglect.

Historical preservation models could be used to determine current work with such repressive architecture, even as some of it lingers without purpose: neither museums nor monuments, such structures remain as vacant sites of destruction. Bereft of historical contestation, they have remained outside public consciousness, absent from events of commemoration. They come to us as buildings torn asunder historically and spatially from their original

Figure 7.4. Main administrative hall, Pass Office, 80 Albert Street, Johannesburg, 2012. Photograph by Jo Ractliffe

context. These buildings might only finally be activated as historical sites by more expansive processes of collective memory rather than official endorsements such as monuments.

In South Africa, there is a surplus of these spaces, buildings and sites of oppression, serving among the memorial sites that have sprung up across the urban landscape of the country since the first democratic elections in 1994. Making memory out of such spaces has, over past decades, underpinned the national cultural constitution in coming to terms with the brutal legacy of apartheid. These spaces include powerful transformed historical sites of oppression such as Robben Island off Cape Town, with the preserved prison cells and the infamous quarry; KwaMuhle Museum in the headquarters of Durban's former Native Administration Department, with an exhibition of the labour system of influx control, the history of forced removal from Mkhumbane, and the development of the townships of KwaMashu and Umlazi; and Constitutional Hill in Johannesburg, with the Constitutional Court on the site of the former prison and Fort (the latter housed white prisoners), including Numbers Four and Five (which held black prisoners), and the Women's Jail.[17] These national projects starkly contrast oppression with liberation, and the iniquities of apartheid with post-1994 democracy.

Significant other contested museum memorial projects include national cultural commemoration sites such as the Hector Pieterson Memorial and Museum in Soweto, and community-driven social history initiatives such as the District Six Museum in Cape Town; the Lwandle Migrant Labour Museum and restored Hostel 33 outside the city; and the Sophiatown Heritage and Culture Centre, The Mix, in Johannesburg.[18] Yet massive parts of the historical apartheid landscape – vacant buffer zones and crowded former hostels – are not easily visible or even comprehensible, bound as they are by borders and lines once imposed in the legislation, or compromised by dire economic needs.

Despite the possibility in the first decade after democracy to consider oppressive sites of apartheid, many more urgent events and stories had first to be told through the Truth and Reconciliation Commission (TRC), focusing on gross human rights violations, killings, exhumations and the disappeared. At the same time, there was the need to record the everyday violations of apartheid, the relentless humiliations and control of urban life.

Unable to readily serve a political or cultural role, 80 Albert Street was left vacant, difficult to resolve with a nation struggling to find a new sense of identity and purpose. But the horror of apartheid was always more than what could be placed on record or contained in a singular response. As Auschwitz survivor Jean Améry elucidates in his memoir *At the Mind's Limits*, facts serving simply as a reminder of what took place do little to temper accumulated antipathies:

> It is not easy to reject the reproach that so simplifies the problem, and it is entirely impossible for me to refute the suspicion that I am drowning the ugly reality of a malicious instinct in the verbal torrent of an unverifiable thesis. I will have to take the risk. When I stand by my resentments, when I admit that I am deliberating our problem I am 'biased' I still know that I am captive of the moral truth of the conflict. It seems logically senseless to me to demand objectivity in the controversy with my torturers, with those who helped them, and with the others, who merely stood by silently. The atrocity as atrocity has no objective character. Mass murder, torture, injury of every kind are objectively nothing but the physical events, describable in the formalized language of the natural sciences. They are facts within a physical system, not deeds within a moral system ... The social body is occupied merely with safeguarding itself and could not care less about a life that has been damaged. At the very best, it looks forward, so that such things don't happen again. But my resentments are there in order that the crime becomes a moral reality for the criminal, in order that he be swept into the truth of his atrocity.[19]

How does one come to terms with a traumatic legacy, and do so in ways that neither revisit nor normalise these historical events and sensitive sites? Internationally at 'sites of conscience', architects have revealed the terrible legacies of places seemingly drained of a past. In Germany in the last decades, there have been restrained projects at pains to confront the horror of the Holocaust and its concentration camps: within the site of Bergen-Belsen, an austere and massive exposed concrete documentation and information centre, and at Sachsenhausen, 'Station Z' preserving under a translucent fabric roof the ruins of the cremation ovens. Why should any of these projects be revisited upon a new generation, one to which further acts and forms of oppression are ever-present? Within a week of demonstrators taking over the Stasi headquarters in Berlin in 1990, a memorial and research centre on the German Democratic Republic (GDR) was established in House 1 on the former grounds of the Ministry for State Security. Civil rights activists later secured the historic site as the renamed Stasimuseum and founded the 'Antistalinistische Aktion e.V (Astak) to present exhibitions and provide information through the Stasi Records Agency. Offering a reflection on historical trauma, this centre has been able to approach difficult and unsettling questions of social collaboration, which, though never fully resolved, are kept active through continuous research and documentation.

For visitors to such sites there is the slight discomfort of passing through yet another place along the historical trail. The amnesia of these events, together with the national trauma, slowly recede from public consciousness. Remembrance that promises healing and relief in the telling offers another way to confront the past. With stark displays of events in places undergoing national reconciliation, history and memory are placed publicly on record in powerful memorial projects developed at the actual sites of terror. At the notorious Escuela Superior de Mecánica de la Armada (Higher School of Mechanics of the Navy) in Buenos Aires, the secret detention centre was converted into a space for memory of the thousands of people who were abducted and tortured on the campus before being killed during the 'Dirty War' in Argentina (1976–1983). The decaying building and abandoned cells are left exposed for visitors to reflect on traumatic events as an architectural deference to unimaginable brutality. In Phnom Penh, Cambodia, the Tuol Sleng Genocide Museum was established at S–21 Security Prison, a former high school building the Khmer Rouge used to interrogate and torture around 15 000 people before massacring them in the infamous Killing Fields. In Rwanda, the Kigali Genocide Memorial Centre was developed as a place of burial for victims of the genocide against the Tutsi, and as a documentation centre to record evidence, provide a repository for testimonies, and support the survivors. This place of memorial and remembrance includes, importantly, a burial place for the mass grave of more than 250 000 victims, a wall of names, and garden of reflection. Such ordinary places – classrooms turned into prison cells and gardens for mass burial – serve powerfully to reflect the poignancy and ongoing presence of harrowing historical events for the many family and citizens left behind and bereft, so as to remember.

RHYTHM OF RECUPERATION

In the case of 80 Albert Street, the absence and neglect that continues to hide the building from our immediate notice may be seen as an indication of other more compelling narratives coming to the fore, and the urgent needs of a developing nation. It can also be seen as indicative of a past that is best not lingered over. Turning away might serve to heal communities rather than haunt them, allowing them to live without the constant reminder of the brutal urban practices of the past. How, then, is the architect to juggle the various voices and languages if, after apartheid, participation and inclusion have become the means to confront the damage it caused? How, given the limited transformation of the profession, are architects to achieve authenticity, and imagine shared spaces of remembrance? Upon reflection, white architects might step aside and instead provide support, turn down historical commissions, practise not-building, and learn from the sidelines. In that way, they might find an architecture equal to both the anguish and hope embedded in the landscape.

Today, 80 Albert Street lies spatially adrift in the city, with a barely repressed material heritage, still resonant with the memory of events that cannot easily be discerned. Could alternative tactics of preservation – abandonment, exposure, formlessness, or recuperation – offer approaches to these difficult spaces that do not take on a single narrative? Is commemoration or remembrance even called for at 80 Albert Street? Do architects always have to physically intervene? Lifting tiles once laid beneath absent counters would not reveal anything further, or obviously allow recall of what took place here, day after day. The architect's responsibilities, both here and across the city, would be rendered singularly grave, given the traumatic nature of such buildings and the damaged urban landscapes of former buffer zones and segregated settlements. The writer Njabulo Ndebele talks in his essay 'Arriving Home?' of the need to fracture the sense of structurally permanent processes cemented into the dormitory settlements and townships of apartheid:

> It is this sense of permanence that has to be broken. Failure to break it would mean the persistence and resilience of soul-wrecking settlements whose continued existence will have a devastatingly corrosive effect on the morale of newly enfranchised citizens, a sense of disillusion that could lead to a fundamental

questioning of the depth of change and the ability of government to direct such change. Social movements that have emerged around the country in the last decade may have their origins in such corrosion. The corrosion has much to do with the fact that the spatial landscape of apartheid, as one of the most enduring features of our country, will not disappear overnight, and as such will continue to exercise a dominant impact on the shaping of our consciousness of the South African landscape. What South Africans perceive of it has a major effect on how they assess possibilities for change. What they can see makes people either excluded or included; trapped or freed; centred or marginalised; observing or observed; despised or respected.[20]

Ndebele is calling for township dwellers to be placed at the centre of self-organising initiatives in creating thriving new environments, and new urban identities. Effecting dialogue, interpreting history, promoting values, raising consciousness, and addressing issues in the public realm are, however, burdens often loaded onto these same communities. We need to be sensitive to rehabilitation, to confrontations of former victims and perpetrators, to healing that struggles to take place, to the painful recall of documents and losses deeply embedded in damaged buildings that have emerged out of the once totally oppressive landscape.

Memory and pedagogy could better be enabled through activation rather than preservation. For these active learning functions cannot be promoted in buildings as neutral vessels simply through reduced architectural palettes of materials and colours, as if such places need be free of any associations. Even here, the narrative, audience and commemoration that are required would not necessarily be manifested in the construction process. Teaching history, remembering the power structures and planning that this entailed, and fostering a critical understanding, are all aspects of public engagement that would be elicited in the preparation of the building. Meaning is not fixed, just as these spaces are not static, bound as they are with the culture and identity of the city's inhabitants, whose presence has radically evolved.

Which communities, and how they would be engaged in acts of remembrance, would lie at the heart of any attempt to address architectural conjectures. Ultimately, the lives and communities growing alongside would demonstrate most poignantly a freedom from the weight of this historical bureaucratic morass. In this long era of decolonisation, a new generation of architects, artists and activists is reclaiming a past that was never fully bequeathed to them, and reconsidering these sites. In drawing together stories of everyday sleights and resistance, building could become a project of collecting, collating and collaboration – and not historical rehabilitation alone. To go further, it remains necessary to think against the grain of solely hardship and deprivation, to get past these assumptions, to get 'The Sense of Township Life' in the words of Jacob Dlamini in *Native Nostalgia*:

> We could call townships impoverished, poor, underprivileged and lacking in social services. We could describe them as 'warehouses for labour' or, as a personal favourite, 'previously disadvantaged areas for previously disadvantaged individuals' as many writers and thinkers do. But that litany of emotive adjectives does not tell us anything about how the people who reside in the 300-odd spaces designated as black townships in South Africa actually live. It does not tell us what it is like to live in a township, given its complex place in South Africa's political economy. It definitely does not enlighten us about the place's rhythms and rituals and how inhabitants are constantly making sense of their worlds and adding meaning to their lives.[21]

Correspondingly, 80 Albert Street is a communal site of remembrance that could be visited and recalled by a previously excluded public who would put together in their own way and collectively a critical and reflective space. We would not be able to turn aside but would instead be aided to delve within the corridors that have become an architectural record, the brutal evidence of the relentless administration of apartheid. We would see that dread has been challenged and overcome with individual acts of bravery, by collective mass action and the passage of time. Empty, forlorn, vacated, revoked: this building has not disappeared. Instead of presenting the hopelessness of apartheid planning, we would see how it was faced down with the stoicism in which a nation turned 'matchbox' houses and deprived townships into intimate homes and vibrant neighbourhoods. Public resilience and activism remain robust and visible in Johannesburg. For this building to reflect urban realities, the political legacy of architecture needs to be drawn down into the intricate details of its material production, though even here some things are best left forgotten, and not all spaces need be revisited.

NOTES

1. Mtutuzeli Matshoba, 'To Kill a Man's Pride ...' *Staffrider* 3.1 (February 1980): 5. *Staffrider* was, from the 1970s, an important literary magazine for aspiring writers.
2. Matshoba, 'To Kill a Man's Pride', 5.
3. Matshoba, 'To Kill a Man's Pride', 5.
4. Matshoba, 'To Kill a Man's Pride', 6.
5. Matshoba, 'To Kill a Man's Pride', 6.
6. Matshoba, 'To Kill a Man's Pride', 6.
7. *Cillié Commission of Inquiry into the Riots at Soweto and Elsewhere from June 16, 1976 to February 28, 1977* (Pretoria: Government Printer, 1980), 12.
8. The vast majority of the witnesses speaking to the Commission were from the South African Police Force and West Rand Administration Board, and none were students.
9. *Cillié Commission of Inquiry*, 12–15.
10. *Cillié Commission of Inquiry*, 15–19.
11. Paul la Hausse, *Brewers, Beerhalls and Boycotts: A History of Liquor in South Africa* (Johannesburg: Ravan Press, 1988), 66.
12. *Cillié Commission of Inquiry*, 29.
13. *Cillié Commission of Inquiry*, 30.
14. Can Themba, 'Nude "Pass" Parade', *Drum*, December 1957, 33.
15. Sifiso Mxolisi Ndlovu, *The Soweto Uprisings: Counter-Memories of June 1976* (Johannesburg: Ravan Press, 1998), 123–24.
16. Dominick LaCapra, *Writing History, Writing Trauma* (Baltimore: Johns Hopkins University Press, 2001), 78.
17. Some other sites of historical struggle and liberation that have also been commemorated are the Sharpeville Memorial and Exhibition Centre; the Kliptown Open Air Museum in Soweto; Liliesleaf in Johannesburg; and Freedom Park, Pretoria. Officially, sites along the 'national liberation heritage routes' are understood as serving 'the purpose of collecting, storing, exhibiting and displaying, and distributing (to other liberation heritage sites) relevant liberation history artefacts and archival material'. See Gregory Houston et al., *The Liberation Struggle and Liberation Heritage Sites in South Africa* (Pretoria: Human Sciences Research Council, 2013).
18. See Annie E. Coombes, *History after Apartheid: Visual Culture and Public Memory in a Democratic South Africa* (Durham: Duke University Press, 2003); Angel David Nieves, 'Places of Pain as Tools for Social Justice in the "New" South Africa: Black Heritage Preservation in the "Rainbow" Nation's Townships', in *Places of Pain and Shame: Dealing with 'Difficult Heritage'*, eds William Logan and Keir Reeves (London:

Routledge, 2009), 198–214; and Noeleen Murray and Leslie Witz, *Hostels, Homes, Museum: Memorialising Migrant Labour Pasts in Lwandle, South Africa* (Cape Town: University of Cape Town Press, 2014).

19 Jean Améry, *At the Mind's Limits: Contemplations by a Survivor on Auschwitz and its Realities*, trans. Sidney Rosenfeld and Stella P. Rosenfeld (New York: Schocken Books, 1986), 69–70.

20 Njabulo S. Ndebele, 'Arriving Home? South Africa Beyond Transition and Reconciliation', in *In the Balance: South Africans Debate Reconciliation,* eds Fanie du Toit and Erik Doxtader (Johannesburg: Jacana, 2010), 4.

21 Jacob Dlamini, *Native Nostalgia* (Johannesburg: Jacana, 2009), 119.

REFERENCES

Améry, Jean. *At the Mind's Limits: Contemplations by a Survivor on Auschwitz and its Realities*. Translated by Sidney Rosenfeld and Stella P. Rosenfeld. New York: Schocken Books, 1986.

Ball, James. '"A Munich Situation": Pragmatic Cooperation and the Johannesburg Non-European Affairs Department During the Early Stages of Apartheid'. Master's thesis, University of the Witwatersrand, Johannesburg, 2012.

Carr, W. J. P. *Soweto: Its Creation, Life and Decline*. Johannesburg: South African Institute of Race Relations, 1990.

Caruth, Cathy. *Unclaimed Experience: Trauma, Narrative and History*. Baltimore: Johns Hopkins University Press, 1996.

Chipkin, Clive M. *Johannesburg Style: Architecture & Society 1880s–1960s*. Cape Town: David Philip, 1993.

Cillié Commission of Inquiry into the Riots at Soweto and Elsewhere from June 16, 1976 to February 28, 1977. Pretoria: Government Printer, 1980.

Dlamini, Jacob. *Native Nostalgia*. Johannesburg: Jacana, 2009.

Evans, Ivan. *Bureaucracy and Race: Native Administration in South Africa*. Berkeley: University of California Press, 1997.

Hlongwane, Ali Khangela. 'The Historical Development of the Commemoration of the June 16, 1976 Soweto Students' Uprisings: A Study of Re-representation, Commemoration and Collective Memory'. PhD diss., University of the Witwatersrand, Johannesburg, 2015.

Houston, Gregory, Shepi Mati, Dineo Seabe, Jeff Peires, Denver Webb, Siphesihle Dumisa, Kombi Sausi, Bernard Mbenga, Andrew Manson, and Nedson Pophiwa. *The Liberation Struggle and Liberation Heritage Sites in South Africa*. Pretoria: Human Sciences Research Council, 2013.

Huyssen, Andreas. *Present Pasts: Urban Palimpsests and the Politics of Memory*. Stanford: Stanford University Press, 2003.

LaCapra, Dominick. *Writing History, Writing Trauma*. Baltimore: Johns Hopkins University Press, 2001.

La Hausse, Paul. *Brewers, Beerhalls and Boycotts: A History of Liquor in South Africa*. Johannesburg: Ravan Press, 1988.

Matshoba, Mtutuzeli. *Call Me Not a Man*. Johannesburg: Ravan Press, 1979.

Matshoba, Mtutuzeli. 'To Kill a Man's Pride ...'. *Staffrider* 3.1 (February 1980): 4–6.

Maylam, Paul. 'The Rise and Decline of Urban Apartheid in South Africa'. *African Affairs* 89.354 (January 1990): 57–84.

Maylam, Paul. 'Explaining the Apartheid City: 20 Years of South African Urban Historiography'. *Journal of Southern African Studies* 21.1 (March 1995): 19–38.

Ndebele, Njabulo. 'Memory, Metaphor, and the Triumph of Narrative'. In *Negotiating the Past: The Making of Memory in South Africa*, edited by Sarah Nuttall and Carli Coetzee, 19–28. Oxford: Oxford University Press, 1998.

Ndebele, Njabulo. 'Arriving Home? South Africa Beyond Transition and Reconciliation'. In *In the Balance: South Africans Debate Reconciliation*, edited by Fanie du Toit and Erik Doxtader, 55–73. Johannesburg: Jacana, 2010.

Ndlovu, Sifiso Mxolisi. *The Soweto Uprisings: Counter-Memories of June 1976*. Johannesburg: Ravan Press, 1998.

Pohlandt-McCormick, Helena. '"I Saw a Nightmare ..." Doing Violence to Memory: The Soweto Uprising, June 16, 1976'. Accessed 15 June 2017, http://www.gutenberg-e.org/pohlandt-mccormick/index.html.

Posel, Deborah. *The Making of Apartheid 1948–1961*. Oxford: Clarendon Press, 1991.

Posel, Deborah. 'Whiteness and Power in the South African Civil Service: Paradoxes of the Apartheid State'. *Journal of Southern African Studies* 25.1 (March 1999): 99–119.

Savage, Michael. 'The Imposition of Pass Laws on the African Population in South Africa 1916–1984'. *African Affairs* 85 (1986): 181–205.

Themba, Can. 'Nude "Pass" Parade'. *Drum* (December 1957): 28–33.

Young, James E. 'The Texture of Meaning: Holocaust Memorials and Meaning'. In *Writing and Rewriting the Holocaust: Narrative and the Consequences of Interpretation*. Bloomington: Indiana University Press, 1988.

INTERVIEW

Matshoba, Mtutuzeli. Personal interview with author. Johannesburg, 20 September 2018.

8 INDIAN TRADING, ART DECO AND URBAN MODERNITY IN A SEGREGATED TOWN: JUBILEE HOUSE IN KRUGERSDORP

ARIANNA LISSONI AND ROSHAN DADOO

The address is 36 Commissioner Street, Krugersdorp. The building standing on the corner of Commissioner and Market streets, two busy thoroughfares in Krugersdorp's Central Business District (CBD), is a tyre shop and garage called 'Solly's' (figure 8.1). This Art Deco building was erected in 1940 by Kallenbach, Kennedy and Furner, an influential architectural firm in early Johannesburg with links to the Indian nationalist movement. Jubilee House, as it used to be known, was once regarded as the 'jewel of Krugersdorp'. For most of the twentieth century, it was owned by one of the town's wealthiest Indian families, the Dadoos, who conducted business in Krugersdorp for at least three generations.

Across the road from Jubilee House is the south-eastern corner of Krugersdorp's original Market Square and Town Hall, one of its oldest architectural attractions and the site of the local municipality. Krugersdorp was founded in 1887 as a white mining town approximately 30 kilometres west of Johannesburg, following the discovery of gold on the Witwatersrand in the 1880s. It was named after Paul Kruger, the Boer leader and president of what was then the South African Republic. The Mogale City Local Municipality today incorporates what used to be the white town of Krugersdorp; the townships of Munsieville (built in 1912 to house Krugersdorp's African residents

Figure 8.1. Solly's (formerly Jubilee House), corner of Market and Commissioner streets, Krugersdorp, 2015. Photograph by Arianna Lissoni

who had been forcibly removed from the Old Location and relocated to the new site outside the town); Kagiso and Azaadville (built under apartheid's Group Areas legislation to accommodate Africans and Indians respectively, located even further away from white areas across the West Rand); and surrounding commercial farming areas such as Magaliesburg, Tarlton and Hekpoort. While the new expanded democratic municipality has taken the name of Kgosi Mogale of the Batswana ba Po – who had inhabited the area until Mzilikazi's Ndebele and the Voortrekkers broke up their polity in the 1820s and 1830s – Afrikaner right-wing organisations have so far successfully resisted the renaming of Krugersdorp itself.[1]

THREE GENERATIONS OF DADOOS

Indian traders started arriving in Krugersdorp from the 1890s, attracted by the business opportunities opened up by the booming mining economy of the Witwatersrand. Among them was Mahomed Mamoojee (M. M.) Dadoo, a young Muslim immigrant from Kholvad, near the port city of Surat in

Gujarat. He came to South Africa as a 'passenger Indian', following the path of indentured labourers who crossed the Indian Ocean to work in different parts of the British empire in the late nineteenth and early twentieth centuries. As the historian Thomas Metcalf argues, Indians were at the forefront of the exploitation of resources of Britain's colonial empire, whether they were recruited as indentured labourers or migrated because of trading opportunities opening up in other colonial territories.[2]

In spite of the restrictions on Indian trading and residence in the Transvaal, Indians managed not only to obtain a foothold in many towns scattered along the Reef but also to expand and prosper, not least because they supplied cheap goods and extended credit.[3] After the establishment of the Union of South Africa in 1910, M. M. Dadoo was able to bypass anti-Indian legislation that prevented Indians from owning immovable property and to buy a number of stands in the Krugersdorp municipality. Among these properties was Jubilee House, where Dadoo opened a general dealership. Over the decades, he turned the business into a sophisticated clothing retailer called Dadoo's, importing goods from as far away as England and Japan. The store attracted the custom not only of mineworkers – both black and white – in the town, but also of Boer farmers and patrons at the upper end of the market, thus competing with white shopkeepers who 'considered whites to be their privileged clientele'.[4]

Initially erected in 1898, the original Jubilee House had been a two-storey Victorian structure. But in 1940, this was completely overhauled and remade into the Art Deco building that still stands today. This had been the wish of M. M. Dadoo, the head of the family, a few years before he died in 1944. His descendants continued to own and run the store for another five decades, through the entire apartheid era and into democracy, as he had ensured that his estate would remain in the hands of his descendants, through a trust, for seven generations after his death. The family finally sold the business in 2005, as no family member was willing to take on the running of the shop; this was due partly to the declining economy in Krugersdorp but also to the provisions of the will, which allowed for no individual ownership or accrual of wealth as all profits went into the trust.

M. M. Dadoo was the father of Dr Yusuf Mohamed Dadoo (1909–1983), a prominent leader of the South African Indian Congress and of the Communist Party, and one of Krugersdorp's most famous sons. In the democratic era, the town's hospital, formerly known as Paardekraal,⁵ was renamed Dr Yusuf Dadoo Hospital. M. M. Dadoo had planned for his first-born son, Yusuf, to join him and eventually take over the business. Although he chose a life of politics over business, young Yusuf, like the other family members, did his share helping in the shop after returning to South Africa in 1926 from India, where he studied at the prestigious Aligarh College. Soon, however, he clashed with his father: he wished to continue studying, and even helped workers in the shop organise a strike against working on Sundays. Eventually, he convinced his father to send him to university overseas, on condition that he studied medicine (and not law, as Yusuf wanted).⁶ Jubilee House was thus a prominent space in Dr Dadoo's formative years, and holds a central place in the history of the Dadoo family more broadly: at least three generations of Dadoos were born and grew up in the family home at the back of the shop (fronting Joubert Street) and contributed their share to the family business.

If the Dadoos' family history is inextricably tied to Jubilee House, so is the history of Indian trading on the Witwatersrand. These interconnected histories need to be understood against the backdrop of the unfolding of South Africa's capitalist economy and the segregationist state. Dadoo's shop is emblematic of the resistance of Indian traders to racial laws that sought to confine Indian commercial and residential spaces to 'Asiatic bazaars' and other racially segregated locations in the first half of the twentieth century. Indian traders responded to legislation designed to restrict their trading and residential rights by themselves making ingenious use of the law to both evade and to actively resist these measures.

While Jubilee House does not fall into the category of oppressive buildings, it may be viewed as a site of defiance against the segregationist (and later apartheid) spatial planning and socio-political order. The history of the building – including a reading of its architectural aesthetics – provides a unique window not only into Dr Yusuf Dadoo's family history, but also into the socio-economic forces that contributed to the making of modern South Africa, the development of South African Indian politics, and the character of urban life on the Witwatersrand during the segregation era. Its reconstruction as a modern Art Deco building in 1940 coincides with the birth of what the social anthropologist Parvathi Raman has described as a new 'political consciousness that combined a transnational Indian identity with a firm commitment to the fight for rights of citizenship in the South African state', which Yusuf Dadoo came to embody.[7] The architectural choices of the building's owners – which we have reconstructed here through photographs, drawings on business letterheads in the archives, and oral histories – reflect a shift from a plea for Indians to be accepted and justly treated as British subjects migrating from one part of the empire to another, to an assertion of a modern Indian identity linked to nationalist claims for full citizenship rights in South Africa.

Roshan Dadoo is M. M. Dadoo's granddaughter and Dr Yusuf Dadoo's daughter with Winnie Kramer. She was born in exile in London, after both her parents left South Africa in the early 1960s, and grew up hearing stories of the legendary family shop from her father and other family members who were passing through the city. When she was able to come to South Africa for the first time in 1993, one of the highlights of her visit was a tour of the family store in Krugersdorp.[8] By then, the vibrant character and bustling activity of Krugersdorp's CBD had been killed by the gradual decline of the gold mining industry and the effects of apartheid's forced removals, and was to be given the final blow by the arrival of big shopping malls, eventually leading the family to sell the shop. At the time of her visit, it was still owned and operated by the family, although none of them lived in the town any longer. By the 1980s they had all been forced to move to the racially segregated township built to house Indians from Krugersdorp and the West Rand, whose very name, Azaadville – from the Hindustani word *azad*, meaning 'free' – added insult to injury.

'ASIATIC BAZAARS'

M. M. Dadoo was born in Kholvad, in Gujarat, on 19 May 1881 and arrived in South Africa as a passenger Indian via the port of Lourenço Marques in 1896.[9] Mamoojee was only about 15 years old at the time, which makes his foresight and business acumen over the next decades all the more remarkable. In addition to Gujarati, he could speak and write in English. In all probability, therefore, he had attended school before leaving Kholvad.[10] The year of his marriage to his first wife, Aysha, also from Kholvad, is 1894, and while it is possible that he arrived in South Africa with his wife, it is more likely that she joined him later, as was the more common practice at the time.[11] The couple had a daughter, Fatima, who was born in 1902 in Kholvad. Mamoojee visited India in 1900 and returned to the then Transvaal in 1902, at the end of the South African

War; Aysha and Fatima probably followed him to South Africa around this time. But in 1907 the couple were divorced, and Mamoojee married Fatima Ahmed Wajee (born in Kholvad on 24 July 1891) in Kholvad in 1908.

M. M. Dadoo had first settled in Klerksdorp, a white farming town west of Potchefstroom that experienced dramatic – if short-lived – growth following the discovery of gold in the area in 1885. Here, M. M. Dadoo is said to have worked as an assistant in the shop of another Indian from Kholvad, most likely a relative. The common pattern was for one family member to immigrate first, and to be later followed by others, who would work for their relative until they could start their own business. From Klerksdorp, M. M. Dadoo moved to Krugersdorp either in 1898 or 1904;[12] there, he worked for Amod Ebrahim Chotabhai, a fellow Khovadian who was a draper and general merchant in the town.[13]

Krugersdorp was at the time a booming, if violent and unstable, mining town, whose early history has been researched by the historian Charles Dugmore. In the nineteenth century, Indians had been prohibited from owning land or voting in either of the two Boer republics. The Coolies, Arabs and Other Asiatics Act, Law 3 of 1885, prevented Indians from owning land in the South African Republic, whose statute explicitly rejected the equality of its white and black inhabitants either in the Church or the state. In Krugersdorp, Indians were first accommodated in the African location until a separate Indian location was established in 1897 next to Burgershoop, an area for the settlement of bywoners, or landless white farmers. According to Dugmore, compared to its counterparts in small towns on the Rand, Krugersdorp's Indian location was in a relatively favourable commercial position as it was close to the railways, the white miners' houses, as well as the white middle-class suburb of Luipaardsvlei. Yet, as Dugmore notes:

> The more successful and ambitious Indian shopkeepers had their eye on the Market Square, a prime commercial space in the heart of town. This is where the middle- and working-class residents and the local farmers did most of their shopping, and where the real money was to be made.[14]

It was here, close to the Market Square, that Chotabhai began trading on the corner of Commissioner and Rissik Streets and opposite Jubilee House, renting stands 375 and 376 from a certain James Henry Smit, a clerk in the post office. From 1902, A. E. Chotabhai's business was regularly advertised in the pages of the *Rand Daily Mail* as selling 'the cheapest groceries, drapery, clothing, boots and hardware'.[15]

Another surviving trace of Chotabhai's business is a letterhead which M. M. Dadoo used to enquire from the Registrar of Asiatics about his registration certificate in 1908, on the eve of travelling to India.[16] Like many other immigrants, M. M. Dadoo undertook frequent trips back to India and retained a special link and interest in Kholvad. He was one of the founders of the Madressa Islamia Anjuman of Kholvad, a trust formally established in 1914 and still in existence today, promoting educational and welfare activities in Kholvad.

In 1904 Dadoo and Chotabhai entered into a memorandum of agreement, according to which Dadoo was appointed salesman in Chotabhai's business, initially for a period of two years.[17] According to later testimony by M. M. Dadoo, he became a partner in 1906.[18] Chotabhai died in 1912, leaving Dadoo as the sole partner.[19] By now the latter had married Fatima, who, having disembarked from the S.S. *Karoa* in Delagoa Bay (today's Maputo Bay) in July 1909, arrived in South Africa pregnant with their first child.[20] Yusuf Mohamed Dadoo was born two months later in Krugersdorp, in what was then the Colony of Transvaal.[21]

During the years of the British colonial administration in the aftermath of the South African War, Krugersdorp's white English-speaking commercial and professional elite, who had come to southern Africa from Britain and other parts of Europe, was able to exert its control over municipalities and to use this power to remove Indians from towns through legislative methods. These shopkeepers competed with Indian traders for customers, particularly at the upper end of the market. This commercial rivalry had a profound impact on the 'urban and social fabric' of the town and ultimately 'helped "make" Krugersdorp', as Dugmore argues.[22] In the aftermath of the South African War, the Milner administration passed legislation for the establishment of specially designated 'Asiatic bazaars', to which Indian residential and commercial spaces were to be confined.[23] Moreover, the 1908 Precious and Base Metals Act (known as the 'Gold Law') prohibited any 'coloured person' from acquiring rights to gold claims or to reside or trade in a proclaimed area (which in practice meant the entire Witwatersrand).

These renewed restrictions were steeped in colonial discourses and imagery that associated Indians with infectious diseases for which they had to be 'quarantined' and isolated. These discourses were related to broader colonial fears – what Maynard Swanson calls the 'sanitation syndrome' – that drove the government's policy of urban segregation.[24] In spite of the restrictive measures that Indian traders in the Transvaal encountered, many were able to prosper commercially, thanks mainly to their extended credit business strategy and 'polite treatment of customers'. Their success was also the outcome, at least in part, of the divisions that existed among Krugersdorp's white community.[25]

M. M. Dadoo had direct experience of these restrictions and racist attitudes. In 1913 he had to appear as a witness in a court case which saw his landlord, Smit, charged with contravening the 1908 Gold Law for letting his property to Indians and allowing them to reside there. As the *Rand Daily Mail* reported, the property in question stood on a prominent business site and the case raised 'the knotty point of Asiatic occupation in Krugersdorp'.[26] In July 1913, the premises of the business were inspected by a police detective accompanied by a sanitary inspector, who 'found nine adult Asiatics and three children in the sleeping compartments' – suggesting fears of overcrowding typical of colonial sanitation discourses. M. M. Dadoo explained in his testimony that these were his store assistants, bookkeeper and cook, as well as three caretakers who occupied one of the rooms following a recent burglary.[27] Over the years, several improvements had been undertaken with the owner's consent, with a number of rooms erected on the two stands.[28] Smit's defence lawyer argued that Chotabhai was entitled to have his assistants in his store resident on the premises, and the case was adjourned indefinitely.[29]

In spite of the favourable outcome for M. M. Dadoo, it is likely that the experience prompted him to look for new, more secure premises for his business, which was apparently very successful. An article in the *Rand Daily Mail* about a burglary at Chotabhai and Dadoo's store in 1912 mentions an amount of approximately £330 being stolen, with the reporter commenting:

> The sum of money mentioned may sound extravagant when associated with the every-day business of an unpretentious Indian in the dorp, but from enquiries I have reason to understand that the members of the firm are wealthy and they do a ready cash trade equal to that of any two other stores in the town.[30]

Thanks to capital he had accumulated while running Chotabhai's affairs, augmented by several loans, in the years that followed Dadoo was able to buy a number of municipal stands in Krugersdorp.[31] The land was transferred into the name of a limited liability company. As the law considered a company to be a legal entity distinct from its members, registering land in the name of Dadoo Ltd allowed him to circumvent legislation preventing Indians from owning land in the Transvaal, as well as section 130 of the 1908 Gold Law, according to which 'a coloured person could not acquire any rights whatever to gold claims or stands in a proclaimed field'.[32]

DADOO LTD

Among the properties M. M. Dadoo purchased was Jubilee House, then a two-storey building located on stand 370. The original Jubilee House, built in 1898, was a wooden structure with a cast-iron balcony, and housed a draper and outfitter shop owned by MacLoskie and Te Water. Dugmore notes that this business was liquidated in 1912, possibly as a result of competition from Chotabhai's store across the road.[33] The date 1898 inscribed on the top pediment of the building marked Queen Victoria's Diamond jubilee; this is where Jubilee House most likely got its name.[34] As Dugmore explains, 'Dadoo's wealth attracted the attention and resentment of white shopkeepers', and 'was considered the nemesis of the Krugersdorp Chamber of Commerce'.[35] This rivalry resulted in a second court case in 1919 in which the Krugersdorp municipality tried to have the sale of certain municipal stands to Dadoo Ltd reversed. The *Municipality of Krugersdorp versus Dadoo Ltd and Others* turned out to be a landmark case for properties bought by Indians through companies before 1919,[36] going all the way to the Appellate Division of the Supreme Court, where Chief Justice Innes ultimately ruled in Dadoo's favour in 1920.

The municipality had initially successfully argued that Dadoo Ltd was created with the purpose of evading anti-Indian legislation that prohibited Indians from owning fixed property. It further contended that stands in the Krugersdorp township were originally granted under the Transvaal Gold Law as leasehold stands subject to the payment of monthly licences and that the owners of stand 171, Pieter Johannes Fouche and Christoffen Rudolf Howell, held this subject to a prohibition to transfer on their title deed to any 'coloured person'. Nevertheless, Fouche and Howell had transferred the stand to Dadoo Ltd in 1916. According to the legal papers about this intricate case, M. M. Dadoo and his family were, at the time, living on this stand. In December 1919, Supreme Court Justice J. W. Wessels ordered that the transfer of the stand to Dadoo Ltd be set aside for being *in fraudem legis*, meaning with the fraudulent or malicious intention of evading the law: in spite of its being registered in the name of a business, the property was virtually owned by M. M. Dadoo. Wessels found that 'it is quite clear that the company [Dadoo Ltd] was deliberately floated by Dadoo to bring about indirectly a state of affairs which the law would not tolerate to do directly'.[37]

The Transvaal British Indian Association, which Gandhi helped establish in 1903 and was later renamed the Transvaal Indian Congress, protested against the judgement.[38] In 1920, the case reached the highest court of the land at the time, the Appellate Division of the Supreme Court in Bloemfontein. M. M. Dadoo had to apply for a special permit to travel to the hearing, as Indians were not allowed to own land or reside anywhere in the Orange Free State province, and needed a pass to visit provinces outside that of their registration.[39] Here, Chief Justice Innes reversed the previous ruling in favour of Dadoo. He argued in his judgment that by buying properties in the name of a limited liability company, Dadoo had not taken advantage of a mere technicality to avoid the restrictions of the law but had in fact done 'something different in law and substance from what the statute prohibited. And he is entitled to the advantage of that position.'[40]

M. M. Dadoo indeed used this seminal judgment to his advantage. In 1924 he registered a new company, the Krugersdorp Land Company Ltd, to manage and procure new properties. Along with Dadoo Ltd, the company took care of his landed assets, while another company, M. M. Dadoo & Sons Ltd, managed the commercial side of the business. The minute book of the Krugersdorp Land Company Ltd, which is still in possession of the family, chronicles how the company continued to procure and purchase properties in Krugersdorp's CBD. White directors and chairmen were appointed to front the company, which was governed by a board;[41] moreover, numerous loans were taken out with individual moneylenders in order to buy new properties. Capital for these additional land purchases was also raised by mortgaging and re-mortgaging existing properties through the banks. By 1931, the Krugersdorp Land Company Ltd owned numerous stands, all part of the block where Jubilee House stood, and which came to be known as 'Dadoo's Block'.[42]

According to the 1932 census, 424 Indians were then living in Krugersdorp, with an estimated number of 30 Indian-owned shops in Krugersdorp 'proper', and another 12 in Burgershoop. In this period, M. M. Dadoo had become the chairman of the Krugersdorp Indian Association. This had been set up to represent Indian views on the Transvaal Asiatic Land Tenure Act Commission of 1933 and to ask for more land for residential and business purposes for Indians in the Transvaal. In his testimony to the commission, Dadoo argued that, where Indians occupied property, its value had gone up rather than depreciated, as 'these buildings had been sold at a considerably higher price than before'. At the time of the commission, the value of properties owned by 'Asiatic companies' in Krugersdorp was estimated at £32 000, with Dadoo's Block alone valued at £22 000.[43] Moreover, a few years earlier, the Krugersdorp Indian community had contributed £400 for the addition of a ward for Indians at the local hospital (renamed Dr Yusuf Dadoo Hospital after the end of apartheid), which they would otherwise not have had access to. By 1933, 22 people were employed to work in Jubilee House, and 75 per cent of the trade was with whites. In explaining the reasons for the success of Indian traders to the commission, Dadoo referred to their 'polite methods' and the extension of credit to customers.[44]

'THE MODERN STORE'

Figure 8.2. Jubilee House, c. 1925. To this day, a copy of the photograph hangs in the 'office of the manager' in Solly's shop, the only trace of its former owners

This photograph of the original Jubilee House, taken before its 1940 renovation, is clearly staged, with everyone looking towards the camera (figure 8.2). It is not known who took the photograph, or what year this was. Given the Union Jacks and bunting decorating the balcony, the photo may have been taken on the occasion of the 1925 royal visit to South Africa: Edward VIII, then Prince of Wales, visited Krugersdorp on 25 June where he was welcomed by a servicemen's parade.[45] Standing on the balcony are a number of Indian men, who probably include the shop owner, M. M. Dadoo. By this time, 'M. M. Dadoo' was a 'Wholesale and Retail Merchant and Direct Importer' of clothing and other goods, as indicated by the shop sign, partly hidden by a tree.

Jubilee House's original architecture was in many ways an example of the British Imperial trends in vogue at the time, and its appropriation reflects the ambivalent relationship of Indian colonial subjects with the British empire. (By now, Gandhi had returned to India, where the struggle for independence was gaining momentum under the leadership of the Indian National Congress.) In the late nineteenth and early twentieth centuries, Indian colonial subjects who crossed the Indian Ocean became imperial citizens. However, Metcalf argues that the promise of 'imperial citizenship' and expectations of

Figure 8.3. Jubilee House, 1993. Photograph by Roshan Dadoo

equality were shattered by the experience of discrimination, particularly in settler colonies such as South Africa, where 'Indians came to imagine their own identities in new ways'.[46]

The new Jubilee House building that M. M. Dadoo constructed in 1940 was a remarkable example of South African architecture, resembling an Art Deco-styled ocean liner cruising through Krugersdorp (figure 8.3). As such, it conveyed optimism in the fortunes of the town, while also signalling the à la mode fashions to be found within the store. Constructed on the cusp of Art Deco as a popular architectural style in Johannesburg, and the emerging International Style, Jubilee House's modernity, glamour, sophistication and celebration of exuberant capitalism reflect the Art Deco spirit of the age. Federico Freschi's work on Art Deco in Johannesburg shows how its development and rapid spread in the 1930s was shaped by accelerated urbanisation following the economic boom after the abandonment of the gold standard under the Pact Government.[47] This produced a new notion of what it meant to be a white South African, simultaneously nationalist and imperialist, and found public expression in large-scale architectural projects such as the Astor Mansions building.[48] As Freschi notes, within 'a relatively short space of time, the stylistic novelties that it [Astor Mansions] embraced were to become common currency, not only in Johannesburg but throughout the gold-mining towns to the east and west of the city'.[49] Jubilee House is thus an example of the ubiquitous spread of Art Deco in this period as a way of articulating South Africa's modern capitalist identity. What is remarkable about this particular building is the appropriation of Art Deco's self-conscious modernity by an Indian trading family, conveying their permanency within the white town centre and economy and, by extension, that of other Indian communities in South Africa's towns and cities.

M. M. Dadoo died in 1944, a few years after completion of this large construction project. His unusual will bequeathed his properties and business to his wife and children, though not as individual benefactors: instead, he set up a trust in their name. The will specified that his estate could neither be divided nor sold for seven subsequent generations of Dadoos, clearly a statement that Dadoos would remain in Krugersdorp for a few hundred years.[50]

The architects of Jubilee House were Kallenbach, Kennedy and Furner, a firm that had set up a partnership in Johannesburg in 1928. According to the architect Clive Chipkin, Kallenbach and Kennedy's (as the firm was known before Arthur Stanley Furner joined) 'was a major nursery of architectural talent'.⁵¹ Hermann Kallenbach, a Prussian-born Jewish architect who had studied in Germany, was a close friend and associate of Gandhi for over 40 years. During Gandhi's time in South Africa, the two lived together for a period under communal living arrangements, and Tolstoy Farm was established with Kallenbach's help. After participating in the 1913 passive resistance campaign, Kallenbach was arrested together with Gandhi and incidentally imprisoned in Krugersdorp.⁵²

While it is difficult to imagine what possessed a deeply religious Muslim Indian trader, who had performed hajj in 1935–1936, to create a daring structure at the cutting edge of *l'esprit nouveau* in the middle of a small town in the Transvaal, these entanglements may provide some explanation for the choice of architects on his part. Architecturally, Jubilee House reflects the *Zerohour* manifesto issued in 1933 by *Le Group Transvaal*, as the architect Le Corbusier named the Modern Movement in the Transvaal. The manifesto oozes colonial confidence in the future: 'The contemporary spirit is abroad ... we should regard ourselves as drawing near to a remote future rather than receding from a historic past – indeed all living art is the history of the future.'⁵³ As Chipkin points out, this suggests the influence of the Italian Futurist Manifesto of 1909 (many of whose signatories became ardent supporters of fascism). Indeed, Furner himself was a leading exponent of the Modern Movement and authored a series of important papers in which 'for the first time in Johannesburg the name Le Corbusier was publicly mentioned'.⁵⁴ He came to South Africa from England in 1925 to take up a post at the newly established Department of Architecture at Wits University, which he left in 1928 to join the practice of Kallenbach and Kennedy.

The new Jubilee House building was officially opened on 28 June 1940 at a ceremony involving the then mayor of Krugersdorp, E. Gitsham. A three-quarter-spread newspaper advert in *The Star* announced the opening of a 'Magnificent New Department Store for Krugersdorp', with a detailed description of the new building and its interior, and accompanying photographs (figure 8.4). The name 'Dadoo's' was engraved in the marble flooring at the entrance and lettered above the outside window displays. A set of teak doors led into the shop, which featured parquet flooring, an elegant staircase with a wooden bannister leading to the upper-floor showroom, and a balustrade looking down on to the central ground-floor area. On the ground floor

Figure 8.4. 'Magnificent New Department Store for Krugersdorp – M. M. Dadoo & Sons, Ltd.', *The Star*, 28 June 1940. Courtesy Roshan Dadoo

was the ladies' department, while the basement contained menswear. Interior fittings included teak shelves with sliding glass fronts, glass and stainless-steel counters, showcases 'of the latest design' and 'handsome modern chromium steel furniture'.[55]

Jubilee House was, as *The Star* advertisement declared, 'Without doubt one of the most up-to-date structures not only on the West Rand, but in South Africa.' In his speech at the official opening, M. M. Dadoo proclaimed his faith in modernity and a prosperous future:

> It has been a pleasure for me ... to have been in a position to erect this building in Krugersdorp, a building which we feel is in keeping with the progress of Krugersdorp and the West Rand ... We welcome all who care to inspect our wares and to deal with us, and I wish to assure you all that we shall continue to cater for the public of Krugersdorp as we have done in the past, with courteous and efficient service.[56]

This ethos was embraced by his descendants, as is evident from letterhead designs over the years. By the 1970s it boasted a metallic green image of the new Jubilee House building crowned by the slogan 'Dadoo's – The Modern Store'.

IMMIGRATION AND THE MODERN IMAGINARY

Jubilee House simultaneously symbolises the struggle against segregation and the fight for the right to a cosmopolitan city by the black petit bourgeoisie and – at least as consumers – by the working class. The modernist mania that followed the rising price of gold in a growing economy was not only manifest in construction, but also in a frenzy of retail consumerism that was not confined to the white population but was increasingly marketed to black customers. The sociologist and historian Belinda Bozzoli relates how migrant women from Phokeng who had jobs in the cities brought stylish furniture and fashion back with them to the rural areas.[57] Similarly, although the majority of Dadoo's customers were whites, the store sold fashionable clothing and other goods to mineworkers who shopped at month-end and before going home to rural areas. The dashing style drawn from Hollywood movies – Homburg hats and double-breasted suits – would have brought some semblance of personhood and dignity to ultra-exploited black migrant workers. Presiding over a modern retail experience as customers entered the plate-glass doors must also have carried some éclat for the canny immigrant businessman who owned the store.

Jubilee House clearly provides an interesting example of the contradictory urban experience described by the geographer John Rennie Short: 'At a fundamental level there is something inherently fascistic about architecture and urban planning, and something both inhibiting and liberating about city life.'[58] The forward-looking design of Dadoo's was not simply the appropriation of a colonial aspirational style, and nor was it the subjugation to colonial rule. Instead, it embodies the determination of migrants to proclaim a prosperous future through claiming central urban space, and memorialises the court challenge to the segregationist state's removal of Indian traders and residents from Krugersdorp's CBD.

This spirit of modernity imbued the political culture of the times, with the South African Indian Congress, the African National Congress and, indeed, the Congress Movement in India all embracing an imaginary of national liberation, demanding self-determination and full citizenship rights. A glance through the shop window of Dadoo's reveals that within this paradigm there was a mix of urban, rural, migrant, racial, gender and class identities, all permeating the political resistance of the day. Nevertheless, this Art Deco building is symbolic of the urbanisation of Indian traders: in staking a cultural and political claim, they demonstrated a preparedness to organise and fight to live and work in the midst of a malevolent white town centre.

POSTSCRIPT

As we have noted, the Krugersdorp CBD declined along with the waning of the mining industry. However, the arrival of Key West shopping mall just outside the town signalled a further change in fortune for city centre businesses. This project had been agreed to by the municipality prior to the first democratic local elections in 1996, when the council's large right-wing Afrikaner component attempted to shore up the value of their land. Like other satellite towns along the Rand, Mogale City is home to many local and cross-border migrants, particularly Somalis and Ethiopians: some are in transit as they try to make their way to Johannesburg, while others end up staying. Indeed, current patterns of migration, for example Somalis, share many similarities with the early history of Indian traders: starting a joint business outside the city centres, graduating to a single-owned business, living on the shop premises, and often bringing family members to join them in their venture. The next Jubilee House may well appear in the Johannesburg suburb of Mayfair, currently known as Little Mogadishu.

NOTES

1   'What's in a Town's Name?', *News24*, 6 August 2000, accessed 18 October 2019, https://archive.fo/20120904040544/http://www.news24.com/xArchive/Archive/Whats-in-a-towns-name-20000806.
2   Thomas R. Metcalf, *Imperial Connections: India in the Indian Ocean Arena, 1860-1920* (Berkeley: University of California Press, 2007), 2.
3   See Charles Dugmore, 'Dadoo Limited versus Krugersdorp Town Council, 1920: A Case Study in Justice, Policy and Change in a Colonial Context', unpublished paper, colloquium on Justice, Policy and Change in Southern Africa, University of the Witwatersrand, Johannesburg, 3 October 1998; and Charles Dugmore, 'The Making of

Krugersdorp, 1887–1923' (PhD diss., University of the Witwatersrand, Johannesburg, 2006).

4   Dugmore, 'Dadoo Limited versus Krugersdorp Town Council', 5.
5   Paardekraal was the name of the farm where, in 1880, a group of Boers pledged to end British rule, following Britain's annexation of the Transvaal in 1877. Krugersdorp developed on the site.
6   After being awarded the Triple Qualification (TC) in Medicine, Surgery and Midwifery by the Royal College of Surgeons of Edinburgh and the Royal College of Physicians of Glasgow, Dr Dadoo returned to South Africa and moved to Johannesburg, where he began his medical practice in the central suburb of Pageview, later moving to 47 End Street in Doornfontein.
7   Parvathi Raman, 'Yusuf Dadoo: A Son of South Africa', in *South Africa's 1940s: A World of Possibilities*, eds Saul Dubow and Alan Jeeves (Cape Town: Double Storey, 2005), 227.
8   Roshan Dadoo took several photographs of Jubilee House during her 1993 visit, including figure 8.3. The most recent image of the shop (figure 8.1) was taken during a site visit by Arianna Lissoni in 2015 while accompanied by Yusuf Dadoo, a grandson of M. M. Dadoo. The authors wish to thank Yusuf Dadoo for his support, and Goolam Vahed and Pamila Gupta for feedback on this chapter.
9   See folder on Mahomed Mamoojee Dadoo, National Archives of South Africa (NASA), IND, 777, E13900. Some documents have Bombay (Mumbai) as his place of birth.
10 By 1880 there were four *maktabs*, or primary schools, in Kholvad. Madressa Anjuman Islamia Kholvad South Africa Est. 1914, Timeline of Events, accessed 29 October 2019, http://www.kholvad.org.za/timeline-of-events/.
11 Many wives of immigrants remained behind in India, so split households were a common pattern. See Uma Dhupelia-Mesthrie, 'Split Households: Indian Wives, Cape Town Husbands and Immigration Laws, 1900s to 1940s', *South African Historical Journal* 66.4 (2014): 635–55.
12 M. M. Dadoo's 1903 registration permit has Klerksdorp as his place of residence. See Permit, Mahomed Mamoojee Dadoo, Klerksdorp, 21 April 1903, NASA, IND, 777, E13900. Dugmore, on the other hand, dates M. M. Dadoo's arrival in Krugersdorp to 1898.
13 Chotabhai is remembered in some oral accounts by members of the Dadoo family either as a cousin or brother of Mamoojee. See Dugmore, 'Dadoo Limited versus Krugersdorp', 11. Yusuf Dadoo, M. M. Dadoo's grandson, suggests that Chotabhai may have been married to the sister of M. M.'s first wife, Aysha, making them stepbrothers,

which possibly explains how he joined Chotabhai in Krugersdorp. Yusuf Dadoo, interview with Arianna Lissoni and Roshan Dadoo, Johannesburg, 14 April 2015.

14 Dugmore, 'The Making of Krugersdorp', 287.
15 See, for example, *Rand Daily Mail*, 10 October 1902.
16 According to the Asiatics Registration Act of 1906, Indians had to register with the Register of Asiatics and carry a thumb-printed certificate of identity. This resulted in the first *satyagraha* campaign, led by Mohandas Gandhi. In 1921, M. M. Dadoo wrote to the registrar of Asiatics in Pretoria, requesting to change his registration certificate to one with a signature instead of a thumbprint. See Letter from M. M. Dadoo to the Registrar of Asiatics, 17 August 1921, NASA, IND, 777, E13900.
17 The memorandum, a copy of which is still in possession of the Dadoo family, granted Dadoo one fourth of the value of the net business profits at the expiration of the agreement, as well as one fourth in shares from any profits arising from the expansion of the business and acquisition of landed property, but did not give Dadoo any rights to deal with Chotabhai's property other than as a salesman in the business. Memorandum of Agreement, A. E. Chotabhai & M. M. Dadoo, Krugersdorp, 1 February 1904, Dadoo family private papers.
18 See 'Asiatics in Towns: Test Case at Krugersdorp: Important Questions Pending', *Rand Daily Mail*, 20 August 1913.
19 'Asiatics in Towns'.
20 See Principal I. R. Officer, Immigration Restriction Department, Port Natal, to the Registrar of Asiatics, Colonial Secretary Office, Pretoria, 3 July 1909, NASA, IND, 777, E13900; also, entry record for Fatima, wife of Mahomed Mamoojee Dadoo, 11 July 1909, NASA, IND, 777, E13900.
21 Yusuf was the first of nine surviving children, five boys and four girls, with four others dying between 1913 and 1921, some possibly being victims of the Spanish influenza. See Folder on Mahomed Mamoojee Dadoo, NASA, IND, 777, E13900.
22 Dugmore, 'The Making of Krugersdorp', 281.
23 Dugmore, 'The Making of Krugersdorp', 291.
24 Dugmore, 'The Making of Krugersdorp', chapter five; and Maynard W. Swanson, 'The Sanitation Syndrome: Bubonic Plague and Urban Native Policy in the Cape Colony, 1900–1909', *Journal of African History* 8.3 (1977): 387–410.
25 See Dugmore, 'The Making of Krugersdorp'.
26 'West Rand: Asiatics in Towns: Questions of Occupation', *Rand Daily Mail*, 9 August 1913.

27 See 'Work of a Master Hand: Daring Burglary in the Dorp', *Rand Daily Mail*, 6 May 1912.
28 'West Rand: Asiatics in Towns'.
29 'West Rand: Asiatics in Towns'.
30 See 'Work of a Master Hand'.
31 Sale of Stands in Krugersdorp's Municipality, c. 1919, NASA, TPD, 8/250, 721/1919.
32 *The Municipality of Krugersdorp versus Dadoo Ltd and Others*, Judgment by Justice W. Wessels, Supreme Court of South Africa, Provincial Division, 4 December 1919, NASA, TPB 1218, TA5/10234.
33 Dugmore, 'Dadoo Limited versus Krugersdorp', 11 and 17, footnote.
34 The oldest surviving photograph of Jubilee House, showing an enormous swarm of locusts over the building, is dated 1908. A banner along its sides reads 'MacLoskie and Te Water', confirming recollections of the Dadoo family that Jubilee House was bought from an Afrikaner man called 'Tea Water'. See 'Locusts, MacLoskie & Te Water, Krugersdorp', Museum Africa (Johannesburg), PH2006-9448; see also Surendra Bhana and Joy Brain, *Setting Down Roots: Indian Migrants in South Africa, 1860–1911* (Johannesburg: Wits University Press, 1990), 170.
35 Dugmore, 'Dadoo Limited versus Krugersdorp', 11.
36 In 1919, however, the Asiatics (Land and Trading) Amendment Act (Transvaal) of 1919 was passed to put a stop to the practice of Indians acquiring land through companies.
37 This judgment also applied to the sale of stand 340, which had been transferred to Dadoo Ltd in 1916. *The Municipality of Krugersdorp versus Dadoo Ltd and Others*, Supreme Court of South Africa, Provincial Division, NASA, TPB 1218, TA5/10234.
38 Telegram from Secretary of State to Governor General, Pretoria, 6–7 January 1920, NASA, GG, 907, 15/994.
39 Letter from M. M. Dadoo to the Principal Immigration Officer, Pretoria, 18 February 1920, NASA, IND, 777, E13900.
40 *Dadoo Ltd and Others versus Municipal Council of Krugersdorp*, Judgment by Chief Justice Innes, Supreme Court, Appellate Division, [1920], NASA, GG 908 15/109.
41 One of these was a manufacturer, and two were plumbers. While white nominees were frequently used by the Indian community to buy land, M. M. Dadoo and his descendants decided not to expand the business or their properties using the nominee system, which left Indian property owners vulnerable to the whims of the nominal white landowners.
42 Krugersdorp Land Company Limited, Minute Book, 1924–1942, Dadoo family private papers.

43 'Indians Deny Underselling. Success Due to Long Credit. Land Commission at Krugersdorp', *Rand Daily Mail*, 23 June 1933.

44 'Indian Traders at Krugersdorp: Mr Dadoo on Reasons for Success: Evidence before Land Tenure Commission', *The Star*, 29 June 1933.

45 'Prince's Visit, Servicemen Parade', *Rand Daily Mail*, 16 June 1925.

46 Metcalf, *Imperial Connections*, 2.

47 After the National Party and the Labour Party formed a makeshift coalition under the leadership of J. B. M. Hertzog, they won the election in 1924.

48 Federico Freschi, 'Art Deco, Modernity, and the Politics of Ornament in South African Architecture, 1930–1940', in *The Routledge Companion to Art Deco*, eds Bridget Elliott and Michael Windover (London: Routledge, 2019), 254. See also Federico Freschi, 'Art Deco, Modernism and Modernity in Johannesburg: The Case for Obel and Obel's "Astor Mansions" (1932)', *de arte*, 32.55 (1997): 21–35.

49 Freschi, 'Art Deco, Modernity, and the Politics of Ornament', 258.

50 For details of M. M. Dadoo's last will and testament, see Estate of Mahomed Mamojee Dadoo, NASA, MHG, 4635/44.

51 Clive M. Chipkin, *Johannesburg: Style, Architecture & Society, 1880s–1960s* (Cape Town: David Philip, 1993), 68.

52 Two biographies have been written on Kallenbach, one by family members and the other an academic account of his relationship with Gandhi: Isa Sarid and Christian Bartolf, *Hermann Kallenbach: Mahatma Gandhi's Friend in South Africa* (Gandhi-Informations-Zentrum, 1997); and Shimon Lev, *Soulmates: The Story of Mahatma Gandhi and Hermann Kallenbach* (Hyderabad: Orient BlackSwan, 2012). See also James D. Hunt and Surendra Bhana, 'Spiritual Rope Walkers: Gandhi, Kallenbach, and the Tolstoy Farm, 1910–13', *South African Historical Journal* 58 (2007): 174–202.

53 Chipkin, *Johannesburg*, 89.

54 Chipkin, *Johannesburg*, 98.

55 'Magnificent New Department Store for Krugersdorp – M. M. Dadoo & Sons, Ltd.', *The Star*, 28 June 1940.

56 'Magnificent New Department Store'.

57 Belinda Bozzoli, with Mantho Nkotsoe, *Women of Phokeng: Consciousness, Life Strategy, and Migrancy in South Africa, 1900–1983* (Johannesburg: Ravan Press, 1991).

58 John Rennie Short, *Urban Theory: A Critical Assessment* (Basingstoke: Palgrave Macmillan, 2006), 6.

REFERENCES

'Asiatics in Towns: Test Case at Krugersdorp: Important Questions Pending'. *Rand Daily Mail*, 20 August 1913.

Bhana, Surendra, and Joy Brain. *Setting Down Roots: Indian Migrants in South Africa, 1860–1911*. Johannesburg: Wits University Press, 1990.

Bozzoli, Belinda, with Mantho Nkotsoe. *Women of Phokeng: Consciousness, Life Strategy, and Migrancy in South Africa, 1900–1983*. Johannesburg: Ravan Press, 1991.

Chipkin, Clive M. *Johannesburg: Style, Architecture & Society, 1880s–1960s*. Cape Town: David Philip, 1993.

Dhupelia-Mesthrie, Uma. 'Split Households: Indian Wives, Cape Town Husbands and Immigration Laws, 1900s to 1940s'. *South African Historical Journal* 66.4 (2014): 635–55.

Dugmore, Charles. 'Dadoo Limited versus Krugersdorp Town Council, 1920: A Case Study in Justice, Policy and Change in a Colonial Context'. Unpublished paper presented at the colloquium on Justice, Policy and Change in Southern Africa, University of the Witwatersrand, Johannesburg, 3 October 1998.

Dugmore, Charles. 'The Making of Krugersdorp, 1887–1923'. PhD diss., University of the Witwatersrand, Johannesburg, 2006.

Freschi, Federico. 'Art Deco, Modernism and Modernity in Johannesburg: The Case for Obel and Obel's "Astor Mansions" (1932)'. *de arte* 32.55 (1997): 21–35.

Freschi, Federico. 'Art Deco, Modernity, and the Politics of Ornament in South African Architecture, 1930–1940'. In *The Routledge Companion to Art Deco*, edited by Bridget Elliott and Michael Windover, 253–71. London: Routledge, 2019.

Hunt, James D., and Surendra Bhana. 'Spiritual Rope Walkers: Gandhi, Kallenbach, and the Tolstoy Farm, 1910–13'. *South African Historical Journal* 58 (2007): 174–202.

'Indian Traders at Krugersdorp: Mr Dadoo on Reasons for Success: Evidence before Land Tenure Commission'. *The Star*, 29 June 1933.

'Indians Deny Underselling. Success Due to Long Credit. Land Commission at Krugersdorp'. *Rand Daily Mail*, 23 June 1933.

Lev, Shimon. *Soulmates: The Story of Mahatma Gandhi and Hermann Kallenbach*. Hyderabad: Orient BlackSwan, 2012.

Madressa Anjuman Islamia Kholvad South Africa Est. 1914, Timeline of Events. Accessed 29 October 2019, http://www.kholvad.org.za/timeline-of-events/.

'Magnificent New Department Store for Krugersdorp – M. M. Dadoo & Sons, Ltd.'. *The Star*, 28 June 1940.

Metcalf, Thomas R. *Imperial Connections: India in the Indian Ocean Arena, 1860–1920.* Berkley: University of California Press, 2007.

Mottiar, Shauna. 'Yusuf Dadoo: Bafa Begiya'. Master's thesis, University of the Witwatersrand, Johannesburg, 2000.

'Prince's Visit, Servicemen Parade'. *Rand Daily Mail*, 16 June 1925.

Raman, Parvathi. 'Yusuf Dadoo: A Son of South Africa'. In *South Africa's 1940s: A World of Possibilities,* edited by Saul Dubow and Alan Jeeves, 227–45. Cape Town: Double Storey, 2005.

Sarid, Isa, and Christian Bartolf. *Hermann Kallenbach: Mahatma Gandhi's Friend in South Africa.* Gandhi-Informations-Zentrum, 1997.

Short, John Rennie. *Urban Theory: A Critical Assessment.* London: Palgrave Macmillan, 2006.

Swanson, Maynard W. 'The Sanitation Syndrome: Bubonic Plague and Urban Native Policy in the Cape Colony, 1900–1909'. *Journal of African History* 8.3 (1977): 387–410.

'West Rand: Asiatics in Towns: Questions of Occupation'. *Rand Daily Mail*, 9 August 1913.

'What's in a Town's Name?' *News24*, 6 August 2000. Accessed 18 October 2019, https://archive.fo/20120904040544/http://www.news24.com/xArchive/Archive/Whats-in-a-towns-name-20000806.

'Work of a Master Hand: Daring Burglary in the Dorp'. *Rand Daily Mail*, 6 May 1912.

INTERVIEWS

Dadoo, Yusuf. Personal interview with Arianna Lissoni and Roshan Dadoo. Johannesburg, 14 April 2015.

Dadoo, Yusuf Mohamed. Personal interview with Essop Pahad. London, c. 1978.

9 AN UNCERTAIN HERITAGE AND RESISTANCE: TRANSFORMING THE DRILL HALL IN JOHANNESBURG

BARBARA MOROVICH AND PAULINE GUINARD

To the memory of K. C., who died for – and at – the Drill Hall

The Drill Hall is a heritage site in the middle of the city centre of Johannesburg. A former army barracks, it is best known for the preliminary hearings of the Treason Trial which were held there in 1956.[1] Once a symbol of British colonisation, it has, over time, become known as a site of the struggle against the apartheid regime. However, the Drill Hall has not been maintained or protected by public institutions. This is in contrast to other heritage sites in the city, such as Constitution Hill, the former fort and prison that was transformed, after the end of the apartheid regime, into a museum and the new South African Constitutional Court.[2]

This has allowed the Drill Hall to be appropriated by independent and alternative cultural and social organisations since its rehabilitation in 2004. The commitment of these stakeholders has, so far at least, contributed to keeping the place alive. Thus, in addition to becoming a place of creativity in the city centre, the Drill Hall has maintained a heritage dimension. The word 'heritage', used here in the sense of a complex and 'invented' construction, references the concept of an 'invented tradition';[3] it is made up of history, memories and architectural and urban spaces, all linked with artistic, social and residential activities. Memories, in particular of the fight against the apartheid regime, are seen by public actors not only as the vector of national reconciliation but also as a marketing tool of a 'world-class African city'.[4] The tension between a weak institutional commitment to the site and the liveliness of the memories and practices of the people and associations engaged with the Drill Hall makes it an interstitial and fragile heritage site. In 2019, it was allocated to the Johannesburg Metropolitan Police Department (JMPD) for the establishment of a police station, a decision that will maintain this fragility.

Our fieldwork in January 2016 aimed to understand the complex relationship between different conceptions of heritage and the city of Johannesburg.[5] This involved an analysis of the transformation of the Drill Hall as part of a future renovation plan and study of local artistic interventions.[6] Since the renovation of the Drill Hall, public authorities seem to have adopted a laissez-faire attitude towards the artistic and social dynamics developing in the building. The artistic interventions are seen by the authorities as a way to protect the place and to prevent it from illegal occupation by homeless people, as happened on one occasion in the 1990s, and continues to be the case with many other buildings in the city centre.[7] Over the last two decades, the city has been in a process of gentrification. The focus on the Drill Hall helps to highlight the tensions and contradictions of the reshaping of Johannesburg's inner city, and the contradictory nature of inclusivity and competitiveness.

Our principal aim is to understand to what extent artistic and social commitment such as has developed in, and from, the Drill Hall can contribute to the invention of a completely new relationship to heritage, to the city itself, and to memories of dominated groups. We conducted four ethnographic fieldworks in Johannesburg between January 2016 and November 2018 at the crossroads of urban geography and anthropology. In addition, we looked at how the partially invented heritage of the Drill Hall can influence – if not contest – the dominant practices of memorial and heritage production in the post-apartheid city. We also sought to understand and analyse our position among the stakeholders, and our possible contribution to the evolution of the place. We conducted our fieldwork through repeated encounters with specifically selected stakeholders, and with whom relations of mutual appreciation were strong.[8]

PALIMPSEST OF A CONVULSIVE PAST

The Drill Hall was inaugurated in 1904 on the site of a former prison for those designated as 'non-white' people. In particular, it housed the headquarters of the Transvaal Volunteers, South African soldiers serving with the British army who used it for accommodation and as a training ground. It was from this building that soldiers were deployed to repress significant rebellions, such as the Bambatha Zulu uprising in 1906, and the miners' strikes in Johannesburg and the Transvaal in 1913, 1914 and 1922. In 1922, the Drill Hall was given as an 'Imperial Gift' to South Africa by the British, in gratitude for its participation in the First World War. During this period, the Hall was seen by many as a symbol of white colonial power.

Under apartheid, the symbolic function of the site as a place of domination grew, most emphatically during the Treason Trial. This event followed the arrest for treason of 156 activists, including African National Congress (ANC) members such as Nelson Mandela and Communist Party members such as Joe Slovo. In 1955, those arrested had famously met to help write the Freedom Charter in Kliptown, a township located in the south of Johannesburg; the document was the basis not only of a non-racial democracy in South Africa, but also of the Bill of Rights included in the 1996 Constitution. The preliminary trial hearings were held in the Drill Hall in December 1958, before relocation of the proceedings to Pretoria. The Drill Hall was the only secure place in the segregated city suitable to hold the large number of accused people. For the black public, this gathering of opponents to apartheid in a central place of power contributed to a radical shift in the symbolic meaning of the Drill Hall: from a place of repression it began to be referred to as a place of meeting of leaders and a symbol of rebellion against the regime.[9] Nevertheless, this was momentary, as up until the 1980s the Hall remained effectively and symbolically a place of repression. The years following the establishment of the Republic of South Africa and the severing of ties to Britain in 1960 were marked by an increasing suppression of protest movements. In the case of the Drill Hall, this led to the replacement of volunteer with permanent combat units.

In the 1980s, with the change in political conditions, the Hall lost its function as a site of the imposition of white power. At that time, the inner city of Johannesburg and the area around the nearby Joubert Park were gradually abandoned by businesses and the white population.[10] The departure of the military in 1992 corresponded with the end of the apartheid era and of

Johannesburg as a white city.[11] Since then, the Drill Hall has been occupied by socially disadvantaged populations of different nationalities hoping to access the resources of the inner city. As described by the Joubert Park Project (JPP),[12] the 1990s were a difficult period for the Drill Hall and its inhabitants, marked by insalubrity and delinquency: 'In 1992, the SANDF [South African National Defence Force] vacated the Drill Hall and, soon after, homeless people moved in. In 1994, as the world celebrated the dawn of South African democracy, a different and harsher reality began to emerge at the Drill Hall – that of a city trying to cope with rapid and chaotic change, and with the legacy of 40 years of inhumane governance.' Moreover, in the early 2000s, some 350 families lived in the building without water or electricity.[13] The fire which struck the east wing of the building, taking the life of five inhabitants in 2001, almost marked the end of the Drill Hall and an entire period of its existence in the memories of inhabitants. The JPP was established at this time to deal with issues faced by migrants and other disadvantaged people living in the neighbourhood. Their intervention added another layer to the story of the place.

RENEWAL AS A RECONCILIATION PROCESS

After the fire in 2001, the first solution envisaged by public authorities in Johannesburg was to remove the badly damaged building and clear the site.

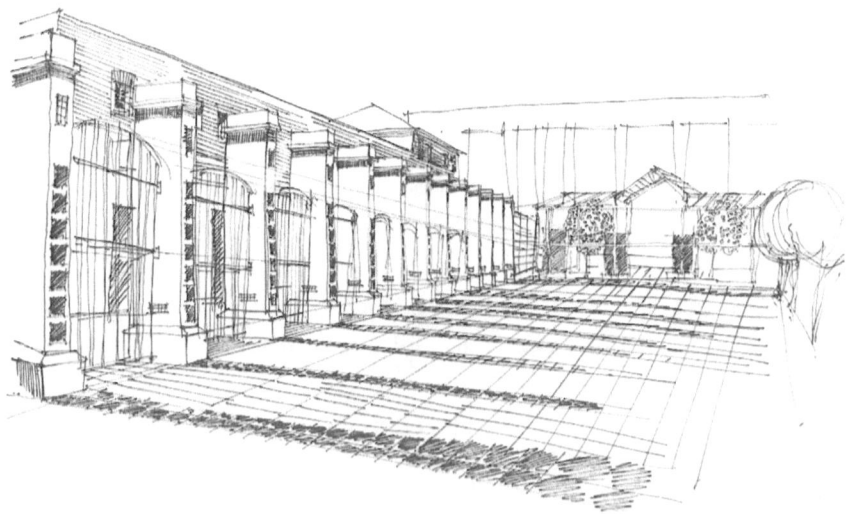

Figure 9.1. Sketch of proposed renovation of Drill Hall by the architect Michael Hart

In an interview with Michael Hart, the architect in charge of the Drill Hall renovation, we were informed that this 'cleaning up' of the inner city led to a wave of opposition in Johannesburg.[14] In part, this was due to the memorial and heritage value attached to the place even during a period of decay and deprivation. People's memories were not (only) of the military occupation but also of the life of a new generation of black citizens and their struggle to survive in the city. They became a potent source of activism when combined with the historical memory of the leaders who were imprisoned here.

Eventually, the city of Johannesburg was forced to change its approach and opted for a R10 million renovation. This project was to be managed by the Johannesburg Development Agency (JDA), a semi-autonomous city division in charge of the city's infrastructure development projects. As noted on the JDA website, the intention was to make the Drill Hall 'a heritage asset and public open space that forms part of the historical and cultural tourism trail of the inner city'.[15] Thus, the Hall was envisaged as a potential heritage site and a public space integrated into a wider tourism project. While the intention to guarantee the accessibility of the place while maintaining its heritage dimension is important, it seems also to have been idealistic on the part of the authorities. It explains, however, their decision to give the management of the renovated site to organisations with a social and cultural focus, thus adding yet another layer of memorialisation.

The aim of the architect was 'the coming to terms and reconciliation of a past history; a celebration and a remembering'. According to Hart, the architectural intervention of transforming the Drill Hall into a site of place-making would enable the memorialisation. The space created would be flexible, implying divergent uses such as 'by the military, community facilities, art exhibitions and events' with a responsiveness to the 'current social and political context'. Certain elements are seen as important by the architect: the glass used in the main building, which was occupied by One Love Skate Expo during the period of our research, represents a 'memory by being transparent' while establishing a dialogue between the building and the environment; also, the main entrance to the site, on Twist Street, is retained as the entrance to the public square (see figure 9.2 for a map of the area). Both inside and outside, linkage and transparency highlight the intention to give back the entire heritage site to all South Africans, partially inventing a common narrative by insisting on the Treason Trial moment,

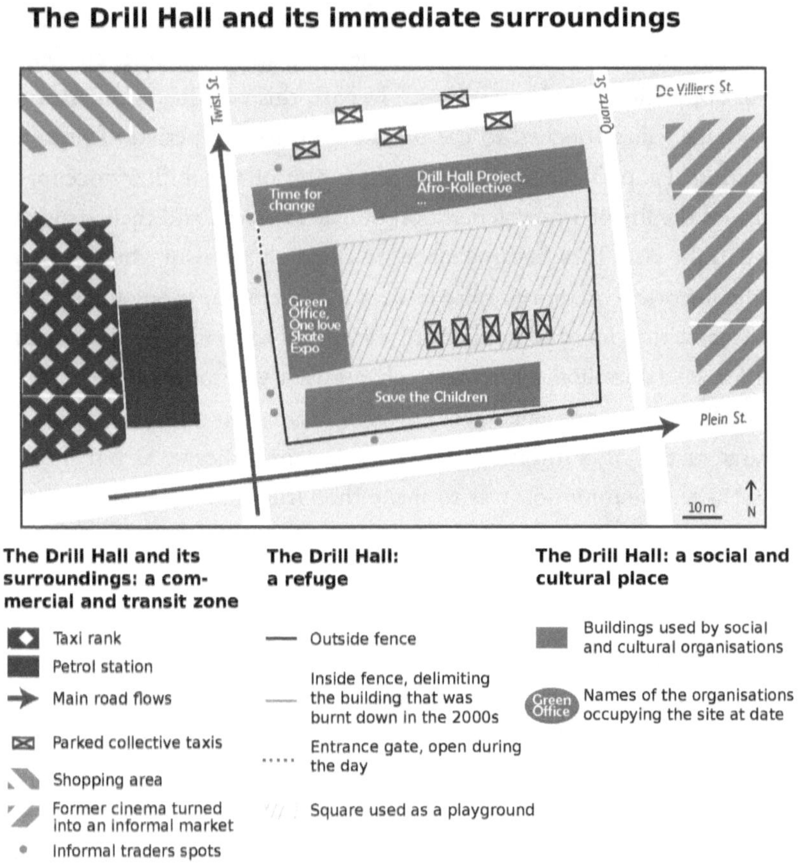
The Drill Hall and its immediate surroundings
Twist St.
Quartz St.
De Villiers St.
Plein St.
Time for change
Drill Hall Project, Afro-Kollective
...
Green Office, One love Skate Expo
Save the Children
10m
N
The Drill Hall and its surroundings: a commercial and transit zone
Taxi rank
Petrol station
Main road flows
Parked collective taxis
Shopping area
Former cinema turned into an informal market
Informal traders spots
The Drill Hall: a refuge
Outside fence
Inside fence, delimiting the building that was burnt down in the 2000s
Entrance gate, open during the day
Square used as a playground
The Drill Hall: a social and cultural place
Buildings used by social and cultural organisations
Green Office
Names of the organisations occupying the site at date

Figure 9.2. Map of the Drill Hall and its immediate surroundings, by Pauline Guinard

even though it was mostly a place of division and violence. The Drill Hall renovation project obtained the Gauteng Institute of Architecture award of commendation 'for a fine example of architecture' in 2005, and was exhibited in the sixth São Paulo Biennial in 2005 and the post-apartheid buildings exhibition in Mendrisio, Italy. The project was internationally seen as fulfilling the requirements of a heritage site while answering to the cultural and social needs of a local population.

Fourteen years after the renovation, Hart confirms that his aim was to respect the historical palimpsest but also 'to take a building used as negative and turn it to something relevant'. In this process, the transformation and selection of heritage was made possible by the existing shift of significance from military and oppressive to political resistance, and by a process of 'conservation turned to the future' and not 'restoration turned to the past'. Hart pushed hard to obtain a public square within the Drill Hall precinct, while the city 'didn't really understand the idea'. Ultimately, it was converted into a semi-enclosed, in-between urban space. The aim of turning the Drill Hall into a public venue is crucial, since these types of spaces are sorely missing in Johannesburg. This is due in part to historical segregation and ongoing racism and division and, in part, to widespread feelings of insecurity. Even though the Drill Hall was explicitly designed by the JDA as a 'public space', it was surrounded by a fence in order to reassure potential users of the safety of the site.

Four organisations were located in the Drill Hall at the end of the renovation in 2004: the Rand Light Infantry, the reserve unit of the South African Army; the Johannesburg Community Chest, an organisation providing a range of training to the community; the Johannesburg Child Welfare Society, an organisation promoting child protection; and the JPP, a collective of artists engaged in contextual, relational and participative art in the inner city. The JDA disengaged from the site after the renovation, as agreed, but found no public entity to take over its management. A year later, the Rand Light Infantry left because the inner city 'was too rough for them'. It was in part for this reason that the JPP departed, but mostly because of the lack of management at the site. For the stakeholders we interviewed, the uncertainty of the ownership and the lack of maintenance of the building were the main reasons for leaving. Even though the JDA had renovated the building, it was in fact owned by the Public Works Department. This situation is reflective of the difficulty of administratively reorganising the country after apartheid, particularly since the three levels of government – state, province and city – were intended to be independent and autonomous.[16]

Because of the uncertainty about the ownership of the site, the Drill Hall was never maintained. Organisations that used this space did not have a lease, and nor did they have the opportunity to request the manager to take care of water and electricity bills, a procedure that was often established when a public site was occupied by non-profit organisations. One of the founders of the JPP told us on 10 February 2016 of the 'years of pain and agony' he experienced during his tenancy at the Drill Hall:

> We never were given a proper lease agreement ... We were actually the only tenants that had a signed lease agreement ... we were the only one and that was part of the problem ... There were also lots of technical problems about who actually owns the site. In fact, it belongs to Public Works that have given it to the City of Johannesburg but that process never had been properly formalised and completed ... So in fact the City – although they signed a lease with us – did not have any power to sign that lease. And that created a whole cascading process of absolute disaster and administrative nightmare, the type I hope I will never encounter again in my entire life.

This situation did not prevent other social and cultural organisations from taking over and continuing to promote activities there, especially activities which encouraged memories attached to the Drill Hall.

SHIFTING MEMORIES

Art and artists, in Johannesburg or elsewhere, often give new meaning to urban environments, especially in times of change.[17] As the activist Theresa Giorza writes:

> What connects the participants is the place: an inner city building and its surrounds. A place that has seen landmark events in the history of a nation and life-changing events for individuals drawn into the struggle for social justice and change. It is also the set for contemporary struggles waged daily by its residents and a crossing point for travellers and new arrivals to the city.[18]

The ritual dimension of art is repeatedly stressed by researchers on the subject. Artists tend to put forward forgotten memories, and in so doing they establish a partially new selection of memories.[19] In South Africa, art and culture were a way for individuals or groups to contest apartheid in the absence of other means of political expression.[20] In the post-apartheid period, artistic engagement remains present in all sectors of society, and particularly in the process of reinventing a South African nation.[21] The Drill Hall is a significant example of a succession of cultural and artistic socially engaged activities over time.

Our focus was the period in which the Drill Hall was appropriated by different stakeholders – artists, researchers and activists – who emphasised values and ideals linked to the struggle against apartheid and the gathering of ANC leaders, rather than the period of occupation by the military or the apartheid and colonial history of the place. This 'invented tradition', which was a kind of pretext to occupy the Drill Hall, is made up of a mix of the history of political resistance, contemporary local stories and everyday life, often linked to migration and the fight against xenophobia.

The Joubert Park Project was the starting point for an innovative use of such a tradition in that part of the city. It was the JPP who began to speak about the appropriation of the area by the neighbourhood through art.[22] After the departure of the JPP, this integration of a new narrative continued with the Keleketla! Library project. It had originally started in the Drill Hall in 2008, when, identifying a lack of books or public library in the east side of the inner city, the artist B. M. decided to create a new project in the Drill Hall during her residency with the JPP. Deeply passionate about books, she told us she wanted local people and especially children to have access to them. This project resonated with the methodology developed by the activists R. H. and M. K. M. based on a 'call and response' type of exchange. Their approach consists in proposing meetings, dialogues and conversations. In fact, it encompasses actions which, for them, correspond to a need of the community with which they are working. They allow the resulting proposal to evolve, based on the reaction of that community. As M. K. M. explained to us: 'We create projects along with the community, and the community will respond in certain ways, how they want to engage, what we are proposing to them.'

With the establishment of Keleketla! Library in the Drill Hall, the site became an even more important place for the transmission of memories linked to the struggle for the rights of black people, and against racism. This project of an open library in the Drill Hall allowed educational institutions, town planners, artists, political activists, teachers, children and students of different ages to engage over six years through educational and artistic activities as part of after-school programmes. In a collective publication, *58 Years to the Treason Trial*, student participants in the various workshops describe their experience of conversing with older activists in the fight against apartheid, thereby forming a new community.[23]

In the book, we can see that the library acts as a node, connecting participants through the sharing of stories and memories. It has given birth to multidisciplinary outcomes, such as lectures, workshops, fanzines, posters and performances. This is not only a question of putting forward the official history but also of telling the small stories of everyday life and of connecting them to the context of recent migrations. In this way, the historical fight against apartheid is linked to the contemporary fight against xenophobia and violence. In tracing the heritage of the Drill Hall from the history of the Treason Trial to the present, art is seen to be a means of transformation as it aims to fight racism, or, more broadly, the 'fear of the other' in all its contemporary forms.

In spite of the termination of the Keleketla! Library project at the Drill Hall, and the partial closing down of the library, the vision of the library continues to survive.[24] Many artists of modest origins from the disadvantaged inner city of Johannesburg and the surrounding townships, as well as migrants from rural areas or other countries, claim (the memory of) the place and its identity. This has a strong influence both on their art and on the stories told by people of all ages who still work and live in the Hall. N. M., a musician with the Enharmonic Collective, translates this as a 'vibrant space to be' which has 'beautiful aura'. B. M., cofounder of the Keleketla! Library project, insists on the character of the place as 'an alternative space, a contact zone', marked by the fact that the artists do not merely pass through, but are 'grounded'. For W. H., a dancer with Afro-Kollectives, the Drill Hall is his 'home', the place he belongs to and fights for. Like the others, he claims to be strongly inspired by the place itself. N. K., co-founder of Afro-Kollectives, speaks of it as 'a beautiful narrative, a summary of the narratives of the surroundings'. The artists we interviewed at the Drill Hall insist on the fact that the site was for them a 'shelter' where they live, and where they also produce and share their art. An urban opportunity such as this clearly offers disadvantaged individuals, aged between 15 and 45, a place to develop or continue their practice: a place where they are in contact with other economic and cultural opportunities in a centre where they can thrive.

TRANSFORMATIONS

The presence of artists in the Drill Hall contributes not only to the maintenance of the place but also, over time, to its transformation. Because access is free and its location central, the Drill Hall is an attractive space for Johannesburg artists and young people, most of whom happen to be male, who are in a precarious situation and cannot afford a place to work or live. The Drill Hall is perceived as a space of creation for emergent artists. It also serves as a place for any social project which ignites action and interaction with the cosmopolitan yet destitute space of the inner city. For artists and stakeholders, the Drill Hall is an ideal place from which to build and legitimise their practice. It is also ultimately a place of encounter and of learning from various practices and people – a place where skateboarders became visual artists, an opera singer learnt to cook, and dancers to draw, as new alliances were forged.

The lack of certainty about the future of the various organisations highlights the precarity of the place itself at a time when the surrounding districts are gentrifying. In this process, the Drill Hall remains a platform for those who sometimes leave to pursue their career elsewhere once they achieve recognition – receiving a grant, being given residency or a job opportunity – and then leave the place to other emergent artists and stakeholders.[25] Such a handover took place after the departure of the JPP, but was jeopardised by the murder of K. C., one of the major figures of the previous generation of artists and social stakeholders. During his stay at the Drill Hall, from 2015 to his death in 2017, K. C. developed skateboarding activities by transforming part of the square into a social spot for skateboarders. Because other activities such as soccer used to take place there, this eventually created tensions between footballers and skateboarders. The organisation One Love Skate Expo grew impressively after arranging funding and the supply of 100 skateboards. This growth changed the utilisation of the central square, with some stakeholders partially retreating from it, and Save the Children prohibiting children from participating owing to a lack of adequate protection such as knee guards. Nevertheless, the flexibility and capacity for transformation of the square as well as the adaptability of stakeholders worked in its favour.

The strongest tensions among the various organisations active in the Drill Hall between 2016 and 2018 concerned the occupation of some spaces by churches for ceremonies and meetings. But even more acute than this was the conflict over the gradual occupation of the square by taxis. Agreements were negotiated by some stakeholders without the consent of all the organisations, drastically changing the atmosphere, safety and viability of the place for most activities. By the end of 2018, churches were no longer admitted but the growth in the number of taxis began to prevent other activities from taking place in the square.

Since 2017, the western part of the Drill Hall has been shared, with the skateboard organisation on the upper level, and the Green Office, which has been there for several years, on the lower level. M. M., who was in charge of the Green Office, continued to live there through 2019. He defines himself as

Figure 9.3. Skateboarding at the Drill Hall. Photograph by Pauline Guinard

'a visual artist by nature' and has been taking care of a part of the site which he has transformed into an outdoor art gallery. His sculptures, about the impact of human action on nature, are installed in the portico, which faces the exterior of the Drill Hall. Besides being his living space, the Hall is also a resource area, since he cultivates a garden, cooks and sells his vegan products, labelled 'Exotically Divine', in various markets in Johannesburg, such as Braamfontein and Maboneng. The Drill Hall is thus a place of expression of various artistic forms that are constantly being renewed, as well as an economic and social space. Furthermore, the presence of Green Office, together with organisations such as Afro-Kollectives, helps to keeping the space alive and thriving even as the surrounding urban situation deteriorates. The space is maintained because the stakeholders use the Drill Hall as an economic resource. Many events continue to take place there – for example, shooting videos for popular TV series, or hosting dance classes – despite the fact that the space is informally occupied by disadvantaged families and individuals seeking shelter.

The organisations based at the site are seen as 'Drill Hall Defenders' and are described as such in an internet article and video about the skateboarders of One Love Skate Expo.[26] It is significant that the Green Office, during our fieldwork in January 2018, had begun to build a memorial in the courtyard of the Drill Hall where K. C. was killed. Indeed, this place continues to act as a palimpsest of memories, of personal and collective stories of survival by and through art and culture. Like the late K. C., M. M. of the Green Office and N. K. of Afro-Kollectives are entrepreneurs whose main resource is the Drill Hall as economic workspace. They combine this opportunity with a capacity for adaptation and a strong link with the community based on the concept of 'giving back'. But these stakeholders of the Drill Hall are not officially recognised and are not in a position to prevent competition and disruption of the place – a situation that leaves them permanently in a precarious position.

UNCERTAIN FUTURE

The mere presence of artists in the Drill Hall seems insufficient, at this point, to bring about social or economic change, either there or in the immediate neighbourhood. This raises the question whether artists are inevitably catalysts of gentrification, or whether such a prognosis should be revised or at least be made more nuanced.[27] After the occupation of the Drill Hall by the JPP, the capacity to adapt remained strong – though not strong enough for stakeholders and artists to avoid eviction. Because they are not officially entitled to stay or manage the place, the artists at the Hall can prevent neither other activities (its use as a parking area, for example) nor private utilisations by individuals or groups (such as churches). The uncertainty at the institutional level is the main cause of this ongoing impasse.

In May 2019, a decision was taken to place the Drill Hall under control of the JMPD. A need was perceived to reorganise and secure the site, due to the lack of management and the difficulties of transferring ownership from the Public Works Department to the City of Johannesburg. A report published in May 2019 makes no mention of the fate of the organisations occupying the site, despite clearly stating that the utilisation of the Drill Hall by the JMPD supports the city's strategy for inner city regeneration.[28] From this, it may be concluded that the artists, and more broadly the people still living or working in the Drill Hall, who remain in a precarious state, are likely to be among the victims of regeneration.

The Johannesburg stakeholders were clearly not able to prevent the deterioration of the Drill Hall, which was first renovated for its heritage value in 2004. At that stage, the artistic activity in the building complex was seen as advantageous to the city. It allowed the city to delegate the daily management of the site, without compensation and without long-term commitment, to a number of artistic, social and cultural groups. Whether deliberate or not, the presence of the artists and other associations in the Drill Hall was a way for the city to manage, at minimal expense, the situation of latency in which this space finds itself. Even if its links with the artists strengthen, and the Drill Hall crystallises feelings of attachment – on the basis of a common narrative of current and past events – its future as an official heritage site remains unclear. Is the Drill Hall thus destined to become a place of abuse, no longer a place of resistance and the invention of a shared tradition?

NOTES

1 During this trial, 156 people, including Nelson Mandela, were accused of high treason by the apartheid regime because of their anti-apartheid activities.
2 See Mark Gevisser, 'From the Ruins: The Constitution Hill Project', *Public Culture* 16.3 (2004).
3 See Eric Hobsbawm and Terence Ranger, *The Invention of Tradition* (Cambridge: Cambridge University Press, 1983).
4 Sabine Marschall, *Landscape of Memory: Commemorative Monuments, Memorials and Public Statuary in Post-apartheid South Africa* (Leiden: Brill Academic Publishers, 2010).
5 We wish to thank all those who agreed to talk to us during our fieldwork; rather than mentioning them by name, we have chosen to use initials only.
6 Pauline Guinard and Barbara Morovich, 'Art, mémoires et engagement au Drill Hall (Johannesburg): l'invention d'un patrimoine incertain', *Information Géographique* 2 (2017).
7 Keith Beavon, *Johannesburg: The Making and Shaping of the City* (Pretoria: Unisa Press, 2004).
8 Those dynamics were strengthened by the involvement of some stakeholders in the discussion on art and public spaces organised by the French Institute of South Africa in May 2017 and by the reaction to the murder that month of one of the main interlocutors at the Drill Hall site.
9 Keren Ben-Zeev et al., eds, *The Drill Hall* (Johannesburg: Joubert Park Project, 2006).
10 See Beavon, *Johannesburg*.
11 In accordance with the Group Areas Act of 1950, which assigned an area of residence based on 'race' (white, black, coloured or Indian), the municipality of Johannesburg – corresponding to the current CBD – was reserved for the white population.
12 Created by Bie Venter, Dorothee Kreutzfeldt and Joseph Gaylard in 2000, and based at the Drill Hall, the JPP was a collaborative artistic programme which aimed at engaging with the local community through workshops, training, and art events.

13 Ben-Zeev et al., *The Drill Hall*, 31.
14 The phrase is attributed to the first post-apartheid mayor of Johannesburg, Amos Masondo. We wish to thank Michael Hart, who provided us with (unpublished) documents from which we have quoted.
15 See https://www.jda.org.za/drill-hall-in-joubert-park/.
16 For further discussion, see Philippe Gervais-Lambony, 'Afrique du Sud: à la recherche de la ville perdue', *Multitudes* 17 (2004): 157–64.
17 See Guinard, *Johannesburg*; and Barbara Morovich, 'Entre stigmates et mémoires: dynamiques paradoxales de la rénovation urbaine', *Articulo – Journal of Urban Research* 5 (2014).
18 Theresa Giorza, 'Keleketla! Library and the Migrant Pedagogies of Time, Place and Social Action', in *58 Years to the Treason Trial: Inter-generational Dialogue as a Method for Learning*, ed. Molemo Moiloa (Johannesburg: Keleketla Media Arts Project NPC, 2012), 7–9.
19 Michèle Fellous, 'Du rite comme œuvre: l'art contemporain', *Médium* 2.7 (2006): 106–16.
20 William Bellamy, *Une identité nouvelle pour l'Afrique du Sud* (Paris: Publications de la Sorbonne, 1996): 129–36.
21 Marschall, *Landscape of Memory*.
22 Guinard, *Johannesburg*, 265–88.
23 Molemo Moiloa, ed., *58 Years to the Treason Trial*.
24 See Keleketla Media Arts Project website, accessed 10 July 2019, https://keleketla.org.
25 See Guinard and Morovich, 'Art, mémoires et engagement au Drill Hall'.
26 These were produced before the murder of K. C. See Kyle Oberholzer, 'The Drill Hall Defenders', accessed 10 July 2019, https://joburgcbd.com/drill-halls-defenders/.
27 Tatiana Debroux, 'Des artistes en ville. Géographie rétrospective des plasticiens à Bruxelles 1833–2008' (PhD diss., Université Libre de Bruxelles, Brussels, 2012).
28 'Drill Hall: Site Allocation to Joburg Metro Police Dpt.', Inner City Technical Cluster Meeting, Community Development Directorate: Art, Culture and Heritage, 17 May 2019.

REFERENCES

Althabe, Gérard. 'Entretien'. In *Conversations sur la ville et l'urbain*, edited by Thierry Paquot, 10–22. Gollion: Infolio, 2008.

Beavon, Keith. *Johannesburg: The Making and Shaping of the City*. Pretoria: Unisa Press, 2004.

Bellamy, William. *Une identité nouvelle pour l'Afrique du Sud*. Paris: Publications de la Sorbonne, 1996.

Ben-Zeev, Keren, Joseph Gaylard, Veronica Klaptocz, and Bettina Schultz, eds. *The Drill Hall*. Johannesburg: Joubert Park Project, 2006.

Bénit-Gbaffou, Claire. 'In the Shadow of 2010: Democracy and Displacement in the Greater Ellis Park Development Project'. In *Development and Dreams: The Urban Legacy of the 2010 Football World Cup,* edited by Udesh Pillay, Richard Tomlinson and Orli Bass, 200–22. Cape Town: HSRC Press, 2009.

Bremner, Lindsay. 'Reinventing the Johannesburg Inner City'. *Cities* 17.3 (2000): 185–93.

Debroux, Tatiana. 'Des artistes en ville. Géographie rétrospective des plasticiens à Bruxelles, 1833–2008'. PhD diss., Université Libre de Bruxelles, Brussels, 2012.

Farouk, Ismail. 'Planning for Chaos: Urban Regeneration and the Struggle to Formalise Trolley-Pushing Activity in Downtown Johannesburg'. In *African Cities Reader,* edited by Edgar Pieterse and Ntone Edjabe, 239–46. Cape Town: African Centre for Cities, 2010.

Fellous, Michèle. 'Du rite comme œuvre: l'art contemporain'. *Médium* 2.7 (2006): 106–16.

Gervais-Lambony, Philippe. 'Afrique du Sud: à la recherche de la ville perdue'. *Multitudes* 17 (2004): 157–64.

Gevisser, Mark. 'From the Ruins: The Constitution Hill Project'. *Public Culture* 16.3 (2004): 507–18.

Giorza, Theresa. 'Keleketla! Library and the Migrant Pedagogies of Time, Place and Social Action'. In *58 Years to the Treason Trial: Inter-generational Dialogue as a Method for Learning*, edited by Molemo Moiloa, 7–9. Johannesburg: Keleketla Media Arts Project NPC, 2012.

Guinard, Pauline. *Johannesburg: l'art d'inventer une ville*. Rennes: Presses universitaires de Rennes, 2014.

Guinard, Pauline, and Barbara Morovich. 'Art, mémoires et engagement au Drill Hall (Johannesburg): l'invention d'un patrimoine incertain'. *Information Géographique* 2 (2017): 121–45.

Hobsbawm, Eric, and Terence Ranger. *The Invention of Tradition*. Cambridge: Cambridge University Press, 1983.

Marschall, Sabine. *Landscape of Memory: Commemorative Monuments, Memorials and Public Statuary in Post-apartheid South Africa*. Leiden: Brill Academic Publishers, 2010.

Moiloa, Molemo, ed. *58 Years to the Treason Trial: Inter-generational Dialogue as a Method for Learning*. Johannesburg: Keleketla Media Arts Project NPC, 2012.

Morovich, Barbara. 'Entre stigmates et mémoires: dynamiques paradoxales de la rénovation urbaine'. *Articulo* 5 (2014). Accessed 10 July 2019, http://journals.openedition.org/articulo/2529.

Oberholzer, Kyle. 'The Drill Hall Defenders'. *The Johannesburg CBD*. Accessed 10 July 2019, https://joburgcbd.com/drill-halls-defenders/.

Parnell, Sue, and Jennifer Robinson. 'Development and Urban Policy: Johannesburg's City Development Strategy'. *Urban Studies* 43.2 (2006): 337–55.

Vivant, Elsa. 'Les événements *off*: de la résistance à la mise en scène de la ville creative'. *Géocarrefour* 82.3 (2010): 131–40.

INTERVIEWS

Hart, Michael. Personal interview with authors. Johannesburg, 22 November 2018.

B. M. Personal interview with authors. Johannesburg, 2 February 2016.

J. P. P. Personal interview with authors. Johannesburg, 10 February 2016.

M. K. M. Personal interview with authors. Johannesburg, 25 January 2016.

N. K. Personal interview with authors. Johannesburg, 26 November 2018.

N. M. Personal interview with authors. Johannesburg, 1 February 2016.

W. H. Personal interview with authors. Johannesburg, 3 February 2016.

PART THREE
STATUES, AS MONUMENTS

10 CREATING SPACES OF MEMORIALISATION: NEW DELVILLE WOOD (FRANCE) AND SS *MENDI* (SOUTH AFRICA)

YASMIN MAYAT AND BRENDAN HART[1]

All monuments and memorials originate as a creative act. As with artworks, they are the product of the time and culture from which they originate, infused with politics and inherent personal and social biases. Monuments and memorials become both symbols of pride and identity as well as triggers for protest and rage. They can be seen to statically embody the injustices of the past or act as an anchor for memory in a rapidly changing modern world. In this context, what does it mean to create a new monument or site of memory? This chapter offers a retrospective exploration and personal critique of the conceptualisation and creation of two new memorials in the South African context, which has seen protest against as well as the recent removal, vandalisation and questioning of the relevance of colonial and apartheid monuments and memorials.

DELVILLE WOOD MEMORIAL

The Delville Wood South African National Memorial site is a layered complex of memorials and museums established by the South African government on the site of the eponymous 1916 battle in Longueval, France. The battle of Delville Wood is one of the most celebrated engagements of the newly formed South African armed forces during the First World War (1914–1918) and an important event in the creation of the young country's identity.² The First World War affected not only the European countries directly involved but also many of their colonies. While the war was triggered by the assassination of Archduke Franz Ferdinand of Austria, a series of treaties and alliances between the various nations involved led to declarations of war when allies were attacked. The war, expected 'to be over by Christmas' 1914, was prolonged and tragic, with a high number of casualties largely due to the trench warfare – a poor tactical response to increasingly modern military technology. The newly formed Union of South Africa joined the war as part of the forces of the British Empire.

The country's contribution to the war was significant. In addition to the 146 000 citizens who volunteered for active service, there were 83 000 members of the South African Native Labour Contingent (SANLC).³ The SANLC was established in 1916 to address the extreme shortage of labour on the Western Front as well as in French ports. It was made up of black volunteers who believed that their support for the war effort would result in better treatment back home. The South African government at the time was, however, concerned about sending the SANLC members to Europe, and the effect that the mixing with European soldiers 'on an equal footing' would have upon their return, from both a social and political point of view. As part of the conditions of its establishment, the government requested that the SANLC be segregated from the rest of the troops, housed in compounds and not allowed to bear arms. It was believed that 'uninhibited contact with Europeans on an equal footing ... would undermine the existing race relations in South Africa'.⁴

The Battle of Delville Wood was part of the greater Battle of the Somme in northern France, which was itself part of the Western Front offensive fought by British forces against the invading German army. The Battle of the Somme resulted in casualties of approximately half a million allied soldiers in France alone. On 1 July 1916, British and Commonwealth infantrymen attacked the German lines across the Somme valley in order to break the German defensive line of fortifications and the trench-warfare stalemate. Part of the battle was concentrated on a cluster of woods that acted as cover and fortifications. Delville Wood was one of these.⁵

Delville Wood is located next to the village of Longueval. The 156-acre wood was densely forested with thick undergrowth further fortified by the

German forces with a network of trenches, tunnels and machine-gun posts. The 1st South African Infantry Brigade was ordered, as part of the battle of Delville Wood, to take and hold the wood 'at all costs' as a means of breaking the stalemate. Of the 3 153 South African soldiers who entered the wood on 15 July 1916, only 780 remained 6 days later, when they were relieved. The remains of many of the men who died in the battle are either buried in the woods or in unmarked graves. Despite the horrific losses, the soldiers were hailed as heroes, holding the woods for six days and five nights under conditions of relentless shelling, flame throwers, as well as machine gun and rifle fire.[6]

From very early on, the South African government wanted to build a memorial at Delville Wood. While initially investigated in 1918, the memorial was only completed in 1926. It was to be dedicated to the 'sons of the Union', and was funded by public subscriptions.[7] The original Delville Wood memorial was intended as a South African national memorial to those who fought as well as a site of memory for the missing. With less than one in five casualties recovered and buried in the cemetery, the wood itself became a cemetery and was consecrated as the 'true resting place of our dead'.[8] Herbert Baker was appointed as the architect for both the memorial and the Delville Wood cemetery.[9] While Baker was a principal architect for the Imperial War Graves Commission, the architectural work from his prolific practice had already become the default architecture of the Union of South Africa in the wake of the South African War.[10] Supposedly representative of the union of the former Boer and British adversaries, the Union Buildings in Pretoria – the administrative seat of the new government – were inaugurated in 1913.

The original memorial and cemetery were designed along a north–south axis. The southern end of the axis is terminated by the Commonwealth War Graves cemetery, with its tombstones orientated perpendicular to the line of the axis.[11] The northern end of the axis terminates in the heart of the wood with the memorial itself. The form of the original memorial is reminiscent of that of the Union Buildings. Its large central triumphal arch is placed on the main axis, with semi-circular walls connecting it to a pair of small pavilion buildings. The pavilions are based on the summer house that Simon van der Stel, the first Dutch governor of the Cape Colony (1691–1699), had built at Groote Schuur, his estate in Cape Town, and now the residence of the President of the Republic of South Africa.[12] These pavilions house books with the roll-of-honour, as well as viewing balconies. Topping the arch is a sculpture representing physical energy and 'the two races of South Africa', which was inspired by the Greek sculpture of Castor and Pollux.[13] Alfred Turner's bronze statue represented the new union between white English-speaking South Africans and the Afrikaners. The memorial also had another, less obvious, political agenda. The Union of South Africa was less than a decade old, with the country still recovering from the social divisions of the South African War (1899–1902). The memorial's opening ceremony was used to speak of the symbolism of both the memorial as well as the battle where 'Boer and Briton fought side by side'. In this way, the memorial became a symbol for the supposed 'union' in the country and a marker that 'there never more will be fratricidal warfare and bloodshed between the two races'.[14] No mention was made of any of the black South African participants in the war.

The memorial faces southwards, towards the cemetery, and down an oak-lined avenue created when the wood was replanted after being totally destroyed during the battle. The acorns from which the oaks were grown were brought in from Franschhoek in South Africa, and as the descendants of oaks brought to South Africa 150 years earlier by French Huguenot immigrants, the trees certainly reinforced the white settler narrative.[15] The Delville Wood memorial complex was further politicised in the 1980s with the addition of a new museum. Built around the original Cross of Consecration, and now terminating the axis of the memorial site, the museum borrows architecturally from South Africa's Dutch colonial past. It was designed as a scaled-down replica of the Dutch colonial Castle of Good Hope located in Cape Town, with a pastiche of Cape Dutch architectural references associated with the vernacular style of the Dutch settlers, which emerged in the Cape Colony. The museum was opened in 1986 by President P. W. Botha amid much anti-apartheid protest. The curator of the Delville Wood Memorial, T. Masanabo, told us in an interview that the previous museum was a tool of self-promotion and defiance by the apartheid state, a form of built propaganda promoting apartheid South Africa's image internationally to reinforce its place among other nations that had participated in the war.

The existing layers of commemoration and memorialisation at the Delville Wood memorial site had two notable omissions: firstly, there was no physical role of honour listing the names of individuals who had lost their lives during the battle (or the war), and secondly, neither the original memorial nor the subsequent museum acknowledged the role and loss of life in the SANLC. The difficulties of enforcing segregation led to the disbanding of the SANLC in 1918 rather than its integration with the rest of its forces in France. The SANLC members were, at the insistence of the South African government, not awarded medals for serving in the war, and their contribution to the war was ignored in the creation of the Delville Wood memorial.[16]

The year 2016 marked the centenary of the Battle of Delville Wood, and a new memorial was unveiled at the site as part of these commemorations. The new memorial, commissioned by the statutory body the South African Heritage Resources Agency (SAHRA), was intended to be a commemoration of the contribution of all South Africans to the war and was seen as a way to realign the skewed historical narratives represented at the already highly politicised memorial site. The development of the new Delville Wood memorial started in 2015. A professional team was appointed by SAHRA to design and implement the project, located over 13 000 kilometres away, to be opened by then President Jacob Zuma to mark the centenary of the battle in July of the following year. The logistical challenges were substantial. The memorial

Figure 10.1. The new memorial looking towards the original memorial arch. Photograph by Anix Consulting

required input and approval from both South African and French authorities. Construction needed to happen over a European winter in rural France on a site still littered with unexploded ordnance and unmarked graves. Despite this, the team did not want to compromise the conceptual thinking and intention behind the design.

The new memorial is seen by its Johannesburg architectural team, The Creative Axis Architects and Mayat Hart Architects, as a scar or wound on the site. As such, it is more a part of the landscape than its built structures, thereby recalling the remains of the trenches that are still visible throughout the wood. The new memorial is located on the axis of the site, following the model set up by both the original memorial and the museum, and forms part of the route taken when walking between the two. It consists of a role of honour of the names of all South Africans who lost their lives in the First World War – close to 15 000 individuals. The names include members of all the different South African armed forces who participated in the war, including the SANLC not previously commemorated on the site, and these are listed alphabetically, without any hierarchy of race, rank or unit.[17]

Notably, the memorial is all but invisible as the visitor arrives in the woods and walks up the long, tree-lined avenue to the original 1926 Herbert Baker memorial. It is perhaps the understatement of the new memorial rather than the overt politicisation of the site that makes it effective. The new memorial was seen as an opportunity to directly counter the prejudices of the old one. The initial response from the client was for it to make a statement and overshadow the original memorial. Restraint was chosen by the architects: it is only as the visitor walks through the triumphal arch of the old memorial that they become aware of the new memorial holding the site line and pathway to the museum. The memorial compels the movement of the viewer; its power comes from the process of moving through; and the visitor experiences the earth rising up around – all of which is suggested in figure 10.1. Visitors read and touch the list of names inscribed on the walls. As they descend and walk through the new memorial, they become submerged, as if in a trench, and are momentarily visually and physically removed from the surrounding woods. The new memorial is not triumphal but experiential; it requires the visitor to personally experience rather than merely to look at it.[18]

SS *MENDI* MEMORIAL

The SS *Mendi* was a mail ship that was converted to function as a troop ship during the First World War. The ship was tasked with carrying members of the SANLC to the front in France. It left Cape Town on 25 January 1917 with the last group of 803 officers and members of the SANLC to be taken to France. Shortly before 5 am on the morning of 20 February, having left the port of Plymouth the night before, the *Mendi* was tragically struck by a friendly ship, the much larger SS *Daro*, as the *Mendi* captain steered his ship through thick fog off the Isle of Wight – a reckless action that resulted in his licence being suspended. Water flooded into the hold where many men were asleep, and the ship tipped to one side and sank within twenty-five minutes. Most of the men on board could not swim and had to jump into the icy cold water. Of the 649 men who died, 607 were members of the SANLC. After the battle of Delville Wood, the sinking of the SS *Mendi* was South Africa's largest loss in the First World War, and it remains South Africa's greatest maritime tragedy to date.[19]

The South African government was informed of the tragedy by telegram, receiving the news three days after the event. The loss of the *Mendi* was announced on 9 March 1917 with parliament standing in silence as a recognition of the loss. Local magistrates called meetings to share the news with chiefs and headmen. Memorial services across South Africa were held, and communities mourned the loss of their sons, husbands, brothers and friends.[20] Despite the magnitude of the tragedy, the loss of the SS *Mendi* was largely forgotten in the post-war narratives and commemorations, with the South African government declining to grant the members of the SANLC their medals after the war.

In post-apartheid South Africa, the loss of the SS *Mendi* has become part of official histories, an alternative narrative to that of the past;[21] it has been marked and memorialised in many ways, with most major centres having some form of an SS *Mendi* monument or memorial.[22] In 2016, shortly after the commemoration of the 99th anniversary of the sinking of the SS *Mendi*, representatives from the City of Johannesburg, the Johannesburg Heritage Foundation, Ditsong Museums and the South African Legion, gathered in Avalon Cemetery in Soweto to consider how to upgrade and expand the Johannesburg SS *Mendi* memorial to commemorate the centenary the following year.

The existing memorial is located within the cemetery – one of the largest graveyards in South Africa, and the final resting place of many anti-apartheid activists – to serve the surrounding, largely black, community, which is itself a legacy of the apartheid policy of racial segregation. The original memorial was opened in 1995 by then President Nelson Mandela and Queen Elizabeth II, who was visiting the country at the time. It takes the form of a simple memorial wall, constructed by members of the local community, which records the names of those who had lost their lives in the maritime disaster, adding these to the original list of SANLC officers, both black and white, arranged according to rank. Despite being buried in a graveyard, none of the remains of those who lost their lives are located in South Africa. Victims were either lost at sea or buried in Commonwealth War Graves Commission (CWGC) cemeteries in Europe in accordance with the intergovernmental CWGC agreement during the First World War. The memorial is sited at a high point in the cemetery, with sweeping 180-degree views southwards across a sea of graves. The architects Mayat Hart put together a scheme which was launched at the centenary commemorations in February 2017, creating a forum for engagement between military veterans, descendants of the victims of the SS *Mendi*, as well as the community at large.

The first decision by the architects when designing the new memorial was to retain and honour the existing memorial wall. As the centrepiece of the new memorial, and a sign of respect to both it and its creators, the existing memorial wall is neither a grand nor monumental construction. It was built by community members out of a combination of stock face brick and sandstone blocks. The new extension to the memorial, in turn, takes its cue from existing domestic materials that are appropriate to the context, durable and intimately familiar. In addition to this, their intentionally intricate use – particularly in the integrated narrative artwork – required hands-on, precise and labour-intensive construction. This made the act of building the memorial a form of homage in itself. In addition to this, the layering of the new memorial on to the old allowed the community to embrace the new memorial as an extension of their original vision and desire for commemoration.

Figure 10.2. Thin members of the concrete pergola create a sense of enclosure when viewing the integrated display panels; they also repeat patterns and shadows that move through the day. Photograph by Papercut Photography

Conceptually, the extension to the memorial is intended to be a physical and spatial experience. This is not a traditional idea of the memorial as object, but rather one of the memorial as place. While the memorial can be seen as a hypothetical ship navigating the landscape of the cemetery, it is designed to be a space for everyday visits and use. The memorial is made up of a large raised platform connecting the original memorial wall with new brickwork panels and niches, which house built-in seating and display panels explaining the often-forgotten history of the SANLC in addition to that of the SS *Mendi*. This area is topped by a slender off-shutter concrete pergola (figure 10.2). The pergola creates a sense of enclosure and separation for the visitor to the monument while also framing and focusing views of the cemetery. The use and occupation of the memorial, be it for commemorative functions, educational school visits, or as a backdrop to funeral services, allows it to become a living site of memory, interpreted and reimagined by its users.

SENSORY DESIGN AND THE COUNTER-MONUMENT

While the Delville Wood and SS *Mendi* memorials are on vastly different continents, in contexts with varying degrees of exposure, they share a common phenomenological approach to the experience of architecture. Such an approach refers to the implementation of sensory design to create an experiential understanding of architectural space. The architect makes use of the considered manipulation of space, materials, texture, light and shadow to create a memorable physical encounter that has a direct and intentional impact on the human senses. Sensory design makes use of human perception, the triggering of memories and emotional responses through the physical experience of a space that goes beyond the merely tangible.[23]

Both memorials have made the physical experience of the viewer essential to their understanding and legibility. Both require the viewer to occupy them: walking through and touching, as well as offering a look-out, with a specific framed view of their physical and historical contexts. They use the physical manipulation of space as part of the experience and communication of the memorial. The Delville Wood memorial requires the visitor to slowly sink underground while moving through it, removing the beauty and stillness of the surrounding woods and immersing the visitor in the names inscribed on the walls. In contrast, the SS *Mendi* memorial raises the viewer up on a platform, as if 'floating' above the sea of graves. Here, visitors are both held and enclosed by the ribbed body of the memorial. Their view is directed to the horizon line beyond the anonymous rows of headstones. The experience of both memorials is intended to be personal, allowing users to frame their own understanding of the tragedy with the surrounding history and politics. It offers history and memory as personal, embodied experience rather than prescribed narrative.

The context in which the memorials were created may well have had an influence on the design approach. In an environment where earlier, prescriptive forms of monumentalisation are under scrutiny, and where there has been a dramatic shift in the official historic narrative, questioning how to frame the creation of the spaces of memory is to be expected. Both memorials are an intuitive response to such questioning. Not a simple rejection of a past narrative and embrace of a new one, they represent, instead, the creation of a new space for ongoing perception, reflection and questioning.

There are clear parallels between the thinking behind the creation of the Delville Wood and SS *Mendi* memorials and that which underpinned the

German counter-monument movement. A monument is meant to remind and to act as an anchor for memory. 'The traditional aim of war monuments has been to valorise the suffering in such a way to justify it, even redeem it historically', according to James E. Young, a leading scholar on postmodern monument theory.[24] Traditional monuments are typically seen as affirmative. They glorify an event, person or ideology, no matter how tragic.[25] They are a prescribed historical narrative usually written by the victors. The idea of a modern monument is, however, similarly problematic. To be modern signals a break from the past, with its burden of historical precedents and pitfalls. This break is near impossible when creating a traditional monument in a modern form or architectural language. As the architectural historian and critic Lewis Mumford once wrote, 'The notion of a modern monument is veritably a contradiction in terms. If it is a monument it is not modern, and if it is modern, it cannot be a monument.'[26]

The counter-monument is a rejection of the very principles of what defines a monument. In Germany, it was a response to both the inherited tradition of grand monuments and the perceived shortcomings of the act of monumentalisation. Monuments by their very nature represent a fixed, or fixing of, memory. This itself was often rejected and criticised, according to Young.[27] Critics felt that the concretising of memory effectively terminated further discussion and dialogue, with traditional monuments taking away the need for continued engagement. The argument advanced by proponents of the movement such as German artist Horst Hoheisel was that monuments should act as a trigger for the viewer to remember. He described the counter-monument as 'history turned into a pedestal, an invitation to the passer by who stands upon it to search for the memorial in their own heads. For there is the memorial to be found.'[28]

A counter-monument seeks to confront or disrupt established meanings and tropes. It celebrates and exploits the absences that are left through loss or the passage of time rather than physically filling these or trying to resolve them. It is an intimate introspective experience rather than distant viewing. Young, discussing the engagement with Holocaust memory in Germany, describes how its 'perpetual irresolution' guarantees engagement. A complete and final memorial would put an end to this, thereby silencing the process of discussion and remembering. This is where the counter-monument is fundamentally different. While it may still be a built form, the counter-monument is not a physical vessel for memory. It does not attempt to resolve. It does not attempt to validate. It places the burden of memory, interpretation and resolution on the viewer.[29] For, as Stevens, et al. also argue, the counter-monument is not static, it requires engagement.[30]

Young describes counter-monuments as those which reject and renegotiate 'the traditional forms and reasons for public memorial art', such as prominence and durability, figurative representation and the glorification of past deeds. He goes on to distinguish features that separate them from traditional built monuments: they tend to express a position which opposes a particular belief, they tend not to have monumental forms, they invite intimate and multisensory engagement, and finally, they require the visitor to work out and define meaning for themselves.[31] Spatially, this fundamental inversion of the principles of monumentalisation encourages the use of voids instead of solids, absence instead of presence, dark rather than light tones. There is an emphasis on the horizontal rather than vertical, and on forms that are sunken rather than elevated, which tend to be shifted off axis, dispersed or fragmented. The forms are multiple rather than singular.[32] The space for memory, however, does not reside in the memorial itself. Instead, it exists in a liminal space, between the memorial and the viewer, which is external to the memorial; at the same time, it exists in the internal space where the viewer engages with their own memory and conscience.[33] If putting up a monument can be seen as a way of forgetting, the creation of a counter-monument actively encourages remembering.

DYNAMIC MEMORY

The act of remembering, be it of personal experience or of a recalled historic past, is the essential and even defining feature of the power and impact of the counter-monument. Memory is more than just the ability to recall the past. Constantly evolving and changing, memory is what historian Pierre Nora describes as 'life, borne by living societies founded in its name', something that is, moreover, in constant flux, 'open to the dialectic of remembering and forgetting, unconscious of its successive deformations, vulnerable to manipulation and appropriation, susceptible to being long dormant and periodically revived'.[34] Cultural theorist Andreas Huyssen describes memory as 'the fissure between the past and the present', and – echoing Nora – something that is alive; it provides coherence to people's lives and structures their identity.[35]

The dynamic nature of memory, as described both by Nora and Huyssen, is due to the fact that memory itself is not a thing but an act, able to 'attach' itself to objects and places. As such, memory has to exist in the present even though it is a representation of the past.[36] It is what Nora refers to as 'a bond tying us to the eternal present'.[37] Regardless of what form memory takes, be it collective or individual, autobiographical or archival, it does not simply endure. Memory is not the past per se. It is an act of representation, of a real or sometimes imagined past. It is something that has to be created and can just as easily be forgotten and disappear. Memory belongs to the present.[38]

The counter-memorial, harnessing memory and requiring the act of remembering by the viewer, has to therefore exist in the present. References to the past exist only through active remembering. This is where a counter-monument differs from a traditional monument. A traditional monument, while being assertive of a particular outlook, can exist passively without any interaction for a static observer. It remains, even if no longer relevant or understood. A counter-monument exists and remains active and relevant as long as the memory, or the will to remember that surrounds it, continues to exist.

REMEMBERING THE NAMES

It is not coincidental that the Delville Wood memorial and, to a lesser extent, the SS *Mendi* memorial, reference the Vietnam Veterans War memorial in Washington designed by the architect Maya Lin. The competition-winning 1982 design broke classical conventions about the typology and transformed future memorials. The memorial takes the form of a sunken chevron-shaped slash in the landscape of the National Mall. Known as The Wall, it comprises two walls of polished granite, each over 75 metres long, dropping from the natural ground level down to 3.1 metres at their point of intersection. On the walls are a list in chronological order of loss of the nearly 58 000 American servicemen confirmed dead or missing in the war.[39] As Lin notes, 'the power of the design lies in the overwhelming presence of individual names, which represent complicated human lives cut short'.[40] The memorial was designed as a place to remember. It is designed to be interactive, with the viewer touching names and taking rubbings, thereby eliciting an emotional response.

In the discourse of counter-monuments and counter-memory, this memorial is significant for a number of reasons. Firstly, it is a memorial and not a monument. The Vietnam War was extremely contentious in American society, with very strong internal opposition to US involvement. As such, the choice of a design that was non-political and healing was significant.[41] Similarly, the listing of names in chronological order, with no hierarchy, gives importance to the power of the individual name over that of the national identity.[42]

The memorial has become a sacred place of healing and reverence. It was never intended as a symbol of solidarity but rather as a structure that renders explicit a nation's conflicting conceptions of itself and its past.[43] The meaning of the memorial and what it represents has similarly evolved. It has changed over time to become a memorial cluster consisting of the memorial wall dedicated in 1982, a flagpole dedicated in 1983, and the *Three Servicemen* statue by sculptor Frederick Hart, placed in 1984 to appease many in the public who called for a traditional sculptural response.[44] The memorial is no longer just a counter-monument. It is a dialogic monument establishing contrasting spatial, thematic and experiential relationships to Washington's existing commemorative topography.[45] It creates spatial relationships and site lines with the Washington monument and the Lincoln memorial. It also sits in dialogue with its newer, contrasting additions. This interaction adds potentially ambiguous layers that need interpretation, creating a new space for the interpretation of memory, meaning and dialogue.

POST-APARTHEID MEMORIALS

While the existing Delville Wood and SS *Mendi* memorials were built to counter the absences found in the historical narrative, they are not prescriptive in message. Unlike earlier memorials on the site, the new Delville Wood memorial is not prominent, but rather sunken and hidden. The SS *Mendi* memorial makes use of common domestic construction methods and materials. Most importantly, both reject figurative representations or the glorification of past deeds. Both memorials require the viewer's engagement with them, physically as well as emotionally. The viewer is required to move through these memorials, read the names, understand, feel, discuss and interpret the historical events commemorated. These are meant to be a trigger for memory rather than a representation of a prescribed and official narrative. The monuments are also spatially discursive: the Delville Wood memorial is in dialogue, spatially, with the original memorial, museum and the wood itself, while the SS *Mendi* memorial is in conversation with the nearby graveyard at the same time as it acknowledges the absence of the graves of those whom it commemorates.

The end of the apartheid regime in South Africa did not lead to a wholesale removal or re-scripting of earlier monuments and memorials. The complex

South African project of multiculturalism and its associated multiple and fragmented narratives presents a range of 'continuities and discontinuities' in the symbolic representation of the past. Marc Howard Ross identifies three models that have been used for transformation: appropriation, modification and addition.[46] Each of these is an engagement with the past and requires an act, be it a dialogue with or a challenging of the pre-existing narrative. It is not as simple, permanent or complete as removal or erasure. Instead, it is an incomplete and ongoing process in which the static spaces of memory are poorly equipped to accommodate the dynamic nature of memory.

The act of memory – essential to the meaning of the counter-monument – which both monuments elicit, has a material component. The phenomenological approach of remembering, interpreting and engaging with both memorials requires the visitor's interaction with the monument. Memory thus becomes an embodied experience. It is possible to look at both memorials as part of a greater trend in the architectural language of memory. Architect David Adjaye, when speaking about his 2019 exhibition 'Making Memory', explains that the exhibition, much like the work of his practice that it showcases, 'is set up as a provocation or a question to the public'. Furthermore, 'The monument is no longer a representation; it is an experience of time and place that is available to everyone.'[47] Similarly, the understanding and interpretation of the meaning of a memorial is shaped by both the time and place of the viewer.

Dismissing memory as a contemporary architectural trope is perhaps oversimplifying something more opaque. In a context as politicised and historically contested as that of Delville Wood or the SS *Mendi* (or, indeed, most contemporary South African monuments or memorials), any act of memorialisation can have significant – and unforeseen – repercussions. Post-apartheid memory and identity in South Africa remain largely unresolved and ambiguous, given the ongoing contestation of historical narratives, power imbalances and social subjugation. The multiplicity of narratives, histories and identities feeds into this, complicating the memory of a painful and difficult past. The counter-monument does not require the clarity or singular narrative of a traditional monument, making it particularly significant in this context. It is supportive of questioning and interrogation, and of multiple and individual viewpoints.

The Delville Wood and SS *Mendi* memorials were consciously designed to encourage such interrogation, and to represent multiple and forgotten narratives. Both allow for the current time, place and experience of the viewer to shape their meaning. They do, however, have limitations: they alone cannot address the injustices or omissions of the past. And while they are physical anchors for memory, fixed points for learning and questioning, they need to be understood as part of a network of events and actions, a collective of creative acts surrounding the remembering of each event. In the case of the SS *Mendi*, the memorial may be understood as a counterpoint to the poetic tales of bravery of the men who went down with the ship, as commemorated in the South African National Order of *Mendi* for bravery. The memorial can thus be viewed as being part of the dialogue with the story of the SS *Mendi* and the SANLC in both popular fiction and official school syllabuses. The counter-monument strives to be a constant point of questioning and reaction, even as formerly marginalised and forgotten narratives become more mainstream. Instead of providing the unified singular narrative (and identity) of past memorials, the Delville Wood and SS *Mendi* memorials can be seen as creating space for flexible and changing – rather than rigid or static – individual interpretation and understanding.

NOTES

1. Yasmin Mayat and Brendan Hart, the founding partners of Mayat Hart Architects, are directly involved in the creation of the Delville Wood and SS *Mendi* Memorials.
2. South Africa had only existed as a Union since 1910. Prior to that, it was a collection of separate British colonies and conquered former Boer republics.
3. Greg Mills and David Williams, *7 Battles That Shaped South Africa* (Cape Town: Tafelberg, 2006), 117.
4. 'World War I and the South African Native Labour Contingent', *South African History Online*, accessed 27 August 2019, http://www.sahistory.org.za/article/world-war-i-and-south-african-native-labour-contingent.
5. Ian Uys, *Delville Wood* (Johannesburg: Uys Publishers, 1983), 52.
6. Mills and Williams, *7 Battles*, 109.
7. South African National Memorial Delville Wood, *The Delville Wood Memorial Book* (London: St Clements Press, 1926), 5.
8. *Delville Wood Memorial Book*, 7–8.
9. Herbert Baker, a celebrated British-born architect made his name in South Africa designing prominent government, civic and private projects after the end of the South African War. His style, an amalgamation of South African colonial traditions, classical

architectural principles and a response to local context and materials, created a new architectural language for the newly unified country.

10 The South African War saw the British Empire taking control of the whole of South Africa after the defeat of the two Boer republics – the South African Republic and the Orange Free State.

11 *Programme of Unveiling Ceremony, South African National Memorial, Delville Wood*, 10 October 1926, 3.

12 *Programme of Unveiling Ceremony*, 4.

13 *Programme of Unveiling Ceremony*, 7.

14 *Programme of Unveiling Ceremony*, 17.

15 *Programme of Unveiling Ceremony*, 17.

16 Mills and Williams, *7 Battles*, 122.

17 For a previous discussion of these ideas, see Brendan Hart and Yasmin Mayat, 'Making a Memorial Matter', *Architecture South Africa* (Nov/Dec 2017): 18–23.

18 The memorial has been awarded the 2016 South African Property Owners Association Award, the 2017 Gauteng Institute for Architecture Award of Merit, and the 2018 South African Institute for Architects Award of Excellence.

19 Norman Clothier, *Black Valour: The South African Native Labour Contingent, 1916–1918, and the Sinking of the Mendi* (Pietermaritzburg: University of Natal Press, 1987); and Kathy Munro, 'Death by Drowning, Tragedy of the SS Mendi', *The Heritage Portal*, accessed 5 May 2017, http://www.theheritageportal.co.za/article/death-drowning-tragedy-ss-mendi.

20 Clothier, *Black Valour*, 77–82.

21 For example, Fred Khumalo's acclaimed novel, *Dancing the Death Drill*, a fictionalised version of the events surrounding the sinking of the SS *Mendi* and the SANLC.

22 'Wreck of the SS Mendi', *Wessex Archaeology*, accessed 1 July 2019, https://www.wessexarch.co.uk/our-work/wreck-ss-mendi.

23 'Theory of Phenomenology: Analysing Substance, Application, and Influence', Kansas University Centre for Teaching Excellence, accessed 1 July 2019, https://cte.ku.edu/sites/cte.drupal.ku.edu/files/docs/portfolios/kraus/essay2.pdf.

24 James E. Young, 'Memory and Counter Memory', *Harvard Design Magazine* 9 (1999): 3.

25 See Quentin Stevens, Karen Franck and Ruth Fazakerley, 'Counter Monuments: The Anti-Monumental and The Dialogic', *The Journal of Architecture* 17.6 (2014): 951–72.

26 Young, 'Memory and Counter Memory', 5.

27 Young, 'Memory and Counter Memory'.

28 As quoted in Young, 'Memory and Counter Memory', 1.

29 Young, 'Memory and Counter Memory', 2.
30 Stevens et al., 'Counter Monument', 954, 962; and Young, 'Memory and Counter Memory', 3.
31 As quoted in Stevens et al., 'Counter Monuments', 952.
32 In Stevens, et al., 'Counter Monuments', 956–59.
33 Young, 'Memory and Counter Memory', 3–6.
34 Pierre Nora, 'Between Memory and History: Les Lieux de Mémoire', *Representations: Memory and Counter-Memory* 26 (Spring 1989): 8.
35 Andreas Huyssen, *Twilight Memories: Marking Time in a Culture of Amnesia* (London: Routledge, 1995), 3.
36 Huyssen, *Twilight Memories*, 2–3.
37 Nora, 'Between Memory and History', 8.
38 Huyssen, *Twilight Memories*, 2–3.
39 Robin Wagner-Pacifici and Barry Schwartz, 'The Vietnam Veterans Memorial: Commemorating a Difficult Past', *American Journal of Sociology* 97.2 (1991): 376–420.
40 Eva Schmeidl, 'The Vietnam Veterans Memorial and Its Impact on US Memorial Culture', *Dateien* 2011, accessed 4 July 2019, https://www.jfki.fuberlin.de/academics/SummerSchool/Dateien2011/Papers/meigs_schmeidl.pdf.
41 Schmeidl, 'The Vietnam Veterans Memorial'.
42 Wagner-Pacifici and Schwartz, 'The Vietnam Veterans Memorial', 400, 405.
43 Wagner-Pacifici and Schwartz, 'The Vietnam Veterans Memorial', 407–08.
44 Schmeidl, 'The Vietnam Veterans Memorial'.
45 Stevens et al., 'Counter Monuments', 954.
46 As quoted in Paul Nesbitt-Larking, 'Culture and Belonging in Divided Societies: Contestation and Symbolic Landscapes', *Political Psychology* 32.4 (2011): 720–23.
47 'David Adjaye Curates Making Memory Exhibition at the Design Museum', *Dezeen*, accessed 4 February 2019, https://www.dezeen.com/2019/02/04/david-adjaye-making-memory-exhibition-design-museum/.

REFERENCES

Clothier, Norman. *Black Valour: The South African Native Labour Contingent, 1916–1918, and the Sinking of the Mendi.* Pietermaritzburg: University of Natal Press, 1987.

'David Adjaye Curates Making Memory Exhibition at the Design Museum'. *Dezeen*. Accessed 4 February 2019, https://www.dezeen.com/2019/02/04/david-adjaye-making-memory-exhibition-design-museum/.

Delville Wood. *Delville Wood.* Available at www.delvillewood.com. Accessed 27 August 2019.

Hart, Brendan, and Yasmin Mayat. 'Making a Memorial Matter'. *Architecture South Africa* 88 Nov/Dec (2017): 18–23.

Huyssen, Andreas. *Twilight Memories: Marking Time in a Culture of Amnesia*. London: Routledge, 1995.

Mills, Greg, and David Williams. *7 Battles That Shaped South Africa*. Cape Town: Tafelberg, 2006.

Munro, Kathy. 'Death by Drowning, Tragedy of the SS Mendi'. *The Heritage Portal*. Accessed 5 May 2017, http://www.theheritageportal.co.za/article/death-drowning-tragedy-ss-mendi.

Nesbitt-Larking, Paul. 'Culture and Belonging in Divided Societies: Contestation and Symbolic Landscapes'. *Political Psychology* 32.4 (2011): 720–23.

Nora, Pierre. 'Between Memory and History: Les Lieux de Mémoire'. *Representations: Memory and Counter-Memory* 26 (Spring 1989): 8.

Programme of Unveiling Ceremony. South African National Memorial, Delville Wood. n.p., 10 October 1926.

South African National Memorial Delville Wood. *The Delville Wood Memorial Book*. London: St Clements Press, 1926.

Stevens, Quentin, Karen Franck, and Ruth Fazakerley. 'Counter-Monuments: The Anti-Monumental and The Dialogic'. *The Journal of Architecture* 17.6 (2014): 951–72.

'The Vietnam Veterans Memorial and its Impact on US Memorial Culture'. *Dateien* 2011. Accessed 4 July 2019, https://www.jfki.fuberlin.de/academics/SummerSchool/Dateien2011/Papers/meigs_schmeidl.pdf.

Uys, Ian. *Delville Wood*. Johannesburg: Uys Publishers, 1983.

Wagner-Pacifici, Robin, and Barry Schwartz. 'The Vietnam Veterans Memorial: Commemorating a Difficult Past'. *American Journal of Sociology* 97.2 (1991): 376–420.

'World War I and the South African Native Labour Contingent'. *South African History Online*. Accessed 27 August 2019, http://www.sahistory.org.za/article/world-war-i-and-south-african-native-labour-contingent.

'Wreck of the SS Mendi'. *Wessex Archaeology*. Accessed 1 July 2019, https://www.wessexarch.co.uk/our-work/wreck-ss-mendi.

Young, James E. 'Memory and Counter-Memory'. *Harvard Design Magazine* 9 (1999): 1–10.

INTERVIEW

Masanabo, T. Personal interview with authors. Longueval, France, 14 September 2015.

11 RE-HISTORICISING CREDO MUTWA'S KWA KHAYA LENDABA CULTURAL VILLAGE IN SOWETO

ALI KHANGELA HLONGWANE AND TARA WEBER

Soweto's township of Central Western Jabavu is home to one of Credo Vusamazulu Mutwa's unique and strange installations – part public art and open-air museum and, according to some, site of spirituality. Kwa Khaya Lendaba cultural village is located just off Mphuthi Street, on the corner of Ntsane and Majoeng Streets, atop a hill beside the Oppenheimer Tower. Not far from this is the June 16, 1976 Interpretation Centre created in 2006 as part of the commemoration of the thirtieth anniversary of the 1976 uprising, and carefully sited opposite the historic Morris Isaacson High School. The latter forms part of the mapping and reimagining of routes that were used by protesting students on that day. There is, however, an uneasy and disconnected relationship between these developments which include the Kwa Khaya Lendaba cultural village, the June 16, 1976 Interpretation Centre, and the Student March Trail.[1] As part of envisaged tourist attractions in this sector of Soweto, they constitute a disjuncture when it comes to Mutwa's site.

Kwa Khaya Lendaba cultural village is the artistic work of Credo Mutwa. Established in 1974 under the patronage of the West Rand Administration Board (WRAB), the village is in many respects an expression of the WRAB's ideological outlook and tribalist rhetoric. Indeed, Mutwa's relationship with

Figure 11.1. Entrance of the Kwa Khaya Lendaba cultural village, c. 1974. Photograph by Gilbert Briscoe. Courtesy of the Johannesburg Art Gallery

the municipality and the village constitutes a blurring of his ideology with that of the apartheid government. His vision for the village was an open-air museum preserving 'African Culture': Museum Africa records from 1967 indicate that Mutwa was consulted as an authority on African objects as he was presumed to have an understanding of museums and their propensity to 'ethnologise' the very practices in which he engaged.[2]

After the 1976 Soweto uprising and ensuing media coverage of the *Cillié Commission of Inquiry into the Riots at Soweto*,[3] where Credo Mutwa's statements were widely interpreted as in direct conflict with the anti-apartheid movement, both the Kwa Khaya Lendaba cultural village and Mutwa's home in Diepkloof were set on fire. Following the incident, Mutwa relocated to Mafikeng, where he established another cultural village, supported by the bantustan of Bophuthatswana. David Chidester, a scholar in the field of comparative religion, writes of this development: 'At Lotlamoreng Dam Cultural Park, beginning in 1983, Mutwa supervised the construction of small adobe villages, each representing the traditional culture of one of South Africa's tribal African peoples.'[4] Following his expulsion from Bophuthatswana, after its re-incorporation into South Africa in 1994, the site was reclaimed as an asset by the National Parks Board. He subsequently relocated to Kuruman in today's Northern Cape province.

The events of June 16 represent the erasure of memory of the site's problematic association with the anti-apartheid struggle, and a new public who engage these sites as township heritage. Unlike at other places along the students' route, there is little in the way of text panels at the site that engage with and contextualise the history of the village. In fact, save for one remaining sign at the entrance, text panels describing and giving context to the cultural village have gone missing. This means that Credo Mutwa's complicated relationship with June 16 is made *invisible* by omission. Mutwa as a historical figure has been rehabilitated post-1994 as he is once again championed as a custodian of indigenous knowledge. This demonstrates the further mythologising of both Mutwa and the site – a vein that runs throughout his complex history.

'HISTORIAN, PLAYWRIGHT, ARCHITECT, PAINTER, SCULPTOR AND HEALER'[5]

There is scant scholarly reflection on Credo Mutwa's place in the artistic, heritage and indigenous knowledge landscapes of South Africa. Nonetheless, the writings and records that this chapter builds upon grapple in various ways with his complex life, thoughts, works and legacy. Chidester, for example, provides biographical information on Mutwa's birth, parentage, and religious and spiritual orientation. He also explores his relationship with the ideology of apartheid, his role as an 'indigenous environmentalist', and his international travels. For the art scholar Ruth Kerkham Simbao, on the other hand, Mutwa 'continues to fall beyond the perimeters of acceptable art, or even art at all'.[6]

Nevertheless, the art historian Elza Miles describes Mutwa's open-air museum as a 'living and tactile document of the use of materials varying from clay, mud, dung, cement, stone, wood and grass to waste building material and recycled metal in the architecture and sculpture of southern Africa'.[7] Furthermore, Miles situates Mutwa's work, particularly his 'huge custodian figures [as] worthy counterparts of Ndebele mud sculptures as well as the *mbari* and cement sculptures of Nigeria'. She also makes reference to a trip Mutwa took to Zimbabwe that might explain some of the aesthetics found in the cultural village. These observations by Miles are significant insofar as they locate Mutwa in a wider national and even pan-African context, thus contesting the narrow ethnic framework of his sponsors – such as the WRAB and Bophuthatswana – and their politics of culture and ethnicity. It is equally important that Miles identifies his wider sources of influence, including recycling 'metal from waste tin cans, a technique he studied in Kenya'.[8] Materials such as cement, as well as recycled materials are, indeed, widely used in South African art production.

However, it is interesting to note that, while Miles does recognise Credo Mutwa as an artist, it is within the confines of a 'life in clay and wood' – the sub-heading in her book, *Land and Lives*. What is curious about her description of the open-air museum is the way in which it replicates the process of the 'production of authenticity'. While paintings form an integral part of the village, they are largely excluded from the narrative in favour of a description that better fits the conception of art in South Africa – in this case, what 'Black art' should look like. Mutwa's paintings are without the visual cues for authenticity in relation to African art as understood in the West. They are gaudy, use acrylic paints, and depict bizarre, surrealist scenes that make little distinction between folklore and 'fakelore'. According to Chidester, authenticity manifests as 'folklore/fakelore' and is produced and mobilised to evoke 'invented traditions' in the service of various interests such as reimagined nationalisms, and providing tourists with a taste of bygone eras.[9] In the 1950s, Credo Mutwa found work at a curio shop in Johannesburg, authenticating and interpreting African objects for sale to a tourist market. It was here that he emerged as a self-proclaimed authority on African indigenous knowledge. As pointed out by Spencer Crew and James Sims, 'Authenticity is not about factuality or reality. It is about authority, and objects have no authority, people do.'[10] It was Mutwa himself who provided authenticity to both the stories and the objects. His storytelling ability and his confidence provided an alternative source of information to that of the official records and reports by missionaries and other colonial officials and ethnologists.

An interesting comparison can be made between Kwa Khaya Lendaba cultural village and the Owl House of Helen Martins in the Eastern Cape province. Both sites are now museums in different forms, and yet each is more than a museum: it is a place of what we might characterise as a deeply personal battle by the artist with history and mythologies. The Owl House in Nieu Bethesda has become a detour destination: not far from the neighbouring town of Graaff-Reinet, it is deep in a Karoo valley. The village is isolated, surrounded by koppies and haunted by the fossils of creatures known to us through that strange bedfellow of myth and legend – palaeontology. Martins was considered an outsider artist and died in 1976. The parallels between the Owl House and Kwa Khaya Lendaba extend beyond the common use of material elements such as concrete and glass bottles repurposed as eyes and clothing, shattered or ground to form paint. Helen Martins was an enigmatic figure, reclusive and depressive, tethered to the small town by an ailing and abusive father for whom she became a reluctant carer. As with Credo Mutwa, there is a mythology around Martins as an extraordinary eccentric figure.

At the heart of the comparison of the Owl House to Kwa Khaya Lendaba lies its famous sculpture garden consisting of over 300 cement figures, many of which are elaborately decorated with glass. As the art scholar Susan Imrie Ross describes in her book *This Is My World*, 'Images from Eastern philosophy and various religions, such as Islam, Christianity, Buddhism, and Hinduism are portrayed in the form of statues, bas-reliefs, bottle edifices, structures, and inscriptions formed in wire on various fences.'[11] Some are human, some animal, and some can only be described as chimeras, not only of different animals but also of different mythologies. This 'blurring' is common to both artists. In Kwa Khaya Lendaba, one section depicts a dinosaur fighting alongside a sabre-tooth tiger against a pair of prehistoric humans. It also has a section known as 'the Arab Village' containing distinctly un-Arabic imagery seemingly inspired by Great Zimbabwe.

To say that the mythologies and figures presented by Mutwa and Martins are 'fakelore' is perhaps an unfair categorisation. After all, are myths and folk tales not all in a sense formed in the oyster of human oral tradition around small grains of truth? In the introduction to his first book, *Indaba, My Children*, Mutwa writes assuredly: 'Many will find it hard to believe much of what I have revealed in this book, but I am not in the least bit concerned, because whether I am believed or not, everything I write here is *true*.'[12] Yet it remains unclear what exactly is meant by 'true'. Is it that the stories are factual accounts of events? Is it that they are true in the sense that this is how they are known to the cultures from where they come? Or true to Credo Mutwa? If that is the case, how can one say these stories are 'fake'?

To the casual observer, Mutwa's paintings are reminiscent of surrealist artworks, particularly those influenced by dreams. They carry many of the characteristics of the movement, including the juxtaposition of images and symbols. According to museum curators Simon Wilson and Jessica Lack, the 'aim of Surrealism was to reveal the unconscious and reconcile it with rational life' both in art and literature.[13] Surrealism, understood as 'beyond real', with the evocative juxtaposition of incongruous elements, could well be applied to Kwa Khaya Lendaba and much of Mutwa's other work. The same figures often appear in both his paintings and the sculptures in the Kwa Khaya Lendaba, the 'home of storytelling'. One example is the turtle, which, according to African legend, carries the world on its back;[14] this is, however, also closely associated with Native American folklore as well as Hindu culture, where the myth is known as Akupār. There is, nevertheless, evidence to corroborate this story, both in terms of African folklore as well as the uses of reptiles for medicinal purposes.[15] It is noteworthy that the contemporary writer Gcina Mhlophe also has a turtle story in her book *Fudukazi's Magic*.[16]

This story is an example of the 'borrowing' and blurring that occurs between cultures and eras. When people come into contact, however small the interaction, a trace is left, sometimes being carried like a bur across mountains and seas to plant itself in the imagination of another storyteller. While Mutwa conceived of Kwa Khaya Lendaba cultural village as a means to preserve culture and tradition, as if these are static, what it in fact exhibits is the opposite. It shows that mythologies collide and change over hundreds of years of storytelling. Mutwa's views around protecting African culture and indigenous knowledge from erasure are still part of contemporary discourse, although the way his ideology played into apartheid rhetoric and the othering of black people have left it tainted. In a post-1994 landscape, the historian Flora Edouwaye S. Kaplan offers useful advice: 'Museums can play an active and vital role in ... raising historical and national consciousness, interpreting displays in broad contexts, and educating the public to the history of indigenous politics.'[17]

Though the Kwa Khaya Lendaba site is excluded from many books about Johannesburg and South African museums, a brief description may be found in *Soweto*, a book of photographs by Peter Magubane, with accompanying text by Charlene Smith. Yet even here there is a failure to contextualise the site: 'Student activists partially destroyed it during the 1976 student uprising, which began a stone's throw away. Today, despite its dilapidated air, this national cultural treasure is still a place of magic and mystery.'[18] Mutwa himself is featured in a book by Lucille Davie in a section titled: 'Oppenheimer

Park – Place of Gods and Tokoloshes'. Davie's book forms part of the growing literature on heritage, memorialisation, tourism, museums and public art produced post-1994. She maps and briefly discusses Kwa Khaya Lendaba, both as an integral part of the Oppenheimer Park and as 'the cultural village' conceived by Mutwa when he was living in Soweto 'as a traditional healer and creating sculptures and figures from recycled metal'.[19]

Reflecting on Mutwa's ideological outlook, Thandeka Mtshali discusses the place he occupies in the age-old tradition of healing and his role as a High Sanusi, or shaman, thus positioning him as a complex figure 'in the sense that he has one foot in tradition and the other in modernity'.[20] By studying Mutwa's writings, Ntongela Masilela attempts to trace his complex personality. Masilela notes that 'perhaps the one singular distinction of Credo Mutwa within the various generations of the New African intellectuals is that he moved from tradition to modernity and back to tradition'.[21] Masilela goes on to write:

> This may be the explanation of why in conceiving himself as a healer [and] shaman he refuses to distinguish between history and myth, between explanation and speculation, between metaphysical and dialectician, between philosophy and politics, between creative writer and philosopher, between animism and Christianity, between autobiography and fiction. While Credo Mutwa's refusal or incapacity to recognise disciplinary boundaries, different epistemological systems of explanation, as well as different modes of discourse, account for his great facility as a storyteller, it is also at the centre of his endless political blunders.[22]

In the 1970s, when the ideology of Black Consciousness was still at its peak, with themes of 'back to the roots', Mutwa produced a play, *Unosilimela*, at the University of the Witwatersrand. Mutwa described this play as 'Umlinganiso – The living imitation', and in an illuminating article of the same title, he writes about theatre 'before the coming of White men to Africa':

> I beg you first of all to know that theatre is as old as Man himself, and that even in the remotest Pre-History men of various races loved to dress up as animals and even as supernatural beings and to behave like those animals and those supernatural creatures for a few moments in order to terrify, educate or simply entertain other men. There are scores of caves both in Africa and in

Europe, caves which were once the homes of prehistoric people, in which you find rock-paintings of men disguised as animals for various reasons.[23]

Two writers, Mango Tshabangu and Vincent Kunene, went on to debate whether *Unosilimela* was indeed authentic black theatre, and in what ways it was a 'revelation ... to the Black men of his ancestral culture and religion'.[24]

A noteworthy view regarding Mutwa and his play in the era of Black Consciousness is that of Robert Mshengu Kavanagh, compiler and editor of *South African People's Plays*: 'Though Mutwa's reverence for the African past and its values is part of what contemporary [mid-1960s to early 1970s] Black Consciousness is about, Mutwa's rejection of the modern city, its technology and its children in favour of a mystical paradise presided over by a religious hierarchy, stamps him as both a romantic visionary and a conservative.' Nonetheless, Kavanagh acknowledges *Unosilimela* 'as the richest in the collection [as] an epic, embracing a great variety of experiences conceived in an imaginative framework of rapidly alternation modes – realistic, satire, dream, symbol, narrative and ritual'.[25] All the latter elements are at play in Mutwa's public histories such as the heritage site Kwa Khaya Lendaba, and the practice of making public histories will be poorer if we continue to ignore his contributions. These elements are, however, underpinned by both progressive and reactionary assumptions, which should constantly be interrogated.

MUTWA'S IDEOLOGICAL OUTLOOK

Mutwa's admirers have managed to rehabilitate and appropriate his ideas by ignoring his ideology and his statements at the Cillié Commission. The journalist Bongani Madondo, for example, positions Mutwa in the contemporary politics of culture by describing a visit –probably his first encounter – with Mutwa:

> 'Why would you be interested in me, a witch doctor like me? ... Since when have I, Credo Mutwa, a liar, a cheat and a fake – so said the whites – become an object of interest? ... I am uneasy. I fought for black African tradition. I was ridiculed, I was robbed and, furthermore, two attempts were made to kill me. Why am I now an object of interest?' He is referring to the infamous, if tragic, act of buffoonery when he was exiled out of Soweto in the mid-1970s by bands of bloodhounds, youth who believed Mutwa was either a collaborator with the Boers or a false prophet, possibly both.[26]

Referring to contemporary struggles as 'the omen of chaos', Madondo chooses to be silent on the crux of the matter: what did Mutwa say to the Cillié Commission?

The South African Literary Awards (SALA) conferred a Lifetime Achievement Literary Award on Mutwa in 2017. On its website, SALA seemingly endorses his world view: 'The greatest unrest [June 16, 1976] in Johannesburg and the popularisation of communism in the black struggle drew Africans away from their traditional roots ... he supported a separation between white and black in order to preserve black traditional tribal customs and way of life.' Furthermore, SALA fails to problematise the so-called 'black traditional tribal customs and way of life', and posits the view that 'in 1976, students partially burnt down the cultural village after [Mutwa] was misquoted on Afrikaans radio'.[27] In taking this position, SALA ignores the historical record.

Mutwa's testimony to the Cillié Commission was, indeed, widely reported. The *Natal Mercury*, for example, quoted Mutwa extensively:

> The Black Consciousness movement in Soweto committed 'sheer shameful murder' by climbing over the bodies of innocent children in their struggle for power, the Cillié Commission was told yesterday ... [Mutwa] said the riots would go down in history as a shameful episode, both for Black and White people ... He said that at Diepkloof he saw a 'little bloody fool' throw a carton of beer into a police-man's face ... The witchdoctor [sic] could not blame the police for firing. 'I am against the monsters behind the riots, the instigators who pushed children into the jaws of death.'[28]

Helen Zille, who was at the time a journalist with the *Rand Daily Mail*, reported on the hearings as follows:

> A Soweto witchdoctor yesterday called on the government to send in the Defence Force to quell the countrywide unrest. Mr Credo Mutwa, who is also a WRAB employee, made the suggestion before the Cillié Commission of Inquiry in Pretoria yesterday. Outlining his plan, Mr Mutwa said: 'When two forces contend; the Bantu always follows the stronger group. At the moment Black Power certainly appears to be stronger. Why doesn't the Government use the Defence Force – not jet fighters and machine guns, but a display

of power to stamp out the unrest from this land?' ... Mr Mutwa said he was convinced Whites had masterminded the riots ... 'Although I throw the bones of divination, I don't know who is behind these riots. The riots were so well organised that it was impossible that Blacks had planned them alone,' Mr Mutwa said, 'Who is teaching our people to make such sophisticated firebombs?'[29]

Credo Mutwa continued to reaffirm his views in books such as *My People: The Incredible Writings of a Zulu Witchdoctor*:

> Apartheid is a word which the world outside South Africa has come to know and hate, but how many people know what it really means? The world has equated this word with discrimination, but in fact it means almost the opposite. To discriminate is to distinguish between two things and decide which of them is best. Apartheid is to distinguish without deciding *which* is best. Apartheid is a law of nature. We do not see different species of birds and animals mingling together indiscriminately, but each remaining with its own kind, its own customs and instincts. Nor do we see them arguing that one species is superior to another. This argument seldom arises among human beings unless two different races, nations or creeds become mingled together in the same place. Are the Afrikaners to be blamed for having made this discovery?[30]

In his introduction to *Indaba, My Children*, Mutwa refers to stories that lay bare 'the strange workings of the mind of the African',[31] thus reinforcing problematic and colonialist visions of Africa and its people as mystical, unknown and the Other.

Since Mutwa's death on 25 March 2020, the project of rehabilitation – or, as some might say, rectification– of his image has gained more traction. Pitika Ntuli writes: 'The persecution stemmed from the fact that he was speaking on African essences, of knowing who we were. Some might have misinterpreted that to think he was supporting the Bantustans. Others, still, thought he was giving white people the secrets to our origins. Either way, it was misguided, misplaced and unlearned prejudice.'[32] Interestingly, Mutwa was granted a state funeral.

THE BRISCOE / WRAB / MUTWA ARCHIVE

The Briscoe / WRAB / Mutwa archive, which can be accessed in the Johannesburg Art Gallery archives, provides a different entry point to Credo Mutwa's creation of the village, both as artist and employee of the WRAB; it offers an opportunity to unpack continuity between contemporary memory-making and the political context and ideological function of the village in buttressing apartheid ideology. This archive has been utilised to conserve the cultural village in line with the Heritage Resources Act of 1989, even though the site itself is not a declared heritage site. The photographic archive includes architectural drawings and re-representations of the making of Kwa Khaya Lendaba cultural village – the 'huts' and the materials used to build them – as well as Mutwa's large human and animal figures, both in the making and as completed. It is also a photographic record of Mutwa and other traditional healers who were either his *amathwasa* (students) or healers in their own right, performing 'traditional' rituals as well as interacting with WRAB officials sponsoring the cultural village (figure 11.2). Given that the images are not labelled, it is impossible to tell who of the onlookers is an official checking the progress of the site's construction and who is a tourist. These photographs can be considered an archive of the 'production of authenticity', one in which Chidester places Mutwa as a complicit figure alongside onlookers whose presence serves to exoticise as well as validate the site and activities.

At its worst, this photographic archive of observers calls to mind the despicable practice of 'living exhibitions' in Europe in the late 1800s and early 1900s. So-called authentic African villages and activities, with living 'occupants', were displayed for the European public to ogle. The art historian Annie E. Coombes writes of these exhibits: 'Integral to the effectivity of almost all these public displays was the rhetoric of "objectivity" and "authenticity". At the same time, however, the promoters were only too keenly aware of the amusement value of these kinds of exhibits and their potential as a massive crowd-stopper …'[33] While it is true that neither Mutwa's village nor his activities can be compared to these exhibits, there are still uncomfortable parallels in which he can be seen as something of an opportunistic figure.

Gilbert Briscoe, who assembled the Briscoe / WRAB / Mutwa archive, was, like Mutwa, a former Johannesburg City Parks and Zoo employee. The major gap in the archive is supplementary records of decisions and reflections on

Figure 11.2. Credo Mutwa and *amathwasa*, with tourist onlookers, c. 1974. Photograph by Gilbert Briscoe. Courtesy of the Johannesburg Art Gallery

the making of the site at the time. It is a critical gap when one takes into consideration Iain Borden's view that architecture – and, one might add, public art and memorials – in post-apartheid South Africa 'emerges … not as the projected image of a single mind, but as it most often is, that is as the product of a hugely complex intersection of ideas, individuals, groups, thoughts, intentions and propositions'.[34] The archive as a concept is one that is, for the most part, characterised by these gaps: though silent, they also speak of the silence around the matter.

Kwa Khaya Lendaba has a fraught history that many in the old administration, and some in the new, prefer to ignore. It is a loose thread on the June 16 narrative tapestry. If tugged, it might unravel the post-1994 rehabilitated image of Credo Mutwa that the government seeks to present. It also points to the lack of a reliable archive, as understood by the West, of African indigenous stories and knowledge as told by African people. Or, perhaps more accurately, it demonstrates a lack of will by government to see or engage with such an archive, especially one that allowed Credo Mutwa to become a mythical figure. Storytelling, of which Mutwa is a self-proclaimed master, relates back to a strong tradition of oral history in South Africa and Africa. This practice continues at Kwa Khaya Lendaba where, in occasionally claiming a family connection to Mutwa, tour guides 'interpret' the site and its artworks for tourists and other visitors.

MUTWA AND THE WRAB IN THE POST-1994 HERITAGE LANDSCAPE

In 1994, policy and practice were re-examined on a national level, including the role of museums in the new democracy. In its report, Museums for South Africa (MUSA) formally accepted that 'governments at all levels should support and promote but should not intrude on the development and expression of culture in South African society, and that museums should be politically non-aligned and serve society as a whole'.[35] The statement is optimistic, since museums are highly politicised spaces, aligned with the national agenda. The statement, perhaps unintentionally, brushes over the fact that spaces such as Kwa Khaya Lendaba were the direct product of the apartheid government intruding on 'the development and expression of culture in South Africa'; it could, indeed, be read as coded language for the rehabilitation of such uneasy and politically fraught spaces as the village.

The report goes on to state that 'in a democratic society, museums are among the most appropriate instruments to support and promote the expression and development of culture', and furthermore that 'the present fragmented dispensation under which South African museums operate serves neither the best interests of the country nor those of the museums'.[36] Clearly, museums were envisaged as a nation-building tool, and the move to consolidate the Mutwa site with other heritage attractions within the area was in line with this policy. Such an attitude is by no means unique to South Africa. According to Kaplan, post-independence, Dr Ekpo Eyo, the first Nigerian Director General of the Federal Department of Antiquities, saw museums, art and archaeology 'as a means of creating a vision of national identity, fostering unity through new museums, as new states were founded'. Kaplan posits that museums 'which shelter culture in its material forms continue to be pivotal places for envisaging collective identity and national goals'.[37]

Since 1994, the City of Johannesburg has embraced the site of Kwa Khaya Lendaba as a place of 'cultural significance' – defined in the National Heritage Resources Act of 1999 as having 'aesthetic, architectural, historical, scientific, social, spiritual, linguistic or technological value or significance'. It has been restored largely in accordance with the Briscoe archive. A former associate of Mutwa, Musa Ntanzi, was brought on board as an adviser, consultant and lead artist in the restoration of the 'huts', the human and animal figures, as well as a created 'burial place'. Ntanzi had earlier attempted to create a similar 'cultural village' in Orange Farm with the assistance of the Gauteng Department of Sports, Arts, Culture and Recreation. Credo Mutwa and his extended family were interviewed, with some members showing an interest in reconnecting with and appropriating the site as Mutwa's legacy. There are also a number of other people who claim to be custodians of his work and who show up from time to time, which has, in a way, given the site a new lease of life.

The City of Johannesburg employs personnel who look after the gardens. For a long period, the facility also had a Heritage Officer, Mighta Makhutle, who attracted volunteers to operate as tour guides. Together, they recreated the myths underlying Mutwa's beliefs for local and international tourists as well as learners who visit Soweto's heritage sites. Healers, individuals and families, mainly from Soweto, use the site for practising ceremonies, including making sacrifices, burning incense, and, at times, singing and drumming.

Significantly, the latter ceremonies tend to be private, rather than for the tourist gaze. The site also deals with controversial requests such as women who, in the name of 'culture', wish to introduce virginity testing into an urban setting.

Certainly, the site has survived and metamorphosed into the larger post-1994 heritage, memory, public culture and tourism landscape. Consequently, it features prominently in tourism promotional brochures that reimagine Kwa Khaya Lendaba as an open-air museum.[38] It is advertised side-by-side with tourism attractions and a range of tour options nationally, such as the Apartheid Museum, Constitution Hill, Hector Pieterson Memorial Museum and the Kliptown Open Air Museum (to mention those located in Johannesburg).

A PRE-1994 TOUR OF KWA-KHAYA LENDABA

We finally explore the site through the notes of a former heritage officer, Mighta Makhutle. According to Makhutle, the village comprised a central area known as Kwa-Khaya Lendaba – 'the place of stories'.[39] Firstly, visitors are shown a panel of handwritten text by Mutwa invoking 'the sacredness' of the place and warning that it is not a mere museum. The central area of the village contains two large, seated statues of the great earth mother, Nomkhubulwane; holding a spear, she has twin boys sitting on her lap. Before her stands a smaller statue of Thandi, an angel of love, her arms outstretched. To her left is a huge statue of God the Father, its four faces directed to the cardinal points – north, south, east and west. This image, the visitor is told, shows that God does not see people as being different, but rather as one society. The tour guide then leads visitors past a bust of Shaka, and another of Ngungunyani of the Tsonga who guards the formal entrance to the site.

The visitor is further shown a replica of a Zulu village adjacent to a Basotho village, each with sculpted human figures either guarding livestock or playing 'traditional' games. There are also animal figures with horns, and in this context visitors are told of Mutwa's knowledge of 'spacemen' and dinosaurs.[40] From there, the visitor is taken to an 'Arab village', whose architecture is described as 'oriental'. Inside, there is a statue of 'Nomkhubulwana and a medium-sized statue of a mermaid'. It is not clear how Nomkhubulwane fits into an 'Arab' village, but the visitor is told that when Mutwa 'sculpted this

Figure 11.3. A grass hut, with the Oppenheimer Tower in the background, c. 1974. Photograph by Gilbert Briscoe. Courtesy of the Johannesburg Art Gallery

statue, Mutwa's wife had contracted cancer. When he was about to mould the breast of the sculpted woman his wife's cancer was cured instantly.' There are also several other figures representing 'prehistoric' animals, aliens, a 'greedy king', a 'traditional healer' and a 'khoisan family'. Finally, the visitor is shown graves, and here they are told that Mutwa predicted the advent of HIV/Aids, one of numerous other supposed predictions of his.

A tour of the cultural village is not complete without climbing the Oppenheimer Tower (figure 11.3); named after Sir Ernest Oppenheimer, it is located in the adjacent Oppenheimer Gardens.[41] According to Davie, this tower, standing on a small hill offering a 360-degree view of the township, was built from bricks harvested from Moroka slum dwellings following their demolition in 1957.[42] The proximity of the tower to the cultural village, together with its appropriation of the aesthetic of Great Zimbabwe, poses an interesting question: what might future historians make of the site? They would probably interpret it as part of the same site, as the municipality considers Kwa Khaya Lendaba as part of Oppenheimer Gardens. This proximity constitutes a blurring between Mutwa's ideology and that of the municipality and the apartheid government.

A PROBLEMATIC LEGACY

The Kwa Khaya Lendaba cultural village has metamorphosed over time and across different national identities. While the site has, in one sense, been made invisible as part of the June 16 Route, it nevertheless represents a tangible legacy, part of the cultural infrastructure of the WRAB and therefore of apartheid. In another sense, though, it sits uneasily as a post-apartheid site representing the 'genius' of Credo Mutwa. It is a living reference and home of 'indigenous knowledge' and 'traditionalist' practitioners within a wider landscape that memorialises the June uprising. It is also a landscape recalling the bloody repression of the 1980s, which does not feature anywhere in the public histories of the area, though community organisations such as the Each One Teach One Foundation have expressed interest in student histories and the community upheavals of the 1980s. The idea of indigenous knowledge systems brings up for reflection notions of authenticity and the creative license of the artist. The uprisings, which dominate the memory of the wider landscape, left a dent and a disavowed dialogue on the site, since its maker, Credo Mutwa, himself became a figure of controversy following the 1976 uprising. While the archival record confirms that Mutwa appeared in the Cillié Commission, his admirers have, in a sense, rehabilitated his standing and personhood to that of sole embodiment of indigenous knowledge systems.

In post-1994 promotional publications, Kwa Khaya Lendaba continues to be described uncritically as an 'outdoor museum of African art, culture and folklore'.[43] This, despite the growing influence of indigenous knowledge systems in public discourse and, to some extent, the decolonisation debate. The Oppenheimer Tower, on the other hand, continues to be described simply as a 'tall conical brick tower that stands on a small hill in Jabavu'.[44] The tower and its proximity to the village serves as a kind of metaphor for how out of touch with reality both sites were – and continue to be – in the context of the broader Soweto landscape. As an employee of the WRAB, Mutwa helped create narratives of African pasts meant to be congruent with apartheid ideology. Post-1994, Kwa Khaya Lendaba has been co-opted for the project of nation-building in a way that lacks real scrutiny and context. Mutwa's village can thus be seen to create a new narrative about heritage in township spaces, within the tensions of a public history. As such, it powerfully seeks to 'liberate the African voice' while simultaneously perpetuating old silences and inducing new ones.

NOTES

1 For a detailed discussion of the June 16, 1976 Interpretation Centre, see Ali Khangela Hlongwane and Sifiso Mxolisi Ndlovu, *Public History and Culture in South Africa: Memorialisation and Liberation Heritage Sites in Johannesburg and the Township Space* (Cham, Switzerland: Palgrave Macmillan, 2019).
2 Museum Africa digital accession records, accessible at Museum Africa.
3 *Cillié Commission of Inquiry into the Riots at Soweto and Elsewhere from June 16, 1976 to February 28, 1977* (Pretoria: Government Printer, 1980).
4 David Chidester, 'Credo Mutwa, Zulu Shaman: The Invention and Appropriation of Indigenous Authenticity in African Folk Religion', *Journal for the Study of Religion* 15.2 (2002): 65-85.
5 Elza Miles, *Land and Lives: A Story of Early Black Artists* (Cape Town: Human and Rousseau, 1997), 50.
6 Ruth Kerkham Simbao, 'Credo Mutwa: Foremost Traditionalist as Futurist', *Art South Africa*, 5.4 (2007): 43.
7 Elza Miles, *Land and Lives: A Story of Early Black Artists* (Cape Town: Human and Rousseau, 1997), 51.
8 Miles, *Land and Lives*, 51.
9 Chidester, 'Credo Mutwa, Zulu Shaman', 66.
10 Spencer R. Crew and James E. Sims, 'Locating Authenticity in Exhibiting Cultures: The Poetics and Politics of Museum Display', in *Exhibiting Cultures: The Poetics and Politics of Museum Display*, eds Ivan Karp and Steven D. Lavine (Washington: Smithsonian Institution Press, 1991), 163.
11 Susan Imrie Ross, *This Is My World: The Life of Helen Martins, Creator of the Owl House* (Cape Town: Oxford University Press, 1997).

12 Credo Mutwa, *Indaba, My Children: African Tribal History, Legends, Customs and Religious Belief* (Edinburgh: Payback Press, 1998).
13 Simon Wilson and Jessica Lack, *Tate Guide to Modern Art* (London: Tate Publishing, 2012).
14 Credo Vusa'mazulu Mutwa, *Isilwane – The Animal: Tales and Fables of Africa* (Cape Town: Struik, 1996), 219–20.
15 See T. S. Simelane and G. I. H. Kerley, 'Recognition of Reptiles by Xhosa and Zulu Communities in South Africa, with Notes on Traditional Beliefs and Uses', *African Journal of Herpetology* 46.1 (1997): 49–53.
16 Gcina Mhlophe, *Fudukazi's Magic* (Cambridge: Cambridge University Press, 1999).
17 Flora Edouwaye S. Kaplan, 'Nigerian Museums: Envisaging Culture as National Identity', in *Museums and the Making of 'Ourselves': The Role of Objects in the National Identity* (London: Leicester University Press, 1996), 47.
18 In Peter Magubane, *Soweto*, text by Charlene Smith (Johannesburg: Struik Publishers, 2002), 120–21.
19 Lucille Davie, *A Journey Through Johannesburg's Parks, Cemeteries and Zoo* (Johannesburg: The City of Johannesburg, 2014), 76.
20 Mtshali, 'Credo Vusamazulu Mutwa', 1.
21 Ntongela Masilela, *An Outline of the New African Movement in South Africa* (Cape Town: Africa World Press, 2013), 2.
22 Ntongela Masilela, 'Vusamazulu Credo Mutwa', accessed 18 July 2018, http://pzacad.pitzer.edu/NAM/newafrre/writers/mutwa/mutwaS.htm.
23 Credo Mutwa, 'Umlinganiso – The living imitation', *Sketch*, Summer 1974/5: 31.
24 Vusi Kunene, 'uNosilimela – A Revelation', *Sketch*, Summer 1974/5: 41. Wits School of Arts students who were part of the #FeesMustFall movement produced and staged this play at the Wits Theatre in 2018.
25 Robert Mshengu Kavanagh, Introduction to *South African People's Plays: Plays by Kente, Mutwa, Shezi & Workshop '71* (London: Heinemann, 1981), iii.
26 Bongani Madondo, 'From Shaman to Star Man: Bongani Madondo Has an Audience with Sanusi Credo Mutwa', *Mail & Guardian*, 29 July 2016.
27 'Vusamazulu Credo Mutwa', SALA Literary Awards, accessed 16 April 2019, https://sala.org.za/Vusamazulu-credo Mutwa.
28 'Credo on the Shame Behind Soweto Riots', *Natal Mercury*, 23 September 1976.
29 Helen Zille, 'Riots So Well Organised Impossible Blacks Planned Them', *Rand Daily Mail*, 24 September 1976.

30 Credo Mutwa, *My People: The Incredible Writings of Credo Vusa'mazulu Mutwa* (Johannesburg: Blue Crane Books, 1969).
31 Mutwa, *Indaba, My Children*, xvii.
32 Kwanele Sosibo, 'Credo Mutwa: Defying the Sting of Death', *Mail & Guardian Online*, 26 March 2020, accessed 20 June 2020, https://mg.co.za/article/2020-03-26-credo-mutwa-defying-the-sting-of-death/.
33 Annie E. Coombes, *Reinventing Africa: Museums, Material Culture and Popular Imagination* (New Haven: Yale University Press, 1994), 85.
34 Iain Borden, foreword to Jonathan Noble, *African Identity in Post-Apartheid Public Architecture: White Skin, Black Masks* (Burlington: Ashgate, 2011), 11.
35 'Museums for South Africa: Intersectoral Investigation for National Policy', Report, April 1994, xv, Johannesburg Art Gallery library, Q 069.0968 MUS.
36 'Museums for South Africa: Intersectoral Investigation for National Policy', xvii.
37 Kaplan, 'Nigerian Museums: Envisaging Culture as National Identity', 45.
38 'Credo Mutwa Cultural Village', 2016, 2017, Moja Heritage Collection Tourism Pamphlets.
39 All quotations are from Mighta Makhutle, 'Tour Guide's Speaking Notes', n.d., n.p., in the possession of the author, Ali Khangela Hlongwane.
40 See *Soweto: The Complete Township Guide* (Johannesburg: Soweto Spaza, 1997), 14.
41 *Soweto: The Complete Township Guide*, 13.
42 See Davie, *A Journey through Johannesburg's Parks, Cemeteries and Zoo*, 76.
43 'Credo Mutwa Cultural Village', 2013, 32.
44 Davie, *A Journey through Johannesburg's Parks*, 76.

REFERENCES

Borden, Iain. Foreword to Jonathan Alfred Noble, *African Identity in Post-Apartheid Public Architecture: White Skin, Black Masks,* 11–12. Burlington: Ashgate, 2011.

Chidester, David. 'Credo Mutwa, Zulu Shaman: The Invention and Appropriation of Indigenous Authenticity in African Folk Religion'. *Journal for the Study of Religion* 15.2 (2002): 65–85.

Cillié Commission of Inquiry into the Riots at Soweto and Elsewhere from June 16, 1976 to February 28, 1977. Pretoria: Government Printer, 1980.

Coombes, Annie E. *Reinventing Africa: Museums, Material Culture and Popular Imagination.* New Haven: Yale University Press, 1994.

'Credo Mutwa Cultural Village'. Moja Heritage Collection Tourism Pamphlets, 2013, 2016, 2017.

'Credo on the Shame Behind Soweto Riots'. *Natal Mercury,* 23 September 1976.

Crew, Spencer R., and James E. Sims. 'Locating Authenticity in Exhibiting Cultures: The Poetics and Politics of Museum Display'. In *Exhibiting Cultures: The Poetics and Politics of Museum Display*, edited by Ivan Karp and Steven D. Lavine, 159–75. Washington: Smithsonian Institution Press, 1991.

Hlongwane, Ali Khangela, and Sifiso Mxolisi Ndlovu. *Public History and Culture in South Africa: Memorialisation and Liberation Heritage Sites in Johannesburg and the Township Space.* Cham, Switzerland: Palgrave Macmillan, 2019.

Kaplan, Flora Edouwaye S. 'Nigerian Museums: Envisaging Culture as National Identity'. In *Museums and the Making of 'Ourselves': The Role of Objects in the National Identity*, edited by Flora Edouwaye S. Kaplan, 45–78. London: Leicester University Press, 1996.

Kavanagh, Robert Mshengu, ed. Introduction. *South African People's Plays: Plays by Kente, Mutwa, Shezi & Workshop '71.* London: Heinemann, 1981.

Magubane, Peter. *Soweto.* Text by Charlene Smith. Johannesburg: Struik, 2002.

Masilela, Ntongela. *An Outline of the New African Movement in South Africa.* Cape Town: Africa World Press, 2013.

Masilela, Ntongela. 'Vusamazulu Credo Mutwa'. Accessed 18 July 2018, http://pzacad.pitzer.edu/NAM/newafrre/writers/mutwa/mutwaS.htm.

Mhlophe, Gcina. *Fudukazi's Magic.* Cambridge: Cambridge University Press, 1999.

Miles, Elza. *Land and Lives: A Story of Early Black Artists.* Cape Town: Human and Rousseau, 1997.

'Museums for South Africa: Intersectoral Investigation for National Policy'. Report, April 1994, xv– xvii. The Johannesburg Art Gallery Library (Q 069.0968 MUS).

Mutwa, Credo. *My People: The Incredible Writings of Credo Vusa'mazulu Mutwa.* Johannesburg: Blue Crane Books, 1969.

Mutwa, Credo. 'Umlinganiso – The living imitation'. *Sketch,* Summer 1974/5.

Mutwa, Credo Vusa'mazulu. *Isilwane – The Animal: Tales and Fables of Africa.* Cape Town: Struik, 1996.

Mutwa, Credo. *Indaba, My Children: African Tribal History, Legends, Customs and Religious Belief.* Edinburgh: Payback Press, 1998.

Ross, Susan Imrie. This Is My World: The Life of Helen Martins, Creator of the Owl House. Cape Town: Oxford University Press, 1997.

Simbao, Ruth Kerkham. 'Credo Mutwa: Foremost Traditionalist as Futurist'. *Art South Africa*, 5.4 (2007): 43–6.

Simelane, T. S., and G. I. H. Kerley. 'Recognition of Reptiles by Xhosa and Zulu Communities in South Africa, with Notes on Traditional Beliefs and Uses'. *African Journal of Herpetology* 46.1 (1997): 49–53.

Sosibo, Kwanele. 'Credo Mutwa: Defying the Sting of Death'. *Mail & Guardian Online*, 26 March 2020. Accessed 20 June 2020, https://mg.co.za/article/2020-03-26-credo-mutwa-defying-the-sting-of-death/.

'Vusamazulu Credo Mutwa'. *SALA Literary Awards*. Accessed 16 April 2019, https://sala.org.za/Vusamazulu-credo Mutwa.

Wilson, Simon, and Jessica Lack. *Tate Guide to Modern Art.* London: Tate Publishing, 2012.

Zille, Helen. 'Riots So Well Organised Impossible Blacks Planned Them'. *Rand Daily Mail*, 24 September 1976.

12 FACING (DOWN) THE COLONISER? THE MANDELA STATUE AT CAPE TOWN'S CITY HALL

CYNTHIA KROS

By the second decade of the twenty-first century, the Cape Town City Hall, which had stood for more than 100 years, was, once again, in dire need of renovation – the last had taken place in the mid-1940s. The main functions of the City Hall had been usurped some time before by the shift of city government to the Civic Centre in 1997. Brett Heron, the chairperson of the City's Naming and Nomination Committee, which was to be one of the principal drivers of the project described in this chapter, explained to me in an interview in 2019 that there was a sense that the City Hall needed to be revived as a place people had a reason to go to 'other than to pay their traffic fines'. Stuart Diamond, a member of the Cape Town mayoral committee, who chaired the asset and facilities management portfolio, similarly referred to the City Hall as having lost its purpose. He was concerned, he told me in a 2019 interview, to recreate a sense of purpose and to get the building 'to tell a story'.

The City decided to install a statue of Nelson Mandela to commemorate what would have been his hundredth birthday in 2018, as well as the first public speech he had made from the balcony of the City Hall on the day of his release after 27 years of incarceration. In his opening remarks, Mandela conveyed 'special greetings to the people of Cape Town', which he referred to as his 'home for three decades'.[1] On the face of it, this was a strange remark since throughout that period he had been in prison, first on Robben Island, and then in two different prisons on the mainland.

The City's plans have now been at least partially realised, and a bronze, life-size statue of a besuited Mandela stands on the balcony, waving amiably to an invisible crowd gathered on the square below known as the Grand Parade. The site was also intended to be part of the Liberation Heritage Route under the auspices of the National Heritage Council and the National Department of Tourism. A permanent exhibition, to be mounted in a newly refurbished space inside the City Hall, was commissioned and developed. Service providers were advised that it should highlight the role of the old Cape Province and Cape Town in the struggle against apartheid, weaving in Mandela's – in fact, rather fleeting – experience of the city as a free man, as well as his long, mostly off-shore incarceration, his release, and the subsequent achievement of democracy.[2]

The idea, Diamond told me, was that visitors would exit from the exhibition onto the balcony where they would find themselves standing next to Mandela gazing over the Grand Parade, imagining what it must have been like on 11 February 1990, the day of his release. Inevitably, they would reach for their cellphones and take selfies here, and also across the Parade (figure 12.1). These selfies would, undoubtedly instantly, be distributed through social media networks. Thus, the 'reproducibility' of this otherwise rather bland image of Mandela turns out to be crucial.[3]

The City Hall has been resuscitated and tasked with new functions, one of which is to tell a more inclusive story of the city. But, if the story is to be more inclusive, how will it make an impression on the existing landscape, which is still deeply etched with signs of the Cape Colony's ties to Britain in the early twentieth century? The first thing I noticed when I visited the site initially was the striking juxtaposition of the unexceptional Mandela statue on the balcony with an overbearing marble likeness of King Edward VII directly opposite it on the Parade. Thinking that the latter would almost certainly overwhelm the much more modestly appointed statue of Mandela, I intended to follow up on this initial impression and pursue a number of questions. Why was an image of Mandela chosen in a city that has not been governed by Mandela's party, the African National Congress (ANC) for some time, but instead by the opposition party, the Democratic Alliance (DA), and in a period, moreover, in which quite widespread disillusionment connected to the figure of Mandela was said to be evident across the country as a whole? Why – after some impressive experiments with more symbolic and interactive memorials – was it decided that the image of Mandela should take the form of a conventional realist bronze statue?

Unsurprisingly, it seems that the installation of the statue of Mandela has to do with political strategy. It is also connected to visions for the city that do not necessarily reflect only particular party-political affiliations. This is where, in French historian Maurice Agulhon's accounts of *statuomanie* (statue mania) particularly during the period of the Third Republic (1870–1940), the distinction between *l'idéologique* and *le politique* (the ideological and the political) may be useful.[4] In explaining the rash of statue installation in the republican phases of nineteenth-century France, especially following the fall of the Second Empire in 1870, Agulhon argues that the statues of great men were tasked with doing ideological work. Although their installation might involve local political contests, generally statues erected in the squares of towns and cities in republican France differed markedly in an ideological sense from the practices of memorialisation characteristic of the authoritarian periods. The idea of an ordinary man who was neither a monarch nor a saint designated by the Catholic Church being worthy of *héroïsation* (heroisation), Agulhon argues, is a core concept of liberal humanism made possible by the French Revolution. The Third Republic saw the advent on a grand scale of '*une pédagogie par le grand homme*' (pedagogy by the great man)[5] or '*un hommage instructif*' (homage that is instructional).[6] Such statues uphold an ideology that is liberal, secular and patriotic, and is also supposed to provide an example for citizens of the Republic. Taking their place among other decorative architectural embellishments to enhance public spaces in towns and cities, these statues of great men in the period of the Third Republic were intended to play a part in educating citizens in the values of the new order.

The statue of Mandela on the balcony of the Cape Town City Hall was, evidently, drafted for the same sort of exercise nearly 30 years after its real-life counterpart had stood there to make his speech. After acknowledging a seemingly exhaustive list of organisations and individuals who had kept up the resistance to apartheid, Mandela had expressed the hope that the establishment of democracy would be made possible through a 'negotiated settlement'. In discussing the way forward, he himself – perhaps deliberately – exhibited the very humility, self-restraint and 'stoic self-discipline' that would make of him, along with his exceptional self-sacrifice, a worthy citizen to emulate. He also emphasised 'the need to unite the people of our country'.[7] Although he explicitly called for structural reforms and 'an end to white monopoly on political power', Mandela also appealed to 'our white compatriots to join us in the shaping of a new South Africa'.[8]

MANDELA AND EDWARD VII

The statue of Mandela may loosely be understood to have risen from the 'ruin' of the Edwardian City Hall and the statuary across the way on the Grand Parade. This statuary – like the City Hall, long deprived of its essential functions – has an air of neglect. It includes the towering marble figure of Edward VII, the once-delinquent son of Queen Victoria, dressed in his investiture regalia when he was crowned King of the United Kingdom of Great Britain and Ireland, and of the British Dominions and Emperor of India two years before, in 1902 (figure 12.1). The Welsh sculptor, William Goscombe John (1860–1952), once hailed for his craft, and an important member of the New Sculpture movement, is now largely forgotten.[9] New Sculpture artists

Figure 12.1. Taking 'selfies' in front of the statue of Edward VII on the Parade. Photograph by Cynthia Kros

were conscious of how their work would be seen by, and incorporated into the experience of, the pedestrian.[10] The visage of the king bears a striking resemblance to that of its real-life counterpart who, due to his mother's longevity, only ascended the throne when he was 59 years old.

In many ways, thanks to the skill and aesthetic principles of its maker, the statue is firmly tethered to the person of a particular monarch at the beginning of the twentieth century, in a way that was intended to allow people to relate to the king as a man rather than a figurehead. One wonders how well it worked in its day, and how the sculptor's attention to the detail of the actual king's physiognomy was registered by viewers. Nowadays, the steps leading up to the enormous plinth upon which the statue of Edward VII stands, provide seating for weary passers-by and itinerants of the Parade. Although aesthetically the statue, in its outline against the imported limestone of the City Hall, with Table Mountain behind it, still makes a powerful statement, its neglect renders its boastful inscription impotent, acting as a rebuke to overweening ambition and arrogance.

The statue of Edward VII is around two and a half metres tall and stands on a plinth that measures about three metres in height from the top step. Its larger-than-life size and its position on the axis of the City Hall, directly opposite the balcony from which Mandela delivered his speech, have understandably provoked discomfort in some quarters. On receiving the announcement that the City Council had voted to support the installation of the Mandela statue, African National Congress leader in the Council, Xolani Sotashe, protested: 'They [Mandela and Edward VII] represent two different histories in the world. Madiba is a champion of the human cause [and] the fellow that is there now came from Europe … we are asking politely so: take that man back to Europe in London. Surely there is enough space there for that statue to be preserved.' He continued: 'It can't be correct madam mayor that Madiba … during his lifetime he fought, and even in his grave he is still facing the colonizer. It can't be.'[11]

In our 2019 interview, Stuart Diamond contended that the fact that the Mandela statue is more or less lifelike and life-size is important in making it feel as if Mandela's presence is still there, carrying with it the significance of 11 February 1990. When asked about the apparent imbalance of power in favour of Edward VII, Diamond responded: 'You don't have to stand on a plinth to have power.' Addressing the relative visibility of the two statues,

Diamond explained that planned upgrades to the Parade, including a kiosk and a project to widen the roads in the vicinity, with traffic-calming features, would give people the space to stand and contemplate the Mandela statue.[12] As for visitors to the exhibition, when they came out onto the balcony, Diamond explained, they would be able to feel what it was like 'delivering that speech to the audience that packed the Parade'. It is from that vantage point, he said, that they would be looking across to Edward VII, and the distance we have travelled from the colonial past.

WHY MANDELA?

Raising statues of anyone might have seemed risky post-#RhodesMustFall, the student movement that effected the removal of a statue of Cecil John Rhodes from its plinth on the campus of the University of Cape Town in 2015. In its wake, as scholars Mcebisi Ndletyana and Denver Webb have pointed out, Rhodes and other figures associated with imperialism or apartheid were not the only casualties of public anger against statues.[13] Furthermore, the summoning of the 'Rainbow Nation' as an aspirational ideal, associated as it is with the first democratic government under Mandela, is increasingly represented as having been a kind of confidence trick. Racially-based inequality and, indeed, racism persist. Some people blame Mandela himself for having struck too many compromises with representatives of the old order. He is accused of having been too eager for reconciliation with apartheid's perpetrators and supporters, to the lasting detriment of post-apartheid society.

Shortly after Mandela's passing in December 2013, the philosopher Slavoj Žižek made several controversial observations in articles published in international newspapers about the failure of socialist transformation in South Africa. Žižek's writings were not, as was sometimes construed, an attack on Mandela himself; instead, they were a critique of the mythology that had enveloped the memory of Mandela and disabled analyses of capitalism which had continued to thrive under his watch. In one such article, Žižek argued that the 'much more radical ANC past [had been] gradually obliterated from our memory', and that structural inequalities were concealed by the 'celebratory' account of liberation with Mandela at its heart. Žižek suggests that what he refers to as Mandela's 'beatification' by Hollywood allowed for the 'miserable life of the poor majority' to remain 'broadly ... the same as under apartheid'.[14]

As far back as 2011, Verne Harris, Director of Archive and Dialogue at the Nelson Mandela Foundation, had written about the damage done to the dream of the 'Rainbow Nation' by, among other things, the outbreaks of xenophobia in South Africa, 'social ills', the rate of HIV/AIDS infection, rising levels of crime, failures in the economy, and the failure of leadership.[15] Rather than putting the blame on Mandela, Harris argues that, to do justice to his legacy, its heirs should engage critically with the archive. Harris's lament about the fading of the ideal of the 'Rainbow Nation' differs from other expressions of disillusionment in that he does not dismiss the idea as mendacious or misleading. He perceives it, rather, as having lost its power because its promise was undermined by the failures of post-apartheid governments and civil society. Harris goes so far as to encourage the development of new metanarratives to help drive the country's reconstruction and development.

While Žižek diagnoses the 'beatification' of Mandela as one of the reasons for failure, obscuring as it does the reality of capitalist relations, Harris and others emphasise that it was not a beatification Mandela himself would have welcomed.[16] But the implications of Harris's argument is that symbolism and metanarrative generate the collective energy and vision required for the arduous task of transformation. While his argument differs from that of Žižek, both recognise the power of symbolic mobilisation – in one case, its potential to sustain radical transformation, and in the other, to obstruct it.

ONLY BEAUTIFUL FOR SOME

The setting of the limestone building of the Cape Town City Hall, with the marble statue of Edward VII in the foreground against Table Mountain, is beautiful. But as poet Gabeba Baderoon once explained before giving a reading of her poem 'A Prospect of Beauty', Cape Town's much-lauded beauty is not immediately apparent to a person like herself who grew up on the desolate sands of the Cape Flats:[17] as she memorably said, Cape Town is and was ever only beautiful for some. In her poem, Baderoon is looking out from a hilltop in today's Bo-Kaap (formerly the 'Malay Quarter'), a vantage point used by artists for the magnificent view it affords of the harbour. Retracing their steps on the anniversary of the abolition of the slave trade in 1807, Baderoon realises that these artists were standing on the burial ground of people who had been enslaved.

The very Parade upon which the statue of Edward VII stands is drenched in the history of slavery that still seems largely invisible, despite the fact that there are several memorials to the enslaved in close proximity – although, as historians Nigel Worden and Kerry Ward have argued, slave memorialisation has generally failed to gain popular traction in South Africa.[18] In a 2018 report on 'inclusive economies', Ivan Turok and Justin Visagie reiterate well-known features of the contemporary South African economic and social landscape, including levels of inequality that rank as the highest in the world.[19] Their main argument is that, while there has been substantial mitigation of social misery through state intervention, the root causes of the vast inequality and substantial obstacles to poor people being able to maximise the demonstrable advantages of living and working in the urban areas of South Africa have not been properly addressed.

Turok and Visagie maintain that solutions to the problems they highlight cannot only be of a technical nature. Achieving real inclusive development necessarily requires, for example, compromise and willingness to agree to meet goals beyond immediate self-interest by the city's better-off residents. They attribute an important role to discursive (or non-technical and material) interventionist strategies. Turok and Visagie imply that it is necessary to develop a vision with the power to convince people to work in the interests of a collective that transcends current divisions, and ask what role city authorities should be playing in trying to direct more inclusive development.

CONTROVERSY AND ACCEPTANCE

Creating an inclusive city was much on the minds of the two former city officials, namely Stuart Diamond and Brett Heron, whom I interviewed in 2019.[20] For them, the Mandela statue belonged to a suite of developments intended to move in this direction. 'We want to work more closely with our residents, and an important aspect of strengthening the relationship between the City and Capetonians is for our residents to participate in matters that affect them and which they feel strongly about', Heron was quoted as saying at the time.[21] In the event, the public responses called for in April and May 2017 eventually numbered about 300 (in various formats) and were fairly mixed.

A report indicates that, for many of the respondents, the R3.5 million allocated to the statue (in fact by the provincial government) seemed an enormous figure.[22] Although a handful confessed that they did not understand the proposal or, in one case, asked for assurance that the statue would attract tourist revenue, a substantial proportion of the participants represented in the survey were incensed. Many believed that the City was wasting the money they paid as ratepayers or taxpayers. By far the most common among the negative responses was that the money might be better spent. These responses primarily seem to have reflected frustration with the City's perceived inability to solve a number of acute problems, including the repercussions of a severe drought; secondly, in the words of one respondent, the statue was 'overkill', with too many already existing statues or other forms of commemoration; the third most common complaint was that the statue was too tourist- or market-orientated.

Some respondents suggested alternative forms of commemoration, or that the statue be located elsewhere, for example next to a new theatre in a township, or on Robben Island, so that it would be 'Africa's Statue of Liberty'. Other alternatives included renaming the City Hall, making a durable copy of Mandela's shoes that a visitor could step into, and laying a commemorative paving stone of slate quarried from Robben Island. There appear to have been fewer yeses to the idea of the statue, and these positive responses tended to be more concise. What is interesting, and worth bearing in mind, is that a few respondents on both sides of the yes/no divide recognised that the statue would inhabit a particular urban landscape. Cognisant of the broader context, a respondent wrote: 'Mandela wouldn't have wanted to be honoured in a colonialist structure.' Another declared, 'Yes, it's about time', complaining that the 'city landscape' was 'dominated by colonial structures', yet stating: 'We do not wish them to fall, but a fairer and more moral history will occupy the public mind in looking at the contrasts.'

At the end of the public participation process, the Council declared that there was sufficient support to go ahead. Heron informed me that, at an estimated initial cost of R3.5 million for the Western Cape Government and another R1.5 million for the City, the proposal for the statue and an associated exhibition to be mounted in the City Hall was accepted, with the siting of the statue on the balcony as its most desirable location.

TATA MANDELA

Alan Winde, then Member of the Executive Council (MEC) for Finance and Economic Opportunities in the Western Cape, played a leading role in the initiation of the project, according to Heron. In 2017, Winde was reported to have observed that Mandela's 'journey, after his release' from the then Victor Verster Prison to the City Hall 'was of important historical significance'; he was, however, quite blunt about how he visualised the statue's potential for earning more tourist revenue: 'Through leveraging this unique heritage, we can build an attraction which will draw visitors to our region and spread Madiba's message of tolerance.'[23] At the unveiling of the statue the following year, Winde was optimistic about the flood of tourists that would soon follow, attracted by the statue, and about the way in which it would help stitch up the National Liberation Route.[24]

According to Heron, then Executive Mayor Patricia de Lille was 'instrumental' in shaping the brief for service providers for the planned City Hall exhibition, ensuring that it was 'very mindful that the story be told from multiple viewpoints'. She brought her own recollections of the struggle against apartheid to the table, together with her experience of visiting museums abroad dedicated to representations of struggles for human rights. Furthermore, she insisted that the exhibition be planned so as to support relevant aspects of the Basic Education curriculum.

De Lille does seem to have brought her very considerable experience, knowledge and concern for human rights to the exercise. However, by the time the statue was unveiled on 24 July 2018, the governing party in the City Council had, for the past few months, been 'in turmoil'.[25] Much of it swirled around the Executive Mayor and her alleged complicity in alleged procurement irregularities. De Lille stepped down only at the end of October 2018 amid rumours that she planned to start her own political party. A speech made little more than a year before the statue was unveiled is revealing:[26] the plan concerning the statue and the 'unfolding' exhibition was, she announced, to 'honour the father of our nation'. It was a formulation she would repeat at the later unveiling ceremony, where she referred to Mandela as *Tata* (father in isiXhosa) while observing that, although they had belonged to different political parties (at that time, she was a member of the Pan African Congress), she had never gathered 'the courage even to fight with *Tata*'.[27] Importantly, she also expressed the hope that those who passed by the statue in the future would remember the 'values that he stood for' and the 'sacrifices' he had made.

'QUITE A LONG STORY'

The Mandela statue did not, however, owe its existence simply to the ambitions of senior politicians. Diamond recalled the question of how to honour Mandela coming up as the centenary of his birth in July 2018 drew near, and discussions about how his history might be identified with Cape Town. It is interesting that the apparent dimming of the 'Rainbow Nation' and Mandela's legacy does not appear to have been an inhibiting factor. For Heron, the Mandela statue was 'quite a long story', going back as far as May 2011.

It was at this stage, according to Heron, that he was asked by newly elected Mayor de Lille to chair the Naming Committee to complete work initiated by her predecessor, Helen Zille, concerning the renaming of roads. He cited a number of examples and, in particular, the renaming of roads in the township of Gugulethu about 15 kilometres from the city centre, which he described as having been enormously successful in terms of public participation. He went on to argue that the naming of streets is one of the 'few tools' a community has to tell its own history. Heron sketched a kind of 'topography of pain',[28] as he spoke of people having to travel roads named after H. F. Verwoerd or National Party Minister of Justice and later Defence, Oswald Pirow, who was also a Nazi sympathiser.

One of Heron's committee members made a proposal about installing a statue of Mandela, but there was no procedure in place to take it forward, which led to an expansion of the committee's mandate and its renaming as the Naming and Nomination Committee. Various ideas were proposed, including removing the statue of former Prime Minister Jan Smuts from its position outside the Slave Lodge, and replacing the equestrian statue of former Prime Minister Louis Botha outside the gates of Parliament with a statue of Mandela. According to Heron, both these sites were rejected for fear of controversy that might be provoked. One of the main intentions was, he said, to 'unify' the city's residents, and not sow further division. Also mooted as a possible site in the city centre was the Company's Garden, established by the Dutch East India Company in the 1650s, but the national Department of Sport, Arts and Culture objected, maintaining that the site was 'overdone with memorials'.[29] Heron mentioned that he recalled the complaint about 'statue clutter'. In fact, the Garden *is* cluttered with memorials, mostly erected in the colonial or apartheid eras, commemorating the 'bravery' or 'vision' of white men. They include Herbert Baker's 1908 bronze statue of Cecil John

Rhodes, with its hortatory hand gesture indicating where conquest lies, and the accompanying directive to white settlers: 'Your hinterland is there.'

Heron met with the secretary of parliament to discuss a joint project and, according to him, they had agreed to work together. In the event, however, parliament went ahead on its own, resulting in the Mandela bust that was erected outside the National Assembly and unveiled in 2014. The next year, Alan Winde and Anroux Marais – provincial ministers in the Department of Economic Development and Tourism and the Department of Cultural Affairs and Sport, respectively – went to see De Lille and Heron himself to discuss the matter of the City Hall. There was general agreement that, as it stood, it was 'just a building' that would mean little to a tourist passing through, and so they began to explore the idea of erecting a statue of Mandela on the City Hall balcony, which the province would fund.

NOT VERY ORIGINAL?

Clearly, it would not have been considered a feasible alternative to have a memorial in the City Hall precinct for the enslaved – or, indeed, for a person whose politics was more immediately concerned with Cape Town, such as Zainunnisa (Cissie) Gool, a prominent civil rights leader who had addressed rallies on the Grand Parade, and the first black woman to be elected to the Cape Town City Council in 1938. What historical figure other than Mandela would be thought capable of bringing Capetonians together across the city's considerable social, economic and racial divides? For despite the reservations expressed in the public participation survey, there was the notion that the colonial landscape had to be remade to accommodate a different history – that the public mind needed to be exposed to instructive contrasts between the old order and the new.

It is also clear, despite some creative suggestions in the public participation survey, that it was unlikely that an abstract or symbolic form of commemoration would be selected rather than a statue in the realist mode. Art historian Brenda Schmahmann has written on the distinctively performative character of the *Release* memorial created by local artist Marco Cianfanelli, and unveiled in 2012 outside the town of Howick in KwaZulu-Natal at what is known as the Capture Site where Mandela was arrested while on the run in 1962.[30] As we have seen, the statue on the balcony, despite its more conventional genre, is also intended to encourage visitors to engage in performative activities. They include re-enactment, contemplation, memory-making and, possibly above all, absorbing the lessons Mandela taught. Lize van Robbroeck has argued persuasively that Mandela himself had a deliberate hand in collaborating on a multimedia, life-long biography, which would exhort people to be the type of self-disciplined and responsible citizen he was, while also being committed to the promotion of human rights, even under conditions of adversity.[31]

Certainly, Dali Tambo – whose company, Koketso Growth, won the tender to create the balcony statue – was no stranger to the idea of performance. The Long Walk to Freedom monument, started in 2010, was his brainchild, and takes the form of Mandela leading a march of other bronze statues of resistance heroes. The son of highly respected struggle leaders Oliver and Adelaide, Tambo had raised eyebrows when he presented his proposal, noting that the public could interact with the realistic, recognisable statues and remarking that 'heritage is the showbusiness of history'.[32] If the statue of Mandela on the balcony was to accomplish all the work it had to do, it was necessary for it, too, to be immediately recognisable and capable of evoking not just universal respect and admiration, but also affection.[33]

AESTHETIC CHOICES

In studying the aesthetic choices that were made, the intentions behind the installation of the Mandela statue become even clearer. Heron recalled that, after the province put out its proposal, 'every artist under the sun' had contacted him. However, it was up to Koketso Growth to select the artists, and the company duly appointed the respected bronze sculptors, Barry Jackson and Xhanti Mpakama, who had also made the Mandela statue that leads the Long Walk to Freedom procession, and the Mandela bust outside Parliament. Far from following a tried and trusted formula, however, Jackson claims that a great deal of deliberation went into the expression to be portrayed on the face of the City Hall Mandela. 'Between us and the two creative directors [Tambo and Sarah Haines], we managed to get the pose correct', Jackson is quoted as having said, recalling that: 'First, they wanted a serious face. Then, not so serious, then a smile.'[34]

Several distinctly different photographic images of Mandela on the balcony exist, which may have provided the model; these include Chris Ledochowski's familiar photograph showing a serious Mandela appearing to make an emphatic point, with ANC comrades behind him, and eager members of the public balanced precariously on the ledges all around him.[35] Leon Muller's photograph shows Mandela reading from the speech he is holding, and wearing the spectacles of his then wife, Winnie Madikizela-Mandela: having forgotten to bring his reading glasses, he was compelled to borrow hers.[36] In this photograph, we also get a much clearer image of future President Ramaphosa's face as he holds the microphone, appearing to look down at the speech. Jackson recalls that there was a debate about whether or not the statue should be shown wearing spectacles, but it was decided that although 'the women's fashion glasses have nice appeal … it takes away from his likeness'.[37]

The final product, then, is a loveable but generic Madiba, rather than the serious statesman, combatant or elderly man who was facing tens of thousands of restless people after 27 years in prison. At the end of his 1990 speech, Mandela attempted a reprise of the most famous part of the speech that he had made from the dock during the so-called Rivonia Trial. As is well known,

Figure 12.2. Mandela statue on the balcony of the Cape Town City Hall. Photograph by Cynthia Kros

Mandela had declared his willingness, if necessary, to die for the ideals of democracy. Although, many years later, he confessed to his long-term comrade and friend, Ahmed Kathrada, how nervous he had been about the very real possibility of being executed, the statue has neither the vulnerability revealed then, nor the drama of the Rivonia moment.[38]

There is another important aspect to consider. Mpakama, who was born in Willowvale, about 90 kilometres from where Mandela grew up, has made his reputation through creating sculptures that explore 'Xhosa' identity.[39] In the 1962 trial, which took place after Mandela's arrest on charges of leaving the country illegally and inciting a workers' strike, he appeared in court wearing an animal-skin kaross generally associated with Thembu royalty. Mandela's dress and his responses to the judge were intended to impress upon the audience an important argument: whereas democracy had existed in the African society of Mandela's childhood, a court operating under a system founded on racial discrimination could clearly make no such claim, and therefore lacked legitimacy.[40]

Given the delicacy of the historical moment and the prescribed role of the City Hall statue, it is inconceivable, however, that it would have been allowed to project anything that might be interpreted as reflecting a specific ethnic identity or a suggestion that there were alternative systems of justice. One of its most important functions was, after all, to contribute to ending divisions in the city. It was also supposed to serve as the exemplary citizen in a well-constructed mythology – one of Agulhon's 'great men' for a new order. Thus, ironically, Mandela had to be attired as an Englishman wearing a suit.[41] While it is true that the suit is similar to the one worn on the day of his release, if replication were the only criterion for deciding how the statue was to be represented, it would have been surrounded by the rest of the assembly on the balcony that day, and the youths clambering up to get a better view.

UNIVERSAL APPEAL

A literal reading of the scenario in front of the City Hall gives the colossal statue of Edward VII the undisputed advantage. But the intentions of at least some of those responsible for the installation of the Mandela statue on the balcony were to think in metaphorical terms about the nature of Mandela's greatness and the power of his presence. They believed that, whatever its frustrations and disappointments, the public's knowledge of, and mostly undiminished affection for, Mandela would prevail. The Mandela created in bronze was sufficiently recognisable as an individual to retain and even re-ignite that affection, yet at the same time was sufficiently generic so that its appeal was universal – marred neither by suggestions of a particular ethnicity, nor of a particular political party, nor of signs of human frailty.

In 2020, the President of South Africa, Cyril Ramaphosa, would return to the balcony of the City Hall for the thirtieth anniversary of the release speech, just before the Covid-19 lockdown. Perhaps he was already thinking about how to prepare South Africans for what they would have to endure. Certainly, his own political position in the middle of factional strife within the ANC's senior ranks was widely considered to be tenuous. He would draw for his moral authority on the legacy of the man next to whom, as he reminded his audience, he was standing once again. His message, though rather diffuse, included a call for reconciliation over retribution, the necessity of making sacrifices and compromises, and the importance of national unity and striving to make a better life for 'our' people. As he recalled the vision for the nation espoused by Mandela, with the statue's arm raised in greeting above him, the president exhorted his fellow citizens 'to live in [Mandela's] image'.[42]

NOTES

1. 'Remarks by Nelson Mandela in Cape Town on 11 February 1990 after his Release from Victor Verster', website resource compiled and authored by Padraig O'Malley, *Nelson Mandela Centre of Memory*, accessed 8 June 2020, https://omalley.nelsonmandela.org/omalley/index.php/site/q/03lv03445/04lv04015/05lv04154/06lv04191.htm.
2. I was hired by Delve Consulting Agency, which was awarded the tender to develop educational materials to support the exhibition, and I also received remuneration on an occasional basis for advisory work on the narrative of the exhibition by String Communication, which was commissioned to develop the text for the exhibition.
3. Steven Nelson, 'Nelson Mandela's Two Bodies', *Transition* 116 (2014): 139. Nelson uses the concept of the 'endless reproducibility' of Mandela's image to explain the 'constant re-articulation and resurrection of the leader's mythical body'.
4. Maurice Agulhon, 'La "Statuomanie" et l'histoire', *Ethnologie Française* 2/3 (1978): 145–46.
5. Agulhon, 'La "Statuomanie"', 147.
6. Agulhon, 'La "Statuomanie"', 149.

7   For further discussion on Mandela's deliberate fashioning of his image, see Lize van Robbroeck, 'The Visual Mandela: A Pedagogy of Citizenship', in *The Cambridge Companion to Nelson Mandela*, ed. Rita Barnard (Cambridge: Cambridge University Press, 2014), 257.
8   'Remarks by Nelson Mandela'.
9   'Goscombe John and "The New Sculpture"', National Museum, Cardiff, accessed 5 November 2018, https://museum.wales/cardiff/art/impressionist-modern/goscombe-john/.
10 See Rebecca Sheehan, '"A Series of Surfaces": The New Sculpture and Cinema', *Interdisciplinary Studies in the Long Nineteenth Century* 22 (2016), accessed 5 June 2020, https://19.bbk.ac.uk/article/id/1462/.
11 Aphiwe Deklerk, 'Mandela's Statue Should Not Face that of "Coloniser" King Edward VII, says ANC', *TimesLIVE*, 24 August 2017, accessed 5 November 2018, https://www.timeslive.co.za/news/south-africa/2017-08-24-mandelas-statue-should-not-face-that-of-coloniser-king-edward-vii-says-anc/.
12 The upgrades have proved controversial since they disrupt a bi-weekly market that has operated for several generations, with stallholders having managed to overcome race classification restrictions even when they were supposedly in full force. See Wendy Wilson, 'Living Heritage in the Historic Urban Landscape: A Case Study of the Grand Parade Market' (Master's thesis, University of Cape Town, 2019).
13 Mcebisi Ndletyana and Denver A. Webb, 'Social Divisions Carved in Stone or Cenotaphs to a New Identity? Policy for Memorials, Monuments and Statues in a Democratic South Africa', *International Journal of Heritage Studies* 23 (2017).
14 Slavoj Žižek, 'If Nelson Mandela Really had Won, He Wouldn't be Seen as a Universal Hero', *The Guardian*, 9 December 2013, accessed 2 June 2020, https://www.theguardian.com/commentisfree/2013/dec/09/if-nelson-mandela-really-had-won.
15 Verne Harris, 'Jacques Derrida Meets Nelson Mandela: Archival Ethics at the Endgame', *Archival Science* 11 (2011): 116.
16 See, for example, Philip Bonner, 'The Antinomies of Nelson Mandela', in *The Cambridge Companion to Nelson Mandela*, ed. Rita Barnard (Cambridge: Cambridge University Press, 2014); and Paul Maylam, 'Archetypal Hero or Living Saint? The Veneration of Nelson Mandela', *Historia* 54 (2009).
17 I relate this incident from memory, having been present at the launch of Baderoon's book *The History of Intimacy*. Many Cape Flats residents are, like Baderoon herself, the descendants of people who were forcibly removed from the city under apartheid legislation.

18 Kerry Ward and Nigel Worden, 'Commemorating, Suppressing, and Invoking Cape Slavery', in *Negotiating the Past: The Making of Memory in South Africa*, eds Sarah Nuttall and Carli Coetzee (Cape Town: Oxford University Press, 1998); and Nigel Worden, 'The Changing Politics of Slave Heritage in the Western Cape, South Africa', *Journal of African History* 50 (2009).

19 Ivan Turok and Justin Visagie, 'Inclusive Urban Development in South Africa: What Does It Mean and How can It be Measured?', IDS Working Paper 2018 (512), accessed 2 June 2020, https://www.researchgate.net/publication/326410270_Inclusive_Urban_Development_in_South_Africa_What_Does_It_Mean_and_How_Can_It_Be_Measured.

20 For the publicly expressed vision of some of Cape Town's Democratic Alliance leaders at the time, see Patricia de Lille and Craig Kesson, *View from City Hall: Reflections on Governing Cape Town* (Johannesburg: Jonathan Ball Publishers, 2017).

21 Lizeka Tandwa, 'City of Cape Town Wants to Honour Mandela with a R3.5m Statue', *News24*, 17 April 2017, accessed 11 November 2018, https://www.news24.com/SouthAfrica/News/city-of-cape-town-wants-to-honour-mandela-with-a-r35m-statue-20170417.

22 'Public Participation Outcomes on the Proposal to Install a Statue of Nelson Mandela at the Cape Town City Hall', 29 June 2017, NN 10/06/17, Report to Naming and Nomination Committee, provided to me by Gillion Bosman, member of the Western Cape Provincial Parliament, who served on its Naming and Nomination Committee.

23 Tandwa, 'City of Cape Town Wants to Honour Mandela'.

24 'City of Cape Town Unveil Statue of Mandela to Honour Struggle Icon', *Eyewitness News*, accessed 20 November 2020, https://ewn.co.za/video/4488/city-of-cape-town-unveil-statue-of-mandela-to-honour-struggle-icon.

25 'DA "in Turmoil" as De Lille Might Not Resign as Mayor After All', *News24*, 24 October 2018, accessed 24 October 2018, https://www.news24.com/SouthAfrica/News/da-in-turmoil-as-de-lille-might-not-resign-as-mayor-after-all-20181024.

26 Patricia de Lille, 'Speech by the City's Executive Mayor, Patricia de Lille, at the Full Council Meeting on 26 April 2017'. http://resource.capetown.gov.za/documentcentre/Documents/Speeches%20and%20statements/SPEECH2BY2EXECUTIVE2MAYOR20AT20THEFUL20COUNCILMEETINGAPRIL2017.pdf.

27 'City of Cape Town Unveil Statue of Mandela'.

28 I refer here to the Topography of Terror Museum and Documentation Centre: built on the sites of the former offices of the Gestapo and SS Headquarters, it focuses on an urban landscape that has been deeply marked by a history of atrocity being repurposed in the service of civic / human rights education.

29 Anél Lewis, 'Grand Plan for Mandela Statue', *IOL News*, 13 June 2013, accessed 11 November 2018, https://www.iol.co.za/news/south-africa/western-cape/grand-plan-for-mandela-statue-1531652.
30 Brenda Schmahmann, 'An Arresting Portrayal: Marco Cianfanelli's *Release* at the Nelson Mandela Capture Site', *African Arts* 51 (2018).
31 Van Robbroeck, 'The Visual Mandela.'
32 Cynthia Kros, 'Twenty Years of Heritage Studies – The Showbiz of History?' *Social Dynamics* 43 (2017).
33 See Bonner, 'The Antinomies of Nelson Mandela'; Maylam, 'Archetypal Hero or Living Saint?'; Nelson, 'Nelson Mandela's Two Bodies'; Van Robbroeck, 'The Visual Mandela'; and Deborah Posel, '"Madiba Magic": Politics as Enchantment', in *The Cambridge Companion to Mandela*, ed. Rita Barnard (Cambridge: Cambridge University Press, 2014).
34 Jenna Etheridge, 'Bronze Mandela Erected on Balcony at Cape Town's City Hall', *City Press*, 24 July 2018, accessed 5 November 2018, https://www.news24.com/SouthAfrica/News/bronze-mandela-erected-on-balcony-at-cape-towns-city-hall-20180724.
35 For Chris Ledochowski's photograph, see 'Photo Blog: South Africa's Democracy – Mandela's "Cherished Ideal"', accessed 10 June 2020, https://blogs.lse.ac.uk/africaatlse/2014/09/03/photo-blog-south-africas-democracy-mandelas-cherished-ideal/.
36 Arlene Getz, 'Mandela's Message a Universal One', *IOL News*, 6 December 2013, accessed 5 November 2018, https://www.iol.co.za/news/mandelas-message-a-universal-one-1618447.
37 Etheridge, 'Bronze Mandela'.
38 Nelson Mandela, *Nelson Mandela: Conversations with Myself* (New York: Farrar, Straus and Giroux, 2010), 123–25.
39 'Xhanti Mpakama – Xhosa Bronze Sculpture Artist on the Rise', XhosaCulture.co.za, 10 May 2014, accessed 5 November 2018, https://xhosaculture.co.za/xhanti-mpakama-xhosa-bronze-sculpture-artist-rise/.
40 For an analysis of Mandela's sartorial and rhetorical strategies during the 1962 trial, see Tom Lodge, *Mandela: A Critical Life* (Oxford: Oxford University Press, 2006), 104–06.
41 See Van Robbroeck's 'The Visual Mandela' for her reflections on the meanings of a suit as opposed to the Indonesian print shirts later favoured by Mandela.
42 '#Mandela Returns: President Cyril Ramaphosa Reflects on the Historic Day', *SABC News*, 11 February 2020, accessed 26 May 2020, https://www.youtube.com/watch?v=dqZXOuZzkSM.

REFERENCES

Agulhon, Maurice. 'La statuomanie et l'histoire'. *Ethnologie Française* 2/3 (1978): 145–72.

Baderoon, Gabeba. 'A Prospect of Beauty'. In *The History of Intimacy: Poems*. Cape Town: Kwela, 2018.

Bonner, Philip. 'The Antinomies of Nelson Mandela'. In *The Cambridge Companion to Nelson Mandela*, edited by Rita Barnard, 29–49. Cambridge: Cambridge University Press, 2014.

'City of Cape Town Unveil Statue of Mandela to Honour Struggle Icon'. *Eyewitness News*. Accessed 20 November 2020, https://ewn.co.za/video/4488/city-of-cape-town-unveil-statue-of-mandela-to-honour-struggle-icon.

'DA "in Turmoil" as De Lille Might Not Resign as Mayor After All'. *News24*. Accessed 24 October 2018, https://www.news24.com/SouthAfrica/News/da-in-turmoil-as-de-lille-might-not-resign-as-mayor-after-all-20181024.

Deklerk, Aphiwe. 'Mandela's Statue Should Not Face that of "Coloniser" King Edward VII, says ANC'. *TimesLIVE,* 24 August 2017. Accessed 5 November 2018, https://www.timeslive.co.za/news/south-africa/2017-08-24-mandelas-statue-should-not-face-that-of-coloniser-king-edward-vii-says-anc/.

De Lille, Patricia. 'Speech by the City's Executive Mayor, Patricia de Lille, at the Full Council Meeting on 26 April 2017'. Accessed 4 November 2020, http://resource.capetown.gov.za/documentcentre/Documents/Speeches%20and%20statements/SPEECH%20BY%20EXECUTIVE%20MAYOR%20AT%20THE%20FULL%20COUNCIL%20MEETING%2026%20APRIL%202017.pdf

De Lille, Patricia, and Craig Kesson. *View from City Hall: Reflections on Governing Cape Town*. Johannesburg: Jonathan Ball Publishers, 2017.

Etheridge, Jenna. 'Bronze Mandela Erected on Balcony at Cape Town's City Hall'. *City Press*, 24 July 2018. Accessed 5 November 2018, https://www.news24.com/SouthAfrica/News/bronze-mandela-erected-on-balcony-at-cape-towns-city-hall-20180724.

Getz, Arlene. 'Mandela's Message a Universal One'. *IOL News*, 6 December 2013. Accessed 5 November 2018, https://www.iol.co.za/news/mandelas-message-a-universal-one-1618447.

'Goscombe John and "The New Sculpture"'. National Museum, Cardiff. Accessed 5 November 2018, https://museum.wales/cardiff/art/impressionist-modern/goscombe-john/.

Harris, Verne. 'Jacques Derrida Meets Nelson Mandela: Archival Ethics at the Endgame'. *Archival Science* 11 (2011): 113–24.

Kros, Cynthia. 'Twenty Years of Heritage Studies – The Showbiz of History?' *Social Dynamics* 43 (2017): 358–73.

Lewis, Anél. 'Grand Plan for Mandela Statue'. *IOL News*, 13 June 2013. Accessed 11 November 2018, https://www.iol.co.za/news/south-africa/western-cape/grand-plan-for-mandela-statue-1531652.

Lodge, Tom. *Mandela: A Critical Life*. Oxford: Oxford University Press, 2006.

Mandela, Nelson. *Conversations with Myself*. New York: Farrer, Straus and Giroux, 2010.

Maylam, Paul. 'Archetypal Hero or Living Saint? The Veneration of Nelson Mandela'. *Historia* 54 (2009): 21–36.

Ndletyana, Mcebisi, and Denver A. Webb. 'Social Divisions Carved in Stone or Cenotaphs to a New Identity? Policy for Memorials, Monuments and Statues in a Democratic South Africa'. *International Journal of Heritage Studies* 23 (2017): 97–110.

Nelson, Steven. 'Nelson Mandela's Two Bodies'. *Transition* 116 (2014): 130–42.

'Photo Blog: South Africa's Democracy – Mandela's "Cherished Ideal"'. Accessed 10 June 2020, https://blogs.lse.ac.uk/africaatlse/2014/09/03/photo-blog-south-africas-democracy-mandelas-cherished-ideal/.

Posel, Deborah. 'Madiba Magic: Politics as Enchantment'. In *The Cambridge Companion to Nelson Mandela*, edited by Rita Barnard, 70–91. Cambridge: Cambridge University Press, 2014.

'Remarks by Nelson Mandela in Cape Town on 11 February 1990 after his Release from Victor Verster'. Website resource compiled and authored by Padraig O'Malley, *Nelson Mandela Centre of Memory*. Accessed 8 June 2020, https://omalley.nelsonmandela.org/omalley/index.php/site/q/03lv03445/04lv04015/05lv04154/06lv04191.htm.

Schmahmann, Brenda. 'An Arresting Portrayal: Marco Cianfanelli's *Release* at the Nelson Mandela Capture Site'. *African Arts* 51 (2018): 56–69.

Sheehan, Rebecca. '"A Series of Surfaces": The New Sculpture and Cinema'. *Interdisciplinary Studies in the Long Nineteenth Century* 22 (2016). Accessed 5 June 2020, https://19.bbk.ac.uk/article/id/1462/.

Tandwa, Lizeka. 'City of Cape Town Wants to Honour Mandela with a R3.5m Statue'. *News24*, 17 April 2017. Accessed 11 November 2018, https://www.news24.com/SouthAfrica/News/city-of-cape-town-wants-to-honour-mandela-with-a-r35m-statue-20170417.

Turok, Ivan, and Justin Visagie. 'Inclusive Urban Development in South Africa: What Does It Mean and How Can It Be Measured?' IDS Working Paper 2018 (512). Accessed 2 June 2020, https://www.researchgate.net/publication/326410270_Inclusive_Urban_Development_in_South_Africa_What_Does_It_Mean_and_How_Can_It_Be_Measured.

Van Robbroeck, Lize. 'The Visual Mandela: A Pedagogy of Citizenship'. In *The Cambridge Companion to Nelson Mandela,* edited by Rita Barnard, 244–66. Cambridge: Cambridge University Press, 2014.

Ward, Kerry, and Nigel Worden. 'Commemorating, Suppressing, and Invoking Cape Slavery'. In *Negotiating the Past: The Making of Memory in South Africa,* edited by Sarah Nuttall and Carli Coetzee, 201–20. Cape Town: Oxford University Press, 1998.

Wilson, Wendy. 'Living Heritage in the Historic Urban Landscape: A Case Study of the Grand Parade Market'. Master's thesis, University of Cape Town, 2019.

Worden, Nigel. 'The Changing Politics of Slave Heritage in the Western Cape, South Africa'. *Journal of African History* 50 (2009): 23–40.

'Xhanti Mpakama – Xhosa Bronze Sculpture Artist on the Rise'. XhosaCulture.co.za, 10 May 2014. Accessed 5 November 2018, https://xhosaculture.co.za/xhanti-mpakama-xhosa-bronze-sculpture-artist-rise/.

Žižek, Slavoj. 'If Nelson Mandela Really had Won, he Wouldn't be Seen as a Universal Hero'. *The Guardian*, 9 December 2013. Accessed 2 June 2020, https://www.theguardian.com/commentisfree/2013/dec/09/if-nelson-mandela-really-had-won.

INTERVIEWS

Diamond, Stuart. Personal interview with author. Holocaust and Genocide Centre, Cape Town, 28 May 2019.

Heron, Brett. Personal interview with author. Good Party Offices, Western Cape Parliamentary Building, Cape Town, 28 June 2019.

13 'WHERE'S OUR MONUMENT?' COMMEMORATING INDIAN INDENTURED LABOUR IN SOUTH AFRICA

GOOLAM VAHED

Between 1860 and 1911, 152 641 indentured migrants arrived in Natal, primarily to work on the colony's sugar plantations. They were part of the 1.3 million Indian contract labourers who were shipped mainly to British sugar colonies after the end of slavery in most of the British Empire in 1834. This alternative source of cheap labour was required for the globalising capitalist system's food production and mining operations for European markets.[1] In terms of their contract, indentured migrants had to labour for five years for the employer to whom they were assigned. At the end of that period they could re-indenture or seek work elsewhere in Natal. After ten years they were eligible for a free passage home. The majority, however, chose to make Natal home. Their difficult working and living conditions, as well as their histories, have been extensively chronicled.[2]

The 150th anniversary of the arrival of Indian indentured labourers in 2010 saw the launch of a project to build a monument to acknowledge the role of the indentured in building the provincial economy and their centrality in the history of Indian South Africans. The struggle over this monument must be located within wider local and global debates. In the South African context, during the long history of British colonialism, Afrikaner nationalism and racial oppression of black South Africans,[3] art objects in the public domain were, as the art historians Kim Miller and Brenda Schmahmann assert, mainly 'associated with ideologies that are out of favour, such as British imperialism or Afrikaner nationalism'. In the spirit of reconciliation, the practice in the post-apartheid period is to keep existing public monuments and art, and to add new works that recognise the previously marginalised histories of the oppressed.[4] The results are mixed: while some new works have been widely acclaimed, others are marked by contestation over consultation, what is to be commemorated, and the location, design and funding, among other issues. Furthermore, since the 2015 #RhodesMustFall movement, the policy of retaining old monuments has come under scrutiny.[5]

The quest for recognition by the descendants of indentured migrants to Natal also has a global dimension. Indians elsewhere have been seeking recognition of the journey of their indentured ancestors. As in South Africa, Indians have had troubled racial histories in places such as Guyana, Trinidad and Tobago, and Fiji. Many feel aggrieved that Indian indenture has not received the same recognition as slavery in their respective countries, or, indeed, by the United Nations. The formation of an organisation such as the Global Organisation of People of Indian Origin (GOPIO) by 'twice-migrants', Indians who have emigrated from the former colonies to other Western countries, together with the rise of India as a global power in the past three decades and its embracing of the Indian diaspora, has given impetus to the move to capture the group history of bonded labour.[6] Mauritius, with its majority Indian population, has been at the forefront of the quest for global recognition of indenture. The Aapravasi Ghat in Mauritius, the Immigration Depot where indentured labourers disembarked, was declared a World Heritage site in 2006, and a proposal was presented at the UNESCO session in Paris in 2014 for an Indentured Labour Route Project (ILRP) where the Aapravasi Ghat would become the secretariat.[7]

During the apartheid era, the history of black South Africans was marginalised in written works as well as public history. The democratic terrain offered scope to change this, but as historians Leslie Witz, Gary Minkley and Ciraj Rassool point out, new monuments and artworks 'open debates about the representations of pasts'. They add that 'perhaps even more than history that is produced within the academy, public pasts are debated, criticised, and contested by a wide range of individuals and interest groups'.[8] This is the case with the heretofore non-existent monument to the indentured which has generated debate over how the indentured past should be remembered, and given rise to political wrangling.

The quest for a memorial in recognition of indenture may be viewed as part of the post-apartheid flourishing of 'the heritage of those previously marginalised',[9] but the impetus also comes from concerns about the place of Indians in the post-apartheid nation. While the African National Congress (ANC) government speaks of non-racialism, race remains an important marker of identity because citizens are required to state their 'race' when applying for documentation, jobs, grants and so on. As part of a minority group, many Indians feel vulnerable. Most trace their roots to the indentured workers who arrived in South Africa from 1860. Until 1961, the policy of successive governments was to repatriate them to India or, failing that, to limit their social, political and economic rights. Even when accepted as citizens in 1961, Indians were subjected to second-class treatment.[10]

When Nelson Mandela became president of South Africa in 1994, Indians hoped that they would take their place as fully-fledged citizens in the 'new' South Africa. However, almost three decades into the new democracy, they are beginning to feel excluded, as their place in the 'Rainbow Nation' has come under scrutiny from a rising African nationalism. Anthropologist Thomas Blom Hansen notes that melancholia has taken hold of many Indians in the post-apartheid period: '[There is] a multilayered sense of loss: loss of economic security; loss of the township as "our place"; loss of perceived existential and physical security.'[11] The political scientist Marc Howard Ross tells us that people call upon 'shared narratives ... when they are disoriented and struggling to make sense of events in situations combining high uncertainty and high stress ... Group narratives and the familiar shared images they draw upon link people together providing reassurance, relieving anxiety.'[12] As is evident from a scanning of the letters to the press and radio call-in programmes, many Indian South Africans take great pride in their economic success as the outcome of hard work in the face of enormous odds, and dispute the notion that they were advantaged in any way by differential treatment under apartheid. Memorialising the sufferings of indentured Indians and their economic contribution is seen by some as a means to secure recognition of the right of Indians to be in the country and affirm their South Africanness. In this, there are parallels with coloured people in the Cape.[13]

2010 AND THE IMPETUS FOR A MONUMENT

In 2010, political and civil society groupings were galvanised to mark the 150th anniversary of the arrival of the first migrants on 16 November 1860. The only other time that there was similar interest in commemorating the indentured was the centenary commemoration in 1960, which took place in difficult political circumstances and mainly comprised educational lectures about the history of Indians in South Africa, symposiums on politics, and events that emphasised Afro-Indian unity.[14] The centenary commemoration inspired J. P. Gokool, whose father was an indentured migrant, to form the 1860 Indian Settlers Association, which later became the 1860 Settlers Association and, in 1999, the 1860 Heritage Foundation. Gokool's son Krish replaced him as president in 1986. Both J. P. and Krish organised annual commemorations. Krish Gokool told me in an interview that around 60 'old folks gather annually and do a thanksgiving ceremony at Addington Beach more or less where they [Indians] landed'. There, they offer a prayer, meditate while looking across the Indian Ocean towards India, exchange stories about indenture, and share a meal together.

Another important community organiser, Seelan Archary, has deep roots in indenture. He grew up on a sugar estate in Mount Edgecombe, north of Durban, as a fourth-generation descendant of indentured migrants. His father left school at an early age to work for the sugar mill (Huletts Sugar) while his mother worked as a kitchen hand for the Sugar Association Training Centre, Archary informed me in an interview. He joined the National Education, Health and Allied Workers Union (Nehawu) in the early 1990s, and founded a construction company about a decade later. His community involvement began in the mid-1990s when the local community was beginning to 'lose a lot of assets', such as the clubhouse, school and temple in Mount Edgecombe, to developers wishing to build golf estates and businesses. When a second temple, the Shree Mariamman Temple, was also threatened, he joined its committee and helped prevent its destruction. He has been chairperson of the Temple Committee ever since. In 2000, Archary formed the 1860 Commemoration Council and organised the 140th anniversary celebration of the arrival of the indentured, which has since become an annual event. As chairperson of the ANC in Ward 48 in Phoenix, with its strong trade union connections, he has made a point of inviting African politicians and union organisers to address its gatherings.

The 2010 commemoration attracted the attention of a wide segment of the Indian population. I attended some of the early meetings, where a keenly debated issue was whether indenture was slavery or, as one of the resolutions proposed, 'akin to slavery'. There was a strong backlash from descendants of indentured migrants who insisted that indenture, as historian Hugh Tinker contended, was a 'new form of slavery'.[15] This position was adopted by the 2010 committee. Reflecting on those debates in his 2018 interview with me, Archary remained adamant that 'indenture was a smart word for slavery. The British with their English language were able to sacrament the issue of slavery. They abolished slavery but they needed slaves here from India. And so they offered a contract not even worth the paper it was written on in terms of indenture.'

The field of indenture studies has evolved considerably since Tinker published his study. In a festschrift in honour of Fijian historian, Brij V. Lal, I make the point that Lal (and other scholars of indenture) have 'turned to biographies to provide a sense of how the indentured negotiated a system barely one step removed from slavery. From numbers, he was now turning the indentured into people with ambitions, cultures, and agency even while accepting that the structural nature of indentured industrial agriculture was essentially unfree.'[16] Academic arguments were, however, futile in these public settings; as historians, we had to bow to public sentiment. It is important for Indians in contemporary South Africa to underscore past sufferings in order to counter stereotyping of them as rich and racist, and previously privileged by the apartheid regime.

MONUMENTS COMMITTEE

The meetings for the 2010 commemoration resulted in the launch of the (national) 1860 Legacy Foundation in Durban in 2009. The KwaZulu-Natal (KZN) Legacy Foundation was chaired by Satish Dhupelia, community activist and great-grandson of Mohandas K. Gandhi, with Seelan Archary as vice-chairperson.[17] As Dhupelia told me in an interview, 'Indian' was deliberately omitted from the name: '1860 denotes where we came from, and this is a story of how we went on to become South Africans. So, we're a part of the 58 million people who live in this country, and we are South Africans. So we pay homage to our heritage and where we went from there.' He emphasised the Africanness of Indians, as Archary had done. The latter told me that he had addressed a gala dinner for the May Day celebrations in 2009, declaring: 'India is the motherland for our ancestors, and we respect them. Our motherland is South Africa, we are born and bred here, there's no other country that we know that is our home.' According to its launch presentation, the vision of the 1860 Legacy Foundation is for 'continued involvement of people of Indian origin in all facets of South African Society with the emphasis on nation building.'[18] One of the specific goals of the 2010 commemorations was to build a monument in acknowledgement of the suffering and contribution of indentured migrants.

The KZN Legacy Foundation's three-person Monuments Committee was chaired by Archary. A Memorandum of Understanding (MOU) was signed with the Heritage Directorate in KZN's Office of the Premier and with the eThekwini Municipality, in terms of which the premier's office would fund the monument and the municipality would provide land and implement the project.[19] This became the project's steering committee. For Archary, recognition of indenture was not only about the past but also aimed to acknowledge the plight of many descendants of indentured migrants in the post-apartheid period. 'The sugar mill was very cruel to us', as he explained to me: 'When they decided to close shop in KZN … we were left stranded. Our only source of work was the sugar mill and when the mills closed, there's nothing for you there, you're living in a house but there's no source of employment.' Archary considered it important to highlight this because many ordinary Africans and political parties such as the Economic Freedom Fighters (EFF) associate Indians with affluence, ignoring the legacy of indenture, historically and into the present.

In the lead-up to the 2010 commemorations, Zweli Mkhize, then premier of KZN, set aside R10 million for the commemoration and erection of a monument. Government support could be attributed to factors such as the historically close relationship between Indian and African activists in the Congress movement, the ANC's need to woo Indian voters in KZN, as well as close ties between India and South Africa. According to Archary, the first step that the Monuments Committee took was to place plaques 'in the precincts of the City Hall in ten towns (among these were Durban, Stanger, Port Shepstone and Ladysmith). The reason for going to City Hall is that it is protected, and its maintained.' This gave Indians a central place in the narrative of these towns. Critics claimed, however, that many ordinary people are not aware of these plaques and regard the expenditure as a waste of valuable resources.

More than the plaques, it is the failure to build the monument that is the subject of numerous letters to the press as the commemoration date approaches each year, censuring the Monuments Committee for this fiasco. The delay has, however, been caused by a myriad of factors, including locating a suitable site, securing funding, differences over the design, and ongoing political wrangling.

In 2010, the eThekwini Council formally approved a motion for an Indian monument to be erected on the beachfront. Councillor Duncan Du Bois of the Democratic Alliance (DA) objected in a letter to the editor of the *Daily News* that, while the indentured deserved a monument, 'the more appropriate locality for such a structure would be the Point area because that is where the passengers from the Truro were first lodged'. Despite this objection, the committee proceeded to identify several sites but came up against Mike Sutcliffe, ANC member and then city manager who, according to Archary, 'had plans for the beachfront and he was not going to let an Indian statue get in the way'. Following Sutcliffe's departure, Mayor James Nxumalo and the new city manager, Sibusiso Sithole, were, according to Archary, 'very helpful' and identified a site along the South Beach Walk promenade at the Durban Point Waterfront, which was, nevertheless, only confirmed at the end of 2013.

Members of the Monuments Committee hoped that the location and positioning of the statue, in the vicinity of uShaka Marine World, which draws large numbers of visitors annually, would result in casual visitors being exposed to the Indian monument, with the monument itself drawing a different set of visitors who would contribute to the economy of the area. These would include domestic tourists, as large numbers of Indians now live outside of KZN, and usually visit Durban annually. Once the site was assured, efforts were made to procure funds from the Premier's office. But, as Sinothi Thabethe of eThekwini Municipality noted in an interview with me, 'there was no movement on the project because the Premier's office never made a formal commitment ... funds were not transferred'. The Premier's office eventually wrote to the municipality in 2015, indicating that funds were available for the monument and requesting a project plan. This was provided to Dr A. V. Shongwe, KZN general manager of Heritage, for a project lasting six months.[20] The committee also embarked on fundraising to increase this amount. The response of the sugar companies disappointed Archary, who complained to me: 'They are absolutely silent, man. One of our guys suggested that we should ask them for the monument itself. They made billions on our parents' back, blood, sweat and tears, they should actually contribute to it.'

POLITICAL TENSIONS

Widespread political tension, however, resulted in the project stalling. In March 2015, students at the University of Cape Town demanded the removal from campus of a statue of Cecil John Rhodes. Protesting students gained massive support through a social media campaign #RhodesMustFall, and their demand was met. A month later, in April 2015, a statue of Mohandas K. Gandhi, who had lived and worked in South Africa from 1893 to 1914 and is globally lauded for his non-violent anti-colonial stance, was defaced because of allegedly negative comments he made about Africans.[21] Archary recounted to me that, in light of these attacks, Dr Nhlanhla Thusi, a director in the Premier's office, had said: 'It's too hot ... they wanted Gandhi's statue to fall, also Rhodes, so [Thusi] said let's delay this thing, so we delayed it.' Having worked closely with Thusi, who suffered an untimely death in 2018, Archary lamented to me: 'We [Indians] lost somebody very important ... especially in terms of Indo–African relations. Dr Thusi was totally focused on social cohesion and the integration of different communities. He had a strong passion for the Indian community.'

For Imraan Buccus, a weekly columnist at the *Sunday Independent*, the delay was a blessing in disguise: 'As our political climate becomes more fraught', he wrote, 'race-specific monuments in public spaces might not be the most prudent'.[22] Indeed, Zweli Sangweni of the Mazibuye African Forum (MAF), an anti-Indian organisation established around 2012, issued a statement that it would be a 'monumental insult to (African) leaders ... who uncompromisingly defended the length and breadth of KZN, to commemorate the arrival of indentured labourers'.[23] The MAF argued that indentured labour had reduced African bargaining power with whites, and that Indians continue to be racist towards Africans and an impediment to African economic progress. They are thus undeserving of official acknowledgement.[24]

The history of Afro–Indian race tensions, with riots in 1949 and 1985, together with the xenophobic attacks on migrants and refugees from Africa and South Asia that have intensified since 2008, has forced stakeholders to pay heed to grassroots sentiments. There were clear differences among stakeholders in the African and Indian communities over what should be represented, and how. As Daniel Walkowitz and Lisa Knauer remind us, divided societies are marked by 'divergent and often competing interests and different stakes in how histories are represented', so that the 'multiple publics' make it difficult to reconcile contested pasts.[25]

In interviews with Archary, however, he makes it clear that he is not concerned about possible attacks on the monument. He believes that Indians must continue to forge links with trade unions, political leaders, civil society groups and other 'authoritative voices' among the majority African population, including the Zulu king: 'I don't think any fence is going to help because people will go and damage it if they want. You can't put a fort around a statue, then you rather not build a statue.' In her study of the defacement of public symbols in South Africa, Sabine Marschall concludes that, on the whole, there have been few attacks, and that such attacks generally reflect 'forms of socio-political protest' at the government's failure to deliver rather than an attack on the group per se.[26]

DIFFERENCES OVER THE DESIGN

Further to these externally driven challenges, one of the key causes of the delay has been the finalisation of a design. There was no consensus among the different stakeholders on what the monument for the indentured should look like. As Miller and Schmahmann point out, in post-apartheid South Africa, 'public sculpture has generated robust controversy in regard to questions about how beloved icons are best represented and remembered in the public sphere'.[27] Thabethe had explained to me that his task was to ensure that the project was properly implemented, and so, at a steering committee meeting in June 2015, it was resolved that Frank Reitz of the municipality's Architecture Department would be asked to take the project forward. Ruben Reddy Architects was appointed in September 2015 to supervise implementation of the programme. Reitz informed me in an interview that, since this was considered 'specialised work', the Council's Executive Committee agreed in January 2016 that procurement procedures could be bypassed.[28] He went on to explain that the department decided on a limited rather than open competition, both to expedite the process and to ensure a high standard.

Meanwhile, the community was applying pressure for the monument. Cognisant of this, Thabethe assured Dr Thusi in March 2016 that he would work with representatives from the Premier's office and the appointed architects to achieve its speedy completion. The delay was, however, further politicised. The *Daily News* reported that Minority Front leader Shameen Thakur-Rajbansi described the entire process as an 'insult' to Indians. She labelled government's promises since 2010 as a 'cynical ploy' to win Indian votes. Although there were no designs, then acting director-general for the KZN government, Frikkie Brooks, was quoted as saying that 'everybody was now in agreement'. He gave the assurance that he had 'received the latest report from the eThekwini Municipality, and it is in construction at the moment', and so he expected the statue to be ready by July 2016.

Ruben Reddy Architects approached ten local artists for designs for the proposed monument.[29] According to their brief, the monument should be 'inclusive and one that unifies all South Africans'; have 'significance and relevance' for all South Africans and not just Indians; and 'transcend the historical confines of a single community [and] commemorate a chapter in a broader South African narrative'. It went on to state:

> What is being envisaged … is a powerful living monument that encapsulates the drama and historical importance of their arrival; the humiliation and pain of their experience as indentured workers; the sacrifices they made to survive in unwelcoming surroundings; and the path they laid for the development of a community that is now a proud and integral part of a new democracy.[30]

Carl Wright of Ruben Reddy Architects emphasised that the artists 'will be tasked with not only commemorating the arrival of the 1860 indentured labourers, but creating a landmark tourist destination for the city'.[31] On the whole, the brief tied in with post-apartheid linking of heritage and economic development with nation-building. As Marschall points out, monuments are 'very consciously built as tourist attractions and perceived as mechanisms for community development'.[32]

The artists submitted their designs by 21 June 2016 to give the Bid Adjudication Committee time to decide on a winning entry for the planned sod-turning ceremony in November of that year. The committee, which included architects Frank Reitz and Carl Wright, met in November and decided that none of the designs was suitable.[33] In Archary's view, 'these fellows didn't have a clue as to what we wanted. During all our deliberations, we had been saying we want to commemorate 16 November, the first people who put foot on this soil. The other history [of Indians] is captured in the museums.' Archary told me he found the designs 'so far-fetched, you would have to walk twice or thrice or four times to make out what the hell is in there, what is the word for that, like modern art is ... abstract.'

Reitz, on the other hand, informed me that the delay was caused by the fact that there was 'no clarity' on what the monument should symbolise, whether it should 'focus on the new South Africa or the past, on those who grew up here or those who had arrived, and it was difficult to proceed further because of these different expectations'. Likewise, Thabethe explained to me that it was only after the artists' submissions that he became aware of a sketch of the kind of monument the Monuments Committee envisaged:

> What actually happened was that there was this design, which was given to the province, but that information was not actually cascaded to us ... so I think there was that particular problem of miscommunication. But we also wanted their own expressions, as to how they actually view this in relation to the area where the monument was going to be.

In Archary's vision (depicted in figure 13.1), the statue would 'depict an Indian male sugar cane plantation worker cutting the cane in traditional clothing of the time, his wife carrying sugarcane on her head, attired in traditional clothing of the time, and a child playing or sitting on the ground in traditional clothing of the time'.

Unlike Archary, Reitz did not advocate for something 'too obvious, too literal, those things have been done elsewhere',[34] but he agreed that the expressions of interest 'were definitely not up to the prominence of the site'. What is evident from these statements is that while Reitz wanted a 'world

Figure 13.1. Sketch by Nanda Soobben for the 1860 Monuments Committee for the statue of an Indian sugar cane plantation worker, 2013. Provided to author by Sinothe Thabethe, KwaMuhle Museum

class' monument that in itself would draw visitors, the preference of the Monuments Committee was for a structure that made a clear statement about indenture. Such disagreements are not uncommon: in KZN, a disagreement over a statue of King Shaka, which was deemed not to be 'heroic' enough, led to the statue being removed and replaced.[35] Following rejection of the designs, representatives from the Premier's office, the municipality, and the Monuments Committee agreed that the artists would be sent non-award letters and be paid for their submissions, and that the committee would re-advertise for artist impressions.[36] Although the designs had been rejected, the steering committee proceeded with the sod-turning ceremony, probably to appease the public.

COMMUNITY FRUSTRATION

In November 2016, an editorial in the *Post*, a weekly newspaper that primarily caters for the Indian community, issued the following warning:

> [A] clear message needs to be sent out to the organising committee that these endless delays and excuses cannot be tolerated any further. If there is apathy or a lack of political will within your ranks, get rid of the dead wood immediately. If there is a hint of political interference behind the delays, let's bring this out into the open. Monuments like the 1860 project are important to South Africans wanting to celebrate a shared history, so get your house in order.[37]

Figure 13.2. 1860 project sod-turning ceremony at the beachfront, Durban. From the left are Vic Pillay, Mayor Zandile Gumede (partially obscured), KZN Premier Willies Mchunu, A. V. Mahomed and Seelan Archary, 15 November 2016. Photograph by Gcina Ndwalane

At the sod-turning ceremony on 15 November 2016, then KZN Premier Willies Mchunu stated: 'We remain indebted to the Indian indentured labourers for their contribution, especially in establishing the agricultural potential of KwaZulu-Natal making it the world-renowned region of the sugar industry.' He went on to say that the monument would 'express our deep appreciation to our fellow brothers and sisters from India who unequivocally declared South Africa and KZN in particular, their preferred place to live in'.[38] Selvan Naidoo, a voluntary curator of the 1860 Heritage Centre, told me in an interview that he is convinced that the ceremony was 'a PR exercise in covering up for the bungles along the way and the delay. It was the normal thrills and frills associated with a PR government municipality event … People were bussed in from the townships. The event had about 3 000 people, some from the African townships of Umlazi and KwaMashu, and most from the Indian townships.'

Six months later, there was still no sign of a statue, and public anger forced the adjudication committee to resolve in May 2017 that a call for designs would go out to the 'general public, artists, learners, and students'. However, before this could be done, the municipality received a letter from the Premier's office requesting a 'political decision' to expedite the monument as the procurement processes were 'tedious, long-winded and mired in delays'. The Monuments Committee had, moreover, agreed on the details of the statue and was ready to submit its plan. The city manager's office would appoint a service provider to commence work by August 2017. However, there was no further directive to the municipality from the Premier's office.[39] Dr N. O. Mkhize, director-general in the Office of the Premier, wrote in March 2018 to L. S. Magagula, head of the KZN Provincial Treasury, to recall the funds from eThekwini Municipality. Agreeing to do so, Magagula informed Mkhize that the monies would be held until a satisfactory plan of action was provided.[40] Mkhize wrote to the eThekwini city manager requesting that the funds be returned to the province. At this point, Thabethe recommended that the MOU with the Premier's office be cancelled.[41]

These delays were clearly annoying the (Indian) public, and weekly columnist Dennis Pather demanded, 'Where's our monument?' His article emphasised the political importance of the monument at a time when the place of Indians was under scrutiny by African nationalists: 'Most South Africans knew or cared little about the struggles of the indentured. They do not feel the pain of the unbearably miserable conditions and punishment the labourers experienced … I'm hopeful such a memorial will help dispel unfair stereotypes about a community whose commitment and resilience through successive generations have made it an integral part of the new democracy.'[42] As head of the Monuments Committee, Archary has, he told me, been subjected to intense pressure from within the Indian community: 'All the different political parties were saying, "why are you not showing respect for the Indian community and building the monument as you say you would?"'

EXCLUSION AND THE 'SENSE OF LOSS'

Commemoration of Indian indenture in South Africa has taken many forms, ranging from public lectures, to beachfront vigils, exhibitions, memoirs and fictional work. Since the 150th anniversary of indenture in 2010, the demand for a monument has become louder due to both local and global influences. The memory of indenture is a painful one: Archary believes it should be commemorated through a public monument for the edification of all South Africans as well as for future generations, while Satish Dhupelia is hopeful that the monument will be 'good for social cohesion; people are drifting apart as South Africans, we come together when we need to, but we definitely need to come together again'.[43] In line with archaeologist Christina Luke's notion of monuments as 'cultural diplomacy',[44] the desire of Archary and Dhupelia is for the story of Africans and Indians to be interwoven, so that the exploitation of both is seen through the common lens of the global development of capitalism and British colonial expansion, which appropriated forms of unfree labour.

Given this, it might be asked why the monument that the committee has in mind is not inclusive. Indeed, the lack of progress in building the monument underscores the importance of political context in determining public representation. The political climate was ripe for a monument in 2010, considering the country's sound economic performance, the euphoria over the football World Cup, and then President Jacob Zuma's close relationship with certain Indian businessmen within South Africa and with the notorious Gupta family from India. But as Walkowitz and Knauer have reminded us, the state is constantly changing and is subject to internal fissures.[45] While commemoration of the past can help to build bridges within nation states, a discussion of Indian indenture reveals deeper Afro–Indian tensions. Descendants of indenture wish to emphasise the horrors of bondage labour, and seek recognition of the role of their forebears in building the economy of South Africa. Others, however, see the arrival of the indentured as undercutting the bargaining power of the Zulu people, and thus question paying homage to the indentured. As the historian of memorials and sacred spaces Edward T. Linenthal concludes in *Culture and Belonging in Divided Societies*, 'contestation' is often at the heart of public memorialisation: 'What for some people is an enrichment of narrative registers for others as ... attempts to claim ownership of story and site.'[46] In the same volume, Marc Ross contends that 'inclusion or exclusion from a society's symbolic landscape ... tells us about the politics of acceptance, rejection, and access to a society's resources and opportunities'.[47] Many Indians feel excluded not only from the nation state in a context of rising African nationalism but also from the benefits of affirmative action and black economic empowerment opportunities. Non-inclusion in the 'symbolic landscape' will likely continue to enhance feelings of what Thomas Blom Hansen has referred to as many Indians' 'sense of loss'.

NOTES

1. Robin Butlin, *Geographies of Empire: European Empires and Colonies c. 1880–1960* (Cambridge: Cambridge University Press, 2009), 147.
2. See Ashwin Desai and Goolam Vahed, *Inside Indian Indenture: A South African Story, 1860–1914* (Cape Town: HSRC Press, 2010).
3. 'Black' is used here as it was in the late-apartheid period to refer jointly to Africans, Indians and coloureds. Racial categorisation was adopted by the post-apartheid government, with the South African state officially dividing the country's population into four racial groups: black African, white, coloured, and Indian / Asian.
4. Kim Miller and Brenda Schmahmann, 'Introduction: Engaging with Public Art in South Africa, 1999–2015', in *Public Art in South Africa: Bronze Warriors and Plastic Presidents*, eds Kim Miller and Brenda Schmahmann (Bloomington: Indiana University Press, 2017), viii.
5. The South African government announced in November 2020 that it would conduct a national audit of all the statues in the country by March 2021, to decide which heritage symbols should remain and which should be removed.
6. See Ashwin Desai and Goolam Vahed, *A History of the Present: A Biography of Indian South Africans, 1990–2019* (New Delhi: Oxford University Press, 2019), 212–20.
7. Jayshree Mungur-Medhi, 'The Reconstitution of Aapravasi Ghat, a Nineteenth-Century Immigration Depot in the Capital City of Port Louis, Mauritius, through Archaeology',

International Journal of Historical Archaeology 20.4 (2016): 781–803. An International Scientific Committee (ISC) was established at a meeting in Mauritius in October 2017 to investigate ways to implement the project, and the author was invited as the South African representative but was unable to attend. Nalini Moodley-Diar became the representative on the committee, which has been working on strategies towards memorialisation of the ILRP.

8   Leslie Witz, Gary Minkley and Ciraj Rassool, 'South Africa and the Unsettling of History', in *Unsettled History: Making South African Public Pasts*, eds Leslie Witz, Gary Minkley and Ciraj Rassool (Ann Arbor: University of Michigan Press, 2017), 1–26.

9   Sabine Marschall, 'Commemorating "Struggle Heroes": Constructing a Genealogy for the New South Africa', *International Journal of Heritage Studies* 1.2 (2006): 176.

10 Desai and Vahed, *A History of the Present*, 188.

11 Thomas Blom Hansen, *Melancholia of Freedom: Social Life in an Indian Township in South Africa* (New York: Princeton University Press, 2012), 16.

12 Marc Howard Ross, 'Cultural Contestation and the Symbolic Landscape. Politics by Other Means?', in *Culture and Belonging in Divided Societies: Contestation and Symbolic Landscapes*, ed. Marc Howard Ross (Pennsylvania: University of Pennsylvania Press, 2009), 8.

13 Ward and Worden pointed to the 1 December movement in the Cape in the immediate post-apartheid period as one initiated by middle-class coloured people seeking to recover their slavery heritage for contemporary purposes. The movement was named after the day commemorated by freed slaves. See Kerry Ward and Nigel Worden, 'Commemorating, Suppressing, and Invoking Cape Slavery', in *Negotiating the Past: The Making of Memory*, eds Sarah Nuttall and Carli Coetzee (Cape Town: Oxford University Press, 1998), 201–17.

14 See Goolam Vahed, *Chota Motala: A Biography of Political Activism in the KwaZulu-Natal Midlands* (Pietermaritzburg: University of KwaZulu-Natal Press, 2018), 132–38.

15 Hugh Tinker, *A New System of Slavery: The Export of Indian Labour Overseas, 1830–1920* (London: Oxford University Press, 1974).

16 Goolam Vahed, 'Brij V. Lal: Rooting for History', in *Bearing Witness: Essays in Honour of Brij V. Lal*, eds Doug Munro and Jack Corbett (Canberra: Australian National University, 2017), 73.

17 Sadly, Satish Dhupelia died from Covid-19 complications on 22 November 2020. His death is a huge loss to the 1860 Heritage Centre on whose board he served, as well as to a host of community organisations.

18 Brij Maharaj, 'Commemoration, Celebration or Commiseration? 150th Anniversary of Indentured Labourers in South Africa', in *Legacies, Identities and Dilemmas: Understanding Contemporary India and South Africa*, eds Sujata Patel and Tina Uys (New Delhi: Routledge, 2012), 84.
19 This was in line with the municipality's Monument's Guideline adopted in 2010, which aims to 'embrace our cultural diversity ... [and] stimulate economic growth, social cohesion and unity in diversity'. Report from S. Thabethe, Director of Local History Museums, to Executive Committee, eThekwini Municipality, 6 November 2018. A copy of the Report is in the author's possession.
20 The municipality of eThekwini and the Premier's office signed a formal agreement on 26 March 2015, and the money was transferred to the municipality on 31 March 2015. One condition was that the money had to be utilised by September 2015 or it would be recalled by the Provincial Treasury. See 'Memorandum from S. Sewrathan, Director of Management Accounting, to D. A. V. Shongwe, Heritage, 26 June 2018'. A copy, provided by S. Thabete, is in the possession of the author.
21 For a critique of Gandhi's South African years, see Ashwin Desai and Goolam Vahed, *The South African Gandhi: Stretcher-Bearer of Empire* (Stanford: Stanford University Press, 2016).
22 Imraan Buccus, 'Monumental Misinterpretation of Indian Indenture', *Sunday Independent*, 20 November 2016, accessed 2 November 2020, https://www.iol.co.za/sundayindependent/monumental-misinterpretation-of-indian-indenture-2091680.
23 For a detailed discussion of Mazibuye's role in the KwaZulu-Natal political landscape, see Ashwin Desai and Goolam Vahed, 'Stuck in the Middle: Indians in South Africa's Fading Rainbow?', *South Asian Diaspora* 9.2 (2017): 147–62.
24 Nicholas Barbeau, 'Mazibuye Forum a No-show at Hate Speech Trial', *Independent Online*, 22 July 2016, accessed 10 September 2018, https://www.iol.co.za/news/mazibuye-forum-a-no-show-at-hate-speech-trial-2048622.
25 Daniel J. Walkowitz and Lisa Maya Knauer, Introduction to *Contested Histories in Public Space. Memory, Race and Nation*, eds Daniel J. Walkowitz and Lisa Maya Knauer (Durham: Duke University Press, 2009), 1–27.
26 See Sabine Marschall, 'Targeting Statues: Monument "Vandalism" as an Expression of Sociopolitical Protest in South Africa', *African Studies Review* 60.3 (2017): 204.
27 Miller and Schmahmann, Introduction, viii.
28 Section 36 of the Municipal Supply Chain Management Regulations permits the accounting officer to 'dispense with the official procurement processes' under certain conditions, one of which is 'for the acquisition of special works of art or historical

objects where specifications are difficult to compile'. The city manager agreed to the request on 15 December 2015, and it was approved by EXCO on 26 January 2016.

29 Only seven artists submitted designs. Those originally named were Poori Bhana, Marco Cianfanelli, Lungelo Gumede, Peter Hall, Banele Khoza, Doug Jahangeer, Amita Makan, Nandipha Mntambo, Usha Seejarim and Nanda Soobben. '1860 Indentured Labour Public Art Piece – Adjudication Methodology Report', Ruben Reddy Architects, *Post*, 4 November 2016.

30 '1860 Indentured Labour Public Art Piece'.

31 '1860 Indentured Labour Public Art Piece'.

32 Sabine Marschall, *Landscapes of Memory: Commemorative Monuments, Memorials, and Public Statuary in Post-apartheid South Africa* (Leiden: Brill, 2010), 320.

33 The submissions were judged according to eight criteria: whether they unify South Africans; contribute to nation building; capture the broader South African history / narrative; are appropriate for the site; use appropriate materials; use a narrative that captures indenture; are interactive and legible; add value to the city.

34 The sculpture that Reitz indirectly refers to here is Marco Cianfanelli's *Release*, located on the spot where Nelson Mandela was captured on 5 August 1962 outside Howick in KwaZulu-Natal.

35 See Liese van der Watt, 'Public Art as Political Crucible: Andries Botha's Shaka and Contested Symbols of Zulu Masculinity and Culture in Kwazulu-Natal', in *Public Art in South Africa: Bronze Warriors and Plastic Presidents*, eds Kim Miller and Brenda Schmahmann (Bloomington: Indiana University Press, 2017), 73–94.

36 Report from S. Thabethe.

37 'Indenture Monument: Stop the Delays', *Post*, 2 November 2016, 6.

38 Quoted in Lorna Charles, 'Sod Turning Ceremony for Addington Beach Indenture Monument', *Berea Mail*, 16 November 2016.

39 Report from S. Thabethe.

40 'Memorandum from S. Sewrathan'.

41 Report from S. Thabethe. In October 2020, KZN Premier Sihle Zikalala tasked Ravi Pillay, KZN MEC for Finance, with taking the process forward, and an interim committee comprising 12 community leaders was formed. See 'New Hope for Monument to Mark Arrival of Indians', *Post*, 14 October 2020, 3.

42 Dennis Pather, 'Where's our Monument?' *Sunday Tribune*, 19 November 2017.

43 Quoted in Charles, 'Sod Turning Ceremony'.

44 Christina Luke, 'Cultural Sovereignty in the Balkans and Turkey: The Politics of Preservation and Rehabilitation', *Journal of Social Archaeology* 13.3 (2013): 353.

45 Walkowitz and Maya, Introduction, 16.
46 Edward T. Linenthal, Epilogue to *Culture and Belonging in Divided Societies: Contestation and Symbolic Landscapes*, ed. Marc Howard Ross (Pennsylvania: University of Pennsylvania Press, 2009), 283.
47 Ross, 'Cultural Contestation and the Symbolic Landscape', 1.

REFERENCES

Barbeau, Nicholas. 'Mazibuye Forum a No-show at Hate Speech Trial'. *Independent Online*, 22 July 2016. Accessed 10 September 2018, https://www.iol.co.za/news/mazibuye-forum-a-no-show-at-hate-speech-trial-2048622.

Butlin, Robin. *Geographies of Empire: European Empires and Colonies c.1880–1960*. Cambridge: Cambridge University Press, 2009.

Charles, Lorna. 'Sod Turning Ceremony for Addington Beach Indenture Monument'. *Berea Mail*, 16 November 2016.

Desai, Ashwin, and Goolam Vahed. *Inside Indian Indenture: A South African Story, 1860–1914*. Cape Town: HSRC Press, 2010.

Desai, Ashwin, and Goolam Vahed. *The South African Gandhi: Stretcher-Bearer of Empire*. Stanford: Stanford University Press, 2016.

Desai, Ashwin, and Goolam Vahed. 'Stuck in the Middle: Indians in South Africa's Fading Rainbow'. *South Asian Diaspora* 9.2 (2017): 147–62.

Desai, Ashwin, and Goolam Vahed. *A History of the Present: A Biography of Indian South Africans, 1990–2019*. New Delhi: Oxford University Press, 2019.

Hansen, Thomas Blom. *Melancholia of Freedom: Social Life in an Indian Township in South Africa*. New York: Princeton University Press, 2012.

'Indenture Monument: Stop the Delays'. *Post*, 2 November 2016, 6.

Linenthal, Edward T. Epilogue to *Culture and Belonging in Divided Societies: Contestation and Symbolic Landscapes*, edited by Marc H. Ross, 281–85. Pennsylvania: University of Pennsylvania Press, 2009.

Luke, Christina. 'Cultural Sovereignty in the Balkans and Turkey: The Politics of Preservation and Rehabilitation'. *Journal of Social Archaeology* 13.3 (2013): 350–70.

Maharaj, Brij. 'Commemoration, Celebration or Commiseration? 150th Anniversary of Indentured Labourers in South Africa'. In *Legacies, Identities and Dilemmas: Understanding Contemporary India and South Africa*, edited by Sujata Patel and Tina Uys, 77–95. New Delhi: Routledge, 2012.

Marschall, Sabine. 'Commemorating "Struggle Heroes": Constructing a Genealogy for the New South Africa'. *International Journal of Heritage Studies* 1.2 (2006): 176–93.

Marschall, Sabine. *Landscapes of Memory. Commemorative Monuments, Memorials, and Public Statuary in Post-apartheid South Africa*. Leiden: Brill, 2010.

Marschall, Sabine. 'Targeting Statues: Monument "Vandalism" as an Expression of Sociopolitical Protest in South Africa'. *African Studies Review* 60.3 (2017): 203-19.

Miller, Kim, and Brenda Schmahmann. 'Introduction: Engaging with Public Art in South Africa, 1999-2015'. In *Public Art in South Africa: Bronze Warriors and Plastic Presidents*, edited by Kim Miller and Brenda Schmahmann, vii-xxxviii. Bloomington: Indiana University Press, 2017.

Mungur-Medhi, Jayshree. 'The Reconstitution of Aapravasi Ghat, a Nineteenth-Century Immigration Depot in the Capital City of Port Louis, Mauritius, through Archaeology'. *International Journal of Historical Archaeology* 20.4 (2016): 781-803.

'New Hope for Monument to Mark Arrival of Indians'. *Post,* 14 October 2020, 3.

Pather, Dennis. 'Where's our Monument?' *Sunday Tribune*, 19 November 2017.

Ross, Marc Howard. 'Cultural Contestation and the Symbolic Landscape: Politics by Other Means?' In *Culture and Belonging in Divided Societies: Contestation and Symbolic Landscapes*, edited by Marc Howard Ross, 1-24. Pennsylvania: University of Pennsylvania Press, 2009.

Tinker, Hugh. *A New System of Slavery: The Export of Indian Labour Overseas, 1830-1920*. London: Oxford University Press, 1974.

Vahed, Goolam. 'Brij V. Lal: Rooting for History'. In *Bearing Witness: Essays in Honour of Brij V. Lal*, edited by Doug Munro and Jack Corbett, 65-86. Canberra: Australian National University, 2017.

Vahed, Goolam. *Chota Motala: A Biography of Political Activism in the KwaZulu-Natal Midlands*. Pietermaritzburg: University of KwaZulu-Natal Press, 2018.

Van der Watt, Liese. 'Public Art as Political Crucible: Andries Botha's Shaka and Contested Symbols of Zulu Masculinity and Culture in KwaZulu-Natal'. In *Public Art in South Africa: Bronze Warriors and Plastic Presidents*, edited by Kim Miller and Brenda Schmahmann, 73-94. Bloomington: Indiana University Press, 2017.

Walkowitz, Daniel J., and Lisa Maya Knauer. Introduction to *Contested Histories in Public Space: Memory, Race and Nation*, edited by Daniel J. Walkowitz and Lisa Maya Knauer, 1-27. Durham: Duke University Press, 2009.

Ward, Kerry, and Nigel Worden. 'Commemorating, Suppressing, and Invoking Cape Slavery'. In *Negotiating the Past: The Making of Memory*, edited by Sarah Nuttall and Carli Coetzee, 201-17. Cape Town: Oxford University Press, 1998.

Witz, Leslie, Gary Minkley, and Ciraj Rassool. 'South Africa and the Unsettling of History'. In *Unsettled History: Making South African Public Pasts*, edited by Leslie Witz, Gary Minkley and Ciraj Rassool, 1-26. Ann Arbor: University of Michigan Press, 2017.

INTERVIEWS

Archary, Seelan. Personal interview with author. Durban, 30 August 2018.

Dhupelia, Satish. Personal interview with author. Durban, 11 September 2018.

Gokool, Krish. Personal interview with author. Durban, 6 September 2018.

Naidoo, Selvan. Personal interview with author. Durban, 30 June 2018.

Reitz, Frank. Personal interview with author. Durban, 6 June 2019.

Thabethe, Sinothe. Personal interview with author. Durban, 6 June 2019.

14 DECOLONISATION, MONUMENTS, AND A NEW ARCHITECTURAL LANGUAGE

NNAMDI ELLEH

Kwame Nkrumah, the first leader in sub-Saharan Africa to achieve decolonisation for his country, Ghana, recognised that the struggle for the continent's emancipation was just beginning in 1957. He theorised that while the emergence of newly decolonised states in the 1960s was removing 'open control' of African countries by European powers, the former colonisers were also developing a neocolonialism by using financial capital to wield power in these new nations.[1] However, in 2020 new cultural iconoclasm movements arose, with citizens broadly implicated in memorials not only of their communities but also the world.

Nkrumah's Independence Arch, with its plaque declaring 'AD 1957' alongside the motto 'Freedom and Justice', could be standing in any European city, given its neoclassical visual language.[2] How could Ghanaians be rejecting colonial rule while at the same time celebrating freedom with European monumental architecture? The Independence Arch signals ambiguous visual messages to Ghanaians and Africans at large. It fails to signify that what independence achieved was merely a stage in the long struggle for economic and political emancipation. It is noteworthy that poet and former president of Senegal Léopold Sédar Senghor, and his Pan-Africanist peers, were already interrogating ways of representing African cultures prior to independence in the 1960s. In 1996, Amado Sidibe and V. Galioutine designed and completed the Independence Monument in Bamako, Mali. This time, the visual language of the monument referenced the well-known Sudanese style of architecture in West Africa, and it showed that the pioneering cultural decolonisation project by Senghor and his peers was beginning to take root.[3]

These monuments recall projects undertaken in South Africa after the first democratic election in 1994.[4] Several structures were built to commemorate the end of apartheid: Freedom Park in Pretoria; Red Location Museum in Port Elizabeth; the Provincial Legislature Complex of the Northern Cape in Kimberley; the Provincial Legislature Complex, Mpumalanga, in Mbombela (formerly Nelspruit); and the Constitutional Court in Johannesburg.[5] Archaeological understandings from cave paintings, history, landscapes, earthenware, wall art and even body art were the tools for rejuvenating arts that indicated the diverse cultural identity of South Africans. While acknowledging that the majority of the new monuments were designed by 'white architects', architectural historian Jonathan Alfred Noble makes the salient point that it takes a long time to formulate tectonic identity. In other words, independence and elections are stages in the process, with full emancipation in the fields of art and architecture being achieved at some future point, with tectonic shifts in economic and political consciousness.

The recognition and representation of partially decolonised spaces in appropriate visual languages is not only an African experience. As far back as 1928, the International Congress for Modern Architecture (CIAM) examined urbanism as partially liberated spaces that should be investigated from multiple perspectives and preserved for the wellbeing of the living. CIAM declared: 'Urbanism is the disposition of different premises and places to shelter the development of material, sentimental, and spiritual life in all of its individual and collective manifestations.'[6] The emphasis was placed on human experience, embodied in the monument. CIAM was clear that urbanism was an evolving human experience that included 'the historic heritage of the city that should be preserved'.[7] It understood that all aspects of human experience – including civil technology and society itself – are in a continuous state of evolution.

In his essay, 'Modernity: The Unfinished Project', the philosopher Jürgen Habermas presents decolonisation as stages of development in his defence of the projects of modernity at the Venice Biennale. He underscores the differences between 'the old and the new' and 'cultural modernity and social modernization'. In regard to the old and the new, Habermas contends that modernity is transient: 'Those who, like Adorno, conceive of "modernity" as beginning around 1850 look at it through the eyes of Baudelaire and the avant-garde art.' However, 'neoconservatism displaces the burdensome consequences of a more or less successful capitalist modernisation of economy and society onto cultural modernity'.[8] Habermas argues that modernity is an evolving project and no aspect of it, including the building of schools, hospitals and monuments, should be reduced to stylistic references and what we now call culture wars: 'What the one side considers as problems of style, the other side perceives as problems of the decolonization of lost human habitats.'[9]

While Habermas's exposition links to the neo-iconoclastic culture wars of the time, we often associate iconoclastic clashes with past debates about the veneration or destruction of religious monuments.[10] In the African experience, the emergence of partially decolonised spaces accompanied by iconoclasm occurs in three phases. The first was the immediate decolonisation era of the 1960s when the flags of the colonising powers were lowered in national squares in liberated cities, as streets, places and countries were renamed, either at the time or after subsequent revolutions. The Gold Coast was renamed the Republic of Ghana, Rhodesia became Zimbabwe, and Congo became Zaire (and later the Democratic Republic of Congo). With cities, Leopoldville became Kinshasa, and Lourenço Marques became Maputo. The second phase was ushered in by the end of the Cold War in 1989 – when several socialist monuments fell in cities like Addis Ababa – which preceded the eventual demise of apartheid in 1994. The third phase began with the Arab Spring in the early 2010s, and was followed in 2015 by the #RhodesMustFall student movement.[11] While the world was coming to terms with the Arab Spring, the Republic of Sudan, which had gained independence in 1956, split apart with the birth of the Republic of South Sudan in 2011.

Outside of the African continent, the fall of the Berlin Wall and the unification of East and West Germany in 1989 remains one of the most famous recent iconoclastic cultural acts against the monument. Tearing down the wall to enable people to move across the boundary between the once separated countries was seen as a necessary and symbolic destructive act against an oppressive government.[12] People chipped away, with many removing pieces of the graffiti-covered wall for souvenirs, and it took months before it dawned upon the authorities that the barriers that separated the two Germanys should not be completely dismantled. In a way, it set a precedent on how to overthrow unwanted regimes in public squares around the world. Ironically, while certain monuments were being pulled down, new ones were being erected.

'ANTI-RACIST RACISM'

The partially decolonised spaces and current global neo-iconoclastic movements raise the question whether we can memorialise revolutionary experiences in Africa without the dominant visual narratives of ethnicity, race, religion and tribalism. Though scholars routinely examine artworks in terms of the visual language of representation, it is nevertheless important to unpack what we mean by the new languages of decolonisation on a continent where the historicisation of culture remains the preferred method for representing monuments in partially decolonised spaces. Architects and artists regularly draw from known conventions to signify the meanings of their creations. While Ghana's 1957 independence monument draws from the Roman visual language of the triumphal arch, Sidibe and Galioutine's 1966 independence arch for Mali draws from West African Sudanese visual vocabulary and materiality. Both are signifiers of independent victories, though they differ in terms of the design concepts, metaphors and narratives that they signify. The visual vocabularies of the two arches denote different periods, styles, symbols and themes of representation, but both are derived from known historical and social conventions. There are times, however, when architects adopt abstract methods in representation. Abstract designs task the imaginations of viewers when visual clues are not given about what the images and objects represent, with each discipline having its mode of cultural representation.

In *Black Orpheus*, Jean-Paul Sartre interrogates the poems of African, Caribbean and Malagasy writers. It was originally the preface to *Anthologie de la Nouvelle Poésie Nègre et Malgache de Langue Française*, the anthology edited by Léopold Sédar Senghor. After posing the question whether Senghor made himself the spokesman for his 'brothers of colour', Sartre encourages these writers to assert themselves in their respective societies by 'a sort of poetic psycho-analysis' – a process of self-awareness and affirmation of the relationship the 'coloured' person has with society as a whole. However, subtle meanings may be overlooked in the context of Sartre's references to the 'psycho-analysis' of the 'negro's' self-awareness. Is Senghor's call to his 'coloured' brothers a 'necessity or liberty'? To Sartre, the answer is obvious: the call is a treacherous necessity for attaining liberty for the individual. Freedom for one and for all is the highest form of monument any society can build. But why is it treacherous? The path to liberty, Sartre observes, is always a contentious struggle: 'The Negro, as we have said, creates an anti-racist racism. He does not at all want to dominate the world; he wishes the abolition of racial privileges wherever they are found; he affirms his solidarity with the oppressed of all colours.'[13] The path to liberty could, in a contemporary sense, involve the massive protests and neo-iconoclasms in cities around the world. It is treacherous because there are citizens and leaders who see the movements as threatening and destructive to their way of life.

Sartre's 'anti-racist racism' is not about racial hatred, nor does it concern people of African origin only. It is about the rejection of all forms of oppression that are normalised, regardless of location. Two unrelated incidents in the United States of America that continue to divide citizens are important in this regard. In 1990, Scott Tyler (the artist known as Dread Scott), while studying at the School of the Art Institute of Chicago, exhibited *What is the Proper Way to Display a U.S. Flag?* By placing the American flag on the floor, he invited viewers to address the question by recording their views in a book which could only be reached by walking on the flag. Widespread condemnation followed Tyler's provocative piece, and a group called Veterans of Foreign Wars staged a prolonged protest.[14] Tyler has continued to create artwork that foments controversial discussion in order to raise awareness on injustices such as slavery and police brutality.[15] The second incident was in 2017, when San Francisco football quarterback Colin Kaepernick knelt on one knee during the national anthem during the game's opening ceremony as a form of non-violent protest action against police brutality. His 'taking a knee' during the national anthem parallels Tyler's invitation to desecrate the flag. A comparable historical event took place on 25 May 2020 in Minneapolis: George Floyd was suffocated while lying on the ground with a policeman's knee on his neck. The weeks that followed his death saw mass protests against police brutality across the globe. Thus, #TakeAKnee became a ritual for protesters: an improvised performance was now a new global monument in the form of a live mass sculpture. Initiated by one person, it is recognised by people around the world for refusing to accept police brutality. While certain entrenched traditions are under attack from one side of society, new traditions are continuously being initiated, which take the form of iconoclastic free speech against two iconic monuments: the US flag and anthem. Hoisting the US flag is widely accepted and normalised, but Tyler's exhibition interrogates this, suggesting that it masks injustices against minorities. In this sense, Tyler exposes the racism and injustice associated with the flag. In adopting an anti-racist racism, Tyler condemned the values of the majority who imbue the US flag with too much reverence, failing to recognise that it masks social injustice. And while there is a general assumption that standing up for the US national anthem is a patriotic duty, Kaepernick's #TakeAKnee interrogated the ritual. As in all social acts, a number of outcomes are predictable: those who found it offensive to step on the US flag, or to #TakeAKnee during the US anthem, mobilised and protested against such acts; some were baffled by the performances, pondering as to their meaning; and others bravely joined in the protests, declaring their support. Any resistance against social injustice may be seen as an act of anti-racist racism.

Such momentous events are changing the world, and monuments that represent them should be conceptualised as the start of a conversation. Such events should not necessarily be frozen in sculptures in the way we were once used to making public objects in our communities. In fact, they are comparable to Tunisian Mohamed Bouazizi's act of setting himself on fire on 10 December 2010 that led to protests and the downfall of President Zine El Abidine Ben Ali. Bouazizi's action, in turn, recalls the Vietnamese monk, Thich Quang Duc, who set himself alight in 1963 in Saigon to protest the treatment of Buddhists. The protests that began in Tunisia triggered the region's revolutionary events: in Egypt, Hosni Mubarak's government fell in 2011, and that same year, in Libya, Muammar Gaddafi was deposed by rebel forces before being killed. These neo-iconoclastic battles against systems and institutions cut across nation, class, culture, ethnicity, race, gender and religion, deleting boundaries between the so-called First World and developing countries. Despite the American Civil War having ended in 1865, the removal of statues of four Confederate leaders from public squares in New Orleans, Louisiana, resulted in protest action in 2017. That year, a protest in Charlottesville, Virginia, against the removal of the Confederate General Robert E. Lee's statue exploded into violence among the pro- and anti-monument groups. And by 2020, the statues of Ulysses S. Grant, George Washington and even

Winston Churchill became the subject of intense debate and angry protest as to whether they should remain in public squares.

We should, however, note that Sartre's 'anti-racist racisms' would be problematic in cases where separatist movements are founded entirely on culture, nationalism, race or religion so as to differentiate from the 'Other' and to reclaim lost glories and histories. The psychologist Steven Pinker cautions against using 'anti-racist racism' to advance nationalism, which, he says, 'should not be confused with civic values, public spirit, social responsibility or social pride'. Moreover, since humans are social beings, the 'well-being of individuals' depends on co-operation among people within and across communities: 'When a "nation" is conceived as a tacit social contract among people sharing a territory, like a condominium association, it is an essential means for advancing its members' flourishing.'[16] This concept of 'nation' interrogates, for example, the actions of Hindu nationalists who demolished the sixteenth-century Babri Masjid in the Indian city of Ayodhya in 1992, claiming that the mosque stood in the birthplace of the Hindu god Rama. The demolition led to the death of thousands in India, Bangladesh and Pakistan, by a movement motivated by deep-rooted histories of injustice, identity suppression and disenchantment with the status quo. In a review of Hans Magnus Enzensberger's book on recent civil conflict, Nader Mousavisadeh writes that Enzensberger is nostalgic for the 'good old days of ideology' when 'meaning was everywhere and it was easily legible', and therefore sees the problems in cities around the world in these 'post-ideological days' as tribal wars that are 'virtually meaningless'.[17] If this is indeed the case, what are the meanings and benefits of what we are fighting for in our public squares around the world?

MONUMENTS AS IDEAS AND DEBATES IN PROGRESS

Rather than simply the representation of victory over adversity, or the celebration of collective experiences, partially decolonised spaces could be memorialised as ideas being debated for the development of human potential. In 1977, barely 17 years after the Central African Republic gained independence from France, Jean-Bédel Bokassa, the military officer who had seized power in a coup d'état in 1966, crowned himself emperor for life. His coronation saw the birth of an extravagant catastrophic national monument in the form of a stage set complete with mediaeval symbols such as a crown and a sceptre, with the emperor seated on an oversized, solid-gold throne in the shape of an eagle, and wearing a cape with a long, flowing train – which would become, ironically, an incendiary path to civil war. Metaphorically, the cape swallowed up his figure, so that what Bokassa I, Emperor of Central Africa against the will of his fellow citizens, in fact presented to the populace was a model of imperial government overcome by violent revolutions such as Ethiopia in 1974, America in 1776, France in 1789, and Russia in 1917. Did Bokassa really believe that he had the support of the people, or imagine that he could prolong his imperial rule by crushing dissent? In the end, the country was plunged into civil war, and Bokassa fled to France after he was overthrown in 1979.

In 1974, Emperor Haile Selassie was overthrown in a military coup, with the Marxist Derg government led by Mengistu Haile Mariam gaining control. In 1983, during the peak of a famine, the 10th anniversary of the revolution was celebrated, and monuments to Karl Marx, Friedrich Engels and Vladimir Ilyich Lenin were constructed by acclaimed artists from Warsaw Pact countries. When the Mengistu government fell in 1991 – after the fall of the Berlin Wall and the collapse of the Warsaw Pact alliance – the socialist revolutionary monuments were demolished. Although each socialist figure had been idealised in the form of a neoclassical sculpture, what was effectively removed from the public squares in Addis Ababa were the ideas they stood for (the current whereabouts of the statues is unknown, the National Museum of Ethiopia has informed me). Only one of the anniversary objects still stands: the 50-metre tall Tiglachin Monument in the Ethiopia–Cuba Friendship Park (figure 14.1A). However, it is now challenged by the 51-metre tall Memorial for Martyred Freedom Fighters and Patriots, built by the Tigray People's Liberation Front (TPLF) at Mek'ele at the end of the Cold War (figure 14.2A).

On the Tiglachin monument, two wall reliefs on either side of the column depict scenes from ancient times up to the 1974 revolution to show how socialism uprooted the feudal monarchy (figure 14.1B). The later TPLF monument (figure 14.2A) uses sculptures on two plinths to narrate stories of how the outgunned liberation front overcame the mighty Ethiopian socialist army. Between the plinths, three cast concrete stems emerge from the ground like giant mangrove roots, forming a column that is surmounted by a golden orb. The monument is rhizomic in the sense that it does not have a single point of origin.[18] Furthermore, whereas the bold Tiglachin monument boasts

Figures 14.1A and 14.1B. Tiglachin (our struggle) monument was built in the Ethiopia-Cuba Friendship Park, Addis Ababa, in 1984 to celebrate the 10th anniversary of the socialist revolution of Ethiopia. Photographs by Nnamdi Elleh

of violence and bravery under the leadership of Mengistu, the TPLF monument has a melancholic air, showing the victims' war, and their resilience. It is hardly coincidence that the latter stands one metre taller than Tiglachin, since it suggests the shift of power after the fall of the Derg. What began as a national healing and reconciliation process reawakened ethnic-based rivalries that were represented in such provincial monuments.

Tiglachin was built at the peak of the Cold War when the country was engaged in land reforms relating to farming while thousands of people were dying of hunger and malnutrition. The idealised wall reliefs represent the past and also the transformation of Ethiopian society from a feudal monarchy to a modern nation state ruled by a military autocrat. Cultural icons, including the rock-hewn thirteenth-century churches of Lalibela, woven baskets and fabrics, huts and fauna, and an envisioned industrial society, are arranged on the panels in the manner of a procession, with the ancient stelae from Tigray represented prominently. While the columns in both monuments lay claim to Ethiopian history, the later one sets itself apart by claiming a provincial history and narrating the sufferings of a people during the socialist revolution and long war.

The Tiglachin column has a five-point star pinnacle, and a coat of arms – a medallion (insignia) – at the midpoint integrated into the wreath. The wreath has green leaves, a sword and an arrow at diagonals, a five-point star, and the hammer and the sickle inside a ring. The juxtaposition is evocative of the symbols of communist ideology that the Derg government projected to the world (figures 14.3A and 14.3B). The coat of arms of the TPLF monument also has a wreath formed by lightly etched laurel leaves on the rose granite. However, instead of the hammer and the sickle on the medallion of the Tiglachin, an automatic rifle and a sledgehammer are laid diagonally across each other inside the wreath. Like the Tiglachin column, a five-point star is placed on the wreath. The two monuments in fact tell similar stories, although the former is from a nationalist rather than a provincial perspective. The medallion of the Tiglachin and the crest of the TPLF monument each demonstrate how the political actors inspire the artists on either side to exploit the visual, the 'oral', and the 'written traditions' of the Aksumite stelae as 'palimpsest of changing memories and interpretations' to fudge their respective identity and modernity.[19]

Figures 14.2A and 14.2B. The 51-metre column of the Memorial for Martyred Freedom Fighters and Patriots, Mek'ele, built by the Tigray People's Liberation Front (TPLF) at the end of the Cold War (after the socialist government had fallen in May 1991). Photographs by Nnamdi Elleh

Figures 14.3A and 14.3B. The medallion of Tiglachin and the coat of arms (insignia) of the Memorial for Martyred Freedom Fighters and Patriots, Tigray People's Liberation Front (TPLF), Mek'ele. Photographs by Nnamdi Elleh

Whereas the Tiglachin monument represents objects and human figures in a manner that recalls Soviet-type realism, the Memorial for Martyred Freedom Fighters and Patriots uses traditionally carved and moulded objects to show that, despite all the sufferings of the Tigray people, they had won the war (figure 14.2B). The figures tell a story of human suffering, hunger and pain. Although positioned as a background to the two objects in the coat of arms, the column, or obelisk, derives design precedent from the stele, an icon of both the Tigray and the Ethiopian people. The stele in the insignia is the visual symbol of the ancient memory with which the Tigray people identify, and it differentiates them from other ethnic groups in Ethiopia. It is deployed to send a message that the Tigray people own the Aksumite stelae heritage that has a cultural pedigree well known in 'Graeco-Roman, Byzantine, and Arabic literature'.[20] The most emphatic aspect of the TPLF insignia, however, is the gun and sledgehammer on the stele: both are symbols of resistance, strength, violence, and tools in the war waged by the TPLF to achieve its political objective of toppling the Ethiopian government in 1991. History, then, is its foundation and memory, although its intention is to bridge the gap between past and present. The gun and hammer are emboldened by ancient historical events to send the message that the people of Tigray can overcome oppression by means of armed struggle. The fall of the Tigray people dominated the Ethiopian national government in 2018, with the election of a prime minister from the Oromo ethnic group. The insistence of the provincial government to hold elections, against the wishes of the national government, has unfortunately spiralled into civil war between the federal government and the Tigray provincial government. While it is not argued here that the two monuments are exact representations of the artistic and the political culture of Ethiopia, the contest of power between the Tigray region and the federal government of Ethiopia is, nevertheless, evident in the respective symbols of the monuments.

HEALING AND MEMORY KEEPING

Bridget Conley of the World Peace Foundation has shown how monuments embody ideas of justice, memory keeping (documentation), truth telling, and the slow journey towards healing for victims. Documenting atrocities for 'transitional justice' assists in holding perpetrators accountable for their crimes, and for reminding succeeding administrations in countries that have suffered trauma to adopt democratic governance 'through a range of policy tools'.[21] Conley's inclusion of the traumas of both Hirut Abebe-Jirut and her torturer, Kelbessa Negewo, at Kebele prison in Addis Ababa, shows how memorials can be vehicles for justice. Kelbessa was eventually found in Atlanta, and while the atrocities against Abebe-Jirut and her prison inmates were committed in Ethiopia, their lawyers relied on the Alien Tort Claims Act of 1789 in their efforts to seek justice in the United States legal system.[22] Conley explains how some European countries have used their own courts to prosecute perpetrators, while the International Criminal Court has tackled similar cases in the former Yugoslavia and Rwanda. She writes how, eventually, Abebe-Jirut was inspired by the Documentation Centre for Cambodia to establish the Ethiopia Red Terror Documentation and Research Centre, whose aim and purpose is the 'collection, preservation, translation, and indexing of official documents and survivor testimonies of the Derg's Red Terror'.[23]

Memorials can be about enabling 'various forms of truth-telling', assisting 'victims' and 'survivors' in mourning their losses, and 'keeping memory alive for future generations'.[24] Conley's insight into how memorials become public courts for judgment recalls two national experiences with distinct political and economic systems. One involves the leader of the Spanish Nationalist government, General Francisco Franco, who ruled Spain for 36 years. The other involves President Robert Mugabe of Zimbabwe, who led his country to freedom in 1980 and ruled for 37 years. Citizens of these countries debated and fought over the final burial place of the two dictators. In September 2018, the Spanish Socialist Workers' Party-led government decided that the body of the fascist leader should be exhumed from the Valley of the Fallen, the national heroes' cemetery where he had been interred. After the Supreme Court of Spain confirmed the removal in 2019, conflict arose between those who were in favour of the decision and family and supporters who wanted the body to remain in its original resting place.[25] The battle was fought through the courts as well as in the court of public opinion. In Zimbabwe, after three weeks of waiting and preparing for the burial of the deposed president, the government announced that he would not be buried at the National Heroes Acre in Harare, as it had initially proposed. It stated that it was respecting the family's wishes for a private burial ceremony at Mugabe's birthplace, Kutama, in the district of Zvimba.[26] The apathetic funeral attendance, together with the public jubilation when he was overthrown, may have signalled to his family the imprudence of burial in the National Heroes Acre. In both Spain and Zimbabwe, the memory-keeping sites for traumatic events became de facto courts of justice, with both dictators expelled from their country's heroes' resting places.

The cases presented here should not be conflated with anti-monument or minimalist monument movements; instead, they show how memorials often employ the documentation of trauma, or attempts at justice and healing, as well as memory keeping. However, among contested anti-monument monuments employing trauma and healing, Maya Lin's 1982 Vietnam Veterans Memorial Wall in Washington, D.C. stands out. Many veterans, whom the memorial was supposed to represent, protested because it did not feature the usual neoclassical visual icons and symbols characteristic of Washington memorials. Instead, its two walls lie sunken in the ground, gradually rising in a V-shape until they meet at its highest point. The polished granite wall with the names of more than 50 000 dead soldiers etched into it is one of the most-visited monuments in Washington. The architecture critic Catesby Leigh praises it as a place of healing fostered by its tactile finish, regardless of its 'aesthetic minimalism'. However, Leigh also blames it for prompting a 'plague of anti-monuments' by designers attempting to emulate Lin in designing minimalist places of contemplation.[27] Anti-monument monument prescriptions do not reject the ideas of monuments. Instead, they represent monuments as minimalist objects.

Unlike anti-monument monuments that tend to espouse minimalist representations, the statues of Marx, Engels and Lenin, which have a long history that is universal in its scope, are about modernity even though they have been exploited by oppressive governments. Regarding the current reception of projects with their roots in the eighteenth century, Steven Pinker writes: 'Since the 1960s, trust in the institutions of modernity has sunk, and the second decade of the 21st century saw the rise of populist movements that blatantly repudiate the ideas of the enlightenment.' Echoing Enzensberger's disenchantment with tribal wars, Pinker goes on to describe those who resist the projects of modernity as 'tribalist rather than cosmopolitan' and 'authoritarian rather than democratic'. Here, Pinker also recalls Habermas's neoconservatives who favoured visual idioms from neoclassical architecture over the projects of modern architecture. As Pinker puts it, the neoconservatives are 'contemptuous of experts rather than respectful of knowledge, and nostalgic for an idyllic past rather than hopeful for a better future'.[28]

WE NEED NEW LANGUAGES

Monuments commemorating independence from former colonial powers are often represented as fully emancipated social and physical spaces; however, architects should strive instead to convey the idea of stages in the struggle for liberation and human development, and the processes through which this is achieved. Although economic resources and the stability of governments differ from country to country, the upheavals we have witnessed since Bouazizi's self-immolation in 2010 show that partially decolonised spaces are still to be found around the world.

Often, memorials represent episodes of history in our communities as final narratives, and they draw on lessons from the past so as to avoid the recurrence of certain events. The predominant visual mode is merely one aspect of our desire to memorialise. Building memorials is an expression of faith in humankind's capacity to grow intellectually and spiritually, even though lessons to be learnt are not apparent in the present moment. Inevitably, contemporary monuments lack the conceptual vocabulary for conveying unknowns to viewers. The notion of a new language for memorialising collective spatial and social experiences is as old as the emergence of the modern world, the call for democracy, and the liberation of citizens from autocratic and monarchical rule. Moreover, it is about human rights, free speech, justice, access to education, health, employment and social security. Since memorials are often initiated at the end of catastrophes or to commemorate major victories, the communities involved often fail to see their projects as part of the continuum of the human struggle for a better life. Instead, they conceptualise their edifices in time and space to capture specific collective experiences: the end of apartheid in 1994, for example, prompted the development of the Constitutional Court in Johannesburg, as indicated above; and the end of the South African War in 1902 resulted in the creation of the Union Buildings in Pretoria in 1912.

The real monuments commemorated at any setting are, however, not the mere events and experiences. Memorials are inanimate objects; they are not capable of maintaining themselves and perpetuating the ideas for which they were built. Memorials are idols. The real memorials are the human beings who continue the ideas of monuments, and as such, they are the real monuments. Therefore, we need new languages – be they textual, reflective or symbolic modes of expression – for commemorating the collective struggles, traumas and celebratory experiences of humankind. Citizens, civic and political leaders, artists and architects, as well as scholars, bring diverse perspectives to the concept of the monument, but all are united in the promotion of human monuments. Monuments are mere concepts of ideas such as democracy, freedom, human rights, employment, education, inclusivity and safety. Together, these ideals empower various human beings in different ways to live fulfilled lives, helping to bring different perspectives to the idea of the monument.

Sartre proposes the universal language of 'anti-racist racism', that is, standing up for what is right, even if this is uncomfortable for certain segments of society. Habermas looks at the effects of the industrial revolution on the citizens of European countries in the nineteenth century, and the emergence of a new architectural language based on materials and construction techniques. He suggests that large segments of communities are yet to benefit from the industrial revolution. For Habermas, the stylistic proposition by neoconservatives who advocate postmodern architectural projects is a distraction from the decolonisation of lost human habitats and citizens who are yet to benefit from the projects of modernity. Pinker grounds the universal language in an eighteenth-century Enlightenment project like the United States of America, which advocated liberty, democracy and freedom from monarchical rule, and is concerned that it is being eroded. Instead of proposing that the Enlightenment was a utopia, Pinker recognises that it was not a universal emancipation since it did not grant freedom to slaves and women, for example. Yet the perspectives of Marx, Engels and Lenin, underpinned by workers' freedom and state monopoly of the means of production, have also been contested as universal languages of collective emancipation. Conley's study proposes, inter alia, aspects such as justice, good governance and ethnic solidarity which could be drawn into the universal language of monuments. Writing from a social science perspective, Fukuyama examines what he calls 'an idea for a universal history', though emphasising that 'a Universal History of mankind is not the same thing as a history of the universe'.[29] Fukuyama's search for the universal language goes back to Aristotle and acknowledges that early Christian thinkers were among the first to state that all are equal in the eyes of God. As with Pinker, Fukuyama's universal history reaches a crescendo in the Enlightenment, with the 'sovereignty of the people' founded on inclusivity and on lasting 'liberal democracy'.[30]

There is always the temptation to reduce universal history into memorials of great events. However, we are increasingly aware that this tendency should be resisted, since humans are yet to be liberated in many spaces in the world. Architectural historian Manfredo Tafuri examines the search for a universal language of emancipation as a conspiratorial alliance between capitalist and bourgeoisie that pays lip service to the projects of modernity. For Tafuri, the bourgeoisie have found various ways of covering up the real discourses of art and architecture, which have, since the eighteenth century, been in the service of capitalist markets rather than deploying creativity and design as the real instruments of social change. Moreover, modern architecture takes cover in the 'ideals' of the scientific 'rationalisation' of the profession. And if it is in 'crisis', this is not because it lacks creativity, nor is it because of the 'tiredness or dissipation' of creativity. Instead, the problem is due to the 'ideological function' it has assigned itself to serve the market.[31]

Architects and artists often use nature, art and tectonic forms – the visual languages of representation – as decoys for covering up the deeper problems of partially decolonised spaces. Examined carefully, these forms are mostly used to drive consumption and raise market values. Tafuri laments that the instruments of the capitalist's cover-ups have been used to dazzle the public and co-opt it into accepting monuments as the universal languages of emancipation and progress. Tafuri puts the blame squarely on 'bourgeois ambiguities' – their hypocritical dedication to the cause of the working class.

The consequence can be seen in the 'fall of modern art'.[32] Artists are caught up in market ups and downs, and, as Frederic Jameson puts it, visual forms and 'aesthetic productions' are used in converting culture into 'commodity production'.[33] Thus, monuments often serve specific group purposes guided by prevailing opinions and the market, rather than taking on a broader, more complex human view.

For Tafuri, 'this task lies in putting the working class, as organized in its parties and unions, face to face with the highest levels achieved by the dynamics of capitalist development, and relating particular moments to general designs'.[34] Furthermore, 'just as there cannot exist a class political economy, but only a class criticism of political economy, so too there cannot be founded a class aesthetic, art, or architecture but only a class criticism of the aesthetic, of art, of architecture, of the city itself'.[35] We understand that different classes and groups may have different tastes and expectations in art and architecture. Nevertheless, monuments and aesthetics should be designed for all. The process is to employ a broad perspective in design, with the larger society in mind. As Tafuri suggests, a proper 'revolution of architectural language, method, and structure', beyond mere formal representation, is needed in order for architecture to achieve its goals. The current language of art and architecture is not inclusive. Rather than their being memorialised in stone, we need new visual languages which see people and their experiences as being in themselves monumental.

NOTES

1   See Kwame Nkrumah, *Neo-Colonialism, The Last Stage of Imperialism* (London: Thomas Nelson & Sons, 1965), 41.

2   Nnamdi Elleh, 'Architecture and Nationalism in Africa, 1945–1994', in *The Short Century: Independence and Liberation Movements in Africa 1945–1994*, ed. Okwui Enwezor (Munich: Prestel, 2001), 234–45.

3   Suzan B. Aradeon, 'Al-Sahili: The Historian's Myth of Architectural Technology Transfer from North Africa', *Journal des Africanistes* 59.1–2 (1989): 99–131.

4   For a discussion on the relationship between decolonisation, apartheid and monuments, see Okwui Enwezor, *The Short Century: Independence and Liberation Movements in Africa 1945–1994*; and Manuel Herz, *African Modernism: The Architecture of Independence* (Zurich: Park Books, 2015).

5   For an examination of the ways in which such projects explore cultural tectonics and modernity, see Jonathan Alfred Noble, *African Identity in Post-Apartheid Public Architecture: White Skin, Black Masks* (London: Routledge, 2011).
6   As quoted in Le Corbusier, *The Athens Charter* (New York: Grossman Publishers, 1973), 6–7.
7   As quoted in Le Corbusier, *The Athens Charter*, 86.
8   Jürgen Habermas, 'Modernity: An Unfinished Project', in *The Post-Modern Reader,* ed. Charles Jencks (London: Academy Editions, 1992), 158–61.
9   Jürgen Habermas, 'Modern and Postmodern Architecture', in *Rethinking Architecture: A Reader in Cultural Theory,* ed. Neil Leach (New York: Routledge, 1997), 227.
10 For an explanation of the concept of iconoclasm, see Laurie Adams, *A History of Western Art* (New York: McGraw-Hill, 2010), 169; and Fred S. Kleiner, *Gardner's Art Through the Ages: A Global History* (New York: Wadsworth, 2011), 257.
11 Donal Lowry, 'The "Rhodes Must Fall" Campaign: Where Would the Destruction End?' *The Round Table*, 105.3 (2016): 239–331.
12 See Tom Smith, 'Berlin's Other Anniversary', *History Today* 69.11 November 2019.
13 Jean-Paul Sartre, *Black Orpheus* (Paris: Présence Africaine, 1948), 49–58.
14 Daniel Grant, 'The Art of the Controversy', *The New Criterion*, 13 December 2013: 35.
15 Demetria Irwin, 'Controversy and Conversation for MOCADA Art Exhibition', *New York Amsterdam News*, 20–26 March 2008: 19.
16 Steven Pinker, *Enlightenment Now: The Case for Reason, Science, Humanism and Progress* (New York: Allen Lane, 2018), 31.
17 Nader Mousavizadeh, Review, '*Hearts of Darkness: Civil Wars from L.A. to Bosnia* by Hans Magnus Enzensberger', *The New Republic*, 28 November 1994: 70.
18 Elizabeth Schmidt, *Foreign Intervention in Africa: From the Cold War to the War on Terror* (Cambridge: Cambridge University Press, 2013), 159.
19 Schmidt, *Foreign Intervention in Africa*, 160.
20 David W. Phillipson, Introduction to *The Monuments of Aksum*, ed. David W. Phillipson (Addis Ababa: Addis Ababa University Press in collaboration with the British Institute in Eastern Africa, 1997), 1.
21 Bridget Conley, *Memory from the Margins: Ethiopia's Red Terror Martyrs Memorial Museum* (Switzerland: Palgrave Macmillan, 2019), 9.
22 Conley, *Memory from the Margins*, 13.
23 Conley, *Memory from the Margins*, 19.
24 Conley, *Memory from the Margins*, 9.

25. 'Franco Exhumation: Spanish Dictator's Remains Moved', *BBC News*, 24 October 2019, accessed 3 July 2020, https://www.bbc.com/news/world-europe-50164806.
26. 'Zimbabwe Ex-President Robert Mugabe Buried in his Native Village', *Aljazeera.com*, 28 September 2019, accessed 10 June 2020, https://www.aljazeera.com/news/2019/09/robert-mugabe-set-private-burial-home-village-190928104251383.html.
27. Catesby Leigh, 'The Plague of New ANTI-Monuments', *The American Enterprise* 11.2 March 2000: 42.
28. Pinker, *Enlightenment Now*, 29.
29. Francis Fukuyama, 'An Idea for a Universal History', in *The Idea of History and the Last Man* (New York: Perennial, 1993), 55.
30. Fukuyama, 'An Idea for a Universal History', 45.
31. Manfredo Tafuri, *Architecture and Utopia: Design and Capitalist Development* (Cambridge: MIT Press, 1976), 181.
32. Tafuri, *Architecture and Utopia*, 181.
33. Frederic Jameson, *Postmodernism, or the Cultural Logic of Late Capitalism* (Durham: Duke University Press, 1991), 4.
34. Tafuri, *Architecture and Utopia*, 172.
35. Tafuri, *Architecture and Utopia*, 179.

REFERENCES

Aradeon, Suzan B. 'Al-Sahili: The Historian's Myth of Architectural Technology Transfer from North Africa'. *Journal des Africanistes* 59.1–2 (1989): 99–131.

Conley, Bridget. *Memory from the Margins: Ethiopia's Red Terror Martyrs Memorial Museum*, 1–46. Switzerland: Palgrave Macmillan, 2019.

Elleh, Nnamdi. 'Architecture and Nationalism in Africa, 1945–1994'. In *The Short Century: Independence and Liberation Movements in Africa 1945–1994,* edited by Okwui Enwezor, 234–45. Munich: Prestel, 2001.

Fanon, Frantz. *Black Skin, White Masks.* New York: Grove Press, 1967.

Fanon, Frantz. *The Wretched of the Earth.* New York: Grove Press, 1968.

'Franco Exhumation: Spanish Dictator's Remains Moved'. *BBC News*, 24 October 2019. Accessed 3 July 2020, https://www.bbc.com/news/world-europe-50164806.

Fukuyama, Francis. 'An Idea for a Universal History'. In *The Idea of History and the Last Man*, 55–70. New York: Perennial, 1993.

Grant, Daniel. 'The Art of the Controversy'. *The New Criterion*, 13 December 2013: 34–8.

Habermas, Jürgen. 'Modernity: An Unfinished Project'. In *The Post-Modern Reader*, edited by Charles Jencks, 158–61. London: Academy Editions, 1992.

Habermas, Jürgen. 'Modern and Postmodern Architecture'. In *Rethinking Architecture: A Reader in Cultural Theory*, edited by Neil Leach, 225–35. New York: Routledge, 1997.

Herz, Manuel, ed. *African Modernism: The Architecture of Independence: Ghana, Senegal, Côte d'Ivoire, Kenya, Zambia*. Zurich: Park Books, 2015.

Irwin, Demetria. 'Controversy and Conversation for MOCADA Art Exhibition'. *New York Amsterdam News*, 20–26 March 2008, 19.

Jameson, Frederic. *Postmodernism, or the Cultural Logic of Late Capitalism*. Durham: Duke University Press, 1991.

Kultermann, Udo. *New Directions in African Architecture*. New York: George Braziller, 1969.

Le Corbusier. *The Athens Charter*. New York: Grossman Publishers, 1973.

Leigh, Catesby. 'The Plague of New ANTI-Monuments'. *The American Enterprise* 11.2 March 2000: 38–43.

Lowry, Donal. 'The "Rhodes Must Fall" Campaign: Where Would the Destruction End?' *The Round Table* 105.3 (2016): 329–31.

Mousavizadeh, Nader. Review, '*Hearts of Darkness: Civil Wars from L.A. to Bosnia* by Hans Magnus Enzensberger'. *The New Republic*, 28 November 1994: 70–3.

Nkrumah, Kwame. *Neo-Colonialism: The Last Stage of Imperialism*. London: Thomas Nelson & Sons, 1965.

Noble, Jonathan Alfred. *African Identity in Post-Apartheid Public Architecture: White Skin, Black Masks*. London: Routledge, 2011.

Phillipson, David W., ed. Introduction. *The Monuments of Aksum*, 1–4. Addis Ababa: Addis Ababa University Press in collaboration with the British Institute in Eastern Africa, 1997.

Pinker, Steven. *Enlightenment Now: The Case for Reason, Science, Humanism and Progress*. New York: Allen Lane, 2018.

Sartre, Jean-Paul. *Black Orpheus*. Paris: Présence Africaine, 1948.

Schmidt, Elizabeth. *Foreign Intervention in Africa: From the Cold War to the War on Terror*, 159–60. Cambridge: Cambridge University Press, 2013.

Smith, Tom. 'Berlin's Other Anniversary'. *History Today* 69.11 (November 2019): 42–9.

Tafuri, Manfredo. *Architecture and Utopia: Design and Capitalist Development*. Cambridge: MIT Press, 1976.

'Zimbabwe Ex-President Robert Mugabe Buried in his Native Village'. *Aljazeera.com*, 28 September 2019. Accessed 10 June 2020, https://www.aljazeera.com/news/2019/09/robert-mugabe-set-private-burial-home-village-190928104251383.html.

CONTRIBUTORS

Faeeza Ballim is a senior lecturer in the Department of History at the University of Johannesburg. She is broadly interested in science and technology studies and African political economy, and is currently writing a book about Eskom and the activities of South African state corporations in the coal-rich Waterberg region. She is also engaged in new research on artificial intelligence on the African continent, and serves as the review editor for the *South African Historical Journal*.

Roshan Dadoo worked for the Department of Foreign Affairs (now DIRCO) where she served on the Middle East desk and as political counsellor at the South African Embassy in Algiers. She subsequently worked as a regional advocacy officer and director of a civil society migrant rights organisation, the Consortium for Refugees and Migrants in South Africa. She submitted an MA thesis in development studies at Wits University in 2020.

Nnamdi Elleh, the head of the School of Architecture and Planning at the University of the Witwatersrand (Wits), was professor of Architecture, University of Cincinnati, Ohio, USA, from 2002 to 2017. He trained as an architect at the University of Wisconsin-Milwaukee, USA, and received his PhD in art history from Northwestern University, Illinois, USA. His publications include *African Architecture, Evolution and Transformation* (1996), the first comprehensive text on African architecture from antiquity to the present, as well as *Architecture and Power in Africa* (2001) and *Reading the Architecture of the Underprivileged Classes* (2014).

Sally Gaule is a photographer, curator and lecturer in the School of Architecture and Planning at Wits University. Her work has focused on the city and architecture of Johannesburg, where she has lived most of her life. Currently, she is researching the work of William Matlala and Victor Matom, two unsung heroes of South African photography. In addition, she is researching and co-curating an exhibition about the Hong family, who emigrated from China to South Africa in the 1950s and who lived and worked in the suburb of Brixton for 56 years.

Kelly Gillespie is a political and legal anthropologist at the University of the Western Cape with a research focus on criminal justice in South Africa. She is concerned with the ways criminal justice has become a vector for the continuation of apartheid relations. Dr Gillespie writes and teaches about urbanism, sexualities, race, and the praxis of social justice in South Africa. She co-founded the Johannesburg Workshop in Theory and Criticism, an experimental project tasked with re-crafting the work of critical theory beyond the global North.

Pauline Guinard is an associate professor in geography at the École Normale Supérieure in Paris, and a member of two research units, UMR LAVUE-Mosaïques and UMR IHMC. Her work focuses on the relationships between cities and arts, especially in the South African context. In 2014 she published a book entitled *Johannesburg: l'art d'inventer une ville*. Currently, she is also developing a new field of research about the geographies and spatialities of emotions.

Ali Khangela Hlongwane is a researcher in the History Workshop at Wits University. He was previously deputy director: Museums and Galleries at the City of Johannesburg, and chief curator at Museum Africa in Newtown, and also at the Hector Pieterson Museum in Soweto. His research interests include the memorialisation of forced removals, the Pan Africanist Congress (PAC) radio broadcasts during the exile period, and cultural struggles in the 1980s. Hlongwane is currently completing a biography of PAC leader Zeph Mothopeng.

Eric Itzkin is an official at the Directorate of Arts, Culture and Heritage at the City of Johannesburg. As deputy director: Immovable Heritage, his role has included conservation of historical sites, structures and monuments, developing heritage trails, and promoting public art. Born in Johannesburg, he spent a period in exile while working as a teacher in Zimbabwe in the 1980s. After returning to South Africa, he worked as a research librarian, museum curator and cultural historian. He holds an MA in heritage studies from Wits University.

Hilton Judin is an architect and director of postgraduate architecture in the School of Architecture and Planning at the University of the Witwatersrand. Together with the History Workshop, he developed the exhibition *[setting apart]*, and was curator and co-editor of *blank____Architecture, apartheid and after*. He has worked on the Nelson Mandela Museum in Mvezo and the Living Landscape Project in Clanwilliam. His book *Architecture, State Modernism and Cultural Nationalism in the Apartheid Capital* is due to be published by Routledge in 2021.

Cynthia Kros is an historian and heritage specialist. Her academic interest in heritage dates to 1992 when she organised the History Workshop conference 'Myths, Monuments, Museums: New Premises?' Anticipating the political transition to democracy, participants were keen to exchange ideas with progressive curators in cultural institutions. Since then she has written a number of articles on public art and museum representations. The most recent concern the removal of the statue of Cecil John Rhodes on 9 April 2015 as a result of student protest action at the University of Cape Town, and the National Heritage Monument installation 'Long March to Freedom', a procession of bronze statues.

Arianna Lissoni is a researcher in the History Workshop at the University of the Witwatersrand and one of the editors of the *South African Historical Journal*. Her research and publications focus on the history and politics of South Africa's liberation struggle. Her recent books include the co-edited volume *New Histories of South Africa's Apartheid Era Bantustans* (2017), and *Khongolose: A Short History of the ANC in the North West Province Since 1909* (2016), of which she is a co-author.

MADEYOULOOK is a Johannesburg based, interdisciplinary artist collaboration between **Nare Mokgotho** and **Molemo Moiloa**. Their works often reference everyday innovations – aspects of inner-city life that find simple solutions to ordinary challenges. Related to this is their broader interest in art's relationship to audience, concepts of publics, and what constitutes an audience. Notions of knowledge production and access to ownership in the wider sense are also central to their thinking. DIY serves as a typical approach, not only to their interests, but also to their own functioning.

Yasmin Mayat and **Brendan Hart** are staff members of the School of Architecture and Planning at Wits University, where they lecture on the history of architecture and urbanism. In 2012 they co-founded and are principals of the award-winning Mayat Hart Architects. The diverse work of their research, teaching and practice focuses on the understanding of architecture as a product of material culture, as well as the creating of architectural and spatial interventions rooted in both context, historical narratives and the complex realities of heritage and identity in contemporary South

Africa. Both hold Master's degrees in the Conservation of the Built Environment from the University of Cape Town, and professional architectural degrees from the University of the Witwatersrand. Yasmin holds a BSc from the University of Cape Town.

Born in Johannesburg, **Temba John Dawson Middelmann** pursued undergraduate and Honours studies at Wits University, which cemented his love of history. A Master's degree in African studies at Oxford University, UK, broadened his appreciation of history while also refining his research interests, with a focus on South African public history and memory, and eventually Constitution Hill and Johannesburg. A growing interest in public space, regarding its history, management, design, perception and use, formed the basis of his PhD studies in public space and spatial justice. Currently, he is a postdoctoral researcher at Wits University's Centre for Urbanism and Built Environment Studies (CUBES).

Barbara Morovich is an associate professor in anthropology at the École Nationale Supérieure d'Architecture de Strasbourg, France, a member of the research unit AMUP, and president of the French Anthropological Association. Her work focuses on the socio-spatial processes of protest and negotiation in disadvantaged and stigmatised neighbourhoods in France, Argentina, and more recently South Africa, including their impact. Her most recent book is *Miroirs anthropologiques et changement urbain: qui participe à la transformation des quartiers populaires?* (2017).

Muchaparara Musemwa is an associate professor of history and head of the School of Social Sciences in the Faculty of Humanities at Wits University. He is a past president of the Southern African Historical Society and a former editor of the *South African Historical Journal*; he also serves on the executive boards of directors of the International Consortium of Environmental History Organisations, the European Society for Environmental History, and the International Water History Association. He serves on the editorial boards of the *Water History* journal and the *Environment and History* journal. He has published widely on environmental history and on water history and politics in Zimbabwe.

Goolam Vahed is a professor in the Department of History at the University of KwaZulu-Natal. He received his PhD from Indiana University, Bloomington, USA, and has published widely in peer-reviewed journals on identity formation, citizenship, ethnicity, migration and transnationalism among Indian South Africans, as well as the role of sport and culture in South African society. His most recent (co-authored) works are *A History of the Present: A Biography of Indian South Africans, 1994–2019*, Oxford University Press (2019); and *Class, Colour and Community: The Natal Indian Congress 1971–1994*, Wits University Press (2021).

Tara Weber works as registrar at the Johannesburg Art Gallery where she has curated a number of exhibitions. She completed a BA in art history, English literature and media studies, and Honours at the Centre for Curating the Archive, at the University of Cape Town. She operates as part of the collective *Johannesburg Lasts*, whose practice lies in creative responses to 'the last, lasts, lasting and losts'. Her research interests are ruins, archives and the future of museums.

INDEX

Page numbers in *italics* indicate figures.

1st South African Infantry Brigade 195
58 Years to the Treason Trial 181
1860 Commemoration Council 259
1860 Heritage Centre 269
1860 Heritage Foundation 259
1860 Legacy Foundation 260–261

A

Aapravasi Ghat 257
abandonment 124–125, 144
Abebe-Jirut, Hirut 290
abstract forms of commemoration 245, 281
accessibility 4, 46–47, 49, 92, 177
activism 2, 7, 146, 177, 181
Adjaye, David 207
affective labour 63, 65, 74, 75
African ancestral beliefs 14–17, 35
African migration 91, 124, 126, 129
African National Congress (ANC) 18, 115, 165–166, 175, 180–181, 235, 249, 258–259, 261
African nationalism 258
Africans, dispossession of 14, 17, 24–25, 72
Africans, forced removals of 17, 20–24, 30, 34
African traditions 52, 68
Afrikaans language 127, 134
Afrikaners 20, 43, 111, 114, 151, 166, 196
    nationalism 44–45, 256–257
    right-wing organisations 151, 166
Afro–Indian race relations 260–261, 264, 270
Afro-Kollectives 182, 184
Aggett, Neil 90
Agulhon, Maurice 236
alcohol 110–111, 134–135
Alien Tort Claims Act (USA) 290
ambiguity 54–55, 90
Améry, Jean 142
amnesia *see* forgetting
ANC *see* African National Congress
ancestral beliefs 14–17, 35
Anglo-Boer War *see* South African War
anthem *see* national anthem (USA)

Anthologie de la Nouvelle Poésie Nègre et Malgache de Langue Française 281–282
anti-monument monuments 291
'anti-racist racism' 281–284, 293
Antistalinistische Aktion e.V (Astak) 143
apartheid *see also* Pass Office, Johannesburg
    architecture of 1–3
    Delville Wood South African National Memorial site 196
    Drill Hall 173, 175, 180–182
    end of 279–280, 293
    forced removals 15, 17, 22–24, 29–30, 33–34, 69, 151, 154
    Gandhi Square 53–54
    Indian indentured labour 257
    Johannesburg Central Police Station 84–86, 90–95, 98
    Juliwe Cemetery 29–30
    Kwa Khaya Lendaba cultural village 213–214, 217, 221–222, 224, 228–229
    Mandela statue 239, 244–245
    Medupi Power Station 14–15, 17–19
    prisons 117–118, 120
    Robben Island prison 106–109, 114
    struggle against 45, 98, 153–154, 173, 180–182
Apartheid Project, The 90
appropriation 181, 207
Arab Spring 280
archaeology 45, 279
Archary, Seelan 259–264, 266, *268*, 270
archives 109, 222–224
Arendt, Hannah 85
Argentina 143
Aristotle 294
'Arriving Home?' (essay) 144–145
Art Deco 152, 153, 162, 166
artists 180–185, 228
artworks 174, 180–186, 193, 200
'Asiatic bazaars' 153, 154–158
aspiration 69
Astak *see* Antistalinistische Aktion e.V
Astor Mansions building 162

Atget, Eugene 98
atrocities 142, 290
At the Mind's Limits 142
Augé, Marc 73
authenticity 138, 144, 215, 222, 228
Avalon Cemetery, Soweto 199–200
awards 178, 220
Azaadville township 151, 154

B
Babri Masjid 284
Baderoon, Gabeba 240
Baker, Herbert 195, 244–245
Bakhtin, Mikhail 109
Bandiet 96
Bantustans *see* homelands
Battle of Delville Wood 193–197
'beatification' of Mandela 239–240
beer halls *130*, 134–135
Beinart, William 20
Belgium 7
belonging 4, 16, 66, 69, 73–74
Ben Ali, Zine El Abidine 283
Benjamin, Walter 88, 98
Bentham, Jeremy 94–95, 97
Berlin Wall, fall of 280–281, 285
Bird, Flo 44–45, 48
black citizenship 53, 93
Black Consciousness 218–219, 220
Black Lives Matter 2
black migrants 74, 165–166, 176, 181–182
Black Orpheus 281–282
'black spots' 22, 24, 34
black urban gardening *see* Ejaradini project
black volunteers, First World War 194, 196, 197–201, 208
blue heritage plaques 30, 37, *37*, 67
Bo-Kaap 240
Bokassa, Jean-Bédel 284–285
Bonner, Philip 95, 100
Bophuthatswana 213–214, 215
Borden, Iain 224
Botha, Louis, statue of 244
Botha, P. W. 196
bottle stores 134–135
Bouazizi, Mohamed 283, 292
Bozzoli, Belinda 165
bribes 127, *128*
Briscoe / WRAB / Mutwa archive 222–224, 225
Britain
    Afrikaners and 43
    colonialism 66, 117, 152, 156, 161, 173, 235, 256–257, 270

First World War 175, 194–195
    Indian indentured labour 260
Brooks, Frikkie 265
brutality 49, 109, 117, 120, 143, 282
Buccus, Imraan 263
Bunn, David 53
burial sites *see also* Juliwe Cemetery, Roodepoort, Johannesburg
    Delville Wood South African National Memorial site 195
    exhumation of human remains 17, 34–36
    Kigali Genocide Memorial Centre 143
    Kwa Khaya Lendaba cultural village 227
    Medupi Power Station 14, 17, 25
    in Spain 290–291
    in Zimbabwe xv–xvi, xviii–xix, 290–291
bus terminus, Gandhi Square 43, 53–55
Butler, Judith 91

C
Cambodia 143, 290
Cape Town 240, 242, 244 *see also* Mandela statue, City Hall, Cape Town
Cape Town Opera 106, 108
capitalism 42, 107–109, 111, 117–118, 120, 162, 239, 256, 270, 294–295
Capture Site 245
Castle of Good Hope 196
casualties, names of 194, 196, 198, 200, 205–206, 291
Catholic Church 236
cattle 21
CCB *see* Civil Co-operation Bureau
cemeteries *see* burial sites
census of 1932 159
Central African Republic 284–285
Chidester, David 213, 214, 215, 222
Chipkin, Clive 85, 162–163
Chotabhai, Amod Ebrahim 155–158
Christianity 35, 66, 110–111, 294
Church Square 42, 43 *see also* Gandhi Square, Johannesburg
CIAM *see* International Congress for Modern Architecture
Cianfanelli, Marco 245
Cillié Commission *see Commission of Inquiry into the Riots at Soweto and Elsewhere*
citizenship 161–162, 166
City Hall, Cape Town 234–235, 242 *see also* Mandela statue, City Hall, Cape Town

Index

City of Cape Town *see* Mandela statue, City Hall, Cape Town
City of Johannesburg 30–32, 37, 50, 72, 177, 185, 199–200, 225
Civil Co-operation Bureau (CCB) 43
class 69, 295
clinics *130*, 134
coal 13, 17
Cold War 280, 285, 287
Cole, Teju 86
collective memory 40–41, 52–53, 125, 141
colonialism
    architecture of 1–2
    Constitution Hill 41–42
    Drill Hall 173, 175
    Gandhi Square 41–42
    gardening 65–66, 68, 71–73, 75, 77
    Indians in South Africa 152, 156–157, 161, 165
    Mandela statue 238, 242, 244–245
    Mutwa, Credo Vusamazulu 221
    prisons 109–111, 118
    Zimbabwe xvii–xviii
Commissioner for Bantu Affairs 22–24
Commission for the Promotion and Protection of the Rights of Cultural, Religious and Linguistic Communities (CRL Rights Commission) 14
Commission of Inquiry into the Riots at Soweto and Elsewhere (Cillié Commission) 129, *130–133*, 135, 213, 219–221, 228
Commonwealth War Graves cemeteries 195, 200
Communist Party 152, 175
communities
    Drill Hall 181, 185
    Ejaradini project 62–63, 69
    engagement of 5–7
    Indian indentured labour, commemoration of 265, 268–270
    Juliwe Cemetery 32
    Medupi Power Station 16–18
    Pass Office, Johannesburg 145–146
    SS *Mendi* memorial 200
Company's Garden, Cape Town 244–245
Confederate leaders, statues of 7, 283
conflict 8, 34–36, 54, 136, 157, 178–179, 183
Conley, Bridget 290, 294
Constitutional Court 43, 45, 48, 141, 279, 293
Constitution Hill, Johannesburg 40–61, *46*
    accessibility 40, 46–47, 49
    background on 43–44
    changing status of 44–47
    contingencies of commemoration 54–55
    development at 47–49
    memory 40–42, 47–48, 54–55
    nation-building 40
    ruination at 47–49
consumerism 165
control 66, 68–69, 94–95, 124, 126, 141
Coolies, Arabs and Other Asiatics Act, Law 3 (1885) 155
Coombes, Annie E. 47, 222
counter-memory 138–139, 205–206
counter-monuments 202–208
Covid-19 lockdown 249
Creative Axis Architects 198
Crew, Spencer 215
crime 86, 97–98, 100
CRL Rights Commission *see* Commission for the Promotion and Protection of the Rights of Cultural, Religious and Linguistic Communities
cultural events 75, 177, 180
'cultural significance', definition of 225
Culture and Belonging in Divided Societies 271

D

DA *see* Democratic Alliance
Dadoo, Aysha 154–155
Dadoo family 150–154
Dadoo, Fatima 154–155
Dadoo, Fatima Ahmed 155, 156
Dadoo Ltd 158–160
Dadoo, Mahomed Mamoojee (M. M.) 151–162, 164
Dadoo, Roshan 154
'Dadoo's Block' 159–160
Dadoo's (clothing retailer) 152–154, 160–166
Dadoo, Yusuf Mohamed 152–154, 156
Daily News 262, 265
Daro, SS 199
Davie, Lucille 217–218, 227–228
Davis, Sharlene 53–54
death 35, 73, 95 *see also* casualties, names of
Deats, Michael 19
decay 49, 73
De Certeau, Michel 54
decolonisation 2, 146, 228, 278–281, 284–285, 292–295
De Lille, Patricia 243–245

Delville Wood South African National
 Memorial site 193–211, *197*
  Battle of Delville Wood 193–197
  cemetery 195
  counter-monument 202–208
  description of 195–198
  memory 204–205
  names of casualties 196, 198, 205–206
  pavilions 195–196
  post-apartheid 206–208
  sensory design of 202–204
Democratic Alliance (DA) 235, 262
demolitions 44, 45, 48, 176–177
Department of Bantu Administration 134–135
Department of Correctional Services 115
Department of Justice 43
Department of Public Works 45, 179–180, 185
Department of Sport, Arts and Culture 244
Department of Tourism 235
Department of Traditional Affairs 17
De Villiers, J. C. 135
Dhlame, Zakhe 69–71, 74
Dhupelia, Satish 260, 270
Diamond, Stuart 234–235, 238–239, 241, 244
Diepkloof 68, *130*, *132*, 134
'Dirty War' 143
Discipline and Punish 94
diseases 16, 23–24, 94, 117, 156–157
dispossession of Africans 14, 17, 24–25, 72
Dlamini, Jacob 146
Dobsonville 29–34, 36, 68, *131*
'*dop* system' 110–111
Drill Hall, Johannesburg 173–189
 community 181, 185
 conflict 178–179, 183
 'Drill Hall Defenders' 184
 heritage value of 173–174, 177–179, 182, 185–186
 history of 173–174, 175–176
 maintenance of 173, 179–180, 182–184
 map of *178*
 memory 173–174, 177, 180–182
 renovation of 176–180, *176*, 185
 skateboarding 177, 183, 184, *184*
 sketch of *176*
 stakeholders 173, 174, 182–185
 struggle against apartheid 173, 175, 180–182
 transformation 174, 182–185
 Treason Trial 173, 175, 177–178, 182
 uncertainty 183, 185–186
Drum 111, *128*, 137
Dr Yusuf Dadoo Hospital 153, 160
Dube, Soweto 67–69, *131*, 134
Du Bois, Duncan 262
Dugmore, Charles 155–156, 158
Dutch colonialism 196
Dutch East India Company 110
Dutch Reformed Church 43
Du Toit, Boetie 113–114
dynamic nature of memory 204–205, 207

E
Each One Teach One Foundation 228
Economic Freedom Fighters (EFF) 261
economic growth 25, 30, 33, 162, 165, 265
Edward VII, King, statue of 235, 237–239, *237*, 248
Edward VIII, King 161
EFF *see* Economic Freedom Fighters
Egypt 283
Ejaradini project 62–80
 affective labour 63, 65, 74, 75–77, 78
 belonging 66, 69, 73–74
 community 62–63, 69
 description of 62, 71
 entanglement 65–66, 77
 food farmers 67, 69–71
 gardeners 64–65, 67–68, 69–71
 gardening inheritance 68–69
 Johannesburg Art Gallery 62, 71–78
 museums 62, 72–73, 77–78
 Ngilima Photo Archives *63*, *76*
 ruination 71–73, 77
 sanctuary 74–75
 time 76–77
Elizabeth II, Queen 200
Ellis, Patric 19
Ellis, Ponk 19, 20
Ellisras 17–25
'empathetic unsettlement' 139–143
emptiness 97–98, 146
eNCA 16
Enharmonic Collective 182
Enlightenment 293–294
entanglement 65–66, 77
entrepreneurship 182, 184–185
Enzensberger, Hans Magnus 284, 292
Erasmus, Piet 19
Escuela Superior de Mecánica de la Armada (Higher School of Mechanics of the Navy) 143

Esibayeni 127
Eskom 13–14, 16–17, 24, 25
Essa, Nabeel 49
eThekwini Municipality 261–262, 265, 269
Ethiopia 166, 285–290, *286*, *288–289*
Ethiopia–Cuba Friendship Park 285, *286*
ethnic identity 248, 281, 287
evidence 89, 97–98
Evidence 89
exclusion 40, 94, 270–271
exhibitions 31, *31*, 71, 207, 222, 235
exhumation of human remains 17, 34–36
Eyo, Ekpo 225

F
'fakelore' 216
farming 20, 69–71, 110–111, 118, 287
Fidecaro, Agnese 66, 69
Fidelio 106–109, 120
fires 129–135, *130–133*, 176–177, 213
First, Ruth 111
First World War 175, 193–195, 198–200 *see also* Delville Wood South African National Memorial site; SS *Mendi* memorial
flags 108, 282–283
Floyd, George 282
Flynn, Mr *116*, 117
folklore 215
food farmers 67, 69–71, 256
forced removals 15, 17, 22–24, 29–30, 33–34, 69, 151, 154
forensic photographs 89
forgetting 40–41, 73, 124–126, 137–139, 143, 146, 204
Foto Album van RSA Terroriste ('terrorist album') 86–87, *87*
Foucault, Michel 84, 89, 94–95
Fouche, Pieter Johannes 158
France 193–195, 236
Franco, Francisco 290–291
Freedom Charter 175
French Huguenot immigrants 196
French, Patrick 51
French Revolution 236
Freschi, Federico 162
Freund, Bill 19
Fudukazi's Magic 217
Fukuyama, Francis 294
funerals 35, 221
Furner, Arthur Stanley 163

G
Galioutine, V. 279, 281
Gandhi, Mohandas K. 159, 161, 163, 260
Gandhi, Mohandas K., statues of 51–52, 263
Gandhi Square, Johannesburg 40–61, *52*
  accessibility 41
  background on 43–44
  contingencies of commemoration 54–55
  Gandhi as icon 42, 50–54
  memory 40–42, 52–55
  name changes of 41–43
  nation-building 40, 53
gangs 112
gardening 184 *see also* Ejaradini project
Gauteng Growth and Development Agency 47
Gauteng Institute of Architecture award of commendation 178
GDHF *see* Greater Dobsonville Heritage Foundation
GDHP *see* Greater Dobsonville History Project
gentrification 174, 183, 185
Germany 142–143, 194–195, 203–204, 280–281
Ghana 51, 278, 281
Giorza, Theresa 180
global influences 2, 15, 41, 51, 248–249, 256–257, 270
Global Organisation of People of Indian Origin (GOPIO) 257
glorification 203–204, 206
Gobbato, Angelo 108
Gokool, J. P. 259
Gokool, Krish 259
'Gold Law' (Precious and Base Metals Act) 156–158
gold mining industry 83–84, 150, 154–158, 165
Gool, Zainunnisa (Cissie) 245
GOPIO *see* Global Organisation of People of Indian Origin
Government Square 42, 43 *see also* Gandhi Square, Johannesburg
graffiti 48, *133*
Graham, Lonnie 71
Grand Parade, Cape Town 235, 239, 241
graves *see* burial sites
Greater Dobsonville Heritage Foundation (GDHF) 31
Greater Dobsonville History Project (GDHP) 31–32
Great Zimbabwe 216, 228
Green Office 183–184
Grootestryd farm 24

Grootgeluk coal mine 13, 17–18, 20, 22–23
Group Areas Act 15, 36
Group Areas Board 17, 23, 25
Gugulethu 244
Gule, Khwezi 72, 77
Gumede, Zandile *268*

H
Habermas, Jürgen 279–280, 292, 293
Haile Selassie, Emperor 285
Haines, Sarah 246
Hansen, Thomas Blom 258, 271
Hans Strijdom Dam 20
Harris, Fels, Jankes and Nussbaum 85
Harris, Verne 240
Hart, Frederick 206
Hart, Michael *176*, 177–179
Hay, Michelle 29, 34, 35
healing 143, 290–292
health *see* diseases
heritage plaques, blue 30, 37, *37*, 67
Heritage Resources Act 222
heritage value
    Constitution Hill 43–46, 54
    Drill Hall 173–174, 177–179, 182, 185–186
    Gandhi Square 43–44, 54
    Kwa Khaya Lendaba cultural village 222
    Medupi Power Station 14–15, 25
    notion of 6–7
    Pass Office, Johannesburg 137
Heron, Brett 234, 241–246
hierarchies 75, 110, 115–116
Higher School of Mechanics of the Navy (Escuela Superior de Mecánica de la Armada) 143
Hindu nationalists 284
historiography 109, 111–112, 120
History Workshop, University of the Witwatersrand 2–3, 31–32
Hogan, Barbara 86
Hoheisel, Horst 203
Hollywood movies 165, 239–240
Holocaust 142–143, 203
homelands 22
homeless people 97, 174, 176
Horizon Development Company 33–34, 36
Horizon View 30, 33–34
hostels 22–24, 141
housing 113–115, 126, 136
Howell, Christoffen Rudolf 158
Huletts Sugar 259

human monuments 293
human remains 15–18, 34–36, 200
human rights 41, 243
humiliation 89, 129, 137, 141
Hurd, Leslie 126
Huyssen, Andreas 204

I
iconoclasm 278, 280–281
identity 41, 64–65, 138, 154, 162, 166, 193, 207, 258, 279
ideologies 120, 212–213, 217–222, 228, 236, 284
ILRP *see* Indentured Labour Route Project
Impepho Press 71
Imperial Debris 16
Imperial War Graves Commission 195
inclusivity 144, 174, 241–242, 295
Indaba, My Children 216, 221
Indentured Labour Route Project (ILRP) 257
Independence Arch, Ghana 278, 281
Independence Monument, Mali 279, 281
India 156, 161, 165–166, 261, 284
Indian indentured labour, commemoration of 256–277
    150th anniversary of arrival of first migrants 256, 259–260
    Dadoo family 152
    design of monument 264–267, *267*
    exclusion 270–271
    frustration over monument 268–270
    impetus for monument 256–260
    Monuments Committee 260–263, 266–267, 269–270
    political tensions 258, 263–264
    'sense of loss' 258, 270–271
    slavery 256, 260
    sod-turning ceremony 267, *268*, 269
    stereotypes 260, 261, 270
    sugar companies 256, 259, 261, 263
Indian traders in South Africa 150–163, 165–166
indigenous knowledge systems 228
industrialisation 15, 23
inequality 239, 241
infectious diseases *see* diseases
influx control 124, 126
informal settlements 22–24, 32
inner city of Johannesburg 43–44
Innes, Chief Justice 158, 159
International Congress for Modern Architecture (CIAM) 279

International Criminal Court 290
international influences *see* global influences
International Style 162
'invented tradition' 173–174, 181, 215
invisibility 92–93, 95, 214
Iscor 13, 17–19, 20, 22–24
Italian Futurist Manifesto of 1909 163
Itzkin, Eric 50, 53

J

Jackson, Barry 246–247
Jacobs, Steven 97
JAG *see* Johannesburg Art Gallery
Jameson, Frederic 295
JDA *see* Johannesburg Development Agency
JMPD *see* Johannesburg Metropolitan Police Department
Johannesburg 41, 43, 135, 139, 162, 174
  see also City of Johannesburg
Johannesburg Art Gallery (JAG) 62, 71–78, 222
Johannesburg Central Police Station 83–105, *84*, *85*, *92*, *93*, *96*, *99*
  aluminium screen of 93–94, *93*
  crime 86, 97–98, 100
  emptiness 97–98
  history of 85–86
  mug shots 85–89
  panopticism 94–95, 100
  photography 83–89, 91–94, 97–100
  prison life 86, 93, 95, 100
  punishment 89–90
  rooftop of 99, *99*
  surveillance 95–96, 99–100
  'terrorist album' 86–87, *87*
  torture 89, 95
  transparency 95–97
  Vorster, B. J., bust of 98, *98*
Johannesburg Child Welfare Society 179
Johannesburg Community Chest 179
Johannesburg Development Agency (JDA) 45, 177, 179
Johannesburg Heritage Foundation 44, 199–200
Johannesburg Metropolitan Police Department (JMPD) 174, 185
Johannesburg Prison 43–45, 47–48, 51
John Vorster Square *see* Johannesburg Central Police Station
John, William Goscombe 237
Joubert Park Project (JPP) 176, 179–181, 183

Jubilee House, Krugersdorp 150–172, *151*, *160*, 161, *161*, *164*
  Art Deco building 150, 152, 153, 162–165, 166
  'Asiatic bazaars' 153, 154–158
  Dadoo family 150, 151–162, 164
  Dadoo Ltd 158–160
  Dadoo's 152–154, 160–166
  'Dadoo's Block' 159–160
  forced removals 151, 154
  history of 150, 152–153, 158
  Indian traders 150–163, 165–166
  Krugersdorp 150–151, 155–159, 166
  media coverage of 163–164, *164*
  migrants 165–166
  modernity 154, 160–166
  name of 158
  Solly's 150, *151*, 160
  Victorian building 152, 158, *160*, 161–162
Juliwe Cemetery, Roodepoort, Johannesburg 29–39, *33*, *37*
  ancestral beliefs 35
  Dobsonville 29–34, 36
  exhumation of human remains 34–36
  forced removals 29–30, 33–34
  Horizon Development Company 33–34, 36
  Horizon View 30, 33–34
  land restitution claim 32, 36
  maintenance of 36, 38
  memorial in 30, 36–37, *37*
  oral history 31, 32
  plaques 30, 36–37, *37*
  Roodepoort Museum 31, *31*
  Roodepoort West township 29–34
Juliwe township 30–34, *33*
June 16, 1976 Interpretation Centre 212
justice 53, 136, 290–291

K

Kaepernick, Colin 282–283
Kagiso township 151
Kallenbach, Hermann 163
Kallenbach, Kennedy and Furner 150, 162–163
Kaplan, Flora Edouwaye S. 217, 225
Karoa, SS 156
Kasrils, Ronnie *87*
Kathrada, Ahmed 109, 248
Kavanagh, Robert Mshengu 219
Kelbessa Negewo 290
Keleketla! Library project 181–182

Kigali Genocide Memorial Centre 143
Kincaid, Jamaica 69
Klerksdorp 155
Knauer, Lisa 264, 270
Known and Strange Things 86
Koketso Growth 246
Kramer, Winnie 154
Kruger, Barry 115–116
Kruger, Paul 150
Krugersdorp 150–151, 155–159, 166
Krugersdorp Indian Association 160
Krugersdorp Land Company Ltd 159
Kunene, Vincent 219
Kwa Khaya Lendaba cultural village 212–233
   see also Mutwa, Credo Vusamazulu
      apartheid 213–214, 217, 221–222, 224, 228–229, *213, 223, 227*
      'Arab village' 216, 226
      Briscoe / WRAB / Mutwa archive 222–224
      description of 216, 226–228
      history of 212–213, 228–229
      legacy of 228–229
      location of 212
      mythology 214, 216–217, 225
      Owl House and 215–216
      signs in 214
      Soweto uprising (1976) 212–213, 228
      Surrealism 216–217
      tourism 212, 224–226
      WRAB 212, 215, 222–226, 228–229
KwaZulu-Natal (KZN) Legacy Foundation 260–263

L
labour
      affective 65, 74, 75–77, 78
      farm 110–111
      First World War 194
      Indian indentured 256–257
      migrant labour system 22, 111, 126, 129
      mining 22
      prison 111, 118
LaCapra, Dominick 139
Lack, Jessica 217
La Hausse, Paul 135
Lal, Brij V. 260
Land and Lives 215
land ownership 16, 20–25, 66, 152, 155–160, 287
land restitution claims 32
Latilla, Marc 91

laws 90–92, 156, 158
Lebowa homeland 22, 23, 24
Le Corbusier 163
Ledochowski, Chris 246–247
legislation *see* laws
Leigh, Catesby 291
Lephalale 13–15
Lewin, Hugh 96
liberation *see* struggle for liberation
Liberation Heritage Route 235
lifehood 73, 77
Linenthal, Edward T. 271
Lin, Maya 205, 291
'living exhibitions' 222
Long Walk to Freedom monument 246
Loots, Willie 21–22
Lotlamoreng Dam Cultural Park 213–214
Luke, Christina 270
Lutyens, Edwin 72

M
M1 highway, Johannesburg 93–94, *93*, 95
Madikizela-Mandela, Winnie 247
Madondo, Bongani 219–220
Madressa Islamia Anjuman of Kholvad (trust) 156
MAF *see* Mazibuye African Forum
Magagula, L. S. 269
Magubane, Peter 217
Mahomed, A. V. *268*
maintenance of buildings 36, 38, 173, 179–180, 182–184
Makhutle, Mighta 225, 226
'Making Memory' (exhibition) 207
Malawi 51
Mali 279, 281
malls 154, 166
management of buildings 47, 179–180, 185–186
Mandela, Nelson
      legacy of 52, 239–240, 244, 246, 249
      release from prison 234–237
      at Robben Island prison 107, 109
      SS *Mendi* memorial 200
      tourism and 50
      Treason Trial 175
Mandela, Nelson, bust of 245, 246
Mandela statue, City Hall, Cape Town 234–255, *247*
      aesthetic choices 246–248
      City Hall 234–235, 242
      controversy over 241–243

Index

Edward VII, King, statue of 235, 237–239, *237*, 248
  Grand Parade 235, 239, 241
  history of 244–248
  political strategy 235–236, 243–244, 249
  reasons for 235–236, 239–240
  slavery 240–241
  tourism 235, 242–243, 245
  universal appeal of 248–249
Mandel, Mike 89
Marais, Anroux 245
Marapong township 14–15, 25
Market Square 150, 155–156
Marschall, Sabine 52, 54, 264, 265
Martins, Helen 215–216
Masanabo, T. 196
Masilela, Ntongela 218
Matshoba, Mtutuzeli 126–129
Mauritius 257
Mayat Hart Architects 198, 200
Maylam, Paul xix
Mazibuye African Forum (MAF) 263
Mbembe, Achille 84
Mbofho Consulting and Project Managers 14, 16
M'bula, Winston 114–116, 118–119
Mchunu, Willies *268*, 269
Meadowlands *133*, 134
meaning 145, 180, 207
medals 115–116, 197, 199, 208
media coverage 111, 163–164, *164*
medical examinations 128–129
Medupi Power Station 13–28
  ancestral beliefs 14–17
  coal 13, 17
  construction of 13–14
  Eskom 13–14, 16–17, 24, 25
  forced removals 15, 17, 22–24
  future of 24–25
  graves 14, 17, 25
  Grootgeluk coal mine 13, 17–18, 20, 22–23
  human remains 15–18
  Iscor 13, 17–19, 20, 22–24
  Marapong township 14–15, 25
  white settlers 19–22
Memorial for Martyred Freedom Fighters and Patriots 285, *288–289*, 289–290
memory
  collective 40–41, 52–53, 125, 141
  Constitution Hill 40–42, 48
  counter-memory 138–139, 205–206

Drill Hall 173–174, 177, 180–182, 184–185
  dynamic nature of 204–205, 207
  Gandhi Square 40–42, 52–54
  Juliwe Cemetery 32
  keeping 290–292
  Kwa Khaya Lendaba cultural village 222
  Pass Office, Johannesburg 125–126, 135, 138–139, 141, 145
Mendi, SS 199 *see also* SS *Mendi* memorial
Mengistu Haile Mariam 285, 287
metaphors 72–73, 83, 88–89
Metcalf, Thomas 152, 161–162
Meyer, Joe 17
Mfisa, Johannes 21
Mhlophe, Gcina 217
migrant labour system 22, 111, 126, 129
migrants 74, 124, 165–166, 176, 181–182, 257
Miles, Elza 214–215
Miller, Kim 257, 264
minimalist monuments 291
mining industry 15, 17, 22, 83–84, 118, 150–151, 154–158, 165–166, 175, 256
Minkley, Gary 15, 257
missionaries 110
MK *see* Umkhonto we Sizwe
Mkhize, N. O. 269
Mkhize, Zweli 261
Mkhwanazi, Thoko 14
M. M. Dadoo & Sons Ltd 159, *164*
modernity 14–15, 85, 97, 154, 160–166, 203, 279–280, 291–295
'Modernity: The Unfinished Project' (essay) 279–280
Mogale City 150–151, 166
Mogol River 19–20, 23
Moloantoa, Sara 18
Morris Isaacson High School 212
Motha, Mphathi 69–71, 73–75
Mousavisadeh, Nader 284
Mpakama, Xhanti 246, 248
Mthembu, Theo 67
Mtshali, Thandeka 218
Mudzingwa, Farai xvii
Mugabe, Robert xv–xix, 290–291
mug shots 85–89
Muller, Leon 247
Mumford, Lewis 203
Munsieville township 150–151
Murray, Martin J. 41
MUSA *see* Museums for South Africa

Museum Africa 50, 213
museums 47–49, 62, 72–73, 77, 106–109, 120, 196, 224–225
Museums for South Africa (MUSA) 224–225
Mutwa, Credo Vusamazulu *see also* Kwa Khaya Lendaba cultural village
    career of 213–215
    Cillié Commission 213, 219–221, 228
    death of 221
    ideology of 212–213, 217–222, 228
    Indaba, My Children 216, 221
    Kwa Khaya Lendaba cultural village 212, 216–217
    legacy of 214–215, 221–229
    protests over 213–214
    Unosilimela (play) 218–219
My People 221
mythology 214, 216–217, 225, 239
'Myths, Monuments, Museums: New Premises?' (conference) 3

N

Naidoo, Selvan 269
name changes xvii–xviii, 41–42, 50, 151, 242, 244, 280
names of casualties 196, 198, 200, 205–206, 291
Natal Mercury 220
national anthem (USA) 282–283
National Heritage Council 235
National Heritage Resources Act 225
National Heroes Acre, Zimbabwe xv–xix, 291
nationalism xvii, 44–45, 109, 150, 154, 256–258, 284
National Liberation Route 243
National Monuments Council (NMC) 44–45
National Parks Board 214
National Party (NP) 20, 92
nation-building 40–41, 47, 53, 109, 224–225, 229, 265
Native Nostalgia 146
Ndawana, Cyprian Muketiwa xvi
Ndebele, Njabulo 144–145
Ndletyana, Mcebisi 239
Ndlovu, Sifiso Mxolisi 138
neglect 8, 124–125, 140–141, 144, 238
Nengwikhulu, Randwedzi 135
neocolonialism 278
neoconservatism 280, 292, 293
New Sculpture movement 237–238

Newsday xvi
Nieu Bethesda 215–216
Nkosi, Lewis 91
Nkrumah, Kwame 278
NMC *see* National Monuments Council
Noble, Jonathan Alfred 279
Nomkhubulwana, statues of 226–227
Nora, Pierre 204–205
normalisation 92–93
nostalgia 73, 135, 137
NP *see* National Party
Ntanzi, Musa 225
Ntuli, Pitika 221
Nuttall, Sarah 84
Nxumalo, Henry 111
Nxumalo, James 262

O

objectivity 142, 222
Old Fort, Constitution Hill 43, 44, 47–48
Olitzki Property Holdings (OPH) 43–44, 50
omission 6, 91, 196–197, 214
One Love Skate Expo 177, 183, 184, *184*
On Photography 87–88
opacity 95–97
OPH *see* Olitzki Property Holdings
Oppenheimer Gardens 227–228
Oppenheimer Park 218
Oppenheimer Tower 227–229, *227*
oral history 31, 32, 224
Orange Free State province 21, 159
Orlando East *130*, 134
othering 217, 221
Owl House 215–216

P

Paardekraal hospital 153, 160
Pahama location 22–24
panopticism 94–95, 100
Parade *see* Grand Parade, Cape Town
paradoxes 90, 93–94, 97
Parnell, Sue 3
pass laws 124–127
Pass Office, Johannesburg ii, 124–149, *125*, *128*, *140*
    abandonment 124–125, 144
    counter-memory 138–139
    'empathetic unsettlement' 139–143
    forgetting 124–126, 137–139, 143, 146
    history of 126
    medical examinations 128–129

memory 125–126, 135, 138–139, 141, 145
pass laws 124–127
pride 126–129
reparation 135–137
segregation 124, 139
Soweto uprising (1976) 129–135, *130–133*
West Rand Administration Board 126, 129–135, *130–133*, 137
Pather, Dennis 269–270
perception 91–94, 202
personal experiences 47–48, 135, 202
Phillips, Lady 72
Phillips, Sandra S. 86
photographic archive, Briscoe / WRAB / Mutwa 222–224
photography 83–89, 91–94, 97–100
Pillay, Vic *268*
Pinker, Steven 284, 292, 293–294
Pirow, Oswald 244
place-making 4, 74
plaques 30, 36–37, *37*, 50–51, 67, 261–262
poetry 71, 240
police 86–87, 90–91, 99–100, 134, 174, 282
Police and Prisons Civil Rights Union (Popcru) 116
political prisoners 45, 106, 109
Pollsmoor prison 113
Popcru *see* Police and Prisons Civil Rights Union
population growth 33
Porterville 110–113
portrait photography *76*
Posel, Deborah 3, 90, 94–95
Post 268
poverty 32, 111, 120
power 66, 90–91, 95, 175
precarity 183, 185–186
Precious and Base Metals Act ('Gold Law') 156–158
Premier's office, KwaZulu-Natal 261, 262, 263, 265, 269
preservation 73, 77, 136–137, 140–141, 144–145
pride 126–129, 193
prison administrators 112
prison labour 111, 118
prisons 86, 93, 100, 107–111, 114, 117–120
see also Johannesburg Central Police Station; Johannesburg Prison; Robben Island prison museum

Prison Service 114, 115–116
prison warders 90, 95, 109–110, 112–120
privatisation 41, 44, 118
propaganda 196
'Prospect of Beauty, A' (poem) 240
protests 2, 7, 29, 50, 116, 175, 193, 196, 263–264, 282–283, 292 *see also* Soweto uprising
Public Art Policy, City of Johannesburg 50
public participation 40–42, 50–51, 53, 139, 144–146, 241–242, 244–245, 270
public–private partnerships 44
public spaces 40–42, 46, 51, 92–93, 177, 179
Public Works Department 45, 179–180, 185
punishment 89–90

Q
Quang Duc, Thich 283

R
race relations 110–112, 114–116, 162, 194, 258, 263–264, 281–284
racial capitalism 107, 111, 117–118, 120
racism 3, 7, 42, 50–51, 114–116, 120, 157, 179, 181–182, 239, 281–284
railways 19
'Rainbow Nation' 42, 108, 239–240, 244, 258
Raman, Parvathi 153
Ramaphosa, Cyril 247, 249
Rand Daily Mail 156, 157, 220–221
Rand Light Infantry 43, 179
Rassool, Ciraj 15, 257
reconciliation 1–4, 42, 108, 129, 136, 174, 176–180, 239, 249, 257
regeneration 41, 185
Reid, Graeme 45
Reitz, Frank 264–267
Release memorial 245
relocation 109–113
remembering 5–6, 73, 126, 136, 143, 204–206
renaming xvii–xviii, 41–42, 50, 151, 242, 244, 280
renewal 43–44, 176–180
renovation 54, *176*, 177–179, 185, 234
reparation 53, 135–137
'reproducibility' 235
Reservation of Separate Amenities Act 92
resistance 135, 153–154

respectability politics 69
restoration 1, 73
Rhodes, Cecil John, grave of xviii–xix
Rhodes, Cecil John, statues of xvii, 7, 52, 239, 245, 263
#RhodesMustFall campaign 2, 51, 239, 257, 263, 280
Richards, Colin 92–93
rituals 35, 180
Rivonia Trial 247–248
Robben Island prison museum 106–123
    decommissioning of prison 106–107, 109–113
    Fidelio production 106–109, 120
    relocation of prison 109–116
    violence 5, 116–120
    Voorberg prison 110, 112–119, *116, 119*
Roodepoort 30
Roodepoort Museum 31, *31*
Roodepoort West township 29–34
Ross, Marc Howard 207, 258, 271
Ross, Susan Imrie 216
Ruben Reddy Architects 264–265
ruination 47–49, 55, 71–73, 77, 139
rule of law 90
Rwanda 143

S
Sachs, Albie 49, 51
sacredness 35, 68, 226
SADF *see* South African Defence Force
SAHRA *see* South African Heritage Resources Agency
SALA *see* South African Literary Awards
sanctuary 74–75
Sangweni, Zweli 263
sanitary services 23–24, 157
'sanitisation' 49, 97
SANLC *see* South African Native Labour Contingent
Sartre, Jean-Paul 281–282, 284, 293
Save the Children 183
Schmahmann, Brenda 245, 257, 264
Scott, Dread (Scott Tyler) 282–283
sculptures 184, 196, 216, 248
secrecy 90, 93–94
security 46, *46*, 49, 100, 179
security police 86–87, 90, 100
segregation 17, 25, 92–93, 153–154, 157, 165, 194, 197 *see also* apartheid
Sekati, Sam 20–21, 23
Sekoto, Gerard 72

Sekula, Allan 91
selfhood 70–71, 74, 75, *76*
Senghor, Léopold Sédar 278–279, 281–282
'sense of loss' 258, 270–271
sensory design 202–204
Seodisa, Lazarus 16–18
settlers *see* white settlers
Shaka, King, bust and statue of 226, 267
Sharpeville Massacre 15
Shongwe, A. V. 262–263
shopping malls 154, 166
Short, John Rennie 165
Shree Mariamman Temple 259
Sidibe, Amado 279, 281
Sifumba, Nonhlanhla 30
signs 92, 214
Siko, Simangele 67–68, 73
silence 97–98
Simbao, Ruth Kerkham 214
Sims, James 215
Sithole, Sibusiso 262
skateboarding 177, 183, 184, *184*
sketches *176*, 266, *267*
slavery 240–241, 256, 260
Slovo, Joe 175
Smith, Charlene 217
Smith, Kathryn 89
Smit, James Henry 155–156, 157
Smuts, Jan, statue of 244
social engineering 14, 16
socialism 239, 285–287
social relations 35, 62–63, 71–72, 75, 77–78, 138, 174, 182–184
solidarity 35, 112
Solly's 150, *151, 160*
Somali migrants 166
Sontag, Susan 87–88
Soobben, Nanda, sketch by *267*
Sotashe, Xolani 238
South African Communist Party 152, 175
South African Defence Force (SADF) 175–177
South African Heritage Resources Agency (SAHRA) 197–198
South African Indian Congress 152, 165–166
South African Legion 199–200
South African Literary Awards (SALA) 220
South African Native Labour Contingent (SANLC) 194, 196, 197–201, 208
South African People's Plays 219
South African Police *see* police
South African Republic *see* ZAR

South African War 156, 195–196, 293
Soweto 29–30, 84, 212
Soweto (book) 217
Soweto uprising (1976) 129–135, *130–133*, 212–213, 228
Soweto Uprisings, The 138
Spain 290–291
spatial planning 3, 15, 54, 145
spirituality 70, 212
SS *Mendi* memorial 199–211, *201*
    counter-monument 202–208
    description of 200–201
    memory 204–205
    names of casualties 200, 205–206
    new extension to 200–201
    pergola 201, *201*
    post-apartheid 206–208
    sensory design of 202–204
    sinking of SS *Mendi* 199–200
stakeholders 173, 174, 182–185
Star, The 163–164, *164*
Stasimuseum 143
Stasi Records Agency 143
state corporations 15, 25
state support 70–71
'statue clutter' 244–245
statue mania (*statuomanie*) 236
statues 2, 7–8, 52–53, 244–245, 283–284, 291–292
Stelloop 23, 24
stereotypes 260, 261, 270
Stoler, Ann Laura 16
storytelling 215, 217, 224
street photography 97
struggle for liberation 45, 92, 98, 106, 109, 153–154, 173, 180–182, 292–293
Student March Trail 212
Sudan 279, 280, 281
Sultan, Larry 89
Sunday Express 22
Sunday Independent 263
Sunday Times 85, *85*
Surrealism 216–217
surveillance 95–96, 99–100
Susan, Mam' (gardener) 64–65, 68–69
Sutcliffe, Mike 262
Suttner, Raymond 95, 99
Swanson, Maynard 157
symbolism 67, 69, 136, 175, 240

T
Tafuri, Manfredo 294–295
Tagg, John 90–91

'taking a knee' 282–283
Tambo, Dali 246
'terrorist album' (*Foto Album van RSA Terroriste*) 86–87, *87*
Thabethe, Sinothi 262, 264–266, 269
Thakur-Rajbansi, Shameen 265
Themba, Can 137
This Is My World 216
Three Servicemen (statue) 206
Thusi, Nhlanhla 263, 265
Tibanyane, Johannes 16
Tiglachin Monument 285–289, *286*, *289*
Tigray People's Liberation Front (TPLF) 285–290, *288–289*
time 76–77
Timol, Ahmed 90
Tinker, Hugh 260
Tiso Blackstar Group 85
'To Kill a Man's Pride ...' 126–129
torture 85–86, 89, 95, 117, 120
tourism xviii–xix, 177, 212, 224–226, 235, 242–243, 245, 262, 265
townships 23, 110–111, 118–119, 124, 126, 144–146, 155
TPLF *see* Tigray People's Liberation Front
traditional healers 17, 218, 222, 225–226
traditional monuments 203–205
transformation 41, 145, 174, 182–185, 207
transparency 95–97, 177
Transvaal 152, 157–158, 160, 163
Transvaal Asiatic Land Tenure Act Commission 160
Transvaal British Indian Association 159
Transvaal Indian Congress 159
Transvaal Volunteers 175
trauma 48, 129, 136, 139, 142–144, 291
TRC *see* Truth and Reconciliation Commission
Treason Trial 173, 175, 177–178, 182
trench warfare 194, 198
tribalism 212–213, 281
Truth and Reconciliation Commission (TRC) 15, 141
Tshabangu, Mango 219
Tulbagh prison 112
Tunisia 283
Tuol Sleng Genocide Museum 143
Turner, Alfred 196
Turok, Ivan 241
'twice-migrants' 257
Tyler, Scott (Dread Scott) 282–283

U

UCT *see* University of Cape Town
Umkhonto we Sizwe (MK) 18
uncertainty 183, 185–186
underground movements 84
Union Buildings, Pretoria 195, 293
Union of South Africa 152, 193–195
United Nations 257
United States of America (USA) 7, 86, 205–206, 282–283, 290
unity 196, 244–245, 248, 270
universal appeal 248–249
universal language of monuments 294–295
University of Cape Town (UCT) 51, 239, 263
University of the Witwatersrand (Wits) 2–3, 31–32, 62, 163, 218–219
Unosilimela (play) 218–219
urban development 17, 23
urban gardening *see* Ejaradini project
USA *see* United States of America
uShaka Marine World 262

V

vacant buildings 97, 142
Van den Berg, Clive 48
Van der Bijl, Hendrik 50
Van der Bijl Square 42, 43, 50 *see also* Gandhi Square, Johannesburg
Van Robbroeck, Lize 246
Veterans of Foreign Wars 282
Victoria, Queen 158
Vietnam Veterans War memorial 205–206, 291
viewer experiences 202, 206–207
violence 90, 94, 116–120, 137, 178, 182
Visagie, Justin 241
visibility 92–93, 95, 214
Voorberg prison 110, 112–119, *116*, *119*
Vorster, B. J. 85
Vorster, B. J., bust of 98, *98*

W

Wajee, Fatima Ahmed 155
Walkowitz, Daniel 264, 270
warders *see* prison warders
Ward, Kerry 241
Warsaw Pact 285
Waterkloof farm 19–20
Webb, Denver 239
Werbner, Richard xv, xvii
Wessels, J. W. 158–159
West Rand Administration Board (WRAB) 126, 129–135, *130–133*, 137, 212, 215, 222–226, 228–229
What is the Proper Way to Display a U.S. Flag? (artwork) 282–283
white settlers 19–22, 110–111, 196
Wilson, Simon 217
Winde, Alan 242–243, 245
Wits *see* University of the Witwatersrand
Witz, Leslie 15, 257
Women's Jail, Constitution Hill 48
Worden, Nigel 241
World Peace Foundation 290
World War I *see* First World War
WRAB *see* West Rand Administration Board
Wright, Carl 265–266
Writing History, Writing Trauma 139
'Writing the World from an African Metropolis' 84

X

xenophobia 181, 182, 264

Y

Young, James E. 203–204
young people 69, 74–75

Z

ZAR (South African Republic) 43, 44
Zerohour manifesto 163
Zille, Helen 220–221, 244
Zimbabwe xv–xix, 18, 290–291
Žižek, Slavoj 239–240
Zuma, Jacob 197, 270

www.ingramcontent.com/pod-product-compliance
Lightning Source LLC
Chambersburg PA
CBHW020901080526
44589CB00011B/382